The Function of Song
in Contemporary
British Drama

The Function of Song in Contemporary British Drama

Elizabeth Hale Winkler

DELAWARE
Newark: University of Delaware Press
London and Toronto: Associated University Presses

9100004102

Associated University Presses
440 Forsgate Drive
Cranbury, NJ 08512

Associated University Presses
25 Sicilian Avenue
London WC1A 2QH, England

Associated University Presses
P.O. Box 488, Port Credit
Mississauga, Ontario
Canada L5G 4M2

The paper used in this publication meets the requirements
of the American National Standard for Permanence of Paper
for Printed Library Materials Z39.48-1984.

Library of Congress Cataloging-in-Publication Data

Winkler, Elizabeth Hale.
 The function of song in contemporary British drama / Elizabeth
Hale Winkler.
  p. cm.
 Includes bibliographical references.
 ISBN 0-87413-358-0 (alk. paper)
 1. Incidental music—20th century—History and criticism.
 2. English drama—Great Britain—20th century—History and
criticism. 3. Music in theaters. I. Title.
 ML1731.W67 1990
 782.42'1552'0941—dc20   88-40579
                                                  CIP

PRINTED IN THE UNITED STATES OF AMERICA

Contents

Musical Illustrations

Acknowledgments

My greatest debt of gratitude is due to the playwrights John Arden, Peter Barnes, Edward Bond, Margaretta D'Arcy, and John McGrath, who with promptitude, courtesy and indeed enthusiasm agreed to be interviewed on the subject of song in their drama. Their answers provided me with a wealth of valuable information that could not have been obtained elsewhere. Special thanks go to Arden, D'Arcy, and Bond, who read through not only the interview transcripts but also the first drafts of my chapters on their work and made comments and corrections. It need scarcely be emphasized that any errors or misinterpretations in this book fall entirely within my responsibility.

My thanks also to the staff of the National Sound Archive and the National Film Archive in London for their efforts on behalf of this project. Colleagues and friends at the Free University of West Berlin, at the University of East Anglia in Norwich, and at Texas Tech University have provided support and inspiration. Special thanks go to Peter Steiger of the Free University of Berlin, who read through the manuscript in many of its stages. I also wish to thank my flute teacher in West Berlin, Rotraud Puschmann, for her invariable cheerfulness and spontaneity in helping me with the finer points of musical theory and harmony. Last but not least I owe a debt of thanks to all my loved ones, particularly to my husband, Manfred Sommerlad, without whose committed support over many years this study would not have been possible.

Print Permissions

Every effort has been made to secure the necessary permissions. I apologize for any oversights. In a few cases I was unable to trace copyright holders; they are invited to contact me or the publishers.

Excerpts from the following works are reproduced by permission of Methuen London, Ltd.: John Arden, *Armstrong's Last Goodnight; Serjeant Musgrave's Dance; The Workhouse Donkey;* John Arden and Margaretta D'Arcy, *The Business of Good Government; The Hero Rises Up; The Island of the Mighty; The Royal Pardon;* Edward Bond, *The Cat; Grandma Faust; Human Cannon; Poems 1978–1985; The Pope's Wedding; Restoration; Stone;*

Theatre Poems and Songs; We Come to the River; The Woman; The Worlds with the Activists Papers; Howard Brenton, *Hitler Dances;* Caryl Churchill, *Vinegar Tom;* John McGrath, *The Cheviot, the Stag and the Black, Black Oil;* and Peter Nichols, *Poppy.*

By permission of Faber and Faber, Ltd., London, extracts from the following plays are reproduced: Peter Barnes, *Red Noses;* Trevor Griffiths, *Oi for England;* Peter Nichols, *Privates on Parade.* Extracts from W. H. Auden and Christopher Isherwood, *The Ascent of F6* © 1959 are reproduced by permission of Faber and Faber, London, and Curtis Brown, New York; extracts from John Osborne, *The Entertainer* © 1958 by John Osborne are reproduced by permission of Faber and Faber, London, and S. G. Philips, Inc., U.S.A.

Excerpts from John Arden, *The Happy Haven, Live Like Pigs,* and *The Waters of Babylon* are reproduced by permission of Penguin Books, Ltd., London, from *Three Plays* (Penguin Books) copyright © John Arden 1961, 1962, and 1964.

The song text from Arnold Wesker, *The Friends,* is reproduced by permission of Jonathan Cape, London; Martin Bell's "The Songs" by permission of the literary estate of Martin Bell.

Extracts from Peter Barnes's *The Bewitched* (Heinemann) and Edward Bond's *Orpheus: A Story in Six Scenes* (Würtembergisches Staatstheater Stuttgart) are reproduced by permission of Margaret Ramsay, Ltd., Play Agents. All rights whatsoever in these works are strictly reserved and application for performance etc. should be made before rehearsal to Margaret Ramsay Ltd., 14a Goodwin's Court, St. Martin's Lane, London WC2. No performance may be given unless a license has been obtained.

John Arden and Margaretta D'Arcy granted permission to quote excerpts from *The Non-Stop Connolly Show* (Pluto Press) and from the unpublished manuscript of *The Ballygombeen Bequest.*

John McGrath granted permission to quote from *Yobbo Nowt* and *Little Red Hen* (Pluto Press).

Edward Bond allowed reproduction of an excerpt from his letter to Hans Werner Henze.

Permissions to reproduce extracts from songs come from the following sources:

"A Nightingale Sang in Berkeley Square" (Eric Maschwitz/Manning Sherwin) © 1940 Peter Maurice Music Co. Ltd., renewed. Used by permission of Peter Maurice Music Co. Ltd., London WC2H OLD; J. Albert & Son PTY, Sydney, Australia, and Shapiro, Bernstein & Co., Inc., New York.

Angel's "Alleluia" (Cardinal Newman/Edward Elgar) from *The Dream of Gerontius* by permission of Novello Ltd., England.

"The Battle of Harlaw" is reproduced by permission of Leo Cooper Ltd., London.

"The Camptown Races" (Stephen Foster) is reproduced by permission of Simon and Schuster, New York.

"The Coal-Owner and the Pitman's Wife" is reproduced by permission of Lawrence and Wishart Ltd., London.

"Dives and Lazarus" courtesy of the English Folk Dance and Song Society, London.

"Down in Yon Forest" (arranged by Ralph Vaughan Williams) is reproduced by permission of Stainer & Bell Ltd., London, England.

"Dream," "Fair Tree of Liberty," and "Song of Learning" (Edward Bond/ Nick Bicât) are from *Restoration:* the music is © Nick Bicât; any request to perform the music should be made to his agent, Marc Berlin, at London Management and Representation Ltd., 235/241 Regent Street, London W1A 2JT.

"Dry Bones" (arranged by H. A. Chambers) is reproduced by permission of Blanford Press Ltd., an imprint of Cassell (UK).

"Eton Boating Song" (words by William Johnson Cory, music by Algernon Drummond/Evelyn Wodehouse) © 1930. Reproduced by permission of EMI Music Publishing, Ltd., London WC2H OEA and EMI Music Publishing, Australia.

"Funeral Blues" (W. H. Auden/Benjamin Britten) from *The Ascent of F6* © 1980 by Faber Music Ltd., London. Reproduced by permission.

"Hunt the Wren" © Folktracks c/o the Performing Right Society, 29/33 Berners Street, London W1 4AA, England, from whom permission has been obtained.

"John Brown's Body" (musical arrangement by Kenneth Bray) reproduced by permission of Dover Publications, New York.

"Keep the Home Fires Burning" (by Lena Guilbert Ford and Ivor Novello). Copyright © 1916 by Chappell Music Ltd. Copyright Renewed. All rights for the U.S.A. administered by Chappell and Co. International Copyright Secured. All Rights Reserved. Unauthorized copying, arranging, adapting recording or public performance is an infringement of copyright. Infringers are liable under the law. Reproduced by permission of Warner Chappell (U.S.A.) and Warner Chappell Music Ltd., London, England.

"Ladies' Anthem" and Madman Drummer (Edward Bond/Hans Werner Henze) from Henze, *We Come to the River* © B. Schott's Soehne, Mainz, 1976. All rights reserved. Used by permission of European American Music Distributors Corporation, sole U.S. and Canadian agent for B. Schott's Soehne.

"Last Orders" and "Passing Through" (Tony Bicât/Nick Bicât) from David Hare's *Teeth 'n' Smiles*. Music © Nick Bicât. Any request to perform the music should be made to his agent, Rachel Daniels, at London Management and Representation Ltd., 235/241 Regent Street, London W1A 2JT, England.

"Lillibulero" (arrangement © 1939 by Colm O'Lochlainn), reproduced by permission of PAN Books, London.

"Oh, It's a Lovely War" (J. P. Long/Maurice Scott), © 1917, reproduced by permission of B. Feldman & Co., Ltd., London WC2H OLD.

"Oh The Weary Cutters" reproduced by permission of Lawrence and Wishart Ltd., London.

"On the Sunny Side of the Street" (Dorothy Fields, Jimmy McHugh), © 1930 Shapiro, Bernstein & Co., Inc. © renewed 1986 Aldi Music Company and Ireneadele Publishing Co. All U.S. rights administered by The Songwriters' Guild of America. Reproduced by permission of The Songwriters' Guild of America, New York and Lawrence Wright Music Co. Ltd./EMI Music, London WC2H OLD, England.

"Shine On, Harvest Moon" (Nora Bayes/Jack Norworth) © 1908 Remick Music/Warner Bros., Inc. (renewed). All rights reserved. Reproduced by permission of Warner-Chappell, Los Angeles CA, Francis Day and Hunter Ltd., London WC2H OLD, and J. Albert & Son PTY Ltd., Sydney, Australia.

"There'll Always Be an England" (Ross Parker and Hughie Charles), © 1939 by Gordon V. Thompson Music, a Division of Canada Publishing Corporation, Toronto, Canada. Used by permission of Gordon V. Thompson Music, and Dash Music/Campbell Connelly & Co., Ltd., London.

"They Can't Take That Away from Me" (words by Ira Gershwin, music by George Gershwin) © 1936, 1937 by Gershwin Publishing Corporation. Copyright renewed, assigned to Chappell & Co. Inc., International Copyright secured. All rights reserved. Used by permission of Warner/Chappell Music, Inc., Los Angeles CA, and Warner/Chappell Music, Ltd., London, England.

"The Unquiet Grave" ("The Wind Doth Blow Tonight My Love"), from Arnold Wesker, *The Four Seasons*, used by permission of Jonathan Cape Ltd., London.

"The White Cliffs of Dover" (Walter Kent/Nat Burton) © 1941, renewed, Shapiro, Bernstein & Co. Inc., New York, NY and Walter Kent Music. Reproduced by permission of Shapiro Bernstein & Co., New York, and B. Feldman & Co. Ltd., London WC2H OLD.

Introduction

A study of dramatic song in the contemporary period offers unsuspected and significant insights into the vitality of present-day British theater, its indebtedness to theatrical and musical tradition, and the very nature of dramatic presentation itself. Drama has always derived much of its popular appeal from the intermingling of visual, mimetic, aural, and linguistic resources in live performance. The dramatic song can be showstopping in impact. Through the shift in medium from the verbal to the combined musical and verbal, the playwright immediately captures audience attention. A dramatic song often provides a concentrated expression of the essence of the surrounding scene. It frequently represents the emotional and lyrical highlight of the entire play, a moment that can instantly epitomize its feeling. Very often in modern drama, songs may also contain condensed intellectual or political statements, reaching out in an alienating fashion to shake the audience's consciousness. Within a few bars songs can evoke huge cultural complexes for a listener. Through strategic positioning in the play's structure, especially at the beginning or end of scenes or in the final moments of the entire drama, they create a sense of opening or closure. Songs are particularly effective in helping to establish a community of viewers and listeners participating in live theater performance as an age-old cultural ritual.

Research has been undertaken that attempts to explain the energy of the modern English theater through its affinity to the popular heritage, but the musical heritage is mentioned only in passing.[1] The interrelationship between literature and music has been the object of various scholarly works; the most useful for the purposes of this study was James Winn's *Unsuspected Eloquence: A History of the Relations between Poetry and Music*.[2] Two journal issues are devoted to this subject, but these contain few essays on modern drama. In the *Comparative Literature* issue (Spring 1970) the most interesting article is on W. H. Auden's theory of opera. The *Mosaic* volume on music and literature (Fall 1985) is more up to date and contains two challenging essays on reader/listener response in literature and music.[3] An excellent general study of the nature of song is undertaken by Mark W. Booth in *The Experience of Songs*.[4]

General studies of song in drama are practically nonexistent. Those that do exist tend to be collections of song lyrics from earlier drama,[5] detailed studies of some historical period,[6] or studies of song in individual dramatists: Shake-

13

speare, Ben Jonson, John Gay, W. B. Yeats, Sean O'Casey, and Bertolt Brecht, for example, have all received individual attention. Two collections of essays on music and drama prove to be not suitable as general introductions: *Themes in Drama 3: Drama, Dance and Music* (1981)[7] ranges over such disparate topics as Japanese Nō theater and the American musical, while the *Gambit* issue on *Theatre and Music* (1981)[8] concentrates mainly on alternative theater and the rock scene, with a very brief introduction to the history of music in Western theater.

While all of these books provide valuable clues to the nature of song in drama, they cannot entirely supply the missing theory of dramatic song, a general history of music and drama, or a survey of song in the modern theater. It is the purpose of this study to provide a general theory of dramatic song, to give a brief survey of song in Western drama, and to offer an overview of song in contemporary British drama, to illustrate boh the importance of song for the dramatic form and the essential vitality of present-day theater. To demonstrate the functions of dramatic music, this survey is combined with a detailed study of some of the most inventive of contemporary dramatists. This is, I believe, one of the liveliest periods in English dramatic history with respect to the number of dramatists active, the depth and breadth of their intellectual and artistic pursuits, and the exploitation of all the resources of theater: visual, aural, mimetic, verbal, and musical.

It has not been possible to include a detailed consideration of song in Irish drama, although non-English perspectives do enter in through the Irish plays of John Arden and Margaretta D'Arcy and the Scottish dramas of John McGrath. In Ireland, music and drama have always maintained a close alliance: George Bernard Shaw, William Butler Yeats, Lady Gregory, and Sean O'Casey are examples that immediately come to mind. This musical tradition is carried on by younger playwrights in the modern period: Brendan Behan, M. J. Molloy, Donagh MacDonagh, Brian Friel, Stewart Parker, Patrick Galvin, J. B. Keane, Wilson John Haire, James McKenna, Thomas Murphy, and Peter Sheridan all use song in the dramatic medium with ease and skill. The exclusion of Irish plays is thus justified partly by the overabundance of Irish material, and partly by the basic cultural differences between England and Ireland. Both song and theater are communal and societal forms of cultural expression, and any study designed to include the Irish component would have to include also an analysis of Irish cultural understanding of music that far exceeds the scope of this work.

This intimacy of folk, artistic creation, and musical heritage would not at first glance seem to be so common in England. More precisely, the natural ease of association that once existed in England, too, was lost in the late Renaissance with the decline of oral traditions and the increase of literacy in artistic production.[9] It survived, of course, in the more popular forms of theater, in melodrama and music hall, but did not find a place in the realistic traditions of legitimate theater. It is thus one of the major discoveries of this investigation that the musical heritage in drama has been revived in full force in the postwar period. English dramatists of the present exhibit a firm grasp of the possibilities of live performance—and song exists mainly through performance. The dramatic idiom is again expanded to include all the musical, visual, and ritual possibilities that it once possessed, producing vibrant and varied combinations of music and drama.

The central focus of this study is on dramatic song in works designed for the stage. Radio plays, television drama, and film scripts require different techniques of writing and call for unique production methods, to say nothing of a separate focus and vocabulary needed on the part of the critic. For these reasons I have included dramas intended for media other than the regular stage only if they appear to demand special attention. A different type of question is posed by those dramatic forms with a strong musical element, such as opera or musical comedy. The attention of the present study is focused more on stage performance and textual criticism than on questions of musical form and technique. Thus those genres emphasizing music over text are not explored here, unless they are written by an author who otherwise devotes himself or herself to stage plays. In general, operas and musicals are not considered unless they seem relevant to the experience or development of a specific dramatic author.

Within these limitations the study is intended to expand critical vision and vocabulary. It is not until one understands the integration of the textual, musical, and performance aspects that one can fully appreciate the effect of, and response to, dramatic song. The study is directed primarily toward the literature specialist, the theatergoer and the playreader, not toward the musicologist. I have deliberately avoided musical terminology that the average reader would not understand. For those who can read music, the musical illustrations will help to redress this slight imbalance in favor of the text.

1

Dramatic Song: Theoretical and Historical Considerations

Theory of Dramatic Song

SONG THEORY

What is dramatic song? This question can be adequately answered only after a brief consideration of the nature of song in general as opposed to the lyric poem. The two are not identical, although if printed as texts without music they would appear to be so. In the case of song, however, the intended medium of presentation affects the nature of the text. A scholarly critical apparatus developed in response to lyrical poetry is not adequate in dealing with song. By definition, at least in Western culture, song is a relatively short metrical composition designed for singing, often divided into stanzas, "whose meaning is conveyed by the combined force of words and melody. The song, therefore, belongs equally to poetry and music."[1] Song and lyric poem have grown apart since the late Renaissance. Formerly they were much more closely associated, indeed often identical. From Homer to the Elizabethan period, most poetry was intended for oral recitation, whether formally presented, chanted, or sung in a musical form.

In any case, the intended oral presentation and the envisioned projection through music influence and alter the nature of song lyrics. In his excellent study on *The Experience of Songs*, Mark W. Booth illustrates how the first major element influencing the song text is its participation in oral culture, the second its adaptation to the music:

> Song words bear the burden of oral communication, under the special condition of being set to music. . . . Song verse is not assimilated to music but accommodated to it.[2]

It is not always possible to distinguish precisely between the effects of orality and those of musicality in song lyrics. In many cases they overlap or converge. The techniques of song have been devised over the centuries to make the text meaningful to the listener in the context of time-oriented oral

17

presentation in the musical medium. For many people, song exists *only* in oral performance because they are not musically literate enough to hear the sound when they read the score (and often there is no score). Song critics, however, reach similar conclusions whether their attention is focused on the interaction of music and text or on the influence of oral culture on the words.

In contrast with poetry, song lyrics achieve their effect less through density, irony, ambiguity, and complexity than through simplicity, manipulation of familiar formulas, and strong, short-range rhyming. In particular, the syntax is constructed in such a way that the phrase is accommodated to the short line of music and to the limited length of the singer's breath. A striking feature of songs is their use of cumulative devices, foremost among these the patterning into stanzas and a wealth of repetition techniques that enable the listener to keep pace with the meaning and serve as a mnemonic aid to the singer. Familiar to the ballad student will be internal repetition, incremental repetition, and the use of refrain lines or a separate refrain stanza in which text and tune are particularly well integrated. Not all songs tell a story as ballads do, but repetition serves also in a shorter, more lyrical context to achieve unity, clarity, and a sense of familiarity in a form of performance that does not allow for pauses, rereadings, and aesthetic reconsiderations. Alliteration, antithesis, and annular or chiastic structures also strengthen the unity, especially when seen in connection with musical phrases that are repeated exactly or with melodic, harmonic and rhythmic variation. W. H. Auden, who has worked extensively with song, lyric poetry, and drama, concludes that words designed to be set to music are rhythmically more inventive and less inclined to be obscure than those in lyric poetry.[3] It will be seen, then, that song is fundamentally different from lyric poetry. Designed for oral and musical presentation, without these factors it is not complete.

Song theory has long explored the exact nature of the interrelationship between music and words. Earlier critics postulated a synthesis theory in which each of the independent elements fused to create a new whole. Music was seen in effect as an interpretation or translation of the text, or sometimes as the altogether dominant factor. V. C. Clinton-Baddeley in 1941 speaks of the "incompleteness" of song language.[4] Charles O. Hartman, in a 1975 essay, still represents the older school of thought when he writes:

> Song is the integration—not the mere combination—of music and poetry. . . . If integration of word and note is to be maintained, the words must give up some of their autonomy and allow the music, which is more suited to the task because more limited to it, to control the tone. . . . Take the music away, and the words seem fuzzy with indecisions and half-realizations.[5]

Newer theory of song sees the combination of elements not as integration or synthesis but as confrontation in which each element retains its individuality. Lawrence Kramer's *Music and Poetry* (1984) is representative of these more recent ideas, in stating, for example, the following:

> A poem is never really assimilated into a composition; it is *incorporated*, and it retains its own life, its own "body," within the body of the music.[6]

The relationship between the elements is seen as a contest or confrontation. This theory sees song as involving a *dissociation* or an *agonistic struggle*, in which there is a constant active process of deconstruction of the text through the music and reconstruction in song:

> The song is a "new creation" only because it is also a de-creation. The music appropriates the poem by contending with it, phonetically, dramatically, and semantically; and the contest is what most drives and shapes the song.[7]

What used to be seen as a subtle integration of two different forms of rhythm, the stress-oriented system of poetic rhythm and the length-oriented system of musical rhythm, is now seen as a contest, or as a constant process of dissociation and reformation:

> No matter how muted or naturalized it may become, the primary fact about song is what might be called a topological distortion of utterance under the rhythmic and harmonic stress of music: a pulling, stretching, and twisting that deforms the current of speech without negating its basic linguistic shape.[8]

This dissociative or agonistic theory has distinct advantages when dealing with the phenomenon of dramatic song. The complications of visual spectacle, physical performance, gesture, literary and dramatic context must be considered, in addition to the factors of orality, musicality, and textuality. These elements all vie for attention in the performance of a dramatic song. Even at this stage, it is clear that it would be a major critical error to evaluate song with the same criteria used for the criticism of poetry.

THEORY OF DRAMATIC SONG

Just as the song lyric is not a poem, but a "script for a public event,"[9] a dramatic text is essentially a script for production: neither is complete without performance. The problem of assessing a dramatic lyric begins with the issue of musical literacy. Experienced playgoers may be able to imagine some performance features when they read a drama, but unless they are musically trained and attuned, they will still read the dramatic song lyrics as poetry rather than imagining them as performed song. Mark Booth emphasizes:

> To understand the real nature of the song we must not after all be content with the text as object but must project it into performance and imagine the experience it offers.[10]

One of the central purposes of this study is to awaken the reader's imagination to the musical performance aspect of dramatic song. A study of this phenomenon forces reflection not only on the author's intentions but also on theories of audience response. In this case three levels of reaction to a song must be considered: those of reader response (to the literary text); viewer response (to the visual aspects of presentation); and listener response (to the auditory levels of performance and music).

The dramatic song, of course, participates in the duality of drama itself as both script and performance, literary text and public event. The best of dramas and the best of dramatic songs can be reread as literature and are usually written for a literate audience. A major argument of this study is that dramatic song in the contemporary period is indeed an integral element in the play *as literature*. Although song words themselves may employ a simpler patterning than that of a sophisticated poem, they gain their full literary dimensions through the context in which they are placed. The ironies and the multiplicities of meaning they evoke can be extremely subtle and complex. Certainly not all of these dimensions can be perceived by an audience during performance. When sung on stage, a dramatic song will have a more immediate, emotional effect. When reread in leisure it will participate in the literary structure of the entire drama and contribute to the aesthetic patterning of the whole.[11]

I have just mentioned that newer song theory advances an agonistic, dissociative view of how the disparate elements involved in song collaborate and/or compete with each other. In a similar vein, newer performance theory sees theater as a pluralistic art, in which such elements as acting, gesture, lighting, space, sound effects, and voice do not merge but confront each other; the spectator is charged with performing the semiotic act of creating the meaning of the whole. Thus performance is no longer seen merely as a translation of the text, just as music is no longer seen as translation of the song lyrics. The theater experience is seen as a creative process, a dynamic continuum in which the meaning is established during performance, as the spectator filters the various signs and stimuli and decides which embodies the message or meaning. Bernard Dort explains in "The Liberated Performance" from *Modern Drama*:

> The theatrical performance cannot be thought of simply as a static collection of signs; it must also be viewed as a dynamic continuum which has duration and is effectively produced by the actor. . . . Performance [is] the actual site of meaning. . . . Such a conception . . . may be called *agonistic*, since it implies a contest of meaning in which the spectator is really the judge. . . . Theatricality, then, is . . .

the drifting of these signs, the impossibility of their union, and finally their confrontation before the spectator of this emancipated performance.[12]

Jindřich Honzl, an early semiotician of the Prague School, in "Dynamics of the Sign in the Theatre" (1940, reprinted in *Semiotics of Art*), defines the theatrical sign itself as one which is versatile and changeable in nature. For example, music can indicate place, or an actor's movement can define a stage prop.[13] The constantly fluctuating supply of theatrical signs is called *bricolage* by a more recent theater semiotician, Anne Ubersfeld. She, too, sees the theatrical experience as an active and creative, rather than a passive pleasure.[14] The Italian theoretician Marco De Marinis emphasizes that selection is crucial to the derivation of meaning on the part of the spectator. Given the flux of information to which he or she is exposed, it is

> absolutely essential that spectators discard and even drastically eliminate some of the mass of stimuli to which they are exposed. . . . Without this basic *decoupage* and selection carried out by their attention, the spectators would not be in a position to work out their own "reading" strategies for the performance.[15]

De Marinis focuses in the article, "Dramaturgy of the Spectator," (*The Drama Review* 1987) from which the preceding quotation is taken, on the devices whereby dramatic authors, directors and actors focus audience attention. Music and song are, of course, ideal focusing techniques; it would be unusual for an audience to not concentrate on a singer and his words. Of the usefulness of the semiotic approach in a discussion of dramatic song, more later.

At this juncture it would seem helpful to combine the ideas of song theory with those of performance theory to create a new theory of dramatic song. This study indeed posits the existence of dramatic song as a separate genre. The only modern critic to my knowledge who has advanced this theory is the German dramatist Peter Hacks. In his brief study of songs in dramatic pieces, Hacks points out that while these may belong formally to lyric poetry, in terms of genre, they are dramatic. A song in a play is not a subjective and personal utterance of the lyric poet, he says; rather, it conveys something about the singer or the dramatic context, both of which are fictitious creations.[16] This resistance of dramatic song to classification in the traditional genres, and its participation in several literary modes (lyric poetry, dramatic art) as well as several performance media (musical, vocal projection within the acted stage spectacle), justify an assessment of the genre under new theoretical considerations.

Dramatic song as a genre, then, must be seen primarily as one of many means of dramatic expression, participating in the construction of the play as a whole in a way similar to that of dialogue, plot, and characterization. In form, however, it introduces a lyrical and musical moment into the largely spoken or mimed performance. Whereas dramatic dialogue is determined by interpersonal conflict, the song is often personal. Although confrontation of two or more characters in song is not impossible, dramatic song is most often the expression of one figure. This does not necessarily mean, however, that it is an unambiguous statement of the mood, emotion or views of this fictitious character. It may also embody a statement by the author about the character, or even a statement about the function of this play in the author's society. In fact, although related to the soliloquy in its distinctive manner of presentation, song most often embodies a generalized, rather than an individual, statement. It might be said that while the soliloquy makes the individual subtext explicit, revealing hidden passions and motivations, the dramatic song reveals the social subtext, expressing communal emotions and thoughts. Familiar songs often express feelings or experiences shared by a large body of listeners. Dramatic song, then, may be defined as one of the channels through which total dramatic meaning can be conveyed. It is dramatic in function, lyric in form, and musical in its mode of presentation.

Dramatic song is challenging because it extends the inner confrontations of the genre song, and combines them with the dissociative factors of performance to create a particularly striking and discontinuous moment. If semiotics is the study of how meaning is derived from particular signs or sign systems, an understanding of the function of a dramatic song entails assessment of many different and even contradictory signs and systems. Melody line, possible accompaniment or harmony, timbre of the human voice, semantic meaning of the song lyrics, function of the singing character in the context of the stage play, and the implications of the song in the wider dramatic context are just a few of the important factors involved. Others, such as the positioning of the musicians or singers, the lighting during the performance of the song, or the manner in which it is introduced, will also be discussed. The spectator can derive meaning from any one of these signs, or a combination of these, and at each new viewing or hearing new meaning may be perceived or created. The essence of a dramatic song, therefore, is in no way identical with the semantic meaning of its lyrics, and all of these factors—the song factors, performance factors and dramatic factors—must be called into account when attempting an evaluation.

To understand more fully how song is effective and how dramatic song functions, one must first consider in more detail the semiotic theories of theater and music, the psychology of music and the social psychology of song, and how performance conditions affect song presentation and reception. In addition, brief classification of how songs may work in the fictitious dramatic context will be helpful. Far from being a simplistic form of poetry, dramatic song is among the most complex and evocative conveyors of meaning in the theater. Not just an extraneous ornament in serious drama, song contributes significantly to the perception of theater as a place of public confrontation and dynamic creation.

THE SEMIOTICS OF THEATER AND SONG

Although drama and dramatic performance have not received as much attention as other genres, they are in the view of many theater theoreticians particularly suited to semiotic analysis. In the words of one of the pioneers in the field of semiotics, Umberto Eco, the stage radically transforms all persons and objects appearing on it, so that virtually everything is turned into a sign:

> The very moment the audience accepts the convention of the mise-en-scène, every element of that portion of the world that has been framed (put upon the platform) becomes significant.[17]

Some semioticians categorize the elements of theater. Tadeusz Kowzan (1968) distinguishes thirteen systems at work in any given theatrical production; a system is understood as a repertory of signs or signals, a formal network of elements. According to Kowzan, the systems are: language, tone, facial mime, gesture, movement, makeup, hairstyle, costume, props, decor, lighting, music, and sound effects (including "noises off").[18] Music is thus one of the systems involved in live performance. More recent theater semioticians such as Keir Elam in *The Semiotics of Theatre and Drama* (1980) would add further systems to this list, such elements as architectural form of stage and theater, and technical options as film and back projection.[19] With increasing technology and electronics in theater, even these lists surely are not exhaustive.[20]

Semiotics, as a comprehensive, multidisciplinary science of signs, seeks to break down the elements of performance into as many units as conceivable and to categorize them as precisely as possible. Thus music as a communicational factor can be catalogued according to source (composer); transmitter (voice or musical instruments); signals (sounds); and channel (sound waves) before it transmits its message (music) to the receivers (ears) of the addressee.[21] For the semiotician, dedicated to the scientific study of the production of meaning—both the generation of meaning and the communication of meaning—the concern is equally with the vehicles of communication (or signifiers) and the mental concepts involved (or signified). The particular richness and density of theatrical communication makes attention to a variety of performance systems imperative. Keir Elam asks:

> How can we best characterize the overall or global "message" produced by this multi-channelled, multi-systemic communicational system? It is not, clearly, a single-levelled and homogeneous series of signs or signals that emerges, but rather a

weave of radically differentiated modes of expression, each governed by its own selection and combination rules.[22]

Elam pleads for an understanding of each system on its own terms.

Useful certainly, in view of the confusing number of signs and stimuli in the theater, are the semiotic concepts of foregrounding and framing, whereby any of the signs involved may be placed in a position of prominence. By making a sign seem unusual and unfamiliar, the spectator's consciousness is drawn to recognize it as a sign and observe its functions. Song in a play is by its very nature a prime example of foregrounding. The music serves as a frame; the song words are distanced from the dramatic text, set apart and highlighted. The Russian Formalist notion of defamiliarization was essentially the root of the semiotic concept of foregrounding. It was also from the idea of defamiliarization that Bertolt Brecht developed his well-known theory of alienation. In essence, similar phenomena are designated by these terms. Since foregrounding is, however, a spacial concept and alienation a more general intellectual one, the latter term would seem more suitable in explaining how music and song work in the theater. This study, therefore, generally refers to alienating functions and devices rather than to foregrounding ones.

In terms of semiotic analysis, the difference between dramatic text (the written word) and performance text (the realization on stage) must be recognized. The performance text has traditionally received more attention than the dramatic text, and many semioticians avoid discussion of the interaction of the two. Thus Joseph Melançon tries to divorce the semantic from the semiotic:

> One can imagine, in its theatrical expression, the creation of a semiotics as a repertory of signs dissociated from language. As a place of figurativity, theatre has the possibility of dissociating in time and space the semiotic from the semantic. . . . The specificity of theatre, or theatricality, can be defined as the possibility of creating a positional semiotics syntactically dissociated from the discourse which semantically invests it.[23]

This kind of narrow definition of theatricality, which dissociates it from the word, from semantic meaning, and finally from the dramatic text, is clearly unsatisfactory for the literary critic, who usually begins any investigation with the written word. Still, the semiotic approach can potentially offer a good antidote to the narrow vision of the ordinary scholar who may ignore performance conditions. A consideration of text in interaction with performance is essential to a full understanding of dramatic song.

The most profitable semiotic approach seems to be the one that focuses on the dynamics of interaction, the creation of meaning out of a continuous flux or confrontation of signals and sign systems. This, in turn, facilitates concentration on each of the elements involved in dramatic song to see how they interrelate, are foregrounded, and create meaning. One of the most promising of newer undertakings is embodied in the more recent work of Patrice Pavis, who in *Languages of the Stage* can be seen to be moving away from earlier, more rigid attempts at typology. Indeed, Pavis warns against too rigorous a codification or classification in theater:

> Rather than trying to identify the signs of a system exhaustively, we must stress the important moments in the signifying sequence and clarify the main stages of the process of semiosis. . . . In this way we can avoid chopping the performance into a mass of heterogeneous signs.[24]

Pavis defines the sign itself as a correlation that emerges from the activities of author, actor, director, and spectator:

> Instead of considering the code as a system "hidden" within the performance . . . it would be fairer to talk about a *process of setting up a code*.[25]

Pavis particularly stresses the need for flexibility in method to accommodate the dynamics of theatrical performance. It might be noted, however, that Pavis's book, while more stimulating, is far less structured and cohesive than Elam's.

What are the advantages or disadvantages of approaching dramatic song through semiotic analysis, as it has been practiced to date? First, it does away with the awkward necessity for an imprecise terminology, whereby visual, aural, and mimetic systems are referred to as languages of theater. Each system may be analyzed on its own terms, but seen as contributing to the network that comprises the performance text. Second, the semiotic method draws attention to the performance aspects of drama and of song and to their varied, multidimensional resources; this is valuable and essential in any discussion of dramatic song. Finally, the attention to framing, foregrounding, or alienating devices, whereby language is patterned in such a way that it becomes unusual and attracts attention, seems a helpful way to examine how dramatic song has its impact.

The usefulness of the semiotic method for musical analysis, a relatively late development in the theory of music, is disputed critically far more than the semiotics of theater. One of Rose Rosengard Subotnik's main objections to the method is that a static identification of units is not suited to the explanation of the inner dynamics and temporal relationships of music.[26] Newer musical theory and song theory, however, are moving in the same direction as performance theory—toward a description of the dynamics of performance and creative reception on the part of the listener. Nothing in the method per se precludes an extension of the study of meaning to include psychological, sociological, and political aspects of communication. Here, Umberto Eco seems a pioneer when he writes in "Semiotics of Theatrical Performance" from *The Drama Review*: "A semiotics of the mise-en-scène is constitutively a semiotics of the production of ideologies."[27] Patrice Pavis also sees the need for semiology (the term he prefers) to expand its horizons in this direction:

> Semiology is gradually recovering everything it formerly excluded from its methodological field. It is, therefore, now concerned with *the problem of discourse*, speech acts, theory of possible worlds, presuppositions, socio-semiotics.[28]

He, too, emphasizes the role of ideologies in the creation of meaning:

> The spectator's liberty to maneuver . . . depends . . . on a knowledge of the ideological codes of the reality reproduced: this . . . has especially to do with recognition of the ideological and transformational character of the text and of artistic activity in general. . . . A performance text is only decipherable in its intertextual relationship with a social discourse.[29]

Intertextual as used here by Pavis must be understood in its wider sense as reference to a cultural system, the way in which a work participates in the signifying practices of its culture.[30]

Although the semiotic method could potentially encompass such wider questions of society and ideology, it does not, in its present form, prove entirely adequate in dealing with such phenomena. The perception of music is governed by such complex factors as neuropsychology (the way in which the brain perceives music and speech), the psychology of music (how emotions are activated through music), and the social psychology of song (cultural conditioning), to say nothing of the aesthetic patterning and structuring of music studied by traditional musical theory. The perception of theater is governed not just by aesthetic but also by sociopsychological and ideological factors, to say nothing of economics. Semiology has often avoided such wider complexes. A critical approach to the study of dramatic song must encompass not just the aesthetics of form and the categorization of signs and codes of meaning, but also the relationship between signs and codes, and the relationship of these to other forms of discourse—psychological, sociological and ideological—in both music and theater.

THE PSYCHOLOGY AND SOCIAL PSYCHOLOGY OF MUSIC

The power of song has to do with its confrontation of text and music, of the intellectual with the emotional. Music is not comparable to language, although it is sometimes seen as having its own syntax and grammar. It does not lend itself to strict rational understanding: "It is clear that the 'messages' of music are more in the affective than the cognitive realm."[31] Music has its own aesthetic principles; its intellectual appeal is related more to form and structure than to rational discursive thought. W. H. Auden says that to him singing has erotic evocations:

> To me, vocal music plays the part in music that the human nude plays in painting. In both there is an essential erotic element . . . and, without this element of the erotic which the human voice and the nude have contributed, both arts would be a little lifeless.[32]

While music can be produced by instruments alone, a song cannot be produced without the human voice. The voice is a major conveyor of erotic feeling; erotic emotion is one of the most powerful irrational forces in human experience. Lawrence Kramer, too, speaks of the release of "erotic feeling" through song, and continues:

> By replacing the phonetic/syntactic integrity of the text with the gestural continuity of a melodic line, song re-connects the impulse to speak with its basis in physical sensation and the felt continuity of the ego—the subjective preconditions of communication.[33]

It is easiest to analyze the emotional effect of music at the level of the psychology of sound, of physical properties and sensations. Thus vibrations, resonance, and dynamic changes affect the human senses and the nerve system and stimulate emotional response. But this by no means accounts for the full emotional impact of music. The effects of melody, harmony, rhythm, tempo, mode, and pitch are much more difficult to assess. Tempo seems to be the most important factor governing audience response, followed by modality and pitch. Earlier neuropsychological theory postulated that the human brain had different ways of apprehending discursive speech and musical sound. According to this theory, speech is governed by the left hemisphere, and song by the right hemisphere.[34] It seems that modern medical experiments do not bear out this theory: whereas speech is definitely a function of one hemisphere, music is perceived by both, in extremely subtle and complex ways.[35]

Another problem concerning the reception of music arises from the fact that many of the factors governing emotional response to song are independent of the music itself. In his interesting study, *The Social Psychology of Music*, Paul Farnsworth emphasizes both the individual and the social contexts of the listening process:

> The mood elicited by the music will depend not only on the tonal configurations the listener hears but also on a variety of factors external to the music itself. Among the more important of these variables are the listener's personality structure, the mood held just preceding the listening period, the word-meanings of the libretto . . . and the attitudes built up in the listener toward music in general and toward the piece in question.[36]

The most important external factors governing the listener's emotional reception of song are social, foremost among them cultural conditioning and musical education. If the listeners are roughly from the same subculture, their responses to a given piece of music will be similar. Conversely, the song structures of any given culture will reflect its social structures: "Music . . . expresses the culture from which it comes."[37]

The psychology of mode offers a good illustration for the cultural associations of music. The modern major and minor modes are a relatively recent development in the history of music, and the ideas now held about these modes were not invariably valid in other centuries or other cultures. Indeed, mood expectations connected with certain modes have been reversed between Greek times and the present day. Plato considered the Lydian mode, which developed into our major, as self-indulgent, decadent and harmful and wanted it banned from his ideal republic. In medieval church music this same precursor of the major was called Ionian and was reviled as *modus lascivus*, or wanton mode.[38] Major chords and melodies have, however, in present-day Western culture, connotations of joy, triumph or confidence. Thus our modern associations are by no means inherent in the music but are a matter of cultural traditions and conditioning.

It is not surprising, then, that when contemporary British dramatists employ familiar tunes they almost invariably choose them from the English or American cultural spheres. In fact, they are more likely to integrate American songs than Irish songs into their works. The American sphere of musical culture is closer to that of the English than is the Irish. Usually only a dramatist such as Margaretta D'Arcy, who is of Irish origin, will introduce specifically Irish tunes into a play. Both tune and text of a song, each in its own right, function as codes or passwords for much larger cultural assumptions and deep-seated emotions. As the dramatist Peter Barnes remarks, songs are useful as "shorthand," evoking in just a brief musical phrase entire cultural and social complexes. In the most general sense, then, songs participate in the phenomenon of intertextuality, the signifying processes of cultural systems. Response to a song is intellectual and emotional at the same time; it is a response to both words and music. But under performance conditions the emotional and cultural responses to the music will come more quickly, before the intellectual or aesthetic implications of the words have been fully apprehended.

In his study of song, Mark Booth suggests that the actual activity of singing or hearing someone sing has important psychological and emotional implications. Through the music of song the subjective individual is drawn out of the self, transcends mundane reality, and participates in community, celebrates a collective ritual and achieves a sense of communion with all else. This may go so far as to end in quasireligious ecstasy, an abandonment of self, although the words of the song will usually pull us back and prevent total dissolution of the personality. The element of active communal participation in singing is crucial to our experience of song:

> If the community's songs invite people into the interior of a shared image . . . the image is mythic in a positive and powerful sense. It is an element in the living mythology by which the community constitutes itself and its world.[39]

Even if a song is sung to us rather than actively sung by us, our sense of entering into the song's perspective is similar. The experiences of community, ritual, and celebration that song promotes also are extremely significant when we turn to a specific consideration of how song functions in dramatic performance. In fact, since both song on the one hand and theater on the other are concentrated forms of societal and communal expression, it would seem that the dramatic song, which combines both, can be the very epitome of community experience.

PERFORMANCE CONDITIONS

Certain performance conditions may affect the presentation and reception of song. Although most people have the ability to speak, by no means all can carry a tune. Not every actor can sing. Not every theater can afford a musician or musicians to accompany the singer. Such basic thoughts must enter into any discussion of dramatic song. An author may accommodate a non-singing actor by allowing the actor to speak the song lyrics, or by cutting a song for particular performances. In print, however, the song will remain as part of the literary context and structure.

The form of the theater and of the stage, and the positioning of the actor or actors in relation to the audience will also have an influence on the way in which the song is received. A song sung on the forestage and directed straight at the audience will achieve quite a different reaction from one, say, sung by a group of actors dancing in a round upstage. Similar considerations apply to the positioning of musicians. On the open medieval platform stage, songs inevitably included the audience as part of the community. In the Elizabethan playhouse, with its combination of open stage and formal background structure, the musicians were probably set apart in the music room on the third level (at least at the Globe) and hidden from view by a curtain. But they might also perform on stage, under, or above the stage as needed. In the modern theater the two extremes with respect to the placing of musicians are represented by Richard Wagner and Bertolt Brecht. Wagner insisted on having the musicians invisible in a sunken orchestra pit in order to maximize the emotional effect of the singers. Brecht was determined to have the musicians fully visible on stage throughout a performance so the audience would be conscious of the techniques by which music and song were being produced.

Whereas positioning of singers and musicians may be either a matter of theater structure or a result of aesthetic principles, the question of the number of singers and size of the ensemble is not simply aesthetic but also dictated by theater economics. Effect is not always achieved by money and numbers, as can be seen in some of the Royal Shakespeare Company's musical embellishments to Shakespeare's plays. Depending on the size of the theater and the distance to the audience, however, a chorus does require a certain number of singers to achieve the desired effect. Modern microphones, amplifiers, and tape recording techniques add entirely new dimensions to song presentation and can be used effectively in modern theater. These are just a few of the factors that should be considered when discussing the musical presentation of song on stage.

When Wagner developed his theory of the *Gesamtkunstwerk*, he envisioned a synthesis of the arts, whereby the spectators would be overwhelmed by the effect and not inquire about the mechanics or individual meaning of any of the separate elements involved. This ideal of a creative union of all the arts— song, spectacle, music—became dominant in the late nineteenth century. Brecht, totally opposed to this concept of synthetic music theater, created his own theory and practice of dissociative, alienating epic theater and epic opera in which the spectator was to remain conscious of each individual factor and of the mechanics of performance. Many contemporary dramatists, whether or not they follow Brecht in theory, seem to create plays in which the various elements such as song and spectacle are not totally fused, and in which the audience can, and should, remain aware of ironies, discrepancies, and incongruities. Perhaps the post-Brechtian theater should be seen as dissociative in technique, if not Brechtian in political message. For these reasons, the agonistic theory of dramatic song seems to work especially well when dealing with ironic, satiric, and disorienting plays and songs that comprise the majority of modern examples.

FUNCTIONS OF DRAMATIC SONG

The vast majority of dramatic songs have more than one function. Often they are subtly integrated into the dramatic situation, adapted to the singer, of thematic significance for the play as a whole, and chosen for emotional or satirical reasons. The following categories must not, therefore, be thought of as mutually exclusive. On the contrary, many songs will embody several functions simultaneously. I thought it useful to categorize as precisely as possible to demonstrate the extraordinary multiplicity of effects a dramatic song is capable of achieving.

In its simplest form dramatic song is decorative and entertaining. The experience of hearing a song is usually pleasurable, because of the sensuous qualities of the music. If the song lyrics have no wider significance in the context of the action, a dramatic song may be said to be incidental or ornamental. Still, on a simple level, songs may be introduced for reasons of theater technique or for dramatic structure. Illustrative of a fairly straightforward technical function would be a song sung in order to create time for costume or scenery changes. A lyric may also be used in order to avoid unnecessary repetitions. For example, in *As You Like It* Shakespeare refrains from retelling Orlando's story after the latter reaches the Forest of Arden. While Amiens sings "Blow, Blow thou Winter Wind" (act 2, scene 7), Orlando whispers his tale to the Duke. Songs may technically bridge lapses in time, for example, during journeys or when a number of years go by. The dramatist may use this device illusionistically, in order to distract the audience from the time jump, or he may employ it nonrealistically as an epic recapitulation of events in the intervening years. One can also observe a song function related to the classical techniques of *teichoskopia* and the messenger's report; a song may describe off-stage battles and events too difficult to present in action. The very activity of singing may be used to further the plot, as in *Twelfth Night* when the drunken midnight revelry in the kitchen leads to Malvolio's intervention, and this in turn to the plot of reprisal against him. That is an example of comic complication due to song. Related techniques can of course also be observed in tragedy or in serious plays.

Particularly effective in both technical and structural respects are songs that open and close scenes. Such songs create a marked sense of beginning or ending for the audience through the stylistic and musical heightening. In addition to the structural effect, the technique can have thematic usefulness. Introductory ballads prepare the audience for the action to come, whereas a closing song will often summarize or state a moral to be drawn from the dramatic action. Some plays have a formal musical framework carefully balanced between beginning and end. It has always been a favorite technique of drama to end with a song. This may be the equivalent of the triumphant, joyous grand finale: an example is the wedding song that forms the climax of *As You Like It*. Or it may be employed to create a bridge between stage illusion and everyday reality; one need only think of Feste's epilogue song in *Twelfth Night*. In modern political drama such a closing song will often pass on responsibility for further action to the audience. A tune may also be designed to leave spectators with a bitterly ironic aftertaste. A good example of that would be the World War I lyric "Keep the Home Fires Burning," which terminates both Shaw's *Heartbreak House* and O'Casey's *The Plough and the Stars*. Although the intentions of the playwright may differ considerably, the technique always creates a sense of heightened ending, and a feeling of closure.

Music, as we have seen, has a powerful emotional effect on the listener. This property may be used by a playwright in a variety of ways—to strengthen or create mood and atmosphere in a scene, express an emotional impulse in a character, or to support the communal, ritual effect of theater.

Songs employed in realistic drama most often arise in an emotional context. They will be employed in situations in which human beings sing naturally; scenes of conviviality, birthday celebrations, pub scenes, or scenes of communal drinking all give rise to realistic singing. These are contexts in which a director may be tempted to introduce a song, even if the text does not call for it. The same applies to other group contexts in which dramatic characters are thrown together or held together by external circumstances, for example, in army scenes or work situations.

A song may be directly expressive of emotion in a dramatic character. Most obvious examples would be love songs, songs of courtship, and songs of praise. More indirect in effect are songs sung due to an emotion but not explicitly expressive of that emotion. Gretchen in Goethe's *Faust*, before she finds the jewelry box, sings out of a vague dread of an unknown danger. The ballad she sings is not concerned with fear but is rather thematically foreshadowing: "Es war ein König in Thule" is about love, faithfulness, and death. This technique is akin to the age-old human habit of whistling in the dark. Less frequent are songs of hatred, argument, or provocation, for example, Sir Toby and Feste singing in comic defiance of Malvolio in the kitchen scene of *Twelfth Night*. Also deeply personal and emotional is the use of music to bring back memories of childhood or adolescence. Song is a powerful factor in establishing a sense of nostalgia in many plays of the modern period. Song lyrics often function as social passwords, evoking wider social attitudes and emotions such as patriotism.

Songs with ritual functions are dependent on, and supportive of, communal emotion rather than individual emotion. Song has the power to draw the individual out of the limited self into communal experience. In such singing, the ritual origins of drama merge with the ritual power of music to create a binding sense of community. As in the case of the other emotional functions, this may or may not extend to the audience. The ritual tunes in Bond's *The Fool* and *The Woman* are intended to illustrate the nature of the community to spectators, but not to draw them into the celebration. The music in Peter Shaffer's *The Royal Hunt of the Sun*, in contrast, is capable of overwhelming the audience with collective emotional experience. Very familiar airs such as Christmas carols or popular tunes are sometimes actively sung by the audience together with the actors. On occasion, such communal singing can lead to Bacchanalian abandon, especially when it is combined with dancing or clapping. This song function, that of inviting the audience to participate and molding them into a community as they sing, brings music and theater together quite clearly with their ancient ritual implications.

Ironic and satiric usages of song rely less heavily on the emotional power of music and more on the capacity of the audience to perceive structural, aesthetic or intellectual contrasts. The meaning of the text becomes important. Musical ironies can also be observed. Most straightforward is the use of song to underline and elaborate on character traits already revealed in dramatic dialogue and situation. Sometimes, however, the lyrics can actually undermine the words spoken by a dramatic character, expose facts not already known, or contradict the meaning of a scene. Irony and satire are often involved in the perception of such discrepancies. In its ironic functions dramatic song may unexpectedly disclose the opposite of what the audience expects. Or it may epitomize all the contradictions already inherent in the dramatic situation: "Keep the Home Fires Burning" at the end of O'Casey's *The Plough and the Stars* works in this way.

The satirical functions of dramatic song require the audience to perceive the fact that the text or the melody is in some way inappropriate to the situation, indicating criticism on the part of the dramatist. Sometimes the songs are blatantly misplaced, as in many of Peter Barnes's or Bond's satirical plays. Sometimes the relationship between traditional tune and newly-written text is incongruous. Sometimes it is the musical style of the piece that is out of place in the context. By means of satiric song, criticism both of the singer and of his or her values is conveyed. In some cases, criticism of the words and connotations of the music also is implied.

The recognition of contrasts is important in all of these functions. Even if the audience in performance cannot perceive all of the subtleties and ironies, it should be able to sense the dissonances which are indication of conflicting standpoints. A playwright does not necessarily expect his audience to recognize the exact changes that have been made, but he usually hopes that they will feel a change in mood or context. On occasion, a drama will make use of two contrasting types of music in order to symbolize opposing spheres and values. *The Tempest, Twelfth Night, Serjeant Musgrave's Dance* and *We Come to the River* offer examples of this technique.

Nonrealistic and nonillusionistic techniques of dramatic song are characteristic of the modern period. In this respect modern drama revives certain older traditions such as Greek choral commentary, or the direct audience address and character self-introduction of medieval theater. Songs may contain direct commentary or indirect commentary in the form of parable, may employ other alienating devices or may assume narrative functions, particularly in epic theater. Song may be used in a nonillusionistic way to introduce a character or explain character history. Self-introduction as in medieval plays is also possible. Song sometimes takes over the function of the earlier soliloquy, and serves to reveal hidden motivations, policies, and desires. Bond's technique of the public soliloquy in song is related to this but represents less revelation of the individual character than exploration of character potential. The commentary songs may embody general explanation of the dramatic situation, a consideration of the situation from the standpoint of the dramatist, or a wider social and political evaluation; "Song of Learning" in Bond's *Restoration*, for example, covers fifty thousand years of workingman's history. Indirect commentary through parable and metaphor is typical of the songs in Brecht and in Bond's later work. Anti-illusionistic are also the epic song functions in which the role of narration is taken over. The narration of off-stage action and sung commentary to mimed or danced action are remarkable techniques. Brecht also uses song to express unspoken thoughts, often while the character remains motionless, struggling with himself or herself.

Alienation is a general term used to describe all devices whereby an audience is provoked into a critical detachment from the dramatic action. In this respect not only the nonillusionistic commentary and narrative song techniques but also many satirical, ironic, and structural devices can be said to have an alienating effect. Even a straightforward emotional lyric may become alienated through the dramatic context in which it is placed. A satirical song in a sentimental context will have a similar result. The well-known devices of placing an orchestra in full view of the audience or of singing directly to the audience will generally help to establish alienation, but cannot be said to guarantee it. More important is the inner stance of the playwright; if he desires to create critical consciousness in his viewers, his songs will often be employed in an alienating fashion.

Breaking through the barriers of realism, undermining dramatic illusion, and exploiting the effects of artificial theatricality can be said to be characteristic of a large number of plays in postwar British drama, whether or not the dramatists wish to achieve Brechtian political alienation. In this respect the widespread revival of music and song in theater can be seen as symptomatic of the investigation into alternatives to realism and the revival of older forms of theatrical presentation.

2. Historical Survey of Song in Drama

EARLIER CENTURIES

The greatest singer of classical myth is Orpheus. His songs could influence not only men but also wild beasts, plants, and even gods. Orpheus embodies the divine properties of music. The myth of the Sirens, on the other hand, incorporates music's dangerous and seductive powers. Orpheus, able to sing louder and sweeter than even the Sirens, saved the Argonauts from shipwreck. After his death in the hands of the Maenads, his lyre, according to some versions of the myth, became the constellation Lyra in the heavens. The philosophers of antiquity feared the seductive powers of music. Plato wanted all music in his ideal Republic to be sung; he disapproved of music without text, because he distrusted its irrational, emotional effect.

Western drama originated in Greek ritual performances that integrated poetry, music, and dance. From these performances gradually emerged tragedy, comedy, and the satyr play, all of which continue to show "the same characteristic blend of spoken word and song and dance."[40] The very term *comedy* is derived from the Greek and means roughly *revel-song*. Aristophanes was praised as a fine composer, and his comedies often contained sung choruses and musical parody. The satyr plays that accompanied Greek tragedy also had a singing chorus of *sileni* or satyrs. What is perhaps less well known is that not only Homeric poetry but also tragedy was chanted rather than recited:

> The distance between speech and song was smaller in ancient Greek than in any modern Western language. . . . For Homer's hearers, the voice chanting in the firelight was the voice of a singer.[41]

Greek meters could be called musical rather than quantitative because the element of pitch was so important; both tragic as well as lyric poets followed not only rhythmic but also melodic rules. Sappho, Pindar, Aeschylus, and Euripides "were evidently composer-poets, and their lyric forms . . . demanded melodic ability."[42] John Herington, in *Poetry into Drama* (1985), calls classical Greek culture of the fifth century B.C. "essentially a song culture"; unfortunately, Greek music has been lost almost entirely, except for two fragments of musically notated tragedies by Euripides.[43]

A glance at drama in other cultures shows a similar integration of music, dance and theater. Many oriental forms continue to place emphasis on all three. Japanese Nō theater draws from and combines song, dance and various styles of drama: Nō plays are highly codified and always involve a chorus and musicians. The more popular style of Kabuki theater originated in ritual dance, and also involves a variety of songs performed by trained musicians positioned on a podium on stage.

In the Western dramatic tradition, song was an important feature of Roman drama, particularly of Plautus's comedies, although, again, the music has not survived.[44] When drama re-emerged in Western Europe in the Middle Ages it once again proved its intense and fruitful relationship to ritual song. Modern Western drama originates in the sung portions of the Christian church liturgy, specifically in the *tropes*, or embellishments added to the liturgical texts. Liturgical drama is the product of a creative interaction between text and music. In an article on music in medieval drama, John Stevens describes various stages in this interrelationship between words and music.[45] The dramatic song of the earliest of these plays is Gregorian liturgical plainchant, and the same musical phrases are employed repeatedly for various dramatic situations. This music is nondescriptive and nonemotive, reflecting not the individual character but the function of the drama as a whole in accepting and celebrating God's order. Gradually, popular or secular musical elements were assimilated into the plainchant. At a later stage, when drama had moved just outside the church, spoken vernacular passages were introduced, while the Latin liturgical *responds* were sung by the choir. Here, as in the later great vernacular cycles of the fourteenth and fifteenth centuries, music remains "a norm of spirituality for the play," containing God's words and signalling the appearance of God or his angels.[46] Essentially this music is, as Stevens explains,

> still restrained, impersonal, generalizing and non-expressive. . . . The chants convey all the unquestioned grandeur of a[n] . . . untroubled and all-embracing Order. They are symptoms in sound . . . of community, a community of worshippers past and present, on earth and in heaven—a musical witness to All Saints.[47]

Later yet, nonliturgical, lyrical elements were introduced into the music, such as the Shepherd's song and the Mother's lament just before the slaughter of the innocents in the *Coventry Nativity Play*. The music to the latter has survived and is still sung today as the "Coventry Carol." It must be emphasized that these, too, are not expressive of personal emotions but represent generalized and typical experience.

In Renaissance England, the idea of the divine connotations of music was still present in the notion of the "music of the spheres." This concept, dating back to Pythagoras and Plato, maintains that both the planets in their orbits and the heavenly beings produce divine music that only specially blessed souls are capable of hearing. This music is a symbol of divine harmony and holds together the entire universe and all creation. Man, in performing his own music, participates in the divine order of things. J. M. Nosworthy points out the importance of understanding the

> place of music in the Elizabethan scheme of things, of seeing it not simply as a diversion but as an *act of faith,* and as something no less essential to the overall pattern than the concepts of degree, the body politic, the elements and humours, and the like.[48]

The clearest reflection of this concept of the divine music of the spheres in Shakespeare's work is to be found toward the end of *The Merchant of Venice* when Lorenzo explains the idea to Jessica:

> Sit Jessica,—look how the floor of heaven
> Is thick inlaid with patens of bright gold,
> There's not the smallest orb which thou behold'st
> But in his motion like an angel sings,
> Still quiring to the young-ey'd cherubins;
> Such harmony is in immortal souls,

But whilst this muddy vesture of decay
Doth grossly close it in, we cannot hear it.

(act 5, scene 1)[49]

When discussing song in Elizabethan drama the Renaissance concepts concerning the divinity of music must be kept in mind.

The traditions of music in drama had not been lost in the period since the medieval liturgical play, as John H. Long notes:

> The later mystery cycles were accompanied by municipal and guild musicians; the interludes and moralities, by vagabond minstrels or the musicians of noble households.[50]

Song and dance were popular features of the interludes of Heywood and the comedies of Lyly. But it was Shakespeare, claims Richmond Noble,

> who made the play with song occurring in it a consistent art-form; it was he who first grasped all the possibilities afforded by song for forwarding the action and who made it a vital part in his dramatic scheme.[51]

The diversity and subtlety of song functions in Shakespeare is indeed quite remarkable. In the manner of the most inventive of the modern dramatists, he employed songs and tunes from a variety of different sources. He introduced folk song, street ballads and catches (or rounds) which were already popular; he wrote new words to existing airs; he parodied songs familiar to his audiences; and in some cases both words and tunes were apparently newly written and composed.

This was, of course, the Golden Age of English art song and of English music, and every gentleman was expected to have a musical training and to be able to sing: "There was never an impassable gulf between 'art music' of . . . the Golden Age and its popular music."[52] Some of the great composers of the time, for example, Thomas Morley and William Byrd, wrote occasionally for the theater. Nosworthy assumes that Robert Johnson worked regularly for Shakespeare's theater company, the King's Men, as composer from about 1607 on.[53] Many actors were taught to sing and accompany themselves on the lute, and in addition, most theaters probably had a staff of between six and ten professional musicians. In the earlier years they may have called on the services of the city "waits." The boy actors of the private theaters were usually given an excellent musical training and taught to play instruments as well as sing.

The songs in Shakespearean drama are too numerous and complex to be summarized here. They are treated in detail in the works of Richmond Noble, John H. Long and Peter Seng.[54] Seng usefully collects extracts of critical comment on each individual song.

The singers in Shakespearean drama are usually secondary characters and often of low birth. Because etiquette frowned on a gentleman performing in public, noble characters will usually call for a page or servant to sing rather than performing themselves. When a person of high breeding does sing, it is often a clear indication of some extraordinary situation or state of mind. Ophelia sings in madness, and Desdemona sings shortly before her death, distraught by the accusations brought by Othello.

Among those requested to sing, the fool or jester plays an important role. As a professional entertainer and merrymaker, singing is one of his natural functions. Long speculates that Robert Armin, for whom the characters of the wise fools in Shakespeare's work were apparently created, perhaps inspired the dramatist to strengthen the musical elements in his parts, as he was a better performer in this respect than his predecessor Will Kempe.[55]

Another group of dramatic figures often called on to sing are the supernatural or non-human characters. The fairies in *A Midsummer Night's Dream* sing. Ariel in *The Tempest* not only symbolizes the airy element but is also a spirit of music. He sings important songs and causes the divine magical music to be performed at Prospero's command. Rustic characters, low-bred townsmen or drunken revellers often perform songs: they usually sing folk tunes, street ballads or popular catches rather than the more sophisticated art "ayres."

One can observe a development in Shakespeare's employment of music and song from the more incidental and ornamental use in the early plays, through the dramatically integrated and essential song functions of the great comedies, especially *As You Like It* and *Twelfth Night*, to the more philosophically determined usages in the later plays. The romances in particular employ music to symbolize divine harmony and regenerative forces.

In the later plays of Shakespeare and in Jacobean drama, the popularity of the masque form had an important influence. Musical pageantry, scenic spectacle, copious song and a profusion of dances were all elements of the masque, which became popular in the reign of James I. The masque was performed as ritual celebration of some momentous event. Mary Chan calls attention to the Stuart conception of the masque, based on philosophic and Platonic ideas, "as an ideal union of all art forms to create an image of perfection."[56]

While belief in the divine properties of music was still common in the sixteenth century, Renaissance dramatists, lyric poets and composers quickly began to explore the more emotive possibilities of music and words. By the seventeenth century, psychological theory accepted the view that "music was a spontaneous expression of certain primary emotional states and could induce certain emotional states in its hearers."[57] But much of Elizabethan song was still highly stylized emotion; the emotion of many of Shakespeare's songs, for example, is subtly distanced by the persona of the singer or the circumstances surrounding the singing. It was not until the nineteenth century that it became universally accepted that a song should be the spontaneous and direct expression of the actual emotion of the maker or singer.

The ballad opera of the eighteenth century, at least in the hands of a master such as John Gay, provided an ideal opportunity to have it both ways: many of the songs in *The Beggar's Opera* are sentimental and satirical at the same time. Audience familiarity with the popular airs or folk tunes which formed the musical basis for the work furnished an emotional touchstone. Gay's lyrics, either excessively sentimental or cynically satirical, seldom allow the audience to sustain any one mood for long. While we indulge with Polly in a deluge of sentimentality, we laugh at the same time at the exaggerations of style and emotion. Gay's combination of popular emotion, familiar music and satire managed to laugh the excesses of Italian opera off the English stage, and restored to English drama a healthy and appealing affinity to the popular musical tradition.[58]

In the nineteenth century, the essential forms that combined music with theater were melodrama and music hall. Both fused excessive musical emotionalism with relatively rudimentary dramatic form. Particularly in melodrama, an appeal to audience sentimentality is made in its most blatant forms. Melodrama is by definition drama with music, but it is on the whole spoken dialogue with a background accompaniment, not sung music. What is important here, as David Mayer points out, is the development of music to

> underline and emphasize the emotional content of a play's action, . . . maintaining momentum of the play's headlong rush from sensation to sensation, from crisis to emotional crisis.[59]

In many cases, music masks the improbabilities of the melodramatic plot, covers unrealistic transitions, and even replaces dialogue. In contrast with the ballad opera, melodrama had a newly-composed score and was elaborately orchestrated, using all the resources of huge modern orchestras to support the emotional effect. Just as the content of melodrama was largely conventional, the music of melodrama was pieced together out of preconceived elements. The score provided musical emotion on cue.

In music hall the emotions of songs generally do not range very widely. Sentimentality, patriotism, pathos, and humor were the staples of the halls. The dramatic form of the music-hall performance is simple: basically it consists of a cumulation of independent "turns," with climax and ending determined not by the dramatic structure but by the popularity of the stars.[60] Nevertheless music hall was beloved in its day, and its influence proves to be of importance for later drama in a number of ways. Its loose dramatic structure aided experimentation in open form, for example, in revue shows such as *Oh What a Lovely War*. Music hall performers were masters in capturing and holding a large live audience and in encouraging audience participation. Many of their techniques were later used to help break down the barriers between stage and audience. Above all, music hall carried the traditions of music in popular theater well into the twentieth century. Such younger dramatists as Arden, Bond and Barnes remember the music-hall stars from live performances or from radio series.

Related to music hall was the English theatrical tradition of pantomime, which flourished throughout the eighteenth and nineteenth centuries. Although some of its characters are derived from the *commedia dell'arte*, it basically is a hotchpotch of incongruous elements: romance, fairy tale, slapstick, comedy, acrobatics, dancing, music, and song.

In serious drama, however, the advent of realism meant a virtual exclusion of music and song from theater for many years. Any song which could not be sung naturally in the circumstances and was not motivated psychologically was radically excised. Dramatic song tends to destroy illusion rather than creating it. It has many potentialities to display theatricality and artificiality, and historically, song has more often than not used these possibilities. Basically, drama with purely realistically-motivated song is an exception in the history of Western drama. Theater without song or music is an anomaly and should be recognized as such. As David Mayer points out:

> We in the twentieth century have inherited a comparatively new practice, not a long-established tradition, and, mistakenly, we have taken the older tradition to be some peculiar manifestation of the Victorian stage.[61]

As I hope to show in the following section, the heritage of song in drama was never really lost, in spite of the potency of the realistic form. It does appear, however, that serious drama with music became rather more marginal in the first half of the twentieth century, only to re-emerge with vigor and variety in the postwar period.

THE EARLY TWENTIETH CENTURY

Serious musical drama in the first half of the twentieth century was marginal, but not in terms of dramatic stature, for O'Casey and Brecht, who employ song as integral element, are among the most important playwrights of the early part of the century. The drama is marginal, however, in terms of British experience. Brecht, of course, was foreign born, and did not become well known in England until the Berliner Ensemble visited London in the mid-1950s. O'Casey, although he lived in England during the latter part of his life, continued to write on Irish themes, and, above all, did not find production possibilities adequate to his dramatic achievement. Both Brecht and O'Casey provide important musical impulses for postwar drama.

The third great influence in passing on musical traditions of drama to the postwar period was Joan Littlewood. Already active in theater in the 1930s, Littlewood's early experience was in radical left-wing theater in Manchester and thus outside of the mainstream of British drama. She, too, did not become well known until the establishment of the Theatre Workshop in London after World War II. Other interesting developments—the experimental dramas of T. S. Eliot, Auden and Isherwood in the 1930s—never managed to establish themselves as formative influences in theatrical tradition, although such playwrights as John Arden are aware of them.

Serious drama with music was indeed existent in the early twentieth century, but needed to be rediscovered for the stage by the playwrights of the postwar period. All of these earlier factors have come together and have blossomed in the musical style of the contemporary period.

It is the Irish playwrights, foremost among them O'Casey, who represent one major source of lyricism and musicality in modern drama. O'Casey carries on the great heritage of dramatic song in traditional functions. The counterpoint to these traditional usages is Bertolt Brecht. In his plays, radical experimentation leads to the development of new alienating song functions within Epic Theater. This experimentation is to prove of equal importance to postwar drama.

O'CASEY AND YEATS

There is a strong affinity between Sean O'Casey and John Arden. O'Casey appreciated Arden, and it is through Brendan Behan and John Arden that O'Casey's influence has been most directly transmitted to modern theater. Both O'Casey and Arden are rooted in the popular theatrical traditions from Shakespeare to the nineteenth century, especially melodrama. In a 1975 essay, "Ecce Hobo Sapiens," Arden elucidates O'Casey's fusion of popular theatrical technique with revolutionary social and political analysis in terms which would also serve to describe his own drama. He points out the production difficulties which O'Casey's innovatory style inevitably encountered in commercial theater, and concludes:

> O'Casey's plays as social documents have not yet become out-of-date: as poetic creations they have not even begun to be realized.[62]

Although O'Casey is not far from Brecht in his search for non-realistic, emblematic staging techniques and his revival of older theatrical traditions, he represents an opposite extreme in his plea for emotionalism in theater. This sentiment is most clearly embodied in his songs. As he writes:

> I do not agree with those who would banish emotion from the theatre (Brecht seems to imply this), for, to me, emotion burns within the veins of life. . . . I believe that all the arts should meet in the drama—architecture in the framework of the design,

painting in the scenery, music in an occasional song and dance, and literature in a play's dialogue.[63]

He has said he wishes to increase the element of music in his drama:

> I have no fear of characters breaking into song, accompanied with music, during the performance of the play;—in fact, I think there should be more of it in the newer drama.[64]

O'Casey loved all popular forms of song and included them in his plays: folk song, music hall, sentimental parlor ballad, and street ballad are all represented. In addition, he wrote his own lyrics to be set to traditional or new melodies.

The most basic and fundamental function of song in O'Casey's drama is to convey joy and celebration of life. A close affinity exists between song and dance as affirmative activities. Secondarily there is another significant function that extends throughout O'Casey's work, one in which music is used to explore the idea of manipulation of human emotion. In this context, song becomes a useful vehicle in establishing character irony or dramatic irony. Patriotic songs in particular are exploited in this way. In the early plays of the Dublin Trilogy, familiar songs most often are employed in ironic functions, to expose hollow pretensions and deflate overblown ideals. The best-known example is "Keep the Home Fires Burning" at the end of *The Plough and the Stars*.[65]

The Silver Tassie is the first of O'Casey's plays to take its title from a song sung during performance; *Red Roses for Me* and *Oak Leaves and Lavender* are others. *The Silver Tassie* is a strongly experimental drama which explores such Expressionistic techniques as ritual choral chant and movement in relation to stylized realism. Most of the later dramas end with a song which summarizes major thoughts and intentions. To many of these songs O'Casey has written his own texts. In some of the later plays, as O'Casey's political opinions become more explicit, political confrontation is conducted primarily through song (for example, *The Star Turns Red*). Celebration of life, which becomes a dominant theme, relies strongly on song to draw the audience into the ritual joy. Old Codger in *The Bishop's Bonfire* speaks of worshiping through story, dance and song.

In all of these respects O'Casey can be seen as a dramatist rooted in popular musical tradition, but stylistically and formally inventive. He will be remembered for the traditional and emotional expressiveness of his dramatic lyrics. But on no account should we ignore the ironic songs of the early plays or the more experimental song functions of the later plays.

O'Casey is not the only Irish dramatist to embody a strong lyricism in his plays. Shaw, for many years a music critic, often incorporates song. Most of Lady Gregory's dramas contain songs, and the melodies are conveniently

CHORUS

printed at the end of the texts. It is illuminating to compare O'Casey with
W. B. Yeats. In contrast with O'Casey, Yeats possessed no innate musicality.
Whereas O'Casey was steeped in musical tradition from his earliest years and
prided himself in his role as a singer, Yeats was not a singer and had little
sense of melody or pitch. Yeats's interest in song was primarily determined by
his love of lyrical language. In other words, the linguistic aspects of song are
more important to him than the musical. It cannot be reiterated too often that
the musical and lyrical properties of song are not identical. A song is not a
lyrical poem. In Yeats's work music is of secondary importance to the words,
an aid in the public performance of poetry, and it should never distract from
the meaning. Clinton-Baddeley calls Yeats a "Puritan" with respect to music,
because he was afraid of its sensual qualities and worried that it might
obscure the words.[66]

Thus, although both O'Casey and Yeats include songs in all of their major
plays, the functions differ considerably. In Yeats's work, the songs often
represent the lyrical and linguistic culmination. A later phase is represented
by the dance dramas inspired by Japanese Nō theater. The oriental Nō
combines song, dance, and drama, and includes a chorus and musicians. In
Yeats's dance dramas, such as *At the Hawk's Well* or *The Only Jealousy of
Emer*, the static element becomes prominent. Here, song and dance function
as ritual choreography, providing a stylized structural framework. In
O'Casey, in contrast, song and dance are more often employed to indicate a
spontaneous expression of joy.

Due to these distinctions, the influence of O'Casey and Yeats on later
drama makes itself felt in different spheres. Yeats' use of lyrical song inspired
the revival of verse drama in England. O'Casey, on the other hand, has
proved influential among those younger dramatists seeking to integrate musicality, physical movement, visual imagery and the spoken word into a form of
total theater. In contemporary theater, O'Casey provides by far the more
significant inspiration.

BRECHT AND AUDEN

Aside from O'Casey and the popular traditions such as music hall, crucial
inspiration for dramatic song of the later twentieth century came from the
work of Bertolt Brecht. Although Brecht's drama was known before World
War II to people such as Joan Littlewood who were active in radical and
experimental political theater, his influence in England was not widely felt
until the late 1950s, and even then imperfectly understood. Brecht reacti-
vated many older dramatic techniques; a general acquaintance with a few
alienation devices does not necessarily mean, therefore, that a contemporary
dramatist is influenced by Brecht.

Brecht is both the major practitioner of epic theater and epic opera in the twentieth century and also a major theoretician. Nevertheless, he must not be seen in isolation. Just as Erwin Piscator initiated many of the theatrical techniques of the anti-illusionist style later associated with Brecht, so others pioneered elements of the musical theory and musical style typical of epic opera. Epic opera is the culmination of a series of anti-romantic and, especially, anti-Wagnerian tendencies in the early twentieth century.[67] The initiation of the chamber music festival in Donaueschingen in 1921 provided a forum of musical experimentation in Germany, and it was at this festival (after 1926 in Baden-Baden) that Brecht and Kurt Weill's *Mahagonny* was produced in 1927.

Other influences on the use of song in Brecht's work were the anti-illusionistic experiments of Erwin Piscator, the tradition of agitprop street theater that employed proletarian revolutionary songs as an instrument of political persuasion, cabaret, and the German tradition of street ballad known as *Bänkelsang*.[68] Both Piscator and Brecht also insisted that they were following age-old theatrical traditions of musical drama: oriental theater, especially the Nō plays, classic Greek drama, medieval mystery plays, Elizabethan drama, and eighteenth-century ballad opera.

Brecht produced both operas and dramas with song, and he worked with some of the major composers of his day. *Die Dreigroschenoper* (*The Threepenny Opera*, 1928) was Brecht and Weill's first major production. Brecht later collaborated with Paul Hindemith (for example, in *Badener Lehrstück*, or *Baden Didactic Cantata*, 1929); Hans Eisler, who wrote the song music for *Die Mutter* (*The Mother*, 1932) and other plays; and Paul Dessau, who composed the scores for the most important of the mature plays such as *Mutter Courage* (*Mother Courage*, 1946) and *Der kaukasische Kreidekreis* (*The Caucasian Chalk Circle*, 1949).

Throughout his career, Brecht determined to combine entertainment with didacticism. His is a deeply political theater that aims at a rational discovery of the social and political causes of human behavior, examination of possible alternatives, and creation of a progressive critical consciousness in the spectator. The function of music and song in Brecht's drama is in keeping with these basic principles. All of Brecht's well-known alienation techniques are employed in order to destroy the continuity of emotion and dramatic tension and to prevent unreflected audience identification with stage characters or situations.

Brecht's theory of epic opera is the culmination of his theory of epic theater. Music and song become prime instruments of alienation. Brecht's famous table of differences between Aristotelian drama and epic theater is found in his theoretical essay on the opera *Mahagonny*.[69] To Brecht, traditional opera, especially Wagner, is a "drug" used by the middle classes to escape from the disappointments of modern life. He calls such music "culinary," and his negative attitude is clearly expressed in the pejorative term "narcotic." The aim of music and song in Brecht's theater is to expose and explain social processes; they should activate the audience's rational, critical and analytical faculties.

The alienation techniques that apply specifically to the songs are not all new. What makes them unique is their combination in a comprehensive dramatic theory. Brecht's basic premise is the clear and radical separation of the various levels of speech and song. This distinction prevents the almost imperceptible heightening of emotion into song as in the popular musical. The initial distinction of speech levels may be achieved by various techniques such as change of lighting, change in position of singer, announcement of the song title, or presentation of a song emblem. The band or orchestra is fully visible to the audience. Other techniques achieve a more subtle distancing through music. A strong contrast or even contradiction between the text of a song and the type of music may be used. In *Die Dreigroschenoper*, for example, the Fascist "Kanonensong" is set to a jaunty dance tune. The discrepancy may also be between song and dramatic situation or singer. The most beautiful lyrical love ballad of the same play, "Liebeslied," or "Zuhälterballade" is sung by the pimp Macheath and the prostitute Jenny who will later betray him. Deliberate overexaggeration of either text or music can also help to achieve critical distance.

Weill and Brecht in *Die Dreigroschenoper* often introduce elements of popular music, jazz, cabaret, music hall, or *Bänkelsang* to create a distancing effect. Particularly in his later works Brecht came to prefer a style of music that was not popular, one that might be described as harsh or dissonant. For the epic-narrative songs in *Der kaukasische Kreidekreis* the playwright calls for a music with "cold beauty" and a certain "monotony." Brecht places particular emphasis on the singer's presentation of the songs. The actor is not to identify with the song but to create discrepancy by singing in an inappropriate way or speaking "against the music." Physical placing of the singer is important; songs are often sung directly to the audience, and frequently in front of the curtain.

The use of singing chorus or narrator-singer detached from the action as in *Der kaukasische Kreidekreis* is a later development in Brecht's work. The singing presenter in this drama fills us in on wider perspectives and on action not presented on stage (for example, long journeys, battles, the chaos of civil war). He sings of inner thoughts that remain unarticulated in the action (while the actors stand motionless); and at crucial junctures, as when Grusche decides to take the child, he describes in song actions that are mimed. Certainly in Brecht's drama the songs may sometimes evoke a powerful emotional feeling. But the context in which they are placed creates a distancing effect. The emotion must be rationally reflected upon by the spectator shortly after it has been experienced. Song in Brecht's drama is one of the most useful devices for commenting on the dramatic action and placing it in wider perspective.

Brecht's immediate influence in England in the 1930s and 1940s was limited. Certain developments in English theater, especially the plays of Auden and Isherwood, paralleled developments in Germany, without showing direct influence. Also in this period the Theatre Union formed by Joan Littlewood and Ewan MacColl was familiar with leading continental dramatic ideas, including those of Toller, Piscator and Brecht. Joan Littlewood proved influential in introducing Brechtian ideas, albeit in an eclectic fashion, to postwar British theater.

The postwar phase of influence began with the visit of Brecht's Berliner Ensemble to London in 1956. As few people in English theater at that time knew German, the greatest impact of the performances was felt in the spheres of stage design, lighting and particularly music. John Osborne and John Arden are among the younger English dramatists who may have been influenced by Brecht's use of dramatic song.[70] To these names must be added that of Peter Barnes, whose range of theater deliberately encompasses the opposite poles of modern theater: Brecht and Artaud. The young Arden had only the haziest of notions about Brechtian theory and practice. But the later Arden and D'Arcy collaborations often show interesting parallels to Brecht, especially in their use of song in epic-narrative and commentary functions. The later dramas of Edward Bond also show certain affinities to Brecht in their use of parable and didactic, commentary songs. And, although I am not asserting direct influence, Bond is moving in the direction of Brecht in the intensification of both the epic and lyrical elements in his most recent drama, while at the same time making his social and political commitment more precise. The two playwrights have in common a deep distrust of the emotional power of music and song because of their capacity for manipulation and misuse.

Although they never achieved a similar dramatic stature or influence, the English parallels to Piscator and Brecht should be mentioned. That the early plays of T. S. Eliot, W. H. Auden and Christopher Isherwood have not had more effect lies, I believe, in the fact that they are basically intellectual experiments. In spite of the widespread misunderstanding of Brecht's theater as non-emotional, the greatest of his works embody far more emotionalism, human understanding, and compassion than any of the pieces by Eliot or Auden from the 1930s. Both Eliot and Auden are better known as lyric poets, and their early plays lack a unifying dramatic imagination. Nevertheless they form a fascinating chapter in English theatrical and musical history.

Eliot believed that poetry, music, and dance are essential elements of modern poetic drama. He looked to music hall, ballet, jazz, and musical comedy as inspiration for modern drama. His fragment of an "Aristophanic Melodrama," *Sweeney Agonistes* (1926),[71] influenced not only his contemporaries Auden and Isherwood but also postwar dramatists such as John Arden. It was produced in the 1930s by the Group Theatre and by Hallie Flanagan's Vassar Experimental Theater, and was revived by Peter Wood in 1969. With a jazz score by the composer Dankworth, it combined songs in the style of musical comedy, colloquial phrases, and poetically structured rhythmic language. However interesting they may be, these disparate elements did not congeal into a unified whole, and the drama remained very much a fragment.

The dramatic experiments of Auden and Isherwood for the Group Theatre were more extensive, and resulted in an interesting collaboration with the composer Benjamin Britten. Auden was one of the founders of the Group Theatre in 1932. He wished to recreate theater as a communal and universal experience. For this reason he included elements of music hall, acrobatics, dancing, and song so as to involve the audience.[72] Influenced by German cabaret rather than by Brecht, Auden chose to make music and song play an important part in his dramas.

In *The Dance of Death* (1933), serious political themes concerning the decadence of Western European capitalism and the rise of a Hitler-like dictator are treated in satirical manner as a musical revue with songs and choruses set to a jazz score by Herbert Murrill. The affinity of these techniques to *Oh What a Lovely War* and Arden's melodramas has been noted.[73] *Dog Beneath the Skin* (1935), a collaboration with Isherwood, again with a jazz score by Murrill, was modeled on popular forms of musical theater. Although several of the choruses contain excellent poetry, attempts elsewhere to parody trivial forms of entertainment do not work. Julian Symons, a major critic on the 1930s, believes *Dog Beneath The Skin* too close to the musical comedy form to be effective as satire.[74] In its less successful moments the drama reminds one of John Osborne's disastrous musical *The World of Paul Slickey;* in its better parts it foreshadows Peter Nichols' *Poppy,* which also uses popular theatrical and musical traditions.

The Ascent of F6 (1936) was a collaboration between Auden, Isherwood and Britten, one of England's foremost modern composers. Britten had already written some dramatic music for the Group Theatre in the 1935–36 season and had collaborated with Auden on a symphonic song cycle, *Our Hunting Fathers.*[75] Again, cabaret may be seen as an influence both on the language of the song lyrics and on the style of the music. The most memorable song in *The Ascent of F6*, "The F6 Blues" or "Funeral Blues," occurs at the climactic moment of the death of the hero:

> Stop all the clocks, cut off the telephone,
> Prevent the dog from barking with a juicy bone,
> Silence the pianos and with muffled drum
> Bring out the coffin, let the mourners come.
> Let aeroplanes circle moaning overhead

"Funeral Blues" from *The Ascent of F6*, text by W. H. Auden, music by Benjamin Britten, in Britten and Auden, *Four Cabaret Songs* (London: Faber Music, 1980), p. 7. © 1980 Faber Music Ltd., London. Reproduced by permission.

Scribbling on the sky the message: He is dead.
Put crêpe bows round the white necks of the public doves.
Let the traffic policeman wear black cotton gloves.[76]

The lyrics of this song are patterned on everyday vocabulary and phrases, and
the tune is modeled on popular music; the song thus is associated with life's
triviality. But it also embodies a forceful emotionality. Donald Mitchell
describes the effect of this combination of elements:

> For a few timeless and ironic rather than satiric minutes, the feelings proper to the
> cabaret song and the funeral dirge are experienced *simultaneously* through the
> unifying agency of the music; and it is the disturbing simultaneity of the experience
> that is primarily responsible for the powerful impact the ensemble makes.[77]

Auden, Isherwood and Britten collaborated one final time on *On the
Frontier* (1938). This is a melodrama, with choruses sung before the curtain
that embody the standpoint of the lower classes, factory workers, and humble
soldiers. Auden later worked as a librettist for Igor Stravinsky (*The Rake's
Progress*) and Hans Werner Henze (*Elegy for Young Lovers* and *The Bassarids*)
and translated Brecht, but wrote no further original stage plays.[78] Britten
went on to become England's foremost theatrical composer in the 1940s.
Auden's experiments with musical drama are still interesting, but they do not
possess enough poetic energy or dramatic unity to succeed in modern re-
vivals. The spontaneity Auden envisioned was seldom achieved, even at the
time. But the spirit and some of the techniques of Auden's plays were taken
up and formed more successfully by the dramatic and directorial imagination
of Joan Littlewood after World War II.

JOAN LITTLEWOOD AND THE THEATRE WORKSHOP

Theatre Workshop's production of *Oh What a Lovely War* was one of the
seminal events of postwar British theater history, and it provided impetus for
younger dramatists to introduce song into drama. Joan Littlewood, although
not a dramatist, was the leading spirit of the collective that devised and
produced *Oh What a Lovely War*. The Theatre Workshop, of which she was a
founder and director, was one of the important forces in musical drama in
contemporary British theater.

At the time *Oh What a Lovely War* was presented in 1963, Littlewood had
already been active in theater for thirty years. Trained as an actress at the
Royal Academy of Dramatic Art in London, she joined Ewan MacColl in
Manchester in 1934. Together the two established and ran various groups that
set out to explore the possibilities of popular theater and of left-wing political
theater. MacColl had a long-standing interest in music; later he would become one of the leading figures of the folk song revival. Inspiration for the

techniques of Theatre Workshop and for the songs of *Oh What a Lovely War* came from a variety of different sources: Littlewood and MacColl's prewar experience with workers' theater in the 1930s, especially street theater, agit-prop, and the form of the Living Newspaper; English forms of popular entertainment, foremost among them music hall and the seaside Pierrot shows; Erwin Piscator's theatrical experiments of the 1920s and early forms of epic theater; Brechtian epic theater; and improvisational techniques learned from Italian popular comedy *commedia dell'arte*.[79] Littlewood used an eclectic approach in directing. Relying on her knowledge of theatrical method and technique, she would choose whatever elements seemed most suitable to any given play and production.

When Theatre Workshop was founded in 1945, it was in an ideal position not only to develop modern forms of popular nonillusionistic musical theater but also to pass on earlier techniques to the contemporary stage. Littlewood brought to life in the postwar period the communal, experimental theater that Auden had envisioned. Sandy Craig believes that Littlewood and Theatre Workshop's influence in postwar British theater is most directly seen in the community groups, followed by alternative political companies such as John McGrath's 7:84.[80] But the influence can virtually be observed everywhere in the contemporary scene, from regional documentary theater to the more established London productions. If song is once again accepted as integral part of drama, this is in large part due to Littlewood's activities.

Before Littlewood joined him, MacColl had been a member of the Red Megaphones, a Marxist agitprop street group in Salford. These street groups were a typical feature of the radical workers' theater movement of the late 1920s and early 1930s. Because the essence of such performances was pungency and brevity, the satirical song was one of the most important features of their shows. The Theatre Union that Littlewood and MacColl founded in 1934 experimented with live music, as in Brecht's *Schweyk*, which they produced in 1938. The Living Newspaper, *Last Edition*, which they presented in 1940, employed song as part of the commentary on national and international events. The Living Newspaper is a form of documentary theater that originated in the Soviet Union but found its fullest expression in the Federal Theater Project in the 1930s in the United States.[81] It was patterned on cabaret and revue but had a strong political message and made use of songs to put across its points. At the beginning of World War II, Littlewood and MacColl's Theatre Union was forced to disband. A small nucleus prepared for further activity after the war by systematic study of theater history. MacColl says of the group:

> By the end of the war, we had a group of people who, as a collective, probably knew more about the history of the theatre than any other group of players in the country.[82]

Theatre Workshop was founded in 1945 and was at first a touring company. One of its earliest productions was a ballad opera by MacColl, *Johnny Noble*, an antiwar play with songs based on north country folk music. Once settled in Stratford East in London, the group became well known for its presentations of new plays by young authors, among them Shelagh Delaney and Brendan Behan. Theatre Workshop also became popular for its production of cockney musicals, for example Frank Norman's *Fings Ain't Wot They Used T'Be* (1959), with music by Lionel Bart; and Wolf Mankowitz's *Make Me an Offer* (1959), with music by Monty Norman and David Henker. Theatre Workshop performances almost always included music whatever the type of play. In some cases, as in the jazz trio introduced into Delaney's *A Taste of Honey* (1958), the music now seems extraneous, an unnecessary music-hall trick intended to involve the audience.

In Brendan Behan's productions the situation is different. Here, music and song are essential elements of the dramatic style and structure. *The Quare Fellow* (1956) contains the haunting theme "That Old Triangle," which is heard throughout the drama. The effects of music are much stronger in Behan's *The Hostage*, which Theatre Workshop produced in 1958. A comparison with Behan's original Gaelic text, *An Giall*, as presented in Dublin, indicates that Theatre Workshop altered the text in many respects and added most of the songs for which the play later became famous.[83] However, musicality is innate in Irish drama, and Behan was a spontaneous and irrepressible singer and performer. *The Hostage* has undoubtedly been commercialized and popularized but in a way that is congenial to Behan's artistic temperament, and the tunes added are often those Behan himself suggested. On the whole, the songs contribute strongly to the humor and to the satire of the drama and help to structure the loosely episodic plot in the manner of musical cabaret.

Oh What a Lovely War (1963) represents the high point in Theatre Workshop's development in terms of artistic success and renown, and its low point, according to MacColl, in terms of class solidarity and political consciousness.[84] The piece is compelling theater, and I believe, takes a strong stand against war without sacrificing either entertainment value or seriousness. It was Littlewood's idea to cast this trenchant satire of World War I in the form of a musical Pierrot show. The Pierrot show was a form of entertainment popular in English seaside towns of the early 1900s; it comprised singing, dancing, juggling, and comedy. Littlewood's show uses historical songs and parodies sung during the first decades of the century. The music-hall structure brings out the game-playing idea on all levels very well and, in addition, helps to build the structural contrasts on which the play is based. The singing in particular engenders feelings of solidarity, affirmation, humor, and human resilience—feelings that are essential to the overall message of the drama.

The contrast between the two acts is intended to incite the audience to critical thought. Act 1, portraying the events up to 1914, reflects strongly the element of music-hall humor with its many comic turns. Among the songs, the cheerful, confident, and patriotic airs sung at the beginning of the war predominate. Act 2, which emphasizes the grim realities of the war, is characterized by antiwar song parodies typical of those tunes sung by the common soldiers later in the conflict. Characteristic of the stridently, almost arrogantly patriotic melodies of the beginning is "Belgium Put the Kibosh on the Kaiser."[85] Several of the songs in the first act are playful, carefree, humorous, and sexually suggestive. But the context in which they are sung is sobering; trench warfare has begun, the first wounded arrive home.

Act 2 concentrates on the satiric songs that express the horror of trench warfare and the futility of the entire war undertaking. "Gassed Last Night" (pp. 52–53) and "They Were Only Playing Leapfrog" (pp. 72–73) are significant in that their bitter humor exemplifies psychological techniques of survival under appalling conditions. A completely different effect is created by the singing of "Keep the Home Fires Burning." Here, the lyrical intensity of the tune and the sentimental longing of the text are sharply contrasted with the context:

NEWSPANEL. AVERAGE LIFE OF A MACHINE GUNNER UNDER ATTACK . . .
   FOUR MINUTES
The Nurse sings.

.   .   .   .   .   .
   Keep the Home Fires burning
   While your hearts are yearning
   Though the lads are far away,
   They dream of home.

.   .   .   .
NEWSPANEL. . . . BRITISH LOSS 17,000 MEN GAIN 1,000 YARDS. (pp. 84–85)

The effect is to undermine the sentiment of the song lyrics and to question the values and judgments of the authorities.

One of the most powerful scenes in act 2 is the parody of a religious service (pp. 78–81). As the religious and military authorities misuse prayer to justify their own ends, the soldiers sing parodies of church hymns. These parodies were sung in the trenches during World War I. "Fred Karno's Army" to the tune of "The Church's One Foundation" (p. 79) illustrates the theme of soldiers as music-hall comedians or Pierrots. The parody of "What a Friend We Have in Jesus" is particularly forceful; Haig, the Chaplain and the Nurse use the original words while the soldiers sing their version called: "When This Lousy War is Over" (pp. 79–80). The discrepancy between official view and the soldiers' standpoint is effectively brought out and the hypocrisy and corruptibility of established religion are satirized. The Chaplain's words "depart in *peace*" (p. 80) become bitterly ironic.[86]

CHORUS

From "Oh! It's a Lovely War," by J. P. Long and Maurice Scott, in *Oh! It's a Lovely War: Songs, Ballads and Parodies of the Great War* (London: EMI Music Publishing, 1978), pp. 5–7.

The title song "Oh It's a Lovely War," a song from the year 1917, combines sardonic humor with ironic criticism:

> Up to your waist in water,
> Up to your eyes in slush—
> Using the kind of language,
> That makes the sergeant blush;—
> Who wouldn't join the army?
> That's what we all enquire,—
> Don't we pity the poor civilians
> Sitting beside the fire.—[87]

The cheerfulness of the tune and the song's aggressive humor epitomize the resilience of the common soldier as well as his disillusioned rejection of the war.

The songs in *Oh What a Lovely War* thus serve a variety of functions and moods. Cheerful fun is contrasted with irresponsible sentimentality, political hypocrisy with commonsense rebellion. Perhaps the strongest impressions the performance leaves are those of human resilience and humor, impressions that largely are conveyed through the songs. *Oh What a Lovely War* was theatrically effective and served as a role model for serious political drama presented in popular forms of entertainment, both musical and dramatic. It was crucial in strengthening popular musical theater in the contemporary period.

2

Folk Song Tradition and Theatrical Experimentation: The Drama of John Arden and Margaretta D'Arcy

1. Introduction

In the context of this investigation, John Arden proves to be one of the most outstanding playwrights of the present, not only for the sheer bulk of song in his dramatic work, but also for the multiplicity and significance of the functions of his songs. Throughout his creative career, Arden—and later Arden and Margaretta D'Arcy in collaboration—constantly make use of song and music within the context of drama. Indeed, there is scarcely any Arden play that does not contain at least one song; most plays include many songs, and several are predominantly musical. Arden is an initiator of musicality in theater; in this respect he represents a seminal influence on the postwar generations of playwrights. (Arden was born in 1930, and D'Arcy in 1934.) Joan Littlewood's example, while highly significant, was that of a producer and director, not that of a playwright. Katharine J. Worth notes:

A thoroughgoing musical style didn't really emerge in the postwar theatre . . . until writers like Arden appeared on the scene. So far as form is concerned, he was the great revolutionary among the playwrights of the 1956 burst, the one who made the most sustained and radical break with realism.[1]

Because most songs in the work of Arden and D'Arcy are from, or modeled on, such traditional sources as folk songs and ballads, it may be said that these dramatists are pioneers in the introduction of traditional music into drama in the postwar period, much in the same way that Peter Barnes is a pioneer in the use of popular song in drama. Their plays demonstrate a number of points concerning the theory of dramatic song.

In the course of Arden and D'Arcy's work a definite development can be traced in the degree of conscious artistry with which they employ the musical idiom. Thus in the earliest plays for professionals, Arden often includes songs with words of his own in a ballad-type stanza but does not give more than a general indication of the kind of tune he envisions. In *Serjeant*

Musgrave's Dance he suggests specific tunes but does not insist on them. In other words, in these plays songs are seen primarily as lyric interludes in a very general folk-song context. In *The Business of Good Government*, an early collaboration, the playwrights create much of the charm and atmosphere through the singing of specifically named medieval carols. Arden's *Armstrong's Last Goodnight* was inspired by a rereading of the traditional Scottish ballad. It takes its title from the ballad, and integrates several ballads as well as newly written songs. One of Arden's earlier plays, *The Workhouse Donkey*, and three of the later Arden and D'Arcy collaborations, *The Hero Rises Up, Vandaleur's Folly*, and *The Little Gray Home in the West* are subtitled melodramas and make considerable use of both music and song to augment dialogue and action. In the later collaborative plays, the use of improvised instrumental music increases.

In Arden's early work, songs are used in fairly traditional ways to create atmosphere, build character, and forward the plot. Most importantly, they are introduced at moments of emotional climax. Already present, but not dominant, in these early dramas is also the use of lyrics for generalized commentary or ironic exposure. Song must also be seen in connection with Arden's desire to create a form of Dionysian, anarchic theater. Michael Cohen convincingly demonstrates that the political tendencies in Arden's earlier work must be seen as anarchic pacifism.[2] Music is one of the primary means of introducing disorder and anarchy into the traditional dramatic structure. It is important to note that a loose dramatic structure and an extensive use of theatrical music are already characteristics of Arden's early drama. Although these elements increase in the later collaborative plays, they are not entirely due to D'Arcy's influence. The movement toward more consciously political playwriting in the later collaborations of Arden and D'Arcy widens the variety of song functions. Important is the increase in nonrealistic commentary and epic-narrative lyrics. *The Island of the Mighty* combines epic song techniques with nontraditional tunes, while *The Non-Stop Connolly Show* fuses epic theater with traditional music.

With the multiplication of music and song in the later work, some of Arden's original concentration on song lyrics as poetical interludes seems to abate. Many of the later political song lyrics can scarcely pass as poetry in their own right. Here it is the political message that dominates the whole; the dramatic form and the music merely serve as vehicles for the transmission of this message. In this respect, Arden's later work contrasts greatly with the later plays of Edward Bond, in which song texts become not only politically more outspoken but also lyrically more intense.

POETIC THEATER AND SONG

Arden's early interest in song in drama is intimately related to his plea for poetry in the theater. Arden is perhaps the most articulate advocate of poetic drama in the contemporary theater. For him, poetry and the craft of theater belong inextricably together: "I think of playwriting as an offshoot of poetry. I think it is all part of the same craft."[3] Verse passages or songs very often are embedded in his drama, forming an essential part of the dramatic structure: "I find most of my more satisfactory poems are integrated into the plays in some way, in the form of songs or speeches."[4] Significant is Arden's emphasis on the heightening and formalizing of speech at moments of emotional climax:

> In a play, the dialogue can be naturalistic and "plotty" as long as the basic poetic issue has not been crystallized. But when this point is reached, then the language becomes formal *(if you like, in verse, or sung)*, the visual pattern coalesces into a vital image that is one of the nerve-centres of the play.[5]

The use of verse or song to express heightened emotional tension is characteristic of Arden and is also one element that distinguishes his early practice from Brecht's.

According to the statement just quoted, it seems to make little difference to Arden whether the passage in question is in spoken verse or sung. When asked in interview about the distinctions between verse and song in their drama, however, Arden and D'Arcy go on to say that verse is more immediate and personal, while songs have a more generalized message and draw on "collective experience":

> *D'Arcy.* I'd say that the verse would be making more individual statements from a character, while the song is actually bringing in a more collective experience. The audience can identify with them. . . .
> *Arden.* The songs tend to be more generalized in meaning, I think, whereas the verse is the character talking as a rule. The songs are not necessarily the character talking; it might be the situation talking through the mouth of the character.[6]

This seems to hold true for both early and late plays. The statement illustrates the fact that songs, at least familiar songs, draw on communal resources or speak to general experience.

Extremely important in the plays of Arden and D'Arcy is the function of song to create atmosphere, mood, and period setting, and to tap the collective memory and emotions of the audience:

> *Arden.* Looking for songs in one's memory . . . you find very often a song that strikes one as being particularly suitable for use in that part of the play, because it is bringing out a similar atmosphere to the one you want.

But Arden warns against generalizing song functions: a tune does not always heighten the mood of the scene in which it is sung. On the contrary, it may at times be used to loosen things up, to relax the atmosphere.

The separation of levels of speech proves to be one of the most significant features of Arden's theory and practice. The emphasis on mood and emotion through song does not mean that speech drifts into song without transition (as it often does in the American musical). Arden says,

> Verbal patterns, music, must . . . be strong, and hard at the edges. If verse is used in the dialogue, it must be nakedly verse as opposed to the surrounding prose, and must never be allowed to droop into casual flaccidities.[7]

The desire for a sharp separation of the various levels of speech precludes a completely realistic handling of dialogue. Indeed for Arden poetic theater means essentially a nonrealistic, nonpsychological form of theater, a popular theater that is openly and unabashedly aware of its own artificiality:

> The essential artificiality of the public stage will become apparent again. . . . People must want to come to the theatre *because* of the artificiality, not despite it. . . . I am pleading for the revival of the Poetic Drama.[8]

MUSICAL INFLUENCES

Examining influences on the work of Arden and D'Arcy, it is advisable to distinguish between their divergent backgrounds and their later shared experience. Arden grew up in Yorkshire, D'Arcy in a protected convent environment in Ireland. Foremost among the factors that led the young Arden to integrate song into his dramatic structure was his early love of the traditional ballad. In his northern England environment he found a strong ballad tradition preserved. "The bedrock of English poetry is the ballad," writes Arden in his essay "Telling a True Tale."[9] The ballad represents a combination of musical, lyrical, dramatic, and narrative elements; it is a song that tells a story. The ballad tells its tale in a dramatic fashion, highlighting a few vivid episodes and making use of direct speech and dialogue in its confrontations. Transmitted by means of oral tradition, the ballad was always intended to be sung rather than recited. Whereas earlier scholarship tended to concentrate on the texts, an awareness has grown in recent decades of the significance of the music and of the interrelationship between texts and tunes. The pioneer critic to examine these phenomena is Bertrand Harris Bronson.

Arden experienced the ballad first as poetry, and later as song. His childhood fascination with ballads was inspired, he says, by "the words of the poems before I got interested in the tunes." Arden as dramatist is attracted to the ballad form because of its simplicity in situation, verse form, and music. In "Telling a True Tale," he emphasizes the "simple basic situations" that remain valid over centuries, the highlighting of humanity in crisis, the clarity of the symbolism and the primary colors.[10] Extremely important for Arden also is the continuity of the ballad; it is for him an essential link in English

cultural tradition. It is at the same time, however, transcultural and international: "Other countries have similar traditions, so without deliberately
straining for it, the effect of the poetry *becomes* universal."[11] Arden sees his
own plays as representing an important connection between the traditional
past and the present:

> What I am deeply concerned with is the problem of translating the concrete life of
> today into terms of poetry that shall at the one time both illustrate that life and set it
> within the historical and legendary tradition of our culture.[12]

Another aspect of the ballad that may have appealed to Arden, at least in
the 1960s, is the impersonality of its narration. Given Arden's distrust of
overt social criticism in theater as "dangerously ephemeral and therefore
disappointing,"[13] and his disapproval of an outspoken social standpoint on
the part of the playwright, the tendency of the ballad to embody a moral in
the poetry rather than in "intellectualized comments"[14] was surely congenial
to his way of thinking. Later, Arden moves away from this early standpoint
toward a more openly political stance as a playwright, especially in his
collaboration with D'Arcy. But the ballad and folk song traditions continue to
remain significant because they are expressions of the popular roots of
culture. The ballad form gave Arden a model that was at once musical, lyrical
and intensely dramatic; it influenced the playwright's search for possible
combinations of poetry, music, and drama.

Not only the simplicity of the ballad texts appeals to Arden. The dramatist
shows an awareness of the unique qualities of ballad and folk song music:

> I actually didn't get any knowledge of ballad tunes until I . . . was about eighteen
> years old or something like that. That was the years just after the war. Then the folk
> song revival in England was beginning. . . . I think what really got me going was a
> series of programs on the radio by A. L. Lloyd and Ewan MacColl, and by the Irish
> musician Seamus Ennis, who all did programs on traditional song on the BBC back
> in the late 1940s. . . . When I discovered that these traditional ballads actually had
> tunes which improved their effect no end I got really interested in them.

Arden has a very clear opinion of what stage music should be like:

> In stage songs . . . I prefer simple tunes, and that is why I specify ballad ones,
> because the English and American folk song tunes are terribly good. They are
> simple but they are good, whereas the type of music generally used in musicals is
> pleasant but, to my mind, poor.[15]

In addition, he says, the type of lyrics written for musicals are "of small
poetic value," with scant attention paid to meter and rhyme scheme.[16] Arden
as a committed poetic playwright places the greatest importance on the form
and content of his dramatic poetry, whether spoken or sung. In dramatic song
the music must highlight the meaning of the words, not distract from them.

As Arden writes in one of his later prefaces, the type of folk tune he prefers is one

> in which the line of music reinforces and emphasizes the meaning of the line of verse, so that the whole thing becomes a single poetic statement.[17]

Such an idea is expression of the difference between Arden and Brecht in terms of theatrical music.

Arden is also aware of the later English ballad heritage, including street ballad. He cautions:

> I personally believe that the traditional English ballads, even in their poorer forms such as the nineteenth-century street ballads, are a type of basic poetry which we despise at our peril.[18]

Although he harbors no great enthusiasm for music hall, Arden gained a general familiarity with music-hall songs through radio programs in the 1940s.

Early in his career, Arden admired and learned from Elizabethan playwrights, especially Ben Jonson and Shakespeare. Arden's volume of theatrical essays, *To Present the Pretence*, includes an extended essay on "Playwrights and Play-Writers" (1975), in which he shows sensitivity to Shakespeare's use of music and acoustic effects in drama. He examines the stage music in *Hamlet*, act 3, scene 1, in some detail.[19] Among the modern dramatists Arden mentions as having influenced his work, Sean O'Casey is prominent: a fact that is interesting because O'Casey was strongly affected by Irish melodrama and made widespread use of song and music in his own plays.

Arden and D'Arcy have drawn on other sources to shape their presentation of song and music in drama. Both possessed a fairly extensive knowledge of classical music before they began their playwriting careers. D'Arcy's upbringing in a convent trained her in classical rather than folk music. Arden says of himself that he had "a reasonably good education in classical music at school." Of significance for both are the musical traditions of eighteenth-century ballad opera, nineteenth-century opera and melodrama, and the classical choral society traditions that are strong in the north of England and Wales. The ballad opera provides the model for *The Hero Rises Up*. Opera is seen by Arden and D'Arcy as musical melodrama, and they emphasize the popular appeal of opera outside of London. Arden exhibits an early awareness of the roots of popular theater in his use of the melodramatic traditions in *The Workhouse Donkey*.[20] In a 1963 interview Arden says:

> Of course I am influenced by the nineteenth century theatre to some extent; I don't mean so much the plays as the approach to the theatre, the type of staging, the strong lines of character drawing and plot.[21]

To these points, one might add the music.

From the standpoint of their later, radically political consciousness, Arden and D'Arcy have come to see these popular theatrical and musical traditions as models for the celebration of working-class culture. It is both the strong black-and-white portrayal of melodrama and opera, their heightened cultural expression, and their sense of dignity that the dramatists find valuable. They also see their own work as being influenced by the biblical heightened language of religious oratorio music. They believe that here they are carrying on a working-class tradition ignored by other left-wing dramatists such as John McGrath. They place their work firmly in the tradition of melodrama, opera, and choral music. In contrast with McGrath, who also aims at a musical political drama, Arden and D'Arcy do not emphasize the use of song to stimulate audience participation in the performance.

A later influence, resulting from Arden and D'Arcy's visit to India in 1969, was that of epic Indian folk plays and Indian film music. In the folk plays, prose passages alternate with verse and song so that the "regular use of music" becomes "part of the dramatic structure."[22] Arden adds in interview, "The Indian traditional theatre uses music with very hypnotic effect." The strong percussion beat and emphasis on rhythm had an effect on the improvised music that accompanies their later plays. The Indian film music that they find so powerful is based on traditional Indian music, but adapted to the popular medium. They also relate their perception of Indian music to the function of music in Japanese Nō theater. Another example Arden cites is that of ancient Celtic epic writing in which a tale was told in improvised prose until, at a moment of emotional climax, the bard would sing a formal poem, allowing for no improvisation.[23]

ARDEN AND BRECHT

The relationship between Bertolt Brecht and Arden has received a great deal of critical attention. Here, only the aspects of song and music in drama will be elucidated. When Brecht wrote about music in drama it was within the context of his theory of epic theater. The musical elements were to be distinctly set off from the rest of the play by the manner in which they were presented on stage. But even more important was the new function of music within the dramatic whole: no longer were naturalistic pretexts to be sought for the introduction of music or song, rather the musical items were to be of "a reflective and moralizing nature." In those cases where the music did have a recognizable emotional effect, this emotion was to be alienated; in other words, undercut and rationalized by the dramatic context. In strong contrast with Arden, Brecht generally preferred tunes that created an alienating effect. He favored music and rhythms that had a rational rather than an emotional influence and tunes that were unmelodic or discordant. The earlier

Arden, in contrast, preferred simple folk-song melodies that elicit an immediate emotional response in the listener. Even the improvised music in the later Arden and D'Arcy collaborative plays is never intended to be discordant, grating, or aggressive.

On the whole, Brecht's attitude towards the emotional effect of music is a negative one: emotion in music is a dangerous narcotic that easily prevents an audience from attempting or achieving rational political judgment. Emotion may be present in a song or in music, but it must not be allowed to lull the audience's political awareness to sleep. Compare, then, Brecht's strictures on the negative effects of emotion in music to Arden's acceptance of the semiconscious or subconscious emotional influence of song in "Telling a True Tale." After having praised writers who have written close to the ballad tradition, Arden continues:

> It seems to me that this tradition is the one that will always in the end reach to the heart of the people, even if the people are not entirely aware of what it is that causes their response.[24]

Arden here mentions Brecht as working according to this principle, using the emotional touchstone of tradition, but the younger playwright does not take into account any of Brecht's reservations and differentiations.

Characteristic for Arden in the early stages of his development is his insistence on verse or song at intensely emotional moments in a drama. Indeed, Arden admits to a discrepancy between what he theoretically wishes to achieve (a more Brechtian effect) and what he actually experiences while writing:

> I see prose as being a more useful vehicle for conveying plot and character relationships, and poetry as a sort of comment on them. I find it difficult to carry this out in practice. Brecht, for instance, is usually very, very distinct between the two. I haven't always found it possible to be so. I mean, you are writing a scene . . . which seems to call for prose, then you get a heightened emotion, and *before you know where you are,* the prose has become lyrical.[25]

In other words, in actual fact Arden's early practice is quite different from Brecht's, despite his frequent utterances about Brechtian theory. Later, while continuing to exploit song's emotional expressiveness, Arden and D'Arcy employ sung passages more and more often in commentary, alienating functions.

To sum up the relationship between Arden and Brecht in the use of song and music, Arden himself comes closest to the truth when he remarks on their common attraction to the ballad heritage and their roots in common theatrical tradition: the medieval drama, the Elizabethans and "various exotic styles such as the Japanese and Chinese theatres." Given these roots, there is inevitably "a certain similarity in style between us."[26] In the early stages of his career, however, Arden tended toward a quite different political stand-point from Brecht, and he sees this clearly. Any comparison between Arden and Brecht that fails to take this into account will be both inadequate and distorted. Arden and D'Arcy's later work comes closer to Brecht politically and in some of their theatrical techniques, if not in overall effect. In January 1984 they presented an interesting concert adaptation of Brecht's *The Mother,* using Hans Eisler's original music for the songs, but updating and altering the text to illuminate the situation in Northern Ireland in 1968.[27]

MUSIC IN PRODUCTION

At the beginning of his career, then, Arden endeavored to develop tech-niques that would help to create a contemporary form of poetic, musical drama, without adhering strictly to any dramatic theory. Indeed, his style is highly eclectic. Open as he is to a wide variety of different influences, his experiments take on a multitude of different forms. Each drama seems to take a new direction, its form—and with it its song and verse techniques—adapting themselves both to the theme and to the given setting. Arden attempts to escape the conventional limitations of realistic illusionistic drama and to expand or reinvigorate the theatrical idiom to include the nonillusion-ary vocabulary of popular theater. As Andrew Kennedy sees it:

> Arden's work can be seen as a critically conscious attempt at revitalising drama, partly through the primitive sources of the language: releasing the energies of the ballad, of rough verse and song, set in and against a highly coloured prose dialogue. . . . It is a literary attempt to create a language that has seemingly pre-literary qualities—"primary colours", a tough lyricism, a popular poetry-in-the-theatre.[28]

In the later collaborative plays, Arden and D'Arcy's experimentation with form has not diminished. The elements of music and song have increased, adding new dimensions, but also new difficulties. The lyricism and musi-cality of the earlier Arden dramas have been widely commented on. Critical responses to Arden and D'Arcy's later musical style, however, have been sporadic and often influenced by political tastes. Because the writers have withdrawn from professional theater in London, performance evidence is scanty. It does indeed become increasingly difficult to judge the effect of nontraditional or improvisational music in their work.

The difficulties surrounding production of the later plays have become notorious. It is not just their political aspect that has caused controversy. Arden and D'Arcy also feel that even in the early Arden plays and especially in the later collaborations no one was able to handle the integration of music and song into dramatic performance. Arden compares their problems to those of Sean O'Casey:

Every time they thought they'd got to understand how O'Casey wanted his plays put on, he was writing a new style. . . . It means that the theatrical profession is dragging behind the writer all the time.

A similar complaint is made by Peter Barnes, who compares his own difficulties to those of Arden and D'Arcy. Arden says that "nobody knew how to integrate a traditional folk singer into a stage play." The problems with improvised music are even greater. The music becomes a partner for the actor, an alter ego. The actor takes control of the performance, and the balance changes nightly. Actors, musicians and composers have often not known how to deal with such a situation. Arden and D'Arcy also believe that the unfavorable critical response to their later plays may have something to do with the effect of the improvised music. The hypnotic rhythmical music is intended to mold the audience into a collective; however, as D'Arcy remarks, critics "don't like to be part of a collective. It makes them feel quite alienated . . . emotionally and intellectually."

In the following analysis no effort has been made to treat every play extensively, as virtually all of Arden and D'Arcy's plays contain songs. Instead, I have selected for examination dramas that seem to illustrate in exemplary fashion a variety of different song sources and techniques. As the early plays for professional theater were written by Arden alone (with the exception of *The Happy Haven*), and the plays for community theater were written in collaboration, it seemed advisable to treat these two groups separately, in order to determine whether there are significant differences between them in the functions of song. The authors say, "the collaboration on each play has taken a different form. . . . This is very important in any academic assessment of our work."[29] Among the later collaborative plays, the Irish dramas will be treated summarily, since a thorough analysis, as explained in the introduction, would involve a wider discussion of the Irish song tradition than can be undertaken here. I have limited myself to stage plays and have mentioned the radio and television plays only in passing.

2. Earlier Arden Plays for Professional Theater

EXPERIMENTAL BEGINNINGS

Arden's first unpublished radio play, *The Life of Man* (1956) was said to be a kind of "ballad-play,"[30] creating a "rich 'sound tapestry' out of verse, song, and 'poetic prose,' " in a language firmly rooted in "the ballad world, in folklore and myth."[31] In the new production of 1983,[32] the play proves to be a powerful mixture of myth, musicality and mystery. Here Arden employs such folk tunes as "John Barleycorn," which are to reappear in several of his stage pieces.

The Waters of Babylon (1957), Arden's first published play, takes its title from Psalm 137, which portrays the Jewish nation in captivity and which laments the difficulty of singing a song of home for a people in exile.

By the rivers of Babylon, there we sat down, yea, we wept, when we remembered Zion.
We hanged our harps upon the willows in the midst thereof.
For there they that carried us away captive required of us a song; and they that wasted us required of us mirth, saying, Sing us one of the songs of Zion.
How shall we sing the Lord's song in a strange land?[33]

The play concerns a Polish emigrant, Krank, who has fled to London after World War II. His songs are songs of home, of the past, sung in a condition of present exile. The use of the title is partly ironic, because Krank has not been carried from home by force, and he sings anything but the Lord's song.

In *The Waters of Babylon*, Arden specifies traditional tunes for only two of the play's six songs. Throughout, the dramatist tries to break away from realistic conventions. Krank's first song, "As I Went Down by Belsen-town,"[34] is sung with little or no pretense at realistic preparation through the action. The effect is emotionally chilling, as the theater audience will recognize the historical connotations of holocaust and mass murder. The situation in which the song is sung creates a poignant reminder of the play's title: how can an exile sing a song of home in a strange land? Krank's isolation is given expression, and the audience learns something of his emotional history that will counteract the more negative things discovered about him later.

In act 2, Teresa and Bathsheba work together to create an atmosphere of dissipation and seduction. Throughout, Bathsheba sings lasciviously to a blues tune: "He laid me down, . . . Oh Lord. He laid me down so low" (p.62). The action culminates toward the end of the act in a chaotic and unrealistic episode in which Caligula and Bathsheba prowl around the stage, sizing each other up, circling the unconscious Cassidy, while Teresa sings her song. In terms of stagecraft, the song provides an accompaniment to their ritualized movements and dispenses with the need for dialogue at a moment of heightened emotional and sexual tension. For the first time in this play, Arden specifies a tune: "The Wearing of the Green" (p.71). It is a well-known patriotic Irish folk tune from the rebellion of 1798 and is often used as a recognition song for a patriotic Irishman. (Arden and D'Arcy use it in this way in *The Non-Stop Connolly Show* and in *Vandaleur's Folly*.) Here, it illustrates the fact that Arden was acquainted with some traditional Irish airs long before his collaboration with D'Arcy.

The choice of this tune for Teresa's song reminds the listener that she once was an Irish innocent who has now been separated from her origins, caught up and corrupted in the mill of London prostitution. The striking and cynical contrast between original idealistic words and the present song text provides

The Wearing of the Green

Oh — Pad-dy dear and did you hear the news that's go-ing
round, The sham-rock is by law for-bid to grow on I-rish
ground, No man Saint Pat-rick's Day shall keep his co-lour can't be
seen For there's a cruel-law a-gainst the wear-ing of the
green. I met with Nap-per Tan-dy and he took me by the
hand, Said he "How is old Ire--land and how does she
stand?" "She's the most dis-tress-ful coun-try that ev-er could be
seen, For they're hang-ing men and wo-men for the wear-ing of the green."

1. Oh Paddy dear and did you hear the news that's going round,
   The shamrock is by law forbid to grow on Irish ground,
   No man Saint Patrick's Day shall keep his colour can't be seen
   For there's a cruel law against the wearing of the green.
   I met with Napper Tandy and he took me by the hand,
   Said he „How is old Ireland and how does she stand?"
   „She's the most distressful country that ever could be seen,
   For they're hanging men and women for the wearing of the green."

2. Then since the colour we must wear is England's cruel red,
   No Irishman must now forget the blood that has been shed,
   They may take the shamrock from our breasts and cast it on the sod,
   But it will take root where'er it rests though underfoot it's trod,
   When the law can stop the blades of grass from growing as they grow,
   And when the leaves in Summertime their colours daren't show,
   Then I'll take down the shamrock that I wear on Paddy's e'en,
   But until that day I'll live and die still wearing of the green.

"The Wearing of the Green," from *Irische Lieder und Balladen*, ed. Frederik Hetman (Frankfurt am Main: Fischer, 1978), pp. 18–19.

another oblique reminder of the play's title. The path of ruined innocence lies through a desert of waste, a windy moor of corruption and destruction:

> My love is like a thornbush
> On the middle of the moor.
> The winds have blown it black and bare
> Except for one white flower.
>
> . . . .
>
> The only road to reach it
> Runs mad with rocks of stone
> And underneath the branches lies
> A heap of soldiers' bones.
>
> (p. 71)

In diction and rhythm, if not in content, the text is like folk song. The magic ritual atmosphere and the abandoned irresponsibility with which it is sung help to disperse any easy judgments that the audience might be tempted to make. The primitive vitality and enchantment connected with both Teresa and Bathsheba prevent us from seeing them in an exclusively negative light. The song itself and the way in which it is sung serve to create an ambivalent mood.

In the final scene of the play, Arden mocks his own attempt to tie every-thing up tidily; instead, he prefers to close the drama with a song in the form of a ridiculous four-part round, led by the drunken and disreputable Charlie Butterthwaite. For the second time in this play Arden specifies a tune, "The Ash Grove" (p.97). This is an old Welsh air, but it was popularly sung in English in parlor and concert hall throughout the nineteenth century. The original text is extremely sentimental and nostalgic, a lament for lost youth and comradeship. Thus Butterthwaite's raucous, ungrammatical and vulgar lyrics are intended to create an ironic contrast in the minds of those who are familiar with the elevated tone of the original song:

> We're all down in t'cellar-hoyle
> Wi't'muck-slaghts on t'windows.
> We've used all us coyle up
> And we've nowt left but cinders.
>
> (p. 97)

The atmosphere is one of cheerful doomsday, a devil-may-care disregard for middle-class respectability and responsibility. It is an appropriately provoca-tive note on which to end an exuberant and unconventional play. The form chosen, the round, emphasizes the nonsensical nature of the proceedings. The final song, joined into by all the major members of the cast, is a stagey, theatrical finale that exults openly in its own artificiality.

In *Live Like Pigs* (1958) Arden attempted to achieve a more unified plot and a more formally coherent dramatic structure than he did in *The Waters of*

Babylon. One of the methods he uses to attain this end is the avoidance of verse passages and the adherence to a semirealistic plane of language in the prose dialogue. Another method he employs is the concentration of street-ballad-type songs at the beginning of the scenes. These are all to be sung in the same way: by a nonspecified singer in the darkness before the lights come up on the stage, or just as they are coming up, and they should be sung unaccompanied. Arden explains:

> The same tune, basically, could be used for each scene. It should be a typical melancholy street-ballad, dragging and harsh, and sung with the peculiar monotony associated with the old fashioned street-singers.[35]

Arden accords the later street ballad something of the same importance as the traditional folk ballad. In contrast with the more lyrically and emotionally pleasing type of folk song melodies that he so often prefers, Arden experiments here with the effects of a harsh and monotonous style of music, in a sort of Brechtian manner.

One cannot, however, say that the content of the songs and their manner of presentation are Brechtian. A song sung at predictable intervals at the beginning of each scene, and especially one presented in total darkness or dim lighting by an anonymous singer, is going to have a completely different effect on the audience than one that interrupts the action in the middle of a scene and which is marked by special lighting effects and positioning of the actor in the Brechtian way. In addition, these ballads scarcely have the function of Brechtian scene titles that inform the audience of the outcome of the most important events in order to remove the element of conventional dramatic tension. Compare the crucial nature of the information disclosed in some Brechtian scene titles with Arden's introductory song to the last scene of *Live Like Pigs:*

> The morning comes, they all of them come,
> Now fight them for your life:
> They'll have you out and down and dead,
> So fight fight fight for your life.
>
> (p. 183)

The audience here is put in a state of tension, expecting a violent and perhaps deadly confrontation between the Sawneys and their neighbors. In other words, Arden creates dramatic tension in this song rather than dissipates it, as Brecht would. The ballad also has an ironic function, because the scene it introduces is comic and anticlimactic.

In the original Royal Court production, folk singer and scholar A. L. Lloyd was brought in to set these ballads musically and to sing them. The effect was that he and the songs remained cut off from the play's action. For this reason Arden later specified that they should be integrated more fully, or otherwise eliminated. The ballads provide an unusual formal and poetic framework for the play that should be preserved if possible in the interests of the structure of the whole. With their dragging, melancholy music and suggestive, semiserious content, the ballads represent an effective contrast both to the prose dialogue and to the stage action, which should be fast-paced, precise, and comic. Albert Hunt, I believe, is correct in pointing out that the "poetic" structure of the play is essentially theatrical and artificial, as opposed to its "journalistic" content.[36] Elsewhere Hunt remarks: "Played naturalistically, for illusion, *Live Like Pigs* is crude, and the ballads get in the way, as they did at the Court."[37] In other words, an illusionistic style is completely wrong for this drama. The musical framework may not be ideally realized, but it is certainly not casually dispensable.

In addition to these formal street ballads, a variety of songs are sung in this play by various characters within the context of the action. The world Arden has chosen is contemporary in setting, but the Sawneys are nomads and "an anachronism" in the present day.[38] They embody a primitive vitality, animalism and lyricism. Andrew Kennedy writes of the "Dionysiac rhythm"[39] of the play's songs and continues: "Perhaps there is an element of spell-binding in Arden's primitivism."[40] Spell creation, incantation, defiance, cynicism and irony, animal vitality, and tenderness are just some of the moods and emotions expressed in the songs. There is very little in the way of critical commentary, even in the introductory ballads. The probable influences are less Brechtian than derived from popular English traditions of theatrical entertainment, music hall or pantomime, as well as the common heritage of children's song, street ballad, and folk song.

THE FOLK SONG TRADITION

Serjeant Musgrave's Dance (1959), the best known of Arden's early plays and perhaps his best known play altogether, has often been called ballad-like in structure. Arden himself describes his play in terms of ballad symbolism:

> In the ballads the colours are primary. Black is for death, and for the coalmines. Red is for murder, and for the soldier's coat the collier puts on to escape from his black.[41]

This analogy, however, cannot be carried too far. The basic structure of Arden's play is not epic—a juxtaposition of independent scenes—nor is it even episodic in the way of a ballad. In this drama the scenes are interlocked; one prepares for the next. The play does not jump from one episode or scene to the next without transition as the ballad so often does. The drama is, however, permeated by ballad and folk-song atmosphere. Not only the color symbolism but also the language and especially the songs are clearly influenced by these traditional musical forms. Arden mentions other influences:

in addition to film, the most important of these is the traditional English music hall that had also played some role in structuring Arden's earlier work. The most obvious indication is Arden's explicit reference to a comic " 'Fred Karno' sequence" in act 2, scene 2.[42] Fred Karno was a popular music-hall comedian (in whose troup Charlie Chaplin received his early training). Thus the play's structure incorporates a variety of musical and theatrical influences.

For the songs, Arden not only prescribes the general type of tunes he wants: "The songs should be sung to folk-song airs," (p.5) but also the titles of four specific melodies: "Six Jolly Wee Miners," "Blow Away the Morning Dew," "The Black Horse," and "John Barleycorn" (p. 5). In addition, the Bargee's song, "Michael Finnegan," is sung with its original words. In the case of the songs to which he has provided new words, Arden does not insist on the use of these tunes: "There are many available tunes which equally well suit the various songs—perhaps these are as good as any" (p. 5). In several cases, however, the original words to these airs have special relevance in the context in which they are placed in the play, so that subtle nuances of allusion or irony would be lost if they were not used. In actual performance, such subtleties cannot always be fully appreciated, and Arden's flexibility here may well simply be a helpful gesture for a director.[43] The songs Arden specifies are all lyrical folk songs rather than narrative ballads. It is not until *Armstrong's Last Goodnight* that we encounter a play that quotes extensively from narrative ballads, although the general influence of the ballad form and language is present throughout the early work. In this play it is certainly the lyrical folk song that dominates the tone and diction.

The songs in *Serjeant Musgrave's Dance* are directly related to, and intricately interwoven with, the plot and the major themes. They help to characterize the dramatic figures, they create atmosphere, and they are generally sung at moments of heightened emotion. There is little in the way of commentary function; the most explicit comment on the play occurs in Attercliffe's final ballad. They are thus more traditional in their functions than those in Arden's earlier plays. But they are especially well suited to the historical and northern England setting and help to create a densely woven poetic structure.

The play opens almost immediately with a song; the youngest soldier, Sparky, sings while on watch. The emotions out of which his song arises are clearly indicated: fear and nervousness, boredom and discomfort. It is thus quite realistically motivated within the dramatic context and has much the same psychological origins as Hurst's whistling in the graveyard in scene 3 (p. 27). But the text of the song has a much wider significance for the play as a whole. Its theme is the forceful recruitment of a drunken man, desertion, an informing sweetheart, courtmartial, gallows, and hanging. On the one hand it has a function as indirect exposition: Attercliffe's and Hurst's sharp and nervous reactions at the word "desertion" serve to alert audience attention and arouse curiosity, even if the cause of this nervousness is not yet known. On the other hand the song also has a foreshadowing function: there are later two recruiting scenes (one in which the men are drunk), a 'sweetheart' whose information causes Musgrave's plans to go wrong, and, finally, a courtmartial and a gallows hanging. This foreshadowing function establishes links to episodes throughout the drama and spans an especially meaningful bridge to the final scene, which is also dominated by a song. The framework of *Serjeant Musgrave's Dance* is similar to that of *Live Like Pigs;* it is much less formal and rigid but, at the same time, far more subtle and effective. The tune Arden specifies for Sparky's first song, "Six Jolly Wee Miners" is a cheerful begging song traditionally sung at Christmas. Except perhaps for an association with cold and winter, an allusion to the original words does not seem intended.

Immediately after Sparky's song, the audience is offered a dramatic and musical counterfoil in the figure of the Bargee whistling his theme song "Michael Finnegan." This is a well known children's song, part nonsense, part pure play, a circular song that is designed to be sung in endless repetition. The first verse runs:

> There once was a man named Michael Finnigin
> He grew whiskers on his chin-ni-gin,
> The wind came out and blew them in-i-gin
> Poor old Michael Fin-ni-gin (begin-i-gin).

The fifth and last verse leads back to the beginning:

> There once was a man named Michael Finnigin
> He grew fat und he grew thin-i-gin
> Then he died, and we have to begin-i-gin
> Poor old Michael Finnigin.[44]

The song has a jaunty little tune needing only a limited range of musical expression and emotion, as is frequently the case with children's songs.

As has often been remarked, the Bargee is a character created as a deliberately sinister, comic, and grotesque counterpoint to the soldiers, especially their leader: crooked old Joe confronts, parodies and sets off straight Black Jack Musgrave. What has not been noticed sufficiently about this constellation is that the Bargee's song has the same function musically as his character does dramatically. It contrasts with, and ironically reflects on, the folk song idiom of the soldiers. The Bargee whistles his song provocatively at intervals throughout the play (p. 11, 17, 21, 41, and 56). Finally at the close of the crucial marketplace scene, the Bargee slowly begins to sing the words to his song (p. 99) that until now he has only whistled. Gradually, most of the other characters (with the exception of Musgrave, Attercliffe, Annie, Mrs. Hitchcock and the newly arrived dragoons) join in as they link wrists and begin their formalized chain dance around the cross-like centerpiece where Annie is cradling Billy's skeleton. The song itself, seen in connection with this dance, thus comes to symbolize the repetitive nature of the event. Both this song and the dance express the return of oppressive authority, and because the colliers are effectively forced back into an almost childlike role of dependence, the music also symbolizes the inescapability of the situation. All, the colliers and the authorities alike, are caught up in a vicious circle of "violence and counter-violence,"[45] just as their song is a circular, never-ending song and their dance is a chain dance, moving around and around the stage. Song, dance and dramatic situation all coalesce here to an extraordinarily striking, visual, aural, and symbolical image. In an ideal production, Arden says, the stage at this moment

> would be full of dragoons and the dance would take place in front of them. Then the impression given would be that even the most sympathetic of the colliers . . . has no alternative but to take part in the dance, and that law and order have been re-established by force.[46]

In terms of the poetic and theatrical structure of the play it is all important that the dominant musical idiom of the drama, the traditional folk song, has a musical counterpoint in the childish but at the same time sinister and menacing idiom of the Bargee. The Bargee's "Michael Finnegan" creates a secondary musical arch linking beginning with end.

Most of the other songs in *Serjeant Musgrave's Dance* belong to Sparky and Annie. The most natural and spontaneous use of song is connected with the forces of life, love, and affirmation. Through the medium of song a definite connection is established between Sparky and the dead Billy Hicks. We are told that Billy was young and full of humor, jokes and, especially, song. Now Sparky himself is the singer of the group. He, too, is young, impulsive, and insecure; singing for him is one way of coping with unpleasant realities. It is a way of expressing emotions that he otherwise has difficulty in communicating seriously. This does not mean, however, that he can be identified completely with the "I" in his songs. There is a certain distance, a certain amount of generalized commentary about a soldier's life in these pieces, but not enough to call them Brechtian.

Annie's role as singer is different from Sparky's. She, too, is basically a character of life and love, anarchy, as Musgrave would call it, but she has been more deeply hurt by life's experiences. Thus her songs tend to be more provocative and defiant, even cynical and savage, than Sparky's. She smiles for the first time in the play when she defies Musgrave in a song (pp. 51–52). Like Sparky, Annie seldom, if ever, communicates her emotions openly. Both her songs and her passages of verse, uttered at moments of emotional turmoil, serve to express what she cannot say directly. Little resembles Brechtian alienation effect, although such passages may also contain a generalized statement. Both verse and song passages are written in short, ballad-like stanzas.

One would not expect a character such as Musgrave to sing naturally at all. He is too rigid to have any feeling for musical lyricism. Arden's stage directions specify that he is to sing at the moment of climax and extreme stylization. The moment is, of course, Serjeant Musgrave's dance in act 3. Musgrave is in a state of extraordinary emotional turmoil: his face is "contorted with demoniac fury," and he "sings, with mounting emphasis" (p.84), but such psychological observations are almost beside the point. This is, basically, an openly theatrical moment, the theater audience has become, in effect, the town population, the gun is pointed at them, and Musgrave's song is directed towards them. It is his supreme moment, and all eyes, of the audience in the play and of the theater audience, are concentrated on him. Peter Brook writes of this scene that it is an ideal example of rough, improvised "true theatre":

> The demonstration that he improvises is like a genuine piece of popular theatre. . . . When this does not succeed in transmitting his complete message to the crowd, his desperate energy drives him to find still further means of expression and in a flash of inspiration he begins a rhythmic stamp, out of which develops a savage dance and chant. Sergeant Musgrave's dance is a demonstration of how a violent need to project a meaning can suddenly call into existence a wild unpredictable form.[47]

Arden says in his introduction that this speech worked best with the words "spoken against a background of drum rolls and recorded music" (p. 5). I could readily conceive of this song sung to a harsh, grating type of music. Perhaps, however, the true horror of the situation comes out best when the scene is not overdone musically.[48] The rhythm of the lyrics is certainly not that of the dominant musical idiom of the play, the folk song; it is rather in abrupt, jerking lines of four and two stresses. It is much more driving, powerful, and energetic than the rhythm of the lyrical folk song. A chant, or recitative style seems best suited to the words.

After the passion and the fury of the marketplace scene and the total frustration of the circular dance to "Michael Finnegan," the play closes on a quiet coda, once again of folk-song character. The ballad is sung by Attercliffe, who has taken over Sparky's singing role after the latter's death. The tale he tells is directly related to his own personal fate. At the same time, however, it is the only song that points beyond the play to the future, leaving the audience free to think through the events portrayed and to consider possible developments to come. Attercliffe's ballad provides a moment of calm, almost static, reflection after the excitement and movement of Musgrave's and the Bargee's dancing songs. Its melancholy thoughtfulness provides the audience with a relaxation of tension, dramatically and musically. Its metrical form is typical of the ballad stanza.

It should be noted, too, that the words of the specified tune, "John Barleycorn," are relevant to the spirit of the song. The folk song "John Barleycorn" possibly originated in the ancient myth of the death and resurrection of the corn god. As it survives today, it tells the humorous tale of a humanized, personified barley corn who is murdered and buried, but who miraculously grows up once more, only to be cut off once again and ground to death in a mill; and yet his spirit survives in the "nut-brown bowl" of ale, and no one can live without him. One should note here a connection with the green apple of Attercliffe's song that is eaten, but whose seed

> . . . will grow
> In live and lengthy joy
> To raise a flourishing tree of fruit
> For ever and a day.
>
> (p. 104)

The central theme of both songs is thus the resurrection or the persistence of life, and the miraculous survival of the spirit in the face of adverse conditions. "John Barleycorn" is more mythical and archaic, and also more fatalistic, whereas in Arden's tune the continuation of life results from a conscious choice on the part of the woman speaker. The song thus has a didactic function and provides a final commentary statement about the play and the values represented in it. At the moment in the ballad at which the lover's choice for life is made, the singer changes to "a more heavily accented version of the tune" (p. 103),[49] and the tone becomes more defiant and assertive, both in the language and in the music. Arden says of the affinity between the traditional song and his version:

> If you use a tune like "Barleycorn," if people in the audience know the original song there will be an overtone conveyed. If they don't, they'll just be getting the tune as it were by itself, for its own sake, which may not convey quite the same emotion. . . . As far as my own selection of songs goes, I like to choose songs . . . in which the original meaning of the words seems to produce the same effect as the tune.

The songs in *Serjeant Musgrave's Dance* are predominantly modeled on folk songs both textually and musically. Not only are they intricately related to the atmosphere and themes of the play as a whole, but they are also written and composed so that they create a musical framework as part of the essential poetic structure, with a semicomic, semigrotesque counterfoil of the Bargee's music. *Serjeant Musgrave's Dance* contains fewer interesting musical experiments than the earlier plays, but a more effective and satisfying overall

JOHN BARLEYCORN

Sung by 'Shepherd' Haden, Bampton, Oxon. (C.J.S. 1909)

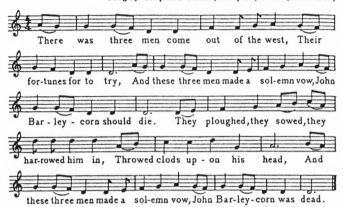

There was three men come out of the west, Their
for-tunes for to try, And these three men made a sol-emn vow, John
Bar-ley-corn should die. They ploughed, they sowed, they
har-rowed him in, Throwed clods up-on his head, And
these three men made a sol-emn vow, John Bar-ley-corn was dead.

There was three men came out of the west,
Their fortunes for to try,
And these three men made a solemn vow,
John Barleycorn should die.
They ploughed, they sowed, they harrowed him in,
Throwed clods upon his head,
And these three men made a solemn vow,
John Barleycorn was dead.

Then they let him lie for a very long time
Till the rain from heaven did fall,
Then little Sir John sprung up his head,
And soon amazed them all.
They let him stand till midsummer
Till he looked both pale and wan,
And little Sir John he growed a long beard
And so became a man.

They hired men with the scythes so sharp
To cut him off at the knee,
They rolled him and tied him by the waist,
And served him most barbarously.
They hired men with the sharp pitchforks
Who pricked him to the heart,
And the loader he served him worse than that,
For he bound him to the cart.

They wheeled him round and round the field
Till they came unto a barn,
And there they made a solemn mow
Of poor John Barleycorn.
They hired men with the crab-tree sticks
To cut him skin from bone,
And the miller he served him worse than that,
For he ground him between two stones.

Here's little Sir John in a nut-brown bowl,
And brandy in a glass;
And little Sir John in the nut-brown bowl
Proved the stronger man at last.
And the huntsman he can't hunt the fox,
Nor so loudly blow his horn,
And the tinker he can't mend kettles or pots
Without a little of Barleycorn.

"John Barleycorn," from *The Penguin Book of English Folk Songs*, ed. Ralph Vaughan Williams and A. L. Lloyd (Harmondsworth: Penguin, 1959), pp. 56–57.

musical structure and unity. In the 1984 revival at the Old Vic, Arden allowed Albert Finney considerable leeway with the music. The result was an over-padding with additional folk tunes, the transformation of verse passages into song, and consequently, to my mind, a destruction of the delicate poetic and musical balance of the original text.

Closely related to these stage plays are Arden's early works for television, *Soldier, Soldier* (1957; performed in 1960), and *Wet Fish* (1960; performed in 1961). *Soldier, Soldier* is subtitled "A Comic Song for Television,"[50] and its music seems specially designed for that medium. Arden's use of a title and theme song, "Soldier, Soldier," is more consistent but also more simplistic than in the stage plays. Like *Serjeant Musgrave's Dance*, with which it shares certain other elements, *Soldier, Soldier* is set in a colliery town. One of its most interesting songs is an old industrial tune from the mining trade, "The Coal Owner and the Pitman's Wife" (p. 53).[51] The original is a slyly humor-ous piece in which a courageous and witty miner's wife gives a horrendous account of how dreadfully the devil treats the "rich wicked race" in hell, and thus scares the coal owner into offering his men a fair wage. What is significant is its dramatic function as a gesture of defiance—just as the original tune was essentially a demonstration of defiance of the small against the mighty.

Wet Fish is associated not only with *The Waters of Babylon* but also points forward to *The Workhouse Donkey*. But it is not dramatically or musically as inventive as the stage plays. The dominant tune in this little piece is "When Father Papered the Parlour," which is whistled and sung throughout and also used as tune to new words. As a comic music-hall song about inept home repairs, it has decided relevance to the overall theme of the play, but its effects are relatively crude and obvious when compared with the songs in the stage plays.

BRECHTIAN SONG AND DIONYSIAN MELODRAMA

The Happy Haven (1960) is in all respects an experimental play. It is one of the earliest pieces written with Margaretta D'Arcy.[52] (*The Business of Good Government* was also produced in 1960.) It contains interesting innovations in the realm of stagecraft, including the use of masks inspired by the *commedia dell'arte*, young actors to play the old people, and a conception for an open stage. As Albert Hunt remarks, it "is a mixture of pantomime, music hall, high comedy and low farce."[53] *The Happy Haven* is not a completely musical drama as is *The Workhouse Donkey*, but it does employ song in new ways. In the context of Arden and D'Arcy's work as a whole, the play's significance lies in the fact that it reflects little of folk song or ballad heritage. Instead, it foreshadows the major collaborative plays with nontraditional music such as

The Island of the Mighty. On the whole, *The Happy Haven* is one of the most Brechtian of the early plays in its use of song.

In this play, Arden and D'Arcy do not indicate any overall tune preference as they do in the folk-oriented dramas. Some of the songs are traditional; the rest, conceivably, could be set to stylized, nontraditional music, in the manner of the later plays. Arden and D'Arcy praise an experimental production by Albert Hunt that sought to find an appropriate musical style. They are also enthusiastic about the music in their own production in Dublin in 1964. There they had, as Arden explains,

> a pianist who improvised on the piano, and he . . . improvised tunes for the songs . . . It was . . . silent cinema music that he was doing. It was rather old-fashioned. It was the kind of music of the people in the play . . . when they were young, . . . the popular music they would have had around 1920, . . . music-hall tunes, or . . . Palm Court music . . . It was all put together in a rather *ad hoc* way, but it worked.

D'Arcy adds, "the music is . . . the thing that gives it the style." In *The Happy Haven*, the formalized presentation and the idiosyncratic "humourous" personalities of the old people, who sing all the songs, make a less traditional manner of singing appropriate to the dramatic style. Interesting is the direct revelation of purpose, personality and motives to the audience through the medium of song. Other functions include irony with respect to both theme and character, and general commentary.

The opening scene is a deliberately artificial dramatic exposition, with actions and songs occurring precisely when they are announced. The impression is that Doctor Copperthwaite is stage-managing the event as another of his demonstrations. Thus when the Doctor explains that the old people are apt to become too excited, they promptly sing "Knees Up Mother Brown," conveniently proving his point. This is a popular music-hall song, sung in encouragement of dancers.

In the same way the Doctor announces his purpose and methods in a lecture to the audience, so both Crape and Letouzel disclose their motivations and passions in introductory songs to the audience.[54] The effect is quite Brechtian in manner. Hardrader's song in defiance of authority takes its vocabulary straight from the popular comic strip: "Ho! Left, right, straight to the chin! / Bang, crash, ho, ooh, wallop, out— / Take him away!" (p. 219). This reminds us not only of Brecht, but also of the less successful efforts of T. S. Eliot, Auden and Isherwood to incorporate popular music and the popular idiom in their lyrics. Arden was familiar with most of these earlier experiments in dramatic song. We laugh not only at this exaggerated, stylized language, but also at Hardrader's following obsequious submission to authority that comically deflates his pretensions.

The various reactions that the prospect of rejuvenation calls forth are conveniently illustrated in song. The lyrics cover a spectrum ranging from a

nostalgic view, through a lusty recreation of youthful vigor, to a children's
nursery song. The vigorous one, sung by Golightly and Hardrader, recalls in
its rhythms and diction a Gilbert and Sullivan operetta tune, sublime in its
cheerful insouciance, and supremely self-confident in its comic use of theatrical artificiality. This kind of tongue-in-cheek theatricality has a light-
hearted comic appeal:

> O I am a man and a very healthy man
> I'm a racehorse in my prime
> Ten thousand fields of the brilliant green
> For my pleasuring they all are mine.
> . . . .
> O I am a man and a very healthy man
> A porpoise upon the storm
> I leap and leap ten thousand miles
> From Australia to Cape Horn.

(p. 247)

The nursery song, "Boys and Girls Come Out to Play," (p. 247) is traditional[55] and illustrates the imaginative leap to the state of childhood, but it is
equally artificial in its way. We have here young, agile actors, wearing stylized
masks of old people, dancing "round and round" the stage singing a nursery
rhyme that calls their playfellows out to the street. The incongruities are in
themselves comic, and the whole is an ironic commentary on the dubious
medical experiment.

Other songs have an emotionally touching effect mixed with their ironic
and comic functions; they are thus ambivalent in the end. This is especially
true of Mrs. Phineus' lullaby, which closes the play. It is the only song she
sings, and is thus given special prominence. A lullaby for the man who
wanted to turn his own patients into small children, it is a piece of supreme
irony. It is also ironic in respect to Mrs. Phineus: all her life she has vainly
wished for a child, and now she gets a "baby." But for this very reason it is
also touching—the illustration of the vanity of human wishes does not make
these desires any less urgent or moving. On the whole, however, the dominant dramatic effect is grotesque: the Doctor, with a child mask, is perched
on the knee of the ninety-year-old "new mother," who sings him to sleep. The
artificiality of scene and of song is in keeping with the style of the entire play.
The songs in *The Happy Haven* are often as ironic as the title itself. They are
decidedly less realistic than the songs in any of the other plays to date. Their
prime characteristic, like that of the entire play, is their exuberant and comic
artificiality. Many of them point forward to Arden and D'Arcy's use of
dramatic song in their later work.

The Workhouse Donkey (1963) is Arden's most thoroughly musical play to
date, and the first one that he openly calls a "melo-drama," "a term I intend

to be understood in its original sense of a play with a musical accompaniment."[56] Arden adds elsewhere: "It's not a musical by any manner of means, but it has this integrated music with it."[57] By saying it is not a musical, he is both emphasizing its difference from the more superficial entertainment of this kind and placing primary importance on the text rather than the music. By calling it a melodrama on the other hand, he wishes to call attention to the integral role of the musical accompaniment and the songs. Arden adds:

> I'm also using some shreds from English music-hall and pantomime tradition, which are more apparent when the play's staged than when you read it because there is a sort of running musical background, . . . which sometimes becomes the accompaniment to songs and sometimes is just played behind speech.[58]

The almost continuous use of music is basically an experiment, and it is one that Arden and D'Arcy will later often repeat.

Musicality is, as mentioned above, part of Arden's wider attempt to recreate vital or Dionysian theater, a theater of disorder, corruption, and fertility, to name a few of the attributes he lists.[59] Music is an indispensable part of the "noise" of this type of theater:

> Vital Theatre consists of plays which must be organic events—to get hold of their audiences by laughter, by pain, by music, dancing, poetry, visual excitement, rhythm.[60]

Dionysian theater is thus a development and extension of Arden's earlier concerns with poetic theater and popular theater. In spite of the labyrinthine plot, the structure of the play as a whole is determined more by its music-hall nature than by plot: "Each scene demands to be played as a turn in its own right, with the emphasis, not on 'character' and 'motivation', but on putting over the songs and the jokes."[61]

For the first time in his work, Arden here calls for a band to play the musical accompaniment. In Chichester, it was placed "on an upper balcony of the stage and remained in view of the audience throughout the action" (preface, p. 7), very much in the Brechtian manner. The actors would signal to the band when they wanted a tune. Arden elaborates on the music of his play:

> We have a sort of little theme tune for each of the characters, used rather like in a musical to establish the beginning of scenes and for certain speeches of importance there's a musical background.[62]

Other scenes experiment with dance or pantomime to music. Except for the traditional tunes, "Ilkley Moor," "See the Conquering Hero," the English national anthem, and the old ballad "Dives and Lazarus," the tunes to the songs and the background music were composed by John Addison. Arden was happy with this. "The music of that was very satisfactory. John Addison was fantastic," he says.

This is the only musical score to an Arden drama that I have been able to examine in detail.[63] In a technique similar to that of melodrama, music is not only frequently used during scene changes but also to cover over transitions within scenes. Musical accompaniment often underscores particularly significant speeches. In act 2, scene 6, the entire verse conversation between the Borough Councillors before Butterthwaite's entrance is conducted in a comic operatic recitative style (pp. 91–93; Addison, pp. 43–47), thus musically conveying a sense of urgency and irritation. In this case, the musical background accompanies verse speeches which are in themselves already linguistically set off and heightened in comparison with the surrounding prose.

On occasion, background music is also employed to accompany prose speeches. In some cases it is introduced not realistically but rather to emphasize moments of heightened dramatic tension or satirical climax. This is very much in the manner of melodrama (or of its successor, modern film music), which almost always uses music to set off, signalize and heighten the dramatic climax. Here, however, most of the climaxes are comic. The entire burglary episode at the Town Hall is set to music, heightening the tension of the moment. It ends in an "allegro agitato" during the chaotic comic climax to the scene (pp. 99–104; Addison, pp. 49–61). The final chorus of the drama is half spoken, half sung as recitative. Here, the music functions not to underline the tension but rather serves as a satirical comment on the superficiality of the agreement. It is the social, political, and musical expression of a harmony that is precariously built on corruption, and thus is totally artificial.

In this drama, the songs tend more strongly than ever to stylization and theatricalism, and are employed in a variety of introductory, explanatory and commentary functions. Band and song contribute to the theatrical ritual when Butterthwaite makes his "processional entrance" (p. 30) to the saloon bar of the Victoria and Albert. Butterthwaite's final exit is also accomplished in a ritual procession. Arrayed as a carnival Lord of Misrule, costumed in a tablecloth, paper chain and with a ring of flowers on his head, he is carried out forcibly through the aisle singing "Out He Goes the Poor Old Donkey" (p. 130). The local down-and-outs who have accompanied him on his last demonstration take up his song in a choric way outside the theater, turning his defeat into another triumphant procession. The processional songs create a formal musical framework for the play, spanning a bridge between beginning and end, and emphasizing the theatrical opening and closing of the action.

As in *The Happy Haven*, song in *The Workhouse Donkey* is used as a means of introduction, explanation, or revelation of past history. Such pieces are often sung in a self-consciously theatrical manner. Declaration of purpose and presentation of basic political policy are also accomplished in song, as in the

case of Blomax who dominates the singing of most of the songs in the first
half of the play:

> I'm a dirty old devil
> Alone in the notions
> Of politics and progress
> . . . .
> You can call me a tortoise
>
> And a dormouse
> And a ostrich in sand
> If it ever gets too hot
> I can pull out my hand . . .

(p. 51)

The lyrics tend toward doggerel. Arden is aiming not at the concentrated
lyricism or folk flavor of *Serjeant Musgrave's Dance* or *Armstrong's Last Goodnight* but at the more immediate humor of political street theater, as in many
of the later collaborative plays.

In the second half of the drama, Butterthwaite gains in prominence, due
partly to the importance of the songs he is given to sing. The history of his
childhood in the workhouse is presented in a song that also gives the play its
title: "In the Workhouse I Was Born" (pp. 99–101). Interesting is his rendition of the traditional ballad "Dives and Lazarus," based on the biblical
parable in Luke 16. This is the first narrative ballad included in Arden's
work; it is to be found in the classic collection of ballads edited by Francis
James Child, *The English and Scottish Popular Ballads* (Child, no. 56). This
tune is presented at the beginning of Butterthwaite's intrusion into the art
gallery reception and is sung unaccompanied in the folk manner. In the
ballad the beggar Lazarus stages a demonstrative sit-in on rich Dives's
doorstep on the day of a feast:

> As it fell out upon a day, rich Dives he made a feast,
> And he invited all his friends and gentry of the best,
> But Lazarus he sat down and down and down at Dives' door,
> Some meat, some drink, brother Dives, he said, bestow unto the poor!

(p. 127)

(This is essentially equivalent with Child no. 56, Variant A, verses 1 and 2.)[64]
In much the same manner, Butterthwaite, who seems to equate himself with
Lazarus, provocatively disrupts the proper Tory party. The religious ballad,
one of the few specifically Christian texts collected by Child, connects
thematically with Butterthwaite's symbolic role as scapegoat and Christ parody ("In the workhouse I was born/ On one Christmas day," p. 99). In the
original, Lazarus is saved, whereas the stingy Dives goes to Hell. Butterthwaite's image as blessed poor man is totally ironic, given his own corruption.

1. [Dives and Lazarus]

Andrews, *JFSS*, II, No. 7 (1905), p. 125. Also in Leather,
1912, p. 190 (1st tune). Sung by Mrs. Harris (80), a mole-
catcher's widow, Eardisley, Herefordshire, 1905; learned
from her father, a noted singer.

a I

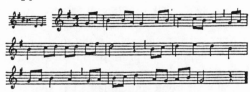

1. As it fell out on a light dully day,*
        high holiday,
  When Diverus made a feast;
And he invited all his friends,
  And grand gentry of the best.

2. Then Lazarus laid himself down and down
  Under Dives' wall:
"Some meat! some drink! brother Diverus?
  For hunger, starve I shall!"

3. "Thou wert none of my brethren as I tell thee,
  Lie begging at my wall;
No meat nor drink will I give thee,
  For hunger, starve thou shall!"

4. Then Diverus sent out his hungry dogs
  To worry poor Lazarus away.
They hadn't the power to bite one bite,
  But they licked his sores away.

5. Then Lazarus, he laid himself down and down,
  And down at Diverus' gate:
"Some meat! some drink! brother Diverus,
  For Jesus Christ His sake."

6. Then Diverus sent to his merry men
  To worry poor Lazarus away.
They'd not the power to strike one stroke,
  But they flung their whips† away.

7. As it fell out, on a light dully day,*
  When Lazarus sickened and died;
There came two Angels out of heaven,
  His soul for to guide.

8. "Arise! arise! brother Lazarus,
  And come along with we;
There's a place provided in heaven,
  (For) To sit on an Angel's knee."

9. As it fell on a dark dully day,§
  When Dives sickened and died;

  There came two serpents out of hell,
  His soul for to guide.

10. "Arise! arise! brother Diverus,
  And come along with we;
There is a place provided in hell,
  For to sit on a serpent's knee!

11. There is a place provided in hell
  For wicked men, like thee;

  .   .   .   .   .   ."

12. "Who had they as many days to live
  As there is blades of grass,
I would be good unto the poor
  As long as life would last!"

* (?) Bright holiday
† Pronounced "weeps"
§ (?) Dark holiday

"Dives and Lazarus" (Child, no. 56), from *The Traditional Tunes of the Child Ballads*, ed. Bertrand Harris Bronson, vol. 2 (Princeton: Princeton University Press, 1962), variant 1, p. 18.

The ballad also has a satirical function: just as Lazarus is turned away from Dives's door, Butterthwaite is carried out of the hall, and the corruption continues among those remaining. Their impending doom is implied through the analogy of the ballad. This is a good early example of satirical song in Arden's drama. The introduction of a traditional religious ballad with parodistic, ironic and satirical functions corresponds stylistically to the biblical language elsewhere in the play; for example, the prose parody of Psalm 108 spoken by Butterthwaite just before his final song.

The closing chorus is dramatically an ironic anticlimax. It is spoken, or rather chanted, in recitative, by all except Feng, and it echoes the words of a World War I army song in a satiric fashion. The theme is whitewashing or metaphorical cleansing:

> If we tell you we've cleaned our armpits
> You'd best believe we've cleaned 'em recent.
> We have washed them white and whiter
> Than the whitewash on the wall.

(p. 133)

The original army jingle runs:

> Wash me in the water that you
> Washed your dirty daughter in,
> And I shall be whiter than the
> Whitewash on the wall.

The implication is that whitewash merely covers over the original dirt with a surface coating. Underneath remains the foulness, just as the corruption remains.

In this play there appears to be little difference between spoken verse passages and sung lyrics. Their functions are roughly parallel. Indeed, John Russell Brown discusses the verse passages without bothering to mention whether a specific speech is spoken or sung.[65] This may be theoretically possible in the study, but it does not do justice to the play as theater. It cannot be stressed strongly enough that the emotional and artistic impact of a song is completely different in performance than it is on the page. This is true of all plays using song, but it is particularly the case in so thoroughly musical a drama as this one. In a melodrama as *The Workhouse Donkey* the reader must necessarily exercise his or her theatrical and musical imagination to appreciate the effect of the songs as opposed to the spoken verse passages. In vital, or Dionysian, theater there really is no complete substitute for live performance.

This type of play forms a strand in Arden's early work, beginning with *The Waters of Babylon* and *Live Like Pigs*. These plays contrast with the more concentrated lyricism of the historical dramas *Serjeant Musgrave's Dance* and *Armstrong's Last Goodnight*. Many critics regret the performance-oriented aspect to Arden's work and blame it on his collaboration with D'Arcy. It should be emphasized, however, that this facet of Arden's dramatic imagination is present from the beginning. Literary critics may find that it does not read as well on the page. While this is true, it indicates a liveliness of Arden's performance imagination which is essential to the vitality of his theater on stage.

THE SCOTTISH BORDER BALLAD

Armstrong's Last Goodnight (1964) is Arden's one play that is almost totally dominated by the world of the traditional narrative ballad. It had its origins in Arden's lifelong love of ballads and his rereading of the border ballad of "Johnie Armstrong" from the disputed lands of the Scottish-English border country. Its plot recounts Arden's semihistorical, semifictional version of the ballad hero's life and death. Above all, it derives much of its poetic charm and emotional impact from the singing of excerpts of two different border ballads, "The Death of Parcy Reed" (Child, no. 193) and "Johnie Armstrong" (Child, no. 169). Arden has written several new stanzas in the style of these traditional ballads, and has also included in his text echoes of numerous other ballads. In addition, there are a few other songs and some bagpipe music. One indication of the permeation of the play with ballad atmosphere is that Arden does not give instructions about the tunes. The airs to be used and the type of presentation (unaccompanied singing in the traditional ballad singer's style) are self-evident.

Arden does not necessarily expect his audience to be familiar with the words of the traditional ballads and their original context: nowhere for example does he mention the title of "Parcy Reed," and it is not crucial to an initial understanding of the play to realize that Arden has altered the words of this song to fit the Armstrong story. An English audience will presumably recognize some names and some ballad lines without knowing exactly what is new or fictional and what is traditional. A Scottish audience, on the other hand, will be more familiar both with the historical facts and with the original ballads and will relish the transformations in the ballad context and the subtle incongruities and ironies intended in Arden's fictional treatment of history. As Arden points out, because of the vague attraction that the border theme exerts on a modern audience it is probably his most popular play:

> I think too that most people are still affected by the romanticism of border ballads, outlaws, and all the rest of what Walter Scott brought in.[66]

For a finer appreciation of the subtleties and ironies of the drama, a detailed understanding of the border ballad world and its songs is imperative. Arden himself was steeped in the ballad lore and was fully aware of the dating, distribution, and connotations of the Scottish border songs. "I certainly used to the full my knowledge of the Scottish ballads when I wrote the play," he says.

This is not to imply that Arden has written a historical museum piece. In his historical parables, he always wishes to draw parallels and awaken audience awareness to contemporary problems. In his introduction he points out the influence of the African Congo conflict on this play.[67] Arden has very subtly built the structure and language of his drama around the contrast and confrontation between the anarchic and self-willed freedom of the border ballad world and the urbane, manipulatory sphere of centralized state diplomacy. Surely this is a conflict that can easily be translated into modern terms.

The Scottish border ballad is present in this drama in plot, atmosphere, character, language, and song. The historical John Armstrong was hanged in the year 1530. The Armstrongs had been a border family of considerable importance since the fourteenth century. They occupied a large portion of the "Debateable Land"[68] on the western edge of the border country and conducted raids into Northern England and—according to some historical accounts—within Scotland too. In this they were typical of the border families as a whole.

> With England to the south, and the wild Highland clans to the north as enemies, the borderers, though constantly at war with each other, made common cause against all foreigners. Thus there runs through all the history, literature, and oral tradition of the Border a continuous sombre note of treachery, murder, cruelty, barbarity—and romantic loyalty.[69]

The borderers built impregnable castles (as in the play, p. 86). They exacted outright tribute money from their raid victims, and demanded protection money or "blackmail," in other words, "rent . . . paid in labor, corn, or base coin, . . . as contrasted to *blanches mailles* or silver"[70] from their feudal subordinates. In the ballad variant that Arden has used for his drama (Child, no. 169, variant C), the captured Armstrong offers to transfer his yearly tribute money to the king if the latter will grant him his life. Note the extent of this tribute:

> "Grant me my lyfe, my liege, my king,
> And a brave gift I'll gie to thee;
> All betwene heir and Newcastle town
> Sall pay thair yeirly rent to thee."[71]

Wells's summary of the family code of the borderers reads like an introduction to the drama:

> Life in the Border was determined first of all by family organization, clan connection being a binding obligation and an unquestioned reason for fierce loyalty. . . .

Tempers were quick, customs brutal, retaliation a part of the code. Quarrels must be instantly taken up and followed to fatal conclusions.[72]

The historical accounts of the Armstrongs differ as to whether they also conducted raids on Scottish territory, but in all probability they did. In any case they were definitely not willing to show unconditional obedience to the Scottish kings:

> The Armstrongs, if nominally Scots, were so far from being "in due obeysaunce" that . . . the representatives of the Scottish king could not undertake to oblige them to make redress for injuries done the English, though a peace depended upon this condition.[73]

The situation became so serious that in the summer of 1530 King James V of Scotland decided to take the pacifying of his borders, and particularly of John Armstrong, into his own hands. The historical accounts of John Armstrong's end all agree that he and his men were hanged, but differ as to whether he was deliberately tricked into appearing unarmed before the king or not. "There is no record of a trial, and the execution was probably as summary as the arrest was perfidious."[74]

The ballad of "Johnie Armstrong" comes down to us in three variants that differ considerably both in story and in language. Both the A and B variants depict John and his men armed, and they fight valiantly until John is treacherously stabbed from behind. Variant C, the one Arden chooses and quotes directly in his play, merely tells us that "John murdred was at Carlinrigg" (stanza 32). All three variants stress the king's ruse in writing John a "loving letter":

> The king he wrytes a luving letter,
>   With his ain hand sae tenderly:
> And he hath sent it to Johny Armstrang,
>   To cum and speik with him speidily.
>
> (variant C, stanza 2)

This verse with its subterfuge is echoed in Lindsay's words in act 3, scene 12: "John, I have ane letter. It is ane leter of love frae the hand of the King. . . . It is ane surety of Royal honour that there will be nae deception" (p. 112).

The play takes its title from one of the ballad variants. A "goodnight" in ballad tradition contains the last words and farewell of a condemned man before he goes to his death. The ballad sometimes bears the title "Johnny Armstrong's Last Goodnight." Arden was familiar with all three text variants. Bronson lists ten tune variants; the dramatist was not, in fact, acquainted with the tune to "Johnie Armstrong" when he wrote the play. In this case the inspiration came from the words as poetry, and the most suitable tune variant was selected during rehearsal. The fact that Arden chose a ballad

theme and a Scottish-English border setting exemplifies the typically northern character of his imagination. In this play Arden succeeds in capturing
both the historical ambience of the border country and its spirit and language, not only in his recreation of a sixteenth-century Scots dialect, but also
through the dramatic lyricism of the ballad. "The North, the ballad, are his
symbols for pre-social reality."[75]

In structure, *Armstrong's Last Goodnight* is considerably more comprehensive and complicated than any ballad; in other words, Arden does not attempt
to recreate a ballad structure in the drama. The traditional ballad begins,
typically, in the fifth act of the drama and tells only of Armstrong's end.
Arden, on the other hand, provides a subtle complex of—sometimes contradictory—background history, emotions and motivations for his characters.
The structure on the whole is not episodic; the scenes are carefully prepared
for and often thematically interlocked.

Crucial to the dramatic and poetic structure of the play is the marked
contrast that Arden creates between the elegant, urbane and rational Lindsay,
and the spontaneous, irrational and irascible Armstrong. This contrast is
worked out theatrically and linguistically from the very beginning of the play.
The first two scenes belong to Lindsay and to his world of policy, of diplomatic wrangling and cultivated behind-the-scenes intrigue. In scene 3 the
world of Armstrong and his clan is presented in sharp contrast. This is an
archaic world, a world of treachery, of spontaneous lust and revenge. In
contrast with the rational, articulate prose of the first two scenes (having only
one verse passage), scene 3 sets in abruptly with a sung traditional ballad,
"The Death of Parcy Reed" (Child, no. 193). Coming as it does with no
introduction and no explanation, the listener's first impression is fascination
with the poetic lyricism and perhaps unease at the sudden mention of the
theme of betrayal:

> To the hunten ho, cried Johnny Armstrang
> And to the hunten he has gaen
> And the man that seeks his life, James Johnstone,
> Alang with him he has him taen.

(p.29)

Following these hints of murder and treachery stand the beautifully lyrical
stanzas of natural description:

> To the hunten ho, cried Johnny Armstrang,
> The morning sun is on the dew,
> The cauler breeze frae aff the fells
> Will lead the dogs to the quarry true.

(p.29)

Arden is here using the second of two variants of the Parcy Reed ballad (Child, no. 193, variant B), and has altered some of the lines and the order of the stanzas, quoting stanzas 7, 6, 10, 11, 12 and later 13. He has, of course, also changed the names and places to fit his tale. The implications of this ballad are subtle and far-reaching. To a listener thoroughly familiar with the original ballad, its use as introduction for Armstrong throws his character into a negative light. In Scottish history Parcy Reed was an honorable man who helped to pacify the borders and who incurred the enmity of the Halls and Croziers by delivering them to the law. His murder, the theme of the ballad of Parcy Reed, caused great public indignation; the false-hearted Halls were driven from their residence and their name became synonymous with treachery. The stanza used to introduce scene 3, which Arden quotes in altered fashion, runs in the original:

> "To the hunting, ho!" cried Parcy Reed,
>   And to the hunting he has gane;
> And the three fause Ha's o Girsonsfield
>   Alang wi him he has them taen.[76]

The Halls then disarm the sleeping Reed so that the Croziers can murder him. Arden has of course here replaced Reed's name with Armstrong's, but by means of subtle transformation of the tale he identifies Armstrong not with the honorable Reed but rather with the treacherous Halls. In the play, Armstrong disarms Johnstone so that Stobs can murder him.

This identification of Armstrong with the Halls is implied more strongly in another stanza of the ballad sung later in the scene. Stanza 13 of the B variant runs:

> There's nane may lean on a rotten staff,
>   But him that risks to get a fa;
> There's nane may in a traitor trust,
>   And traitors black were every Ha.

This stanza contains a strong condemnation of the Halls. In the play, Arden alters the last line and has Armstrong sing: "Yet trustit men may be traitors all" (p. 33). This new line is ironic in multiple ways: it contains implicit references to Stobs, Johnstone *and* Armstrong.

Two new stanzas to the ballad that Arden created (spoken by the betrayed Johnstone's lover, Meg), make Armstrong's complicity seem even more perfidious:

> John the Armstrang is to the hunten gaen
> Wi' his braid sword at his side
> And there he did meet with a nakit man

> Alane on the green hillside.
> And John John John he killt neither hart nor hind
> At the end of the day he hameward rade
> And never a drap of blood did fall
> Frae the tip of his nakit blade.
>
> (p. 63)

Meg means, of course, that Armstrong is as guilty as those who carried out the actual slaying. This kind of reassignment of traditional ballad incidents with ensuing subtle implications for the dramatic characters is deliberate on Arden's part. Other echoes of traditional ballads can be found elsewhere in the dialogue.

The title ballad of the play, "Johnie Armstrong," is not introduced until the end of act 2, and the singing of it continues at the climax of act 3. John has given up the idea of collaboration with the king and has decided on open rebellion. Act 2 ends with the singing of the first and last stanzas of the ballad (stanzas 1 and 33). The First Armstrong begins the song, and "the others all take it up" (p. 92). In this context it is intended as a praise of John's boldness and fearlessness, and functions as a processional song as the men exit into the forest. But the final stanza in praise of Armstrong's patriotism has a decidedly ironic effect, because the audience knows that John is in the process of deliberately sabotaging his own king's political policies.

In the last act, the audience is, in effect, watching the ballad-making process in progress, or rather Arden's fictional version of it. A condemned man's last "goodnight" was in practice never written by the victim himself but by some survivor who could tell the whole tale, including details of the execution, and add some appropriate overall moral. Here, however, Arden gives life to the fiction that the dying man indeed composes his own final words. We witness Armstrong as he begins to invent a new tune, humming it to the bagpipe player; it is the tune that will become his own ballad:

> Ane new-made air: I made it mysel' . . . nae words to it yet, but they'll come—wait, I'll gie you the line of the melody.
>
> *He hums a tune, carefully.* (p. 115)

And with this tune they set off forming "a little procession" (p.115), marching about the stage—and on to the hanging.

As in the traditional ballad, John puts on his "gaudiest garments, . . . a' the claiths of gowd and siller, silk apparel, satin" (p. 114), all booty from his raids into England. The relevant stanza in the ballad runs:

> When Johny came before the king,
>   With all his men sae brave to see,
> The king he movit his bonnet to him;

3. "Johnie Armstrang"

Scott, 1833-34, I, opp. p. 416; text, p. 407. Words from Allan Ramsay, *The Ever Green*, 1724 (Child's C); Ramsay learned them from "a gentleman called Armstrong."

m I

1. Sum speikis of lords, sum speikis of lairds,
   And sick lyke men of hie degrie;
   Of a gentleman I sing a sang,
   Sum tyme called Laird of Gilnockie.

2. The King he wrytes a luving letter,
   With his ain hand sae tenderly,
   And he hath sent it to Johnie Armstrang,
   To cum and speik with him speedily.

3. The Eliots and Armstrangs did convene;
   They were a gallant cumpanie—
   "We'll ride and meit our lawful King,
   And bring him safe to Gilnockie.

4. "Make kinnen and capon ready, then,
   And venison in great plentie;
   We'll wellcum here our royal King;
   I hope he'll dine at Gilnockie!"—

5. They ran their horse on the Langholme howm,
   And brak their spears wi' mickle main;
   The ladies lukit frae their loft windows—
   "God bring our men weel hame agen!"

6. When Johnie cam before the King,
   Wi' a' his men sae brave to see,
   The King he movit his bonnet to him;
   He ween'd he was a King as weel as he.

7. "May I find grace, my sovereign liege,
   Grace for my loyal men and me?
   For my name it is Johnie Armstrang,
   And a subject of yours, my liege," said he.

8. "Away, away, thou traitor strang!
   Out o' my sight soon mayst thou be!
   I grantit never a traitor's life,
   And now I'll not begin wi' thee."—

9. "Grant me my life, my liege, my King!
   And a bonny gift I'll gie to thee—
   Full four-and-twenty milk-white steids,
   Were a' foal'd in ae yeir to me.

10. "I'll gie thee a' these milk-white steids,
    That prance and nicker at a speir;
    And as mickle gude Inglish gilt,
    As four o' their braid backs dow bear."—

11. "Away, away, thou traitor strang!
    Out o' my sight soon mayst thou be!
    I grantit never a traitor's life,
    And now I'll not begin wi' thee!"—

12. "Grant me my life, my liege, my King!
    And a bonny gift I'll gie to thee—
    Gude four-and-twenty ganging mills,
    That gang thro' a' the yeir to me.

13. "These four-and-twenty mills complete
    Sall gang for thee thro' a' the yeir;
    And as mickle of gude reid wheit,
    As a' thair happers dow to bear."—

14. "Away, away, thou traitor strang!
    Out o' my sight soon mayst thou be!
    I grantit never a traitor's life,
    And now I'll not begin wi' thee."—

15. "Grant me my life, my liege, my King!
    And a great great gift I'll gie to thee—
    Bauld four-and-twenty sisters' sons,
    Sall for thee fecht, tho' a' should flee!"—

16. "Away, away, thou traitor strang!
    Out o' my sight soon mayst thou be!
    I grantit never a traitor's life,
    And now I'll not begin wi' thee."—

17. "Grant me my life, my liege, my King!
    And a brave gift I'll gie to thee—
    All between heir and Newcastle town
    Sall pay their yeirly rent to thee."—

From "Johnie Armstrong," (Child, no. 169), in *The Traditional Tunes of the Child Ballads*, ed. Bertrand Harris Bronson, vol. 3 (Princeton: Princeton University Press, 1962), variant 3, pp. 141–42. (In the Chichester production of John Arden's *Armstrong's Last Goodnight*, a different tune variant was used.)

He weind he was a king as well as he.
> (variant C, stanza 6; see also stanzas 25 and 26)

Arden ironically alters the situation: the king is in "plain Highland dress" (p. 116), and Armstrong, expecting magnificence equal to his own, at first does not recognize him. In the ballad Armstrong asks the king for mercy and pleads for his life five times, five times receiving the reply:

> "Away, away, thou traytor, strang!
>   Out of my sicht thou mayst sune be!
> I grantit nevir a traytors lyfe,
>   And now I'll not begin with thee."
> > (variant C, stanzas 8, 11, 14, 16, and 18).

In the play, the king's words: "Ye are ane strang traitor" (p. 119) provide a concise echo of this traditional ballad repetition.

When Armstrong realizes that he is going to be hanged, the words of his new song come to him. Because his piper has already been led away by the soldiers, he must sing, in ballad style, unaccompanied: "Johnny wants his music: He has fand him words to his new air. Nae piper: nae music: Johnny maun sing on his lane" (p. 119). As he is seized and hanged on the tree which occupies the center of the stage, he sings two stanzas of his ballad. For the sake of comparison I will quote the Child version, but it will be seen that it is almost identical to Arden's words (pp. 119 and 120):

> "To seik het water beneth cauld yce,
>   Surely it is a great folie;
> I haif asked grace at a graceless face,
>   But there is nane for my men and me.
>
> "But had I kend, or I came frae hame,
>   How thou unkynd wadst bene to me,
> I wad haif kept the border-syde,
>   In spyte of all thy force and thee."
> > (variant C, stanzas 22 and 23)

The tone of the words is bold, defiant. Armstrong's spirit is unbroken: he epitomizes the proud independence and self-sufficiency of the typical border "laird." The emotional effect of the song at this moment is extremely powerful: not only is all of Armstrong's defiance embodied in it, but also his despair in the face of death and all his bitterness in the face of betrayal. In fact, this song epitomizes the tragedy of the drama. Arden says that in performance the impression was "extremely moving": "It wasn't just sung as a song—it's the man's death song." In the play Armstrong's tune is summarily cut short by the hanging. Almost his last words are: "For God's sake let me finish my sang!" (p. 120).

Just as the play began with two scenes of cultivated diplomacy before the audience was introduced to Armstrong through a ballad, so too after the final ballad stanzas have died away the drama closes with two short prose scenes containing diplomatic business and a moral to the tale. Armstrong remains visible throughout, hanging on the tree. As the ballad and the hanging represent the dramatic and emotional climax of the play, these two scenes relax dramatic tension and establish a rational perspective to the whole. Scene 16 contains a bit of folk legendry:

> There is a legend in the Borders that the trees [on which Armstrong and his men were hanged] withered and died and that the same has happened to any trees planted there since.[77]

This tree, prominent in position throughout the play, provides a visual symbol of treachery and dishonor. *Armstrong's Last Goodnight* thus has a symmetrical poetic framework, with ballad and diplomatic prose evenly balanced at beginning and end.

The principal singer in this play is Armstrong. As in the case of Sparky and Annie in *Serjeant Musgrave's Dance*, Armstrong often sings as a means of expression for thoughts that he cannot otherwise communicate. He has a definite speech impediment, and often needs an interpreter for those who do not know him well. He is unpredictable both personally and politically. Impulsive, irrational, irascible, spontaneous and childlike, he represents forces of love and life—or anarchy as Musgrave would express it. The only times he becomes fluent, almost lyrical, are when his love and lust for the lady loosen his tongue—and when he sings. In song he thus transcends his own personality just as the ballad lyrically condenses and heightens his own story into legend.

Although the ballad idiom and atmosphere remain dominant for the play as a whole, several other types of song are used in *Armstrong's Last Goodnight*. The hymn-singing Evangelist provides a musical counterpoint to the ballad world. In this sphere of the hymn everything is straightforward and clearcut, the distinction between good and evil very pronounced. The hymn thus represents a completely different psychology from the murky, ambivalent, and anarchic border ballad mentality. One song usage that is traditional in theater but that Arden had not previously employed is to cover the passage of time or a spacial change. This is a function that is, for example, common in Shakespeare. Through the lyrical stylization of the song, audience awareness of the unreality of time and place is lessened. Thus McGlass twice sings songs to accompany the journey between the palace and Armstrong's castle.

Armstrong's Last Goodnight is a carefully composed play that derives its poetic structure from the contrast between two differing mentalities, personalities, and political views—and two different linguistic and musical idioms. The diplomatic prose of Lindsay, only occasionally heightened into verse, is contrasted both with the rough, almost inarticulate prose and especially with the heightened, anarchic romanticism and lyricism of Armstrong's ballad world. The singing of stanzas from the traditional ballads of "Parcy Reed" and "Johnie Armstrong" roots the play firmly in tradition. On the other hand, Arden's ironic handling of history and ballad material has a certain distancing effect and helps to relate the medieval ballad sphere to contemporary reality. The prose scenes frame the ballad singing that introduces Armstrong and that accompanies his last farewell.

Following these two very different but each in its own way thoroughly musical plays, *The Workhouse Donkey* and *Armstrong's Last Goodnight*, Arden's next work for the professional London stage, *Left-Handed Liberty* (1965), is theatrically but not musically experimental. This drama was followed by a voluntary three-year exile from the London professional theater establishment. When Arden returned to the London stage, it was with works written in collaboration with Margaretta D'Arcy, works that carried forward both his earlier experiments with dramatic music and Arden and D'Arcy's previous collaborative experiments in community theater. The reappearance on the London stage was accomplished in the form of the controversial semi-operatic *The Hero Rises Up* (1968), a second melodrama. Arden and D'Arcy's work with nonestablishment theater was expanded and deepened in their series of later Irish plays, plays in which the musical element remains prominent. *Left-Handed Liberty* is a transitional play, experimental in a way that Arden decided not to pursue in his later career. It is nonillusionistic theater, but it makes very little use of verse, music, song, dance or spectacle, elements which Arden and D'Arcy accorded an ever-increasing importance in their later works for stage.

3. Earlier Arden/D'Arcy Collaborations for Community Theater

The two plays I have chosen to illustrate this phase of Arden and D'Arcy's work were both written for nonprofessional or semiprofessional performance outside of the proscenium arch theater. They differ in their employment of stage music and song. *The Business of Good Government* has a strong folk flavor, as did many of Arden's earlier works, whereas *The Royal Pardon*, with its improvised percussion music, points forward to the use of stage music in the later collaborative plays.

THE MEDIEVAL FOLK CAROL

As early as 1960, the same year in which Arden wrote *The Happy Haven* with D'Arcy, Arden and D'Arcy coauthored and produced a nativity play, *The*

Business of Good Government, to be performed by amateur actors in a village church with little or no scenery. D'Arcy directed the drama, while Arden appeared in the cast. As Arden emphasizes in his preface, improvisation is vital to any lively amateur production. The drama as a whole, however, depends for its charm and effect on the contrast between the modern and the archaic. For this reason, the biblical, folk, and medieval elements should be left as intact as possible because they form the poetic core of the play. The carols should be sung as indicated. Arden does add, as a concession to amateur actors, that "if Joseph has no voice for singing, his song could be spoken";[78] but his song, "The Cherry Tree Carol," has one of the most beautiful melodies of all English carols, and to speak it rather than sing it would decidedly alter the effect of the scene.

The three carols chosen for the play are positioned almost symmetrically at beginning, end, and near the middle; they are "I Saw Three Ships," "The Cherry Tree Carol," and "The Corpus Christi Carol." "I Saw Three Ships" is specified for the opening procession: "All the characters except Mary and Joseph enter through the audience in procession . . . As they enter, they sing" (p. 17). Herod, however, the hardheaded politician, has a delayed entrance and "does not sing" (p. 17), setting him apart immediately from the rest of the cast. The play concludes with another processional carol, "The Corpus Christi Carol," as the cast leaves the hall or church: "The carol should be timed so that all the actors are clear of the hall before they stop singing" (p. 54). Technically, the function of the carols is to accomplish the entry and exit of an amateur cast in the most dignified manner possible. For both processions, an organ accompaniment may be used, but otherwise the songs are to be sung in traditional folk manner, unaccompanied. These two processional carols establish a formal musical framework to the drama, distinctly marking beginning and end. In this respect they have a somewhat similar musical function to the processional songs at the beginning and end of *The Workhouse Donkey* or the musical framework of *Serjeant Musgrave's Dance*. In character and atmosphere, however, they are quite different. Whereas the musical framework of *Serjeant Musgrave's Dance* was ironic in character, pointing to the unresolved political conflicts of the play, and the processional songs of *The Workhouse Donkey* were anarchic and Dionysian, these carols give the scenes of *The Business of Good Government* a quiet dignity, discipline, and a sense of community devotion suited to the simple folk nature of the play. This is not to deny the complexity of the political conflict in any way, but musically, the emphasis is placed on the communal rather than on the disruptive. It is perhaps the most successful and most accessible of the community plays.

The form of the carol used as the musical basis of this play is closely related to the ballad form: "The carol stands midway between the hymn and the ballad, and may be regarded . . . as a secular hymn or a sacred ballad."[79] Scholars distinguish between medieval manuscript carols and folk carols preserved by oral transmission. Only the folk carols have survived to the present, and they are often in the form of narrative "ballad carols." Thus carol and ballad are interrelated types of folk song that arose in the late middle ages and flourished in the fifteenth and sixteenth centuries. The religious folk carols were driven underground by the Puritan prohibitions of the seventeenth century and were not revived until the nineteenth century.[80] The carol is distinguished from the ballad not only by its religious subject matter but also by the fact that it is more uninhibited and picturesque in detail and more personal in narration. In contrast with the ballad, "the carol . . . is known and loved precisely for its tenderness and fondness for poetic imagery and symbolism."[81] On the other hand, the carol is distinct from the later hymn form that arose in the sixteenth century, which does not belong to folk song. The hymn praises God directly; the carol, in contrast, praises only indirectly.

All three carols chosen by Arden and D'Arcy for this play are medieval in origin, belong to a very old stratum of folk tradition. The refrain of "The Corpus Christi Carol" may indeed preserve much older, even pagan, traditions. The carol form probably originated in a nonreligious circular dance song, including a stanza sung by a leader while the dancers paused for breath, and a refrain or "burden," summarizing the whole and sung by the spectators while the dance progressed.[82] A. L. Lloyd writes:

> To carol, we are told, meant originally to dance in a ring, and it is usually thought that the origins of carolling lie in the pagan round-dances that people performed, especially at midwinter to ensure the re-birth of the sun. If that is so, then our Christian carols have arisen out of the Church's action to . . . take over rituals that it could not abolish.[83]

Although the burden of the carol is usually an independent stanza (as in "The Holly and the Ivy"), it occasionally takes the form of refrain lines interlaced with the narrative lines as in "The Corpus Christi Carol" (here, lines two and four).[84] The ballad carols characteristically narrate stories that have their sources in apocryphal legend or folk legend.

"I Saw Three Ships" belongs to the popular type of lullaby carol and is based on old folk legend. The idea of the holy family sailing to Bethlehem (which is not, of course, a port town) is derived ultimately from the folk legend that the skulls of the Magi were brought to Cologne by three ships in 1162. "The carol has simply transferred the ships from the Magi to Christ himself. . . . So in popular imagination what began as a cortège becomes a triumphal procession by sea."[85] The feeling of naïve folk triumph is best conveyed in the lines:

> Joseph did whistle and Mary did sing,
> Mary did sing, Mary did sing,

And all the bells on earth did ring
For joy our Lord was born.

(p. 17)

"The Cherry Tree Carol" is sung at the first major emotional climax of the play: as Mary withdraws to give birth to Jesus, Joseph sings. The carol's lyricism here heightens the emotional impact of the wondrous moment of the child's birth. Technically, it covers the passage of time during the birth. In addition, it serves as a commentary on the situation. Joseph, singing toward the audience, explains: "Joseph was an old man . . . / When he married Mary" (p. 28). In part, the carol also fulfills the function of divine prophecy:

> As Joseph was a-walking
> He heard an angel sing
> This night shall be born
> Our heavenly king.

(p. 29)

"The Cherry Tree Carol" is the only one of the three carols to be included in the Child collection (no. 54). The story it narrates is derived from the apocryphal gospel of Pseudo-Matthew, chapter 20, in which Mary expresses a desire for dates from a date palm tree during the flight into Egypt, and the infant Jesus causes the tree to bow down.[86] In the English ballad the date tree has been transformed into a cherry tree and the episode takes place before the birth of Jesus during the journey to Bethlehem.[87] From the womb, the unborn Jesus bids the cherry tree to bow down so that his mother may eat. The story has been incorporated into local English folk legend. The gift of a cherry is in itself an element of folk lore, as any fruit carrying its own seed was considered "a divine authentication of human fertility."[88]

Arden and D'Arcy have employed only the emotive stanzas surrounding the birth of the child (Child, no. 54; variant B, stanzas 1, 9, 10, 11, and 12), and not the narrative stanzas that recount the miracle of the cherry tree. They certainly were aware of the full context, however, and in all probability expected their audience to be familiar with the song, for it has maintained widespread popularity even into the twentieth century.

"The Corpus Christi Carol," or "Down in Yon Forest," from the fourteenth century is one of the most remarkable and most mysterious of English carols. It combines no fewer than four religious traditions: the passion, the mass, the legend of the Glastonbury thorn and the Arthurian quest of the Holy Grail. According to folk legend, Joseph of Arimathea brought the Holy Grail, the cup used at the last supper, to Britain and left it in the Hall of Glastonbury. Here he also planted a thorn tree. Thus the hall in stanza 1 and the thorn in stanza 5 can be interpreted with reference to this legend. The bed in stanza 2 may possibly refer to the cross, the deathbed, or the medieval

DOWN IN YON FOREST

(GENERAL)

(R. V. W.)

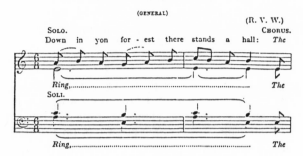

Traditional.　　　　　　　　　　　　　　　　　　　　*Ibid.*

D OWN in yon forest there stands a hall :
　　The bells of Paradise I heard them ring :
It's covered all over with purple and pall :
　　And I love my Lord Jesus above anything.

2　In that hall there stands a bed :
　　It's covered all over with scarlet so red :

3　At the bed-side there lies a stone :
　　Which the sweet Virgin Mary knelt upon :

4　Under that bed there runs a flood :
　　The one half runs water, the other runs blood :

5　At the bed's foot there grows a thorn :
　　Which ever blows blossom since he was born :

6.*Over that bed the moon shines bright :
　　Denoting our Saviour was born this night :

"Down in Yon Forest" ("The Corpus Christi Carol"), in *The Oxford Book of Carols,* ed. Percy Dearmer, R. Vaughan Williams and Martin Shaw (London: Oxford University Press, 1928), carol no. 61, pp. 126–27.

altar of sacrifice. The stone of stanza 3 in a sixteenth-century variant has "Corpus Christi" inscribed on it, hence the title of the carol.[89] As Erik Routley sums up, "The Corpus Christi Carol" represents "the richest example in English of a conflation of Christian belief, church practice and local legend in a folk song."[90] Arden and D'Arcy in this nativity play have thus chosen three traditional carols belonging to the oldest and richest stratum of folk memory and folk song. These impart to the drama a distinctly archaic atmosphere, being so deeply rooted in age-old folk tradition, but they also form a bridge to the present, as all three are still loved and popularly sung in this century.

Three other songs sung in the play also have strong folk flavor, and they are set to familiar folk tunes. The Shepherd's lullaby "Go to Sleep, Little Baby" reflects the playwrights' concern with the cyclical nature of life as reflected in the seasons and expresses the hope for renewal as symbolized in the seed or acorn:

> The deeper it falls then the stronger will it tower
> Bold roots and wide limbs and a true heart of power.
>
> (p. 34)

As in the final ballad of *Serjeant Musgrave's Dance*, this song combines a political hope with an affinity to the folk tradition—two predominant aspects of Arden and D'Arcy's drama as a whole. The tune suggested, "Long Lankin" or "Lamkin" (Child, no. 93), has been chosen for the musical qualities of its melody and not because of any association with the words of the original ballad.

The combination of tune and words is more subtle in the case of the Farm-Girl's song, "The Seed is Set into the Ground" (p. 48). The tune, "John Barleycorn," is the one Arden used before for the closing ballad of *Serjeant Musgrave's Dance*. The theme of the original song, the mythical death and resurrection of the Corn God, was directly relevant to the rebirth idea in Attercliffe's song. Much the same is true here, too. The Farm-Girl sings as a kind of ritual incantation while she sows the corn at the darkest season of the year, a season of physical misery and fear:

> The seed is set into the ground
> At the darkening of the year,
> When the rain runs down in the cold kirk town
> And the roofs are hung with fear.
>
> (p. 48)

Her song takes up the themes of the verse passage immediately preceding it, in which the fear, darkness, and danger of the holy family's flight into Egypt are evoked (p. 47). She also sings as prayer of trust and hope for a bountiful harvest the following summer:

> The grain is scattered on the land
> At the side of Egypt's road.
> God send the proud young harvesters
> A full and golden load.

(p. 48)

Just as the barleycorn grows up again with the help of rain from heaven, and just as Attercliffe's apple seed contains the element of hope for the future, the corn grows up and ripens within an hour, a religious miracle, but also a symbol of an accelerated death and rebirth cycle. "John Barleycorn" is a highly appropriate tune here, as it was in *Serjeant Musgrave's Dance.*

The playwrights do not insist on the use of these suggested tunes, an indication they were not thinking primarily in terms of contrast between original and new words. But they do insist on the type of melody to be used: it must be a simple, unornamented folk melody, sung unaccompanied to enhance, rather than distract from, the meaning of the words:

> If these tunes are not liked and alternative ones are used, I would recommend that they should be airs of the same basic type, in which the line of music reinforces and emphasizes the meaning of the line of verse, so that the whole thing becomes a single poetic statement rather than a passage of attractive singing with some words vaguely attached.[91]

The key phrase is "single poetic statement," a phrase that summarizes the conception of song in the plays to this date: the verse passage and the musical expression should have equal prominence, and both elements should become fused so as to form a new artistic entity, the theatrical song, distinct from spoken verse and set off from the prose passages.

The language of *The Business of Good Government* gains its greatest effect through the contrast between the everyday and modern and the archaic, biblical and age-old folk idiom. As in so many of Arden's plays, a symmetrical structure of linguistic contrasts exists at beginning and end, creating a satisfying stylized formal framework. The movement at the beginning is from song, an intensely heightened and condensed form of utterance, through heightened biblical speech, to the level of everyday prose. The movement at the end of the play is exactly the reverse: from the everyday through heightened biblical quotation to communal, processional song. Communal beginning and end serve to increase the audience's awareness of its part as members of this community.

Both the linguistic and the musical forms of expression in this community play are much closer to folk idiom and folk music than the more complicated, sophisticated forms of expression of the professional dramas. This communal play has a quiet and simple beauty all its own. It illustrates the fact, however, that some of the early Arden/D'Arcy collaborations were close to Arden's lyrical plays in their musicality and carefully planned structures.

IMPROVISED MUSIC

The Royal Pardon (1966) is a play for alternative theater, not necessarily amateur theater, that relies on improvisation and on "a proper sense of communication between performers and audience."[92] It recalls those devices in Arden's earlier plays designed to break down the barriers between audience and actors: for example, direct audience address and disruption of illusion. It anticipates Arden and D'Arcy's later work in which communication between stage and auditorium becomes increasingly important. The music of this play recalls the earlier plays that used a continuous musical accompaniment and it foreshadows the use of song and music in certain of the later plays, most notably *The Non-Stop Connolly Show.* In complete contrast to *The Business of Good Government,* which was firmly rooted in medieval folk traditions, *The Royal Pardon* relies exclusively on improvised music.

> We . . . used music throughout the play, mostly percussion, made by two players in a sort of cage against one wall of the room. This music accompanied many of the speeches and most of the physical movement.[93]

In Brechtian fashion the musicians are to be visible throughout the performance. Whereas in *The Business of Good Government* the improvisational element applied less to the music than to the prose speeches, the improvisation in *The Royal Pardon* extends to the music too: "There is no score of it, as it was improvised during rehearsals and gradually fixed into a final form shortly before the play opened."[94]

In accordance with this different concept of dramatic music, the songs on the whole are not emotional in impact, nor are they placed at moments of particular emotional tension. They serve to introduce, comment on, explain, and summarize. The opening song of act 1, sung from behind the stage as a kind of impersonal chorus before the actors appear, immediately states the play's central theme. It will be about theater and the nature of truth and illusion:

> Sun and moon and stars and rainbow
> Drum and trumpet, tambourine,
>
> . . . .
> All is painted, all is cardboard
> Set it up and fly it away
> The truest word is the greatest falsehood,
> Yet all is true and all in play—

Sun and moon and stars and rainbow
Drum and trumpet, tambourine.

(p. 11)

The repetition in the first two and last two lines with the mention of typical stage instruments gives the aspect of music—especially percussion—thematic prominence.

The dramatic and comic climax of the play comes before the end of act 2, and is initiated by means of a song of incantation that illustrates not only the artificial nature of theater but also its hypnotic powers. Luke, through the medium of his song, lulls the inept constable into a trance so that everything turns out all right in the end. The song with which the play closes is in accordance with the anticlimactic and anti-illusionistic nature of the ending; because in the theater death and hypnosis are merely pretense, the hypnotized constable slowly and stiffly comes to life again and sings a song of comic resignation and bewilderment: "The force of anarchy wins all the time" (p. 109). This is in effect a comic shrug, expressed musically.

The play does make serious points about the nature of authority and anarchy, reality, and theatrical illusion, and many of the major points are made in song, but its music is not as densely or carefully structured as in the major professional plays, or for that matter as in *The Business of Good Government*. It is lighthearted and anarchic, but not as intensely poetic or as deeply musical as the smaller nativity play. It does, however, create a link between the anarchic strand in Arden's earlier work and the later improvisational collaborations.

4. Later Collaborative Dramas

ROMANTIC MELODRAMA AND EIGHTEENTH-CENTURY SONG

The Hero Rises Up (1968) is Arden and D'Arcy's first play in which the musical element is fully as important as the dramatic; indeed, it could be called semioperatic. Its nature is determined by its music to a greater extent than even *The Workhouse Donkey*. At first entitled *Trafalgar*,[95] it was conceived of as a musical to which American composers were to write the music. As Arden elaborates:

The thing was originally going to be a Broadway musical. . . One reason why it fell down was that we disagreed over the type of music that should be used.

In the end, however, it turned out to be a play based firmly in English, rather than American traditions of musical theater.

The Hero Rises Up is subtitled "A Romantic Melodrama"; not only the music but also the juxtaposition of the heroic and romantic with the ironic and low comic reminds one of the nineteenth-century melodramatic heritage. On the other hand, the drama achieves much of its flavor through traditional eighteenth-century tunes, tunes contemporary with the action portrayed. When the Broadway arrangements fell through, the authors decided, as Arden explains,

> to carry it on as a musical play, but to make it into a sort of eighteenth-century type ballad opera, in which you do exactly what Gay did, which is to take tunes either from folk music or from operatic music and use them.

One of the major attractions of a ballad opera is the audience's familiarity with its tunes. Arden and D'Arcy, in employing the technique of the ballad opera, are capitalizing on the effects of musical material already known to the audience. *The Hero Rises Up* thus represents an amalgamation of the musical and dramatic traditions of ballad opera, opera and melodrama. The play was not produced until Michael Kustow of the Institute of Contemporary Arts commissioned it for the Round House in 1968. This production only lasted four days.[96] A later radio adaptation was judged by Arden to be dreadful.

Two songs sung in the play, "Oh the Weary Cutters" and "All Things are Quite Silent" (slightly altered), are traditional folk songs of Horatio Nelson's period. Eight other songs have been set to traditional tunes, and Arden and D'Arcy for the first time in their career insist on their use. Significantly they write: "if they are not sung to those airs something of our dramatic intentions will be lost."[97] To a greater extent than in any other play, the dramatic and satiric effect of these songs depends on audience recognition not only of the tunes but also of the original words so that the discrepancies between old and new texts can be fully appreciated. The tunes specified are not all folk tunes, but most are from the eighteenth century. One is from John Gay's *The Beggar's Opera* (which he in turn borrowed from Händel), several are well known eighteenth-century patriotic airs, others are sea shanties or navy songs. Part of the function of the music is to create period atmosphere. There are also numerous songs written to unspecified tunes. Arden and D'Arcy write of this music: "If you want to do it, you must do it how you like."[98]

A feature of the original Round House production that Arden and D'Arcy liked was the introduction of additional improvised music by Boris Howarth, who was later to provide the musical improvisation for *The Non-Stop Connolly Show*. As Arden elucidates:

> What he did in both cases was to adapt a piano . . . You take the guts out of a piano and then play funny tricks with all the strings by modifying them: tying them together and sticking pins in them and pegging them down with clothes pegs, so that you can make all sorts of strange noises on it that the piano wasn't originally intended to do.

Albert Hunt contrasts this very effective improvised music with music used in a later production of the Nottingham Playhouse: not only had "much of the political content . . . been removed," he says, but also "the music was prettified out of existence."[99]

The conception of *The Hero Rises Up* is based on contradictions and ironies: contradictions in the character of the hero, Lord Nelson, and ironies concerning the whole idea of romantic heroism:

> On the one hand there's all the genuine panache and extravagance of a heroic melodrama: and on the other hand, there's the cool, ironic distancing of the events shown.[100]

The ironic distancing of characters and events is achieved in part through the figure of Nelson's stepson Nisbet. A large part of the distancing is achieved by musical means: discrepancy between tunes and texts, discrepancy between original words and new words, ironical musical quotations, and satiric musical thrusts. In the songs for which traditional tunes are specified, the ironic and satirical intentions of Arden and D'Arcy emerge most clearly.

The beginning of act 2 depicts Nelson's triumphant return to London after his victory in Naples. To the tune of "God Save the King" the people sing a paean to the folk hero as he parades through the streets with Emma on his arm:

> Join we great Nelson's name
> First on the roll of fame;
> Him let us sing!
> Spread we his praise around
> Honour of British ground
> Who made Nile's shores resound:
> God save our King.

> (p. 49)

As irreverent as this may seem, the song is a genuine eighteenth-century adaptation, often sung in Nelson's honor.

Whereas this tune captures a moment of public irony, another piece captures the private irony of Nelson's situation. Parading ostentatiously with his mistress, Emma, Lady Hamilton, Nelson complains that his wife, Lady Nelson, has not come to meet him. His wife's song expresses her hopes and illusions just before they meet. The audience, aware of Nelson's passion for Emma, understands the full dramatic irony. The original, "All Things are Quite Silent," is a melancholy English folk song probably from the late eighteenth century. It is the lament of a wife for her husband who has been forcibly pressed into service with the navy:

In Nelson's day . . . so notorious were conditions aboard the royal ships that the Navy could only be maintained by pressing men to sea. The press-gangs were the terror to life along the coasts of England.[101]

A. L. Lloyd notes: "Nelson himself, as a junior officer, led the press about Tower Hill, Rosemary Lane and Cable Street."[102] The first two stanzas narrate how the press gang tears the man from his home, forcing him to "plough the salt wave." The wife, remaining behind "in sorrow and woe," recalls the idyllic days of their past love in the countryside, and tries to console herself with a note of hope:

> Although my love's gone I will not be cast down.
> Who knows but my sailor may once more return?
> And will make me amends for all trouble and strife,
> And my true love and I might live happy for life.[103]

Lady Nelson here sings stanza 3 almost unaltered, and minor changes are made in stanza 4 to fit her situation (pp. 50–51). But the context throws an ironic light on her song. It is not the wife of the unknown working man who is singing for her kidnapped love, but the wife of the great man responsible for the pressing and himself a member of a press gang in his younger years. The negative aspects of Nelson's power are thus implied. Here the distancing effects of both context and persona of the singer turn the melancholy folk song into something new and ironic.

A dramatically interesting effect is created by the singing of the traditional eighteenth-century folk song "Oh the Weary Cutters" in act 2. Like "All Things are Quite Silent," this is also a woman's lament for her love who has been pressed into Nelson's service. (A cutter is a small fast-sailing boat belonging to a man-of-war.) The tune has a more powerful emotional effect than the earlier folk song. In this case it is not ironically distanced through the persona of the singer. Here it actually is the wife of a humble seaman who sings, and the lament is a direct expression of her personal pain and grief:

> It's oh the weary cutters,
> They ha' taen my love frae me
> It's oh the weary cutters
> They ha' taen my love frae me:
> They've shipped him awa' foreign wi' Nelson
> Beyond the salt sea—
> It's oh the weary cutters,
> They ha' taen my love frae me.

> (pp. 67–68)

The playwrights, however, do not want us simply to sympathize with the working class, but also to reflect on the causes of their distress. For this

Oh,____ the wea-ry cut-ters, they've taen my lad-die fre me.

Oh,____ the wea-ry cut-ters, they've taen my lad-die fre me.

They've pressed him far a-way for-eign wi' Nel-son a-yont the salt sea.

Oh,____ the wea-ry cut--ters, they've taen my lad--die fre me.

O the weary cutters, they've taen my laddie fre me,
O the weary cutters, they've taen my laddie fre me.
They've pressed him far away foreign
Wi' Nelson ayont the salt sea.
O the weary cutters, they've taen my laddie fre me.

O the weary cutters, they've taen my laddie fre me,
O the weary cutters, they've taen my laddie fre me.
They always come in the night,
They never come in the day,
They always come in the night and steal the laddies away.

O the lousy cutters and O the weary sea!
O the lousy cutters that stole my laddie fre me.
I'll give the cutter a guinea;
I'll give the cutter no more,
I'll give the cutter a guinea to steal my laddie ashore.

"Oh, the Weary Cutters," from A. L. Lloyd, *Folk Song in England* (London: Lawrence and Wishart, 1967), p. 267.

reason they effectively distance the song through its context. The entire scene is entitled "The Hero endeavours to recollect himself," and presents Nelson in a state of disarray and confusion. Because the scene titles are projected or announced on placards, the audience will be fully aware of the context. Nelson's sailor-servant Allen explains the situation to the audience in a commentary song:

> They fetched him home and half-disgraced him,
> Said he was not fit to fight:
> England's great reputation foundered
> In a strumpet's cunt so tight.
>
> . . . .
> We all have wives, we all have sweethearts,
> We don't all treat them very well:
> But we must arise and leave them
> When the press-gang's on the prowl.

(p. 67)

As illustration of his generalized moral the audience is offered a melodramatic scene in which "one man is torn in a classical fashion from the arms of his wife" (p. 67), and she responds with her sung lament. Allen then turns back to Nelson to "sort him out."

The scene within the scene is thus not intended as a personal tragedy but as an example of a general condition of the age, a condition about which possibly something could be done. The stylized manner of presentation undermines any sense of true tragedy, and the pressing scene is framed by the tribulations of the admiral, a man who presumably could stop the practice of pressing if he were not so preoccupied with his own loves and lusts. Taken as a whole, then, this scene is very Brechtian in effect and technique: an emotional and lyrical moment is clearly placed in its social and political context in such a way that the audience is forced to reflect on causes of social ills and on their possible solutions.

Another song to be set to a traditional air returns to a more common form of musical irony; the new words stand in deliberate and ironic contrast to the original words. "Heart of Oak," the tune prescribed for the song of Nelson's parasitic relatives (p. 84), is a stirring patriotic air from the eighteenth century, written to celebrate a number of significant military victories in the year 1759. It is "now part of the basic repertoire of British national song."[104] It is a celebration of British pride and British mettle: "Heart of oak are our ships, heart of oak are our men."[105] In the drama, however, the song has been transformed into an ironic celebration of gluttony and political escapism.

It is with the same type of musical irony that Arden and D'Arcy conclude the play. Both the title song of the drama, "The Hero Rises Up," and the final chorus are sung to two other eighteenth-century patriotic airs, the familiar "Rule Britannia" and "Here's a Health unto His Majesty" (p. 110). Instead of the patriotic words, however, texts of sentimental love and exaggerated hero-ism are created. In place of the lines of the chorus:

> Rule Britannia! Britannia rule the waves;
> Britons never, never, never will be slaves,"[106]

a private idyll is sung by Nelson's two loves:

> No more hatred, no jealousy nor fear,
> Nelson's Paradise is here.

(p. 101)

The players become "suddenly conscious of their own artificiality" (p. 102), but they rally to sing the "fa la la" chorus in unison as the hero's chariot rises up above mere earthly reality in a show of theatrical exuberance. In this final scene all the major elements of this romantic melodrama are brought into focus: theatrical and romantic artificiality, ironic contradiction, and, above all, both the emotional and the ironic powers of the musical settings.

Music is a pervasive force throughout *The Hero Rises Up*, and is, of course, not confined to the songs with traditional tunes. To my mind, however, the most distinctive feature of this play is its use of older eighteenth-century airs. Let it suffice, then, to briefly mention a few of the more striking aspects of the other music. As in the earlier plays, songs are sung at moments of heightened emotional tension and confrontation. The emotions are not al-ways pleasant: at one point an argument between Nelson and Emma is given emphasis by an extended passage of alternately sung couplets, which—as the quarrel becomes more heated—turns into sung stichomythia (pp. 85–86).

Very effective dramatically is the combination of song and dance; for example, Nelson's spectacular sword dance and song (p. 25), and the King of Naples's maniacal dance and song (p. 28), both in act 1. In act 2 the "jigging chorus" of the guests, which "threatens to become a riot" (p. 59), actually does erupt into a fanatic dance accompanying the chorus during the book burning (pp. 62–65). This fusion of music and dance conveys the irrational frenzied emotion behind the actions vividly.

Other songs in the play are used in distancing functions that are familiar from Arden's earlier dramas. Thus, Nisbet's critical commentary on the state of England which opens act 2 sets the enthusiasms of Nelson's reception in political perspective (pp. 48–49). The songs in *The Hero Rises Up* are both emotionally heightening and critically distancing. Both functions are of about equal importance, and it is the alternation and combination of functions that characterizes this work.

Seen together with the traditional eighteenth-century songs that imbue the play with its distinctive tone and atmosphere, the musical elements empha-size both the romantic and artificial, and the critical, ironic aspects of the play. Stronger than in any other Arden and D'Arcy drama to date are the satirical and ironic effects achieved by the extensive use of musical allusion and musical quotation. *The Hero Rises Up* is, in effect, an extraordinary mixture of elements: it draws much of its material dramatically and musically from the eighteenth century, treats this material in a theatrical manner derived from nineteenth-century melodrama, and achieves in the end a distinctively twentieth-century critical and ironic perspective. It still awaits an adequate production.

EPIC THEATER WITH IMPROVISED MUSIC

The Island of the Mighty (1972) is a complex trilogy consisting of three full-length plays that underwent numerous revisions for more than a decade before reaching production by the Royal Shakespeare Company in 1972. Arden and D'Arcy were dissatisfied with this production, however, believing that the political issues had been distorted. As Michael Cohen points out, the playwrights' political position had at this time shifted from anarchism and pacifism to radical Marxism. "In the 1974 published text . . . elements of *both* positions coexist, not with entire harmony."[107] These discrepancies may have caused some of their dissatisfaction. The playwrights also disapproved of the style of presentation—costumes, scenery, and the manner in which the music and the songs were being handled.[108]

This trilogy is one of the few Arden and D'Arcy works conceived almost exclusively for non-traditional music. The dramatists had envisioned improvised percussive rhythms such as they had heard in India on a recent visit. But a theatrical composer, Carl Davis, was called in by the Royal Shakespeare Company, and here the difficulties began: "He didn't even know what we were talking about. We were talking about improvised music. We'd just come back from India," D'Arcy complains. In *To Present the Pretence* Arden remarks critically that Davis "was shortly afterwards working on an entertainment at Covent Garden to celebrate the entry of Great Britain into the Common Market."[109] Arden and D'Arcy, with their new Marxist consciousness, would, like Brecht, have preferred a composer who could understand, and be committed to, the political ideas in their play and who could express these in his music.[110] A reviewer comments that the "music slips unfortunately into a quasi-rock sound."[111] Surely, this is not what the dramatists intended.

The musical style foremost in the minds of Arden and D'Arcy at this time was the non-Western music of the Indian folk plays they had witnessed during their stay in India while working on *The Island of the Mighty*. Because the playwrights were also at work on *The Non-Stop Connolly Show*, many of the most striking elements of the Indian plays can also be observed in the latter cycle.[112] There they are combined with traditional song tunes. As Margaretta D'Arcy describes the Indian folk plays in her preface:

> These plays incorporated material of even greater complexity than our own. . . . Yet the style of the staging was simple and direct . . . and where the plot became too diffuse for "dramatization," the action was hurried forward by means of rapid verse-narrative, songs, and instrumental music. It was finally upon similar lines that J. A. and I re-worked the entire trilogy.[113]

The music should be predominantly percussive (p. 25). In her criticism of the Royal Shakespeare Company production D'Arcy emphasizes the Indian model: "The music is all wrong . . . It isn't near the stuff we heard in India."[114] The "overall theatrical concepts" of the Indian plays were

> extreme formality mixed with unexpectedly coarse realism; highly-decorative costumes, make-up and/or masks. . . ; *the regular use of music and dance as part of the dramatic structure;* strongly rhythmical verse-narrative to link passages of action.[115]

The playwrights also link a belief in the divine nature of the events and protagonists in the Indian plays to the "traditional magic of Dionysus."[116] As early as *The Workhouse Donkey,* Arden saw music and song as belonging to the essential attributes of a Dionysian theatrical performance. In spite of the radical shift in political consciousness, there is a certain continuity in experimental dramatic technique between the earlier and later plays. Music had always been a major part of the nonillusionistic technique. In this respect it makes little difference whether these are Arden's own plays or collaborations. What does diminish in the later collaborations is the intense lyricism sometimes found in the earlier Arden. Although the folk song influence remains, the song lyrics become more politically aggressive.

The musicians in *The Island of the Mighty* are to be fully visible to the audience throughout. Some of the verse speeches (and occasionally the prose speeches) are underlined by music, and in addition the music is "to provide a strong rhythm for important pieces of movement and physical action" (p. 25). Most of the music in this trilogy is intended to be nonlyrical, rhythmic, or emphatic.

The playwrights are careful to distinguish between their use of background music and that of melodrama, or its modern successor, film music.

> *D'Arcy.* Now the difference between us and film music is that they have melody in film music. The improvised music . . . is only . . . percussion, so in that sense you're not getting that gooey-gooey kind of thing you have in the movies . . .
> *Arden.* The bad use of film music is when they use it to cover over scenes which have a poverty of dialogue, when actually the dialogue is so poor that it is not telling you anything. And so they use the music to supply the emotion that the actors cannot find in the script.

Their own use of improvised percussion music is to heighten or hurry along a dialogue in which the words are every bit as important as the music. Arden and D'Arcy emphasize that in spite of the lack of melody in this improvised music, the basic incentive in using it is to stimulate and guide audience emotions. They were fascinated by the hypnotic effect of Indian theater music: "It's like dervishes," recalls D'Arcy. This improvised music comes closer to ancient ritual than to the modern melodrama of film.

The songs are predominantly introductory, narrative, explanatory, or commentary in nature. Only few are used in an ironic fashion. Because of the enormity of the material and the large period of time covered, the epic and narrative functions emerge much more distinctly than in earlier plays. Some completely new developments also are to be observed. *The Island of the Mighty* offers the best example in Arden and D'Arcy's work of the extraordinary range of song functions in epic theater with improvised music. The majority is put in the mouths of one or another of the three poets Merlin, Aneurin, and the Pictish Poet. As the dramatists explain, these characters "act as chorus, with songs to relate the narrative and comment upon the action" (pp. 25–26). They alternate in this role, usually with one of them occupying the forestage as narrator at any one time. Visually, they should be immediately recognizable as singer-narrators, for "they each should be equipped with a small instrument—a tambourine or the like—which hangs on their belt and upon which they could accompany their own commentary" (p. 26).

Some of the narrative functions of the songs will be familiar from earlier plays, but others are new and go far beyond techniques in the earlier work. When Merlin sings during his journey to the North, the piece indicates the passage of time and space. Here, however, no attempt is made at illusion; it is really only a report that a journey is taking place:

> I go a smiling travelling man
> To warn them of impeding fate
> And lift their hearts with cheerful word . . .

(p. 35)

In contrast with earlier songs in similar situations, this is much too brief and perfunctory to establish any sense of the passage of time in the audience. The same nonillusionist tendency is true of the airs with new functions; for example, those narrating offstage journeys or shipwrecks too complicated to be shown on stage. Here the lyrics take over the role of the epic narrative. The Pictish Poet sings:

> There was a young man and to Ireland he did sail
> For he thought the wind was fair.

> But it blew him to the south and it blew him to the north
> And it blew him to the Galloway shore.

(p. 89)

A new scene starts, and the Pictish Poet continues:

> And when he came to the Galloway shore
> His boat was broke in three.
> In the strangle of the waves he was thrown overboard
> And they found him by the edge of the sea.

Balin, still clutching his weapons, and soaked to the skin, staggers on to the stage and collapses. (p. 89)

The action carries on from here. In contrast with the "messenger's report" in traditional drama, no pretense is made that the narrator has actually witnessed the events he is relating. These poet-narrators are nonrealistic, all-knowing visionary seers who can report on events past and future, near or far.

Another song function is related to that of *teichoskopia* in traditional drama. A narrative epic element is introduced as Aneurin reports on an offstage battle:

> There was no help for him, no help
> For any man upon that moor:
> Nothing was left but to put breath
> Into the roaring horns of war.
> Upon both sides the soldiers took
> One stride, then two, and then a third.
> At every stride they did let fly
> The loudest cry that ever was heard—

He cries three times, reinforced by the music. (p. 181)

The stylization of the presentation is striking; observe the ritualistic three steps, the use of rhyme. Unlike the *teichoskopia* in classical drama, no pretense is made that the speaker is actually witnessing the offstage events. The poet gives a visionary report, and it is he who utters the soldiers' cries; they do not come realistically from offstage.

Song is employed in a totally anti-illusionistic way in the sung commentary to mimed stage action. Explanatory text to mimed action was also a favorite technique of the later Brecht. He used it extensively, for example, in *The Caucasian Chalk Circle.* In *The Island of the Mighty,* there are several remarkable scenes of this sort. The action thus appears as illustration to some general thesis, rather than as a realistic event.

The love scene between Arthur and Gwenhwyvar, one of the highlights of the trilogy, is performed with extraordinary stylization, supported visually by

John Arden and Margaretta D'Arcy, *The Island of the Mighty:* **the use of masks, mime, and sung commentary in the wedding scene (part 2, scene 5), photo from** *Plays and Players* **(February 1973), p. 31. Photo by Reg Wilson.**

grotesque masks that are handed to the dancers by the singers as the scene begins:

Merlin. *(Singing.)* The bride and her bridegroom
        Now enter their private room
        To put on two faces that are not their own.

    He picks up a mask and carries it to Arthur. Aneurin picks up another one and carries it to Gwenhwyvar.

    Arthur's mask is a grinning demon—great tusk-teeth—bright red face—staring eyes—hair like a golliwog.

    Gwenhwyvar's is a kind of gorgon—protruding tongue—green hair of great length—staring eyes—livid white face. The poets help their patrons to put on the masks and then stand back.

Aneurin. *(Singing.)* They each desire the other should see
        What he or she would wish to be—
Merlin. *(Singing.)* This way there is no sort of victory.
Aneurin. *(Singing.)* Can the fish defeat the river—
Merlin. *(Singing.)* Or the river defeat the sea?

Arthur and Gwenhwyvar indulge in a very violent dance—a mime of battle rather than lovemaking—accompanied by as much thundering percussion as is available. (pp. 126–27)[117]

Not only are the masks symbolical, their symbolism is interpreted by the singers, who also comment on the general nature and meaning of the confrontation. The effect of this scene is thus different, for example, from Musgrave's climactic and frenzied song and dance, or the sung and danced book-burning climax in *The Hero Rises Up.* The frenzy and the emotion here are channelled, controlled, distanced by the two singer-poets who act as stage managers. The fascination stems less from the passion directly than from the manner of its presentation. Because of the intensity of its visual and musical accompaniment, this controlled passion is no less powerful.

Songs of political prophecy are also important and remind us of Brecht. A song of political resistance, composed by Aneurin, is sung with enthusiasm by Aneurin and Morgan, culminating in the chorus lines:

> All that I ever desired will be thoroughly on fire
> And in that fire this bad old man will die!
>
> (p. 149)

It is incendiary and full of venomous emotion, and it is sung throughout the realm by the poorest of the poor in defiance of Arthur. Above all, the closing song of the entire trilogy contains both a parable and a political prophecy of revolution:

> There was a man called Lazarus
> And when he died they said he died at peace with God.
> . . . .
> And this is what Lazarus said to them all
> When he came back to life so hideous and so tall:
> . . . .
> We are going to come back
> And we are going to take hold
> So hideous and bloody greedy
> We take hold of the whole world!
>
> (pp. 234–35)

This strongly resembles the sung prophecy of revolution at the end of the later play, *The Ballygombeen Bequest.* The vast majority of the songs in this long and complex trilogy illustrates variations of commentary or narrative-epic functions. Even the songs at moments of extreme tension tend to be highly stylized and thus critically distanced.

A few pieces in the three plays, however, are reminiscent of the folk tradition, although apparently only one is actually a traditional nursery song. Most of the melodies loosely related to the folk tradition are sung or composed by the poet Aneurin, the youngest of the narrator-singers, and a rebellious and irreverent personality. Aneurin's scorn of authority and hatred of the establishment—political and poetic—place him closer to the folk mentality than any of the other singers. Only one song actually quotes a traditional rhyme; the nursery rhyme that Aneurin sings to lull the mad Merlin, the first step in leading the latter back to sanity. The mad man is in the mental state of a small child, so the use of a nursery tune is appropriate. It is the first stanza of "Tom He Was a Piper's Son,"[118] with slight variations, so that it is here turned into a personal history of Aneurin's childhood:

> I was born a piper's son
> I played my pipe when I was young
> And all the tunes that I could play
> Was over the hills and far away.

(p. 205)

The rest of the stanzas are new, although they incorporate the traditional refrain. The song as a whole becomes a tale of the dangers of poetic expression and of the hostility the world shows toward the poet. The refrain remains an expression of poetic faith. The mad Merlin is enchanted, like a child following the Pied Piper of Hamilton, and he prances off after Aneurin, joining in the refrain of each verse:

> Over the hills and a great way off
> The wind has blown my topknot off.

(p. 206)

With this refrain on his lips Merlin is captured and roped by those who want to exploit his reputation for reasons of political expediency. The momentary vision of childish freedom, gaiety and nonsense is abruptly and brutally overwhelmed by the political opportunists who dominate the play. There is no escape, either in childishness or in madness.

The Island of the Mighty is the most epic of Arden and D'Arcy's dramas to date, and the work that explores most extensively and subtly the various possibilities of nontraditional music and of nontraditional song. Especially distinctive is its use of song in commentary and narrative functions. It takes various usages of the earlier plays to greater extremes; for example, not only onstage journeys but also offstage journeys and other offstage events are reported in an epic-narrative manner. It explores various alienating and commentary functions not previously observed, most notably the sung commentary to mimed action or dance. It contains very few songs even vaguely reminiscent of the folk tradition. In this lack of traditional musical basis it forms a major exception to the typical musical pattern of Arden and D'Arcy's work as a whole.

5. The Irish Plays

Most of the dramatic works Arden and D'Arcy wrote during the 1970s are set in Ireland and concerned with Irish themes. In part, this is due to their radical political awareness from 1968 on and in part to the renewal of political violence in Northern Ireland during the same period. For the playwrights the conflict in Ireland—which they prefer to speak of as a war—has many elements of Third World confrontations. Arden is convinced that "Northern Ireland is Britain's Vietnam."[119] With respect to the Northern Ireland problem Catherine Itzin summarizes:

> For Arden and D'Arcy it was just the kind of colonial war that had sent Black Jack Musgrave mad. The main theme of their lives and work in the seventies was concerned with Ireland—with disastrous results professionally.[120]

All of the playwrights' Irish plays of the 1970s have been presented by fringe or alternative companies. *The Ballygombeen Bequest* was first produced in the Falls Road, Belfast, at a teachers' training college in 1972, and subsequently toured in England and Scotland with the 7:84 Theatre Company until a suit for libel and slander stopped the performances. The 7:84 Company also produced in 1973 *Serjeant Musgrave Dances On*, a reworking adapted to the troubles in Northern Ireland; the Musgrave story was updated to reflect the events of Bloody Sunday in Derry.[121] The work of Arden and D'Arcy on the War Carnival at New York University in 1967, their collaboration with the Cartoon Archetypical Slogan Theatre (CAST) at the Unity Theatre on *Harold Muggins is a Martyr* in 1968, and an improvised eight-hour sequence on the history of American labor presented in 1973 at the University of California at Davis were all experiences that went into the formation of the mammoth twenty-six–hour *Non-Stop Connolly Show* at Liberty Hall, Dublin in 1975. In England, the show received only a drastically cut fourteen-hour production at the Almost Free Theatre in 1976. *Vandaleur's Folly: An Anglo-Irish Melodrama* was performed by the 7:84 Company in 1978. *Little Gray Home in the West* (1978), a revision of *The Ballygombeen Bequest*, was given a reading in 1978 at the Sugawn Theatre with some of the original 7:84 cast.

In structure and style, not all of the Irish plays are epic, but they all represent variations of the dramatists' mature manner based on a nonillusionistic conception of theater, a conception in which music, song, dance, and spectacle form an integral part of the dramatic structure. In this respect they are a logical development of the earlier experiments with dramatic music that Arden alone and Arden and D'Arcy as collaborators have pursued. In contrast with *The Island of the Mighty*, which uses almost exclusively nontraditional music, all the Irish dramas make extensive use of folk tradition, which is combined with improvised music. The song lyrics are aggressively political and have discarded most of the earlier lyricism. Most of the Irish plays make poor reading; their song lyrics are seldom good poetry. Although I like both political drama and theatrical spectacle, I suspect that in some of the Irish plays the raggedness of the political lyrics and the pastiche of performance styles would be problematical. *The Non-Stop Connolly Show* is the most interesting of the Irish plays, but it is surely the most difficult to adequately stage.

MUSICAL REFLECTIONS OF THE NORTHERN IRELAND PROBLEM

The Ballygombeen Bequest (1972), although not so vastly epic in scope as either *The Island of the Mighty* or *The Non-Stop Connolly Show,* covers a period of twenty-six years (1945 to 1971), and exploits some of the devices of epic-narrative song that have already been observed, especially in *The Island of the Mighty.* In contrast with the epic trilogy, however, this Irish play is firmly rooted in the traditions of Irish and English folk music, resulting in a conglomeration of musical styles. Unlike *Armstrong's Last Goodnight* or *The Hero Rises Up,* none of the songs for which traditional tunes are suggested is sung with the original words, so that the play represents a new position in the artistic production as a whole. It is not as strongly traditional as these two plays, and it is not as strictly nontraditional as *The Island of the Mighty.*

As in so many of the plays, particularly the later plays from *The Royal Pardon* on, Arden and D'Arcy once again prescribe a continuous musical background. The authors envision no scenery for *The Ballygombeen Bequest* except for backcloths illustrating the political situation in Northern Ireland since 1968; the dates of the events are to be shown to the audience in typical Brechtian style on placards; the costumes should be stylized, and the whole action delivered "with the greatest possible PACE."[122] Spectacle, even slapstick farce, stylized action, an alternation of prose and verse, and above all music, both instrumental and vocal, have thus become firmly cemented as essential elements of the dramatic structure and method.

Many of the songs in the play can be placed in the category of epic-narrative or commentary. These functions are underlined by the use of a narrator who sings most of the songs of this type. The narrator should be one of the musicians. He differs from the poet-narrator-musicians of *The Island of the Mighty* in that he does not have a role of his own in the action; here the narrator slips in and out of the roles of various different characters. Some of the epic-narrative songs have no prescribed melody, and, as the meter is irregular, are chanted rather than sung.

Several of the narrator's songs are fitted to traditional tunes, creating an effect that is unique in Arden and D'Arcy's drama. Here, traditional folk tunes are combined with new lyrics of a distinctly political nature. Some the playwrights have used before. For example, the air "John Barleycorn" was used in *Serjeant Musgrave's Dance* and *The Business of Good Government* with new words appropriate to the theme and context of the original. Here, however, Arden and D'Arcy have employed the tune for a song evaluating the state of the world in the years 1957–68, a piece which is strongly political and savagely critical:

> From nineteen-fifty-seven
> To nineteen-sixty-eight
> The fat men of the fat-half world
> Had food on every plate.
> The lean men of the naked world
> Grew leaner every day.
> And if they put their faces up
> Their teeth were kicked away.
>
> (scene 4)

The subtle connections of the earlier ballads to the original words of the tune have been lost, and the use of "John Barleycorn" here seems mechanical and arbitrary.

Interesting is the use of songs associated with Northern Ireland, as this is Arden and D'Arcy's first play to deal thematically with the present troubles there. The tune "Lillibulero" (used before in *The Hero Rises Up*) is here employed with its sectarian connotations as an expression of Protestant bigotry. "Lillibulero" is a street ballad dating from the upheavals of the Glorious Revolution in 1687–88.[123] The song is a poisonous satire on Catholic stupidity, superstition, and bloodthirstiness, written in an exaggerated stage Irish dialect, with incorrect grammar and a nonsensical refrain. In this century the tune, with new street-ballad words, is still popular among the Protestants of Northern Ireland and is often associated with fanatic Orange sectarianism. Here, it is sung by an English soldier during the torture and interrogation that lead to Padraic's death, in its modern street version rather than the original: "Slitter slaughter holy water / Scatter the Papishes every one" (scene 7). In this case, there is no alienation between the original and dramatic context.

Siobhan's song of defiance after her brother's death is full of multiple musical ironies. It is set to a favorite melody of the Protestant Northern Ireland majority, "The Sash My Father Wore," one often sung in a spirit of venomous anti-Catholic bigotry. Siobhan sings here "with ferocious emphasis," but the words she sings are directed mainly against thoughtless Republicanism:

> The martyred men you shout about
> Roll over in their graves
> The living men you do not know
> Bewildered work like slaves.
>
> (scene 7)

36.—LILLIBULERO

(⁊) Ho bro-ther Teig, dost hear the de -cree

Lilli - bu-lè - ro bul-len a la   Dat we shall have a

new De-bitt-ie   Lilli - bu-lè - ro bul-len a la.

CHORUS

Lè - ro lè - ro lè - ro lè-ro Lil-li-bu-le - ro

bul-len a la   Lil-li-bu-lè - ro lè - ro lè-ro

Lil-li - bu - lè - ro bul-len a la.

Ho, by my Soul, it is a Talbot;
    Lillibuléro, etc.
And he will cut all de English throat,
    Lillibuléro, etc.

Though, by my Soul, de English do prate,
    Lillibuléro, etc.
De Law's on dere side and de divil knows what
    Lillibuléro, etc.

But if Dispence do come from the Pope,
    Lillibuléro, etc.
We'll hang Magna Cart and demselves in a rope,
    Lillibuléro, etc.
And the good Talbot is now made a Lord,
    Lillibuléro, etc.
And with his brave lads he's coming aboard,
    Lillibuléro, etc.

Who all in France have taken a swear,
    Lillibuléro, etc.
Dat day will have no Protestant heir.
    Lillibuléro, etc.

O but why does he stay behind?
    Lillibuléro, etc.
Ho, by my Soul, 'tis a Protestant wind,
    Lillibuléro, etc.

Now that Tyrconnel is come a-shore,
    Lillibuléro, etc.
And we shall have Commissions go leór,
    Lillibuléro, etc.

And he dat will not go to the Mass,
    Lillibuléro, etc.
Shall be turned out and look like an ass.
    Lillibuléro, etc.

Now, now de hereticks all will go down,
    Lillibuléro, etc.
By Christ and St. Patrick the nation's our own.
    Lillibuléro, etc.

Dere was an old prophecy found in a bog,
    Lillibuléro, etc.
Dat our land would be ruled by an ass and a dog.
    Lillibuléro, etc.

So now dis old Prophecy's coming to pass,
    Lillibuléro bullen a la,
For James is de dog and Tyrconnel's de ass.
    Lillibuléro, etc.

"Lillibulero," from *Irish Street Ballads*, collected and annotated by Colm O Lochlainn (London: Pan Books, 1978), pp. 72–73.

For tactical reasons the official Sinn Fein has withdrawn its support from Padraic's eviction case, thus indirectly allowing him to fall prey to a joint capitalist and Special Branch plot to have him arrested and killed in the North. This traditional song of Orange bigotry is thus turned into an anti-death song. Arden and D'Arcy call the combination of Orange Protestant tune with Republican Socialist text a case of "musical education." Arden says,

> You see, we're trying to rescue a Protestant tune from being a sectarian tune, because in fact those tunes are older than the sectarian situation.

They also emphasize that the original audience would almost certainly have recognized their intentions: "The play was first presented in a Catholic college in Belfast, so the audience would know exactly what that song was," explains Arden.

In spite of the serious political and didactic content of the play, the spirit of comedy—and even farce—is present throughout. Early in the drama the O'Learys join Hollidey-Cheype in a song-and-dance routine to celebrate the idea of renting out the property. This combination of stylized comedy with a serious political purpose is reminiscent of the dramatic method of the later O'Casey, for example in *Purple Dust*. The technique of the later O'Casey regularly combined song and music with political purpose. If I prefer the style of O'Casey to that of the later Arden and D'Arcy collaborations, it is, I think, because O'Casey's humor is based on compassion, whereas comedy in Arden and D'Arcy often appears forced and artificial.

This fusion of politics, theatrical spectacle, and traditional music in the later plays is a visual and aural expression of the dramatists' deeply rooted conviction that political drama must be theatrically entertaining or it has failed its purpose. *The Ballygombeen Bequest*, while using realistic elements, never allows realism to gain the upper hand. Continuous musical accompaniment, numerous songs, and spectacular stylized scenes all distance the realistic sections and bring out the emblematic nature of the story. The songs rely heavily on the principle of contrast or irony to achieve an alienating effect. In their dramas of Irish themes for Irish audiences, Arden and D'Arcy are in a better position than ever to exploit audience familiarity with traditional melodies. Arden claims:

> In general, in Ireland if you use traditional music the audience tends to know what the original songs were all about, and to make any resonances, to accept any resonances that carries. In England that is not necessarily the case.

This illustrates the point made earlier that the musical cultures of England and Ireland vary considerably.

The Little Gray Home in the West, published in 1982, is typical of a new form of collaboration in the Irish plays. The authors' names are reversed; they are now listed as Margaretta D'Arcy and John Arden. This drama is a revised version of *The Ballygombeen Bequest*, reworked after the law suit had been settled. The absentee English landlord, whom the dramatists had satirized (and named with address and telephone number in a leaflet distributed in the theater), brought suit for libel and slander. Arden and D'Arcy, while denying the charges, agreed to settle out of court and to make some changes in their play. Among other things, the name of the landlord character is altered from the satirical Percival Hollidey-Cheype to the more archetypal Baker-Fortescue (also used in *Vandaleur's Folly*).

The revisions affect all aspects of the drama from the political content to the songs, but the basic lines of the play remain the same, and a great many of the speeches are identical to those of the original. The new title is derived from a song, a sentimental music-hall air of the late nineteenth century, used ironically.[124] The political message of the drama has been clarified; new dialogue has been added in which the parallels between the private O'Leary contract with Baker-Fortescue and the political Partition Treaty of 1921 are explicitly pointed out.[125] New staging techniques also aim at didactic clarification; for example, scene titles have been added. Other changes tighten the pace and the logic of the action—Padraic takes over the role of the narrator so that he now appears throughout the play rather than in the second half only, and his nonrealisitc function is strengthened. Padraic "as a dead man" speaks a new opening commentary prologue, creating a formal link to the resurrection scene at the end.

The musical conception of the play has been only slightly altered, and a majority of the most striking songs remains. A new subtitle has been added, identical to that of *Vandaleur's Folly:* "An Anglo-Irish Melodrama," pointing up the consistent musical basis of both plays. In both, a serious political message has been combined with popular theatrical entertainment, the techniques ranging from slapstick farce to political texts with traditional tunes. Both *The Ballygombeen Bequest* and *The Little Gray Home in The West* are rooted musically in English and particularly Irish folk and popular tradition. But they make use of these traditional elements in a different way than the earlier plays. Whereas most of the commentary and epic-narrative pieces in the earlier drama were set to nontraditional tunes, a fusion of political comment and traditional music is found here. This fusion represents a new musical and dramatic style, expressive of the new political and dramatic consciousness of the later work. This style is carried on in both *The Non-Stop Connolly Show* and *Vandaleur's Folly*, more successfully in the former.

EPIC THEATER WITH TRADITIONAL MUSIC

The Non-Stop Connolly Show (1975) has the subtitle "A Dramatic Cycle of Continuous Struggle in Six Parts." Again, D'Arcy's name is listed first. Epic in conception, it covers the entire lifespan of its hero, the Irish labor leader

James Connolly, from his birth in 1868 to his death in 1916 when he was shot by the English as one of the leaders of the Dublin Easter Rising. This cycle represents the culmination of Arden and D'Arcy's experiments in developing nonillusionistic staging techniques. As early as *The Workhouse Donkey* Arden had envisioned a style of production that would last for "six or seven or thirteen hours," during which the audience could come and go as they chose.[126] This is effectively the way in which the *Non-Stop Connolly Show* was staged. The six-part cycle was produced in its entirety, lasting twenty-six hours, over Easter Weekend 1975 at Liberty Hall, Dublin. Both time and place were deliberately chosen: the cycle's hero Connolly was shot for his part in the 1916 Easter Rising, and Liberty Hall is the home of the Irish Transport and General Workers' Union Connolly spent the later years of his life organizing.

One remarkable feature of the staging is the use of stylized costumes and masks and of nonhuman or superhuman emblematic characters. The larger-than-life figures of the Oppressed Nations, Controlling Nations, and Neutral Nations appear in part 6. Recurrent in all parts of the cycle is the archetypal capitalist Grabitall, who takes on the personalities of various historical capitalists. Even less realistic are the figures of the Great Red Bird of Socialism (foreshadowed by the mythical bird of the prologue), and the War Demon with his Subsidiary Demons in part 6. The accumulation of nonrealistic or nonhuman figures is striking in the last part of the cycle. The War Demon is of superhuman stature,

> like an oriental battle-god, all covered with spikes, flags, bits of armour and weapons. He has a small drum at his waist, which he rattles with his fist or knuckles at intervals.[127]

Music is used to support the nonillusionistic staging. As in all the plays from 1966 on, there is a continuous musical background and extensive nonrealistic use of song. Especially effective is the combination of music with highly stylized physical movement, often culminating in song and dance sequences. The entire action should be presented with great "*speed*—and close attention to *rhythm*"[128]—physical rhythm, speaking rhythm, and musical rhythm. In this phase of the playwrights' career, the aims and methods of poetic drama merge with those of political drama. The amalgamation of traditional melody, improvised music, and political texts proves interesting in this dramatic cycle. Verse and song passages are no longer used primarily at moments of heightened emotional confrontation but to achieve a distancing effect.

In *The Non-Stop Connolly Show* prose is most often used for rational political argument. In the sung passages the emphasis is on epic and exemplary functions. Song in this cycle is employed for summaries, narrative accounts, and most distinctively for passages of stylized confrontation. A comparison between verse and song here brings out the more formalized and heightened nature of the song medium. Music and rhythm add an extra alienating element to such symbolical situations. The characteristic grotesque dance routines in the cycle, usually symbolizing frenzied political emotions but with the passions clearly distanced by means of the stylized presentation, are accompanied by song rather than verse.

The types of tunes used in *The Non-Stop Connolly Show* are mostly traditional. For a majority, the playwrights have indicated no specific airs; they write in the authors' preface:

> The music for the songs in the Dublin and London productions was found from traditional sources—there are many Irish, British and American airs which will fit the words. (p. vii)

Arden adds in interview:

> Generally speaking, the songs in *The Non-Stop Connolly Show* weren't written for any particular tunes. We asked the actors to find tunes for them, because most people in Ireland are aware of quite a lot of traditional airs, and if you write songs in conventional ballad meters you can find one or the other air which will fit them. . . . Most of the tunes were traditional Irish tunes. Some of them were opera tunes, some of them were music hall, and all sorts . . . Victorian tunes as well, some Tom Moore melodies.

Arden emphasizes the familiarity with traditional music in Ireland:

> The songs in *The Non-Stop Connolly Show* were almost entirely sung unaccompanied. . . . Irish actors are very good at singing unaccompanied on the stage, in a way that English actors on the whole are nervous of doing.

In addition to the traditional melodies without accompaniment, the Dublin production again had background music improvised by a small group of musicians led by Boris Howarth, who had worked to the playwrights' satisfaction on *The Hero Rises Up.*

As D'Arcy explains:

> In *The Non-Stop Connolly Show* there was a pianist. He improvised music. . . . We had a different style of piano for the American play [part 4]. . . . We had a honky-tonk piano. The rest . . . was Boris Howarth's modified piano. . . . He would play it for marches and funerals and any big scenes where one wanted to swell up the noise.

The individual actors also improvised on their percussion instruments. The conception of the improvised music was influenced by Arden and D'Arcy's experience of Indian epic drama, and resembles closely that of *The Island of the Mighty.* Basically, the music should be percussive and rhythmic rather than melodic. The dramatists appeared pleased with the results, but several critics complained that the music was often at the expense of the text, an effect that the authors certainly did not intend. Paddy Marsh comments on the musicians: "They succeeded all too often in drowning the actors' words without really adding a great deal to the production."[129] The words should of course always be intelligible. On the other hand, the music is important; it is the intent of the music to elevate and to celebrate a large-scale story of working-class history in the style of opera or melodrama. *The Non-Stop Connolly Show* is the presentation of a grand theme in a grand manner.

Although the tunes are traditional, Arden and D'Arcy do not envision the audience joining in in music-hall fashion. D'Arcy emphasizes:

> In our shows, like *The Non-Stop Connolly Show*, . . . the thrust of the story . . . is actually going to a very definite conclusion . . . If you . . . have the audience singing songs it's more . . . like in the music hall . . . I'd say that the participation that we are asking for is more of a political participation.

In rhythm and diction the lyrics are suited to a variety of traditional airs. In some cases the tunes the dramatists had in mind are obvious because the first line, a line of the chorus, or an entire passage is identical with a traditional text. For example, the song that concludes part 1 and opens part 2 is clearly modeled on, and sung to, "Poor Paddy Works on the Railway" (pp. 29–31). Other instances in part 2 are "Oh Dear, What Can the Matter Be" (p. 33), and the song that begins "Oh you'll take the high road/And I'll take the low road" (p. 54); the latter quotes the refrain lines from "Loch Lomond" but transforms the traditional love song into a piece of political resistance. Some of these reworkings have themselves long been traditional. For example, "It's a Long Way Down to the Soup Line" (part 5, p. 73), sung in Dublin during the Great Lockout of 1913, was actually written during the depression of 1914 by Joe Hill to the tune of "It's a Long Way to Tipperary."[130] The finale of part 4 is obviously modeled on the Civil War melody "John Brown's Body," which is itself a reworking of an earlier hymn.

In addition to these songs sung with new words to traditional tunes, a number of familiar airs are sung with the original words. Occasionally, these may be employed in a traditional dramatic context, at a moment when a character might realistically sing as an expression of deeply felt emotion. Fairly often, however, such traditional tunes are used as emblematic musical illustration of a specific political line of thinking. Thus in the American section (part 4), union solidarity is illustrated by American labor songs, for example "Roll the Union On" (p. 41), "Union Maid" (p. 65), or "Solidarity Forever" (p. 66). Other traditional American songs exemplify the situation of the unemployed. "I Don't Want Your Millions, Mister," actually written in 1932 during the Great Depression, is sung in the drama in a 1907 "breadline of unemployed" (part 4, p. 60). "Hallelujah, I'm a Bum," a favorite hobo and

Wobbly song, introduces a campfire in the hobo jungle (p. 32), and is sung again, as it was historically, at the 1908 convention of the International Workers of the World (p. 72). The dramatists say that in part this use of period pieces is to create an appropriate atmosphere. None of these American songs is named by title.

Even more clearly emblematic are the scenes in part 3 in which the visits of the Duke of York and Queen Victoria to Ireland are symbolized by means of puppets trundled hurriedly on and off stage to the appropriate tunes of "The Grand Old Duke of York" (p. 26) and "God Save the Queen" (p. 52). Striking is the closing scene of part 5 (scene 16), in which the conflicting political movements at the end of 1914 in Ireland are introduced and contrasted by means of a flag, a slogan, and, most importantly, a song in a kind of musical summary, with the harassed English Prime Minister Asquith acting as stage manager. Carson's Ulster Volunteers are represented by the traditional Orange tune "The Sash My Father Wore" (p. 89); the National Volunteers by the patriotic 1798 rebel song "The Boys of Wexford" (p. 90); and the Trade Unionists by "The Red Flag" (p. 90).

Because of the epic nature of the cycle, varieties of epic song predominate, although more traditional emotional functions are not completely absent. Occasionally songs are used to express inner thoughts, intentions, or even private emtions. Certainly the most moving example is Lillie's love song for Connolly at the end of part 6.

> James Connolly is my man
> I had rather let him roam
> With the wildest in the world
> Be they women or be they men
> Than lie beside me night by night
> With broken heart and frozen brain.
>
> (p. 93)

Narrative summaries are common. Typical of the cycle are the songs expressing political aims and policies, or political emotions.

One of the most interesting dramatic features of *The Non-Stop Connolly Show* is the combination of song with stylized action or dance. This technique has been present in Arden's work from the beginning—remember Serjeant Musgrave's dance. But it was not until *The Hero Rises Up* and *The Island of the Mighty* that Arden and D'Arcy began to incorporate mimed or danced scenes extensively in their drama. In *The Non-Stop Connolly Show* the most consistent use of this technique can be found.

The method is especially effective when it is used to illustrate power relationships, political conflicts, or confrontations. The manipulatory powers of the employers are exemplified in a sequence accompanied by a "danse macabre" (part 3, p. 10). A simple hat-swapping routine illustrates the extent to which the British labor leader Keir Hardie has become compromised by

1. John Brown's body lies a-mould'ring in the grave,
   John Brown's body lies a-mould'ring in the grave,
   John Brown's body lies a-mould'ring in the grave,
   But his soul goes marching on.

CHORUS: Glory, glory, hallelujah!
            Glory, glory, hallelujah!
            Glory, glory, hallelujah!
            His soul goes marching on!

From "John Brown's Body," in *Songs of Work and Protest*, ed. Edith Fowke and Joe Glazer (New York: Dover, 1973), pp. 170–72.

the employers (part 3, p. 49). Part 4 is given a memorable song and dance finale, performed by Sam Gompers, some American workers, and the bosses, to the tune of "John Brown's Body:"

> *Gompers is marshalling a line of Workers, whom he dresses in a long stars-and-stripes cloth: the head of the line clutches the waist of Grabitall, thus forming a Chinese-style dancing dragon, which begins to perambulate the theatre in time to the music.*
> All. (*Sing.*)
> Glory, glory hallelujah
> Dollar bills will live for ever
> Every man a Rockefeller
> With the NEW CONQUISTADORS!
>
> (pp. 86–87)

The aural and visual powers of live theater combine to create a scene that vividly symbolizes the unbroken domination of the bosses and their manipulatory control of both union leaders and workers. It is not inconsistent with Arden and D'Arcy's analytical purposes that one can frequently detect an element of grotesque humor in such scenes.

The playwrights have chosen to end the entire cycle in part 6 with a passage of rhymed couplets rather than with a song and dance finale as in part 5. The effect of the final scene of part 6 is to dismiss the audience in a quieter and more thoughtful mood, one in which they can ponder the events portrayed in a rational manner and begin to see them in perspective. The final lines of the cycle go beyond 1916 and indicate the connection between the Easter Rising and England's role in events later in the century, in "Cuba, Africa, Vietnam" (p. 106), as well as Northern Ireland after 1968:

> We were the first to feel their loaded gun
> That would prevent us doing it any more—
> Or so they hoped. We were the first. We shall not be the last.
> This was not history. It has not passed.
>
> (p. 106)

The Non-Stop Connolly Show is an epic cycle presented in a predominantly nonillusionistic theatrical style that nevertheless does not forgo the usefulness of traditional elements in its technique. In its use of music and song it exploits a contrast between the traditional and the nontraditional. The songs mostly are sung to familiar airs, but the functions are more often than not epic and emblematic. Some of the most typical illuminate political contexts, constellations, and emotions. Collaboration, confrontation, and manipulation are some of the situations expressed not just dramatically but also through song. Distinctive is the combination of stylized dance with song in symbolical routines. In this cycle, Arden and D'Arcy have reached a stage in their dramatic career where they can express political contexts and ideas without ignoring or neglecting the powers of traditional song. They have moved further away from traditional functions without abandoning them completely. It is this fusion of traditional musical roots and political consciousness which gives the dramas of this cycle their effectiveness and atmosphere.

ANGLO-IRISH MELODRAMA

Vandaleur's Folly (1978) is the latest in D'Arcy and Arden's series of "Anglo-Irish melodramas."[131] As in the other published Irish plays, D'Arcy's name appears first. This drama embodies the wide variety of disparate theatrical elements typical of the playwrights' later style. Its political content is entirely serious: it is the examination of an early historical experiment in communal farming in the west of Ireland. But the manner of presentation includes the juxtaposition of incongruous elements: not only music and song as integral parts of the drama, but also farcical moments, exaggerated type characterization, a complex plot, and multiple ironies. It is "written totally in a theatrical convention," according to Arden.

The melodramatic style that Arden and D'Arcy have come to prefer relates not just to their use of music but also to plot, characterization, and structure. The entire plot structure, based as it is on sudden reversals, sensational hidden secrets, and unexpected juxtapositions of the serious and the low comic is essentially melodramatic in nature. Here, they use improvised music and traditional tunes with new ironic and political texts.

D'Arcy and Arden have termed this play an Anglo-Irish melodrama, and certainly the setting and the main lines of the plot are Anglo-Irish. But they have introduced several fictional threads of subplot that are American, giving the play as a whole, musically and theatrically, a distinct American touch. It might more accurately be termed an Irish-American melodrama. To my mind the combination does not work as well in this play as it has in others. Perhaps the major difficulty is the introduction of the American connection, which seems to confuse the issues, both politically and musically, in this drama.

6. Conclusion

John Arden is an innovator in the field of poetic drama in the postwar period, and Arden and D'Arcy as collaborators are two of the most interesting epic playwrights active in contemporary theater. It was, in fact, the heightened lyricism of the songs in some of Arden's early works, especially *Armstrong's Last Goodnight*, that first awakened my own interest in the topic of song in drama. I was, as I now realize, following in Arden's footsteps in finding myself fascinated with the traditional ballads as poetry before I became aware of their tunes. But the words soon led to the melodies and to a dawning realization of what music is capable of achieving in theater.

Arden is seen as a seminal influence in postwar drama by such younger playwrights as John McGrath. The vigor, originality and poetic density of his drama has inspired those who wished to revitalize and expand the language of theater. The vulgar robustness of the street ballads in *Live Like Pigs*, the folk lyricism of *Serjeant Musgrave's Dance*, and the traditional Northern ballad poetry of *Armstrong's Last Goodnight* added a new musicality to postwar drama and acted as a signal to those who wished to reinvest live theater with some of its original ritual power. Of the earlier collaborative plays *The Business of Good Government* exhibits a similar lyrical intensity due mostly to the beauty of its medieval folk carols.

The anarchic and Dionysian side of Arden as playwright emerges most clearly in the early melodrama *The Workhouse Donkey*. Here, the extensive musical component and the loose dramatic construction foreshadow the later musical epic plays of Arden and D'Arcy. Their first collaborative melodrama, *The Hero Rises Up*, is full of musicality and delights in its artificial theatricality. Their later style, which combines radical political awareness with an experimentation with dramatic and musical heritage, has proved influential particularly for younger playwrights working within political alternative theater. But the diversity of their theatrical idiom is unusual in this sphere. Labyrinthine plots and multiple layers of irony are combined with a variety of musical forms derived from ballad opera, opera, melodrama, the choral tradition, music hall, traditional English and Irish folk music, and Indian epic musical drama. Albert Hunt calls *The Non-Stop Connolly Show* "the major theatrical development in Britain in the 1970's," and claims:

> No other British playwrights have the . . . breadth of historical vision, the dramatic inventiveness and the sheer theatrical *knowledge* of D'Arcy and Arden.[132]

In spite of their clearcut political views and their melodramatic confrontation of good and evil, the later work of Arden and D'Arcy is seldom simplistic in the way that political alternative theater sometimes tends to be. They continuously surprise with the inventiveness of their theatrical and musical imagination.

The playwrights exploit audience awareness of musical heritage. Two major principles are at work: the atmospheric and the satirical. Historical texts or traditional tunes with new texts may evoke a feeling for the mood and context of the original, as, for example, with such songs as "Lillibulero" or "John Barleycorn," that they introduce quite often. In the satiric and parodistic songs, the new text may contradict the spirit of the original. In their exploitation of multiple musical ironies the dramatists clearly hope that audience familiarity with the heritage will increase its appreciation.

In their imaginative vitality, the later Arden and D'Arcy plays are comparable to those of Peter Barnes. All three playwrights display strong visual and musical feeling. Barnes's style is perhaps more grotesque, even gruesome, whereas Arden and D'Arcy are more cheerfully and aggressively political. This distinction emerges, for example, in a comparison of the mock resurrection scenes in *Leonardo's Last Supper* and *The Little Gray Home in the West*. The former leaves us with a feeling of amused horror, while the latter imparts to the end of the play a prophetic hope. Barnes remains throughout his career rooted in the sphere of popular song, whereas Arden and D'Arcy use all the registers of the musical folk tradition or of improvised rhythmic music inspired by the Asian folk play. Barnes is the great innovator in the combination of popular song and drama in the postwar period; Arden and D'Arcy awaken us to the theatrical and musical richness of the folk heritage.

Arden, D'Arcy, Barnes, and Bond may all be counted among the most striking epic playwrights of the present British theatrical scene. Dramatists such as David Rudkin and Howard Brenton must also be included, although they are not treated in comparable detail in this study because their use of music is less extensive. It is the scope of their imagination that distinguishes them from their American counterparts in the contemporary period. Whether it is Bond, using the space of the National Theatre for his rewriting of ancient Greek and Trojan history in *The Woman*, D'Arcy and Arden exploiting Liberty Hall, Dublin, for their monumental panorama of the life of James Connolly in *The Non-Stop Connolly Show* or Barnes evoking the political intrigue and ritual of seventeenth-century Spain in *The Bewitched* with the resources of the Royal Shakespeare Company, the undertakings are all epic and complex. The music reverberating through such dramas becomes a vital partner of the epic imagination. Arden and D'Arcy are foremost among contemporary dramatists in their exploration and development of epic functions of song. Political commentary, summary of world events, the description of journeys and offstage happenings, and narration of mimed or danced action are only a few of their multifold usages.

Masks, music and song, dance, and stylized nonhuman or superhuman characters appear throughout the work, from *The Happy Haven* to *The Non-Stop Connolly Show;* a joy in all the resources of theatrical artifice is constantly apparent. Theater for Arden and D'Arcy remains a communal celebration and ritual festivity, in spite of changing political viewpoints. Needless to say, none of this is easy to put on stage, especially as the artists have very precise ideas about the style of production they want—not just the general thrust of the political message but also the details of kind of music and the type of costumes. They also say that it is difficult to find English actors who feel comfortable about singing unaccompanied in traditional folk manner, or who can improvise spontaneously. The continuous history of production problems is symptomatic of their innovative dramatic style. Even the later political plays are by no means so disappointing or simplistic as is sometimes maintained; on the contrary, they provide a wealth of theatrical and musical ideas within a clearly conceived whole.

3

"Men Run Camps of Mass Murder and Sing Carols": The "Rational Theatre" of Edward Bond

1. Introduction

The playwright Edward Bond (born in 1934) is intensely aware of the multifold possibilities of live theater. One finds in his drama not only an emphasis on visual imagery and on the full exploitation of stage space, but also a conscious employment of acoustic effects and particularly of music. He plans, patterns and structures his plays with extreme care. When he introduces a song in a play he has generally chosen it with deliberation in view of the intended effect on the audience and its function in the dramatic structure as a whole. No one musical sphere dominates in Bond, as folk music does in Arden. Rather, he draws on many varied sources of traditional and contemporary musical experience: English folk song, church hymns, patriotic songs, songs from nineteenth-century music hall and Negro minstrel shows, sentimental parlor songs, and modern pop lyrics. Bond has also written many new songs for his plays to be set to original music. His most extensive and fertile collaboration has been with the German composer Hans Werner Henze. Bond and Henze have worked together on two operas, *We Come to the River* and *The Cat;* a ballet, *Orpheus;* and Henze has composed the music to the songs in Bond's *The Woman*. In addition, Bond wrote a ballet text for Henze to which the latter never composed the music.[1] Recently they collaborated on a cappella choral pieces entitled *Orpheus Behind the Wire*.

BOND AND ARDEN

In contrast to John Arden and Margaretta D'Arcy, Bond almost never attempts to achieve parodistic or satirical effects through new texts to traditional music. Bond, like Arden, makes considerable use of the satiric powers of music, but in a different way. Whereas Arden will exploit audience awareness of the discrepancy between traditional text and new words, Bond derives his satirical effects more from traditional songs in inappropriate

contexts. Although their overall artistic and political aims are not completely
dissimilar, Arden's and Bond's theatrical style and method are entirely different.

Although Arden's plays are carefully planned and patterned, particularly
with respect to language and musical idiom, they appear loose and anarchic
when compared with Bond's taut, precise, pared down, and controlled idiom
and structure. Bond and Arden in effect present a striking contrast both
stylistically and musically. Whereas Arden employs music and song in almost
every play, Bond's use of song is more sparing. With a few exceptions, one
could not say that the dramas of Bond are strongly musical as Arden's are.
Nevertheless, where a song is introduced, it usually has a carefully calculated
impact and a vital dramatic function. Throughout his career Bond has shown
a continuous concern with music and an awareness of the power of music. He
is particularly suspicious of the evil or dangerous possibilities of song and
music.

LANGUAGE AND MUSIC

Bond does not make a distinction between prose and verse or song in the
theater as Arden does. In Bond's conception, all theater language is poetical
language. Stage language is physically suggestive, condensed, multileveled
and metaphorical; it embodies vitality, concreteness, and poetic hardness. In
contrast with Arden, Bond does not feel the need for a heightened form of
language (verse or song) at moments of emotional or dramatic climax. I would
agree with David Hirst in his positive assessment of Bond's poetic power:

> It is to his images—verbal and physical—and to their precision of complex or-
> chestration that we should look for the true poetic drama of today, rather than to the
> minimalist utterances of Beckett and Pinter or the rhetoric of Osborne and Stop-
> pard.[2]

Bond believes that the drama of the future will be not just epic theater but
"epic-lyric" theater.[3] Song in this kind of theater will not have the primary
function of expressing emotion as it does in Arden's earlier work, but is rather
more controlled, distanced, or satirical in purpose. The tendency to use song
in commentary function is similar in the more recent phases of Arden/D'Arcy
and Bond, although their styles continue to be otherwise different.

Bond considers music, like language, to be simply a tool, not something
mysterious or absolute. For the dramatist, the important question is not what
music is, but rather how it works, and to what purposes humans use music.
All music for Bond is made by humans, and is a "humanizing activity":

> Music can seduce people, or charm people, or frighten people. The fact that it can
> do this is not inherent in the nature of music. It has to do with the way human

beings behave. Human beings are susceptible. The moment you get music, you are listening to the music being made. . . . Music can never escape being presented to you in historical and social form. . . . You always have to listen to the music maker as well as the music, and he is using the music for a purpose.[4]

It is of the utmost importance to the playwright to escape from conventional, ritualized, password functions of both language and music. Just as he tries "to make language difficult again, to make it problematic . . . to give language back a meaning of commentary," he also tries to use music to make an audience think about meaning and context and make them conscious of the way in which it is employed. He criticizes as misuse a music that prevents people from thinking; for example, on television, or the background accompaniment in film, or in some of the Royal Shakespeare Company productions of his own plays. In terms of dramaturgy, Bond sees the songs in his work as passages that are isolated, foregrounded, and alienated through the medium of music. The switch from spoken passage to song signals that the language requires special attention and investigation. Particularly in his later plays, Bond tries to "use music as a means of conveying meaning."

ORPHEUS AND "ORPHEUS AND THE WIRE"

Among Bond's printed statements on music, by far the most important are to be found in the ballet text *Orpheus* and in several poems written as comments on his plays. The latter belong predominantly to the category of program poems, those that were composed "after the play or music work had been finished and are a commentary on it or a guide to it."[5] The poems "On Music" and "On Musicians" were created to accompany *We Come to the River;* the poems concerning Orpheus originated in connection with the ballet text *Orpheus* that Henze requested from Bond.

"On Music" is Bond's most suggestive statement both on the power and on the dangers of music and its potential misuse in the hands of tyrannic or fascist regimes. The two opening stanzas, which explore the emotional power of music, are double-edged—the persuasive force of music may have either positive or negative implications. Bond then focuses attention on the negative with a programmatic statement:

> Music cannot ask questions
> It can startle
> That is as good as a question
>
> Music cannot give answers
> It can persuade
> That is as good as the truth
> Music is very dangerous.[6]

He goes on to criticize the dangerous misuse of music by reactionary govern-
ments, giving examples from recent history:

> At Auschwitz they hanged men to waltzes
> In Chile they broke a musician's hands
> With the same irony the church
> Once took away heretics' tongues.[7]

Implied in this latter statement is, however, the conviction that ultimately the
positive renewing powers of music cannot be suppressed. Criticism through
the medium of music can no more be destroyed by brutality than heretical
religious belief was destroyed by the torture of the Inquisition.[8] "On Music"
ends with a demand for a new, progressive type of music:

> So there must be a new music
> A music you can't hang men to
> A music that stops you breaking musicians' hands.[9]

Seen in isolation, this might seem like a naive idealistic appeal. But because
the poem is intended as a commentary on *We Come to the River* it must be
read in connection with the closing scene of the opera. There, the resurrected
victims of tyranny, including the children—symbol of hope—join in a final
chorus of solidarity, expressing the vision of a future in peace beyond the
river. In their song they are in effect beginning to create the new music called
for in the poem.

The companion poem "On Musicians" explores the theme of the complicity of musicians in a reactionary establishment. In a series of questions
Bond examines various possible behavioral patterns in a situation of civic
unrest:

> Is the patron saint of music Nero?
> When the city burns
> Should musicians stand
> On the roof of the opera house
> Bowing and scraping?[10]

If they do so, by implication they make themselves accomplices, supporting
the threatened old order by maintaining the appearance of an intact culture.
Another possible reaction to insurrection is to "sing" alarm, whereby the
alarm of "fire" is subtly turned into an order to soldiers to fire on the
arsonists. In another of the program poems accompanying *We Come to the
River*, "On Art 2," Bond reflects on the function of the artist in society. A
positive challenge is expressed in the last two stanzas of this poem, whereby
the writing of the poet and that of the composer merge into a general creative
activity:

> Write for a new age
> Of a path that leads away from violence.[11]

Both the text of the ballet *Orpheus* and the poems "Orpheus and the Wire" develop this theme of new music for a new society. The poems have undergone numerous revisions over the course of almost a decade. Originally printed as the nine-part "Canzoni to Orpheus" in a program accompanying the Stuttgart ballet production of *Orpheus* (1979), Bond continued to work on them. *Orpheus Behind the Wire*, a series of five a cappella choral songs also written for Hans Werner Henze (1984), treats similar themes and repeats one of the sections of "Canzoni." Finally, Bond revised and combined both sets of poems to form the fifteen-part "Orpheus and the Wire," printed in *Poems 1978–1985* (1987).[12]

In Bond's interpretation of the Orpheus story, the god Apollo illustrates two functions of myth, the emancipating and the repressive. In Bond's view, myth expresses the need for rational explanation and leads to works of aesthetic beauty. Later, however, an old myth can block the continuing need for a still more rational explanation. Thus Apollo is the god of music and the giver of the lyre; but, in time he becomes symbol of the old world and its violence, unable to comfort Orpheus in his passionate grief over the loss of Eurydice. As the composer Henze interprets:

> Der Gott wird für schuldig erklärt: seine Musik hat das an sich, was wir hinter allem Flitter und Glanz als die Klangwelt von Herrschaft erkennen können, Glanz und Gloria des Olymp. Höfisches, Barockmusik, das hier entdeckt wird als etwas mörderisch Feindliches, als Bedrohung, als Ausdruck von Gewalt.

> [The God is found guilty: beneath all the tinsel and gloss his music has an underlying quality which we can recognize as the sound of authority, the magnificence and *gloria* of Olympus. Courtly elements, Baroque music which . . . is here revealed as something murderously hostile, as a threat, as an expression of violence.][13]

At the end of the ballet Orpheus rejects Apollo and breaks the lyre, but from the broken fragments he lures a few notes, the beginnings of new music for new men:

> Orpheus sits beside the broken lyre
> He plays it
> A new music
>
> To the new music the dead rise out of hell
> They are resurrected and changed
> Calm happiness and contented joy
> Children climbing over the edge of the world
> Hell is emptied

> Orpheus dances with Eurydice
> The music of Apollo is the music of men.[14]

As in *We Come to the River*, the symbolic figures of the resurrected dead join with the children to embody the hope of a new music for new men.

In "Orpheus and the Wire" Bond comments on the relevance of the Orpheus myth for the present day. Here, hell is seen not just as the hell of Greek mythology or Christian hell, but the hell of war, imprisonment, concentration camps, and secret policemen. Orpheus and Eurydice are parted in a concentration camp. Bond's theme is contemporary violence:

> In this century day after day
> Many go to hell in war or prison
>
> . . . .
> Of them let Orpheus sing
>
> . . . .
> . . . Orpheus has always sung in hell.[15]

The singer Orpheus is clearly associated with the victims of social and political violence. Section 4 is an evocation of the music of nature before man emerged on the planet. Sections 13–15 sum up the theme of the destruction of an old society that has become cruel and irrational, and the birth of the new:

> Apollo gave Orpheus a lyre
> On which to sing Apollo's hymns
>
> . . . .
> Till in time beauty became cruel
> And music was played at the poisoner's feast
>
> . . . .
> And Orpheus broke Apollo's lyre
> The world was filled with new music
> New dancers
>
> . . . . .
> And therefore I praise this world
> In music.[16]

This is one of Bond's strongest statements on the positive power of music to effect change and to create a new world.

THE POWERS AND DANGERS OF MUSIC

Just as Bond throughout his dramatic career explores the paradoxes of human nature, man's double capacity for brutality and for kindness, he also tries to fathom the paradox of music, its powers, and its dangers. As Xenia remarks in *Summer*, "I didn't know that men who sang so beautifully could hate so deeply."[17] In Bond's view this is not an existential paradox, but rather social schizophrenia: both the good and evil of human nature are determined by society. It is one of the major purposes of his "rational theatre" to explore and lay bare the causes that condition social and political behavior. Song in Bond's plays can be used to express a strong sense of community or solidarity. He also, however, sees a tremendous capacity for the misuse of song: "Men run camps of mass murder and sing carols. So why is this paradox? Why is morality weak?"[18] The paradox of song is directly related to social conditions in the same way that the paradox of morality is. It is not, in fact, a paradox at all, but to his mind a clever manipulation that can be understood, exposed, and thus, he hopes, prevented. The songs in Bond's drama are not used primarily for emotional effect, for atmosphere, or for characterization of his figures. Their major purpose is to expose the social role of the singer and to illustrate the nature of the society to which he or she belongs.

Bond understands that the primary response to music is usually emotional, but he believes it is misleading and dangerous to respond to music in this way alone:

> It is difficult to say of a piece of music, Do I understand it. We usually just say, Do I like it. But it seems to me that all great art is in some way the communication of something understood, not just something enjoyed.[19]

In the same context he points out that music is particularly vulnerable to false romanticizing or sentimentalizing. It is subject to apparent timelessness and hence to a related tendency to escape responsibility; and it is susceptible to manipulation for political purposes:

> Historically we can see that art has always served a political role. It's been used by whoever had political power to create a human consciousness adapted to the convenience of that power.[20]

Central to Bond's drama is the questioning of cultural assumptions in order to understand how the heritage of the past affects present-day society. Thus when he uses historical settings he does not do so out of interest in the past for its own sake, but because he wishes to examine how cultural clichés or ideals determine contemporary thinking. Most of the plays with historical settings are parables with moral and political lessons for the present. Similarly, when Bond introduces familiar songs into his drama, songs that belong to the English cultural tradition, he is both analyzing the way in which society exploits its historical traditions, and he is exposing the general cultural level of that particular society. Traditional songs are often used to indicate depravity or hypocrisy. Church hymns, music-hall, or patriotic songs sung in inappropriate contexts—for example, in conjunction with war, murder or nuclear holocaust—expose cultural, moral and political degeneracy. In a poem of the *Activists Papers*, "The Simple Image," Bond contrasts the more natural past with the ugly, perverted present in terms of song. Speaking of the poor man's children, he says:

> In the time of the hand-held plough
>
> . . . .
> . . . at play his children sang in joy of the world
>
> And now in the time of bombs
>
> . . . .
> . . . children . . . sing commercial jingles.[21]

When Bond employs a traditional folk song, it is not done to create authentic historical atmosphere, but to reveal the cultural assumptions and the class consciousness of the singers.

On the whole, Bond's concept of the function of theater is analytical; his ultimate aim, to help create a new rational and more humane socialist or communist society, which is why he wants his theater understood as "theatre of humanism" or "rational theatre." In the course of his career Bond has been placing increasing emphasis on the public and political nature of the theatrical performance. In a similar way he highlights the public and social functions of music:

> Music isn't something that happens in an isolated sound chamber. It is part of social experience. There is no such thing as pure art—art is the product of the society and the time in which it is made. . . . Music is a public activity—a means of communication between disparate individuals. . . . This places music back in its social context—where it belongs.[22]

With respect to song in drama, Bond's epic theater arrives at a position quite similar to that of Brecht: sometimes a tune may have an emotional effect on the audience, but the context in which it is placed will alienate it, stimulating analysis. Bond's theater is both intellectual and emotional at the same time, and his use of song contributes significantly to both aspects of his theater.

When asked about his early experience of music, Bond's response is striking:

> If I go back to my first experience of music, it was the sound of war . . . the screaming of missiles. Then I wanted to know why . . . the bombs were dropped. I can't dissociate that question from the sound of bombs, and I can't dissociate music from questions.

Bond had a childhood familiarity with the English traditions of music hall:

> I'd watched music hall performances all during my childhood. It's the most incredible way to develop an understanding of timing and control on a stage. . . . A wonderful way to learn about the theatre.[23]

He praises the music-hall comedian Frankie Howerd for his ability to create a sense of partnership between performer and audience.[24] Bond sees theater in general and his own theater in particular as part of this tradition of audience–performer intimacy:

> I don't see the plays I write as being intellectual in the sense of being cut off from a popular expression. I grew up at a time when the theatre was still part of popular experience in the music-hall.[25]

Several of the songs he later chooses for his plays are from the sphere of music hall. Occasionally he will encourage audience participation in a song in order to make a political point.

From the very beginning of his playwriting career, Bond exhibited an awareness of the non-literary, three-dimensional nature of live theater. Particularly important for his early development was the writers' group at the Royal Court Theatre, which Bond joined before achieving his first dramatic success. The work of this group laid emphasis not on the theory of playwriting but on awakening the writers to an understanding of all the available resources of live theater. There were working sessions on the use of masks, mime, games, improvisation, and sound effects:

> We didn't discuss the problems of writing so much as the problems of theatre. What we used to do . . . was to improvise on given subjects, . . . to sort of go through the actors' experience of creating movement, gesture, sound, meaning . . . on the stage.[26]

Certainly Bond's awareness of the usefulness of acoustic effects, music, and song must be seen in the context of this early training in the enrichment of the theatrical idiom.

Positive and negative functions of song can be distinguished in Bond's drama, corresponding to his dual appreciation of music as both powerful and dangerous. Bond, perhaps more clearly than any other contemporary playwright, recognizes and portrays in his plays the dangerous misuse of song and music. The thoughtless and superficial singing of familiar songs creates a false sense of gang solidarity or expresses a hollow conviviality. This is a function that is found in several of Bond's earliest plays, for example, *The Pope's Wedding* or *Saved*. At this earliest stage Bond also recognizes a positive function of song: conveying emotion that cannot be otherwise articulated, a kind of emotional identification. Such singing can, however, potentially develop into a much more dangerous misuse: songs sung to support a tyrannical or unjust regime and to draw attention away from its brutalities. Bond's recognition of fascist misuse of song is best expressed in the words of his poem "On Music" already quoted: "At Auschwitz they hanged men to waltzes."

The traditional songs in Bond's work on the whole illustrate "music as . . . a means of manipulation, rather than of communication." The primary function of the familiar songs is satirical, and they are most often introduced in his comedies. Here, they help to point out the dangerous exploitation of traditional cultural values by a degenerate society, and, at the same time, illustrate the hollowness and hypocrisy of bourgeois morality. In *Narrow Road to the Deep North, Passion, The Sea* and *The Swing* one can find this satirical use of traditional songs. Bond's technique here is primarily that of creating ironic discrepancy between the actions portrayed and the familiar text of the song, be it religious, patriotic or superficially entertaining.

As Bond developed as a dramatist, he began to feel the limitations of the satiric song, and he started to explore the more positive functions. In this connection one finds both traditional and newly written songs. Sometimes they express a simple sense of solidarity, a celebration of the positive powers of community. This function is usually found in those plays with historical settings, for to the dramatist's mind our contemporary society has lost the capacity to sing naturally in praise of the world. The traditional mummers' songs at the beginning of *The Fool* and the newly composed ritual songs of the island community in *The Woman* are illustrations. The playwright more often employs songs today of an objective, commentary nature that he has written and that have been set to music by contemporary composers. Such songs may represent both an informed, detached commentary on the action of the play in which they occur and also a consideration of the wider social and political problems raised by the drama. Several of the songs in *We Come to the River* are of this nature, as well as many of the songs from the unperformed *Text for a Ballet*, in *Stone* and in *Restoration*. Bond most often employs such commentary songs in plays of a serious, even revolutionary nature. *Restoration*, however, represents an exception in that here he experiments with a combination of comedy, or tragicomedy, and informed political comment through song. The technique of the public soliloquy from *The Worlds* is developed further in a musical medium, and the public soliloquy becomes the public song. The content remains political, detached and commentary, but the presentation approaches that of popular entertainment.

Typical of Bond's later technique are not only songs that embody commentary in their text, but also songs based on parable and metaphor that teach a moral lesson in an indirect fashion. Just as the dramatic stories of many of his plays may be comprehended as historical parables and many of his dramatic images as metaphors, Bond uses parable and metaphor in his songs, too. In these plays Bond's understanding of epic-lyric theater takes on new dimensions. The term lyric can here be understood in a wider musical sense, so that one might almost say that Bond achieves a form of musical epic theater. Speaking of one of his most recent dramas, *Human Cannon*, which uses musical choruses, Bond points out the close interrelationship between the lyrical and the musical:

> Note how the use of music infiltrates the language of the . . . play and alters its function. In my latest work the language is becoming more lyrical precisely because this makes possible a more thorough analysis than is possible in naturalism. The language is able to grow from its own in-built commentary to a more explicit commentary.[27]

2. Traditional Songs in Ironic and Satiric Functions: Criticism of Western Values

THE POPE'S WEDDING AND SAVED

Bond intends his plays from *The Pope's Wedding* up to and including *The Sea* to be understood as a cycle. It is interesting that the two dramas that bear the subtitle comedy, *Narrow Road to the Deep North* and *The Sea*, also contain by far the largest number of songs in this early series. Most are traditional English tunes, a few are American. It is their ironic and satirical function that gives them a wider significance; indeed, they serve as commentary on Western civilization and culture. The melodies Bond chooses often are religious, patriotic or sentimental, but the dramatic contexts in which they are placed are outrageously incongruous, thus undermining any sense of seriousness or dignity. At the same time they illustrate the misuse of music in the interests of reactionary established power.

This satirical function is not yet prominent in the first two plays of the series, *The Pope's Wedding* and *Saved*, but discrepancies and multiple ironies can be observed. A further function at this early stage is to indicate an inarticulate need for meaningful explanation. Both dramas are comparable in that they deal with the psychology and social interaction of gangs of young men, in the one case rural, in the other urban. These youths are not very articulate; the gang exchanges are swift-paced, with rapid shifts in topic and almost constant sexual innuendoes. There is an undercurrent of aggression and hostility, but the surface tone is usually one of bantering or joking.[28] Some of the songs in these first two plays are very similar to the jokes in that they express a sense of gang intimacy. Bond himself later speaks of the form and function of the gang language as "a Greek chorus almost," which represents society.[29] Bond summarizes the ironic functions of the songs in his early work:

If you look at the use of music in my first plays, . . . what I think you see is a discrepancy between the song being sung and the singer or the situation in which it is being sung.

In *The Pope's Wedding* (1962) this is most obvious in a hymn that evokes multiple ironies.[30] Scopey, in his search for the significance of Alen's life, at the climax of scene 12 forces the old man to sing, as he cannot talk coherently about himself. There is an ironic contrast between Scopey's search for spiritual enlightenment and his physical violence in this situation.

> *Scopey.* Sing it mate! Sing it. By chriss I'll rip this junk shop up if yoo don't sing! (*He puts his boot through the couch.*)
> *Alen.* (. . . *Starts to sing* . . .). (p. 295)

The text of the song emphasizes the interrelationship of martyrdom and violence in Christian faith:

> Little babe nailed to the tree
> Wash our souls in thy pure blood
> Cleanse each sin and let us be
> Baptized in the purple flood
>
> Bearing thorns and whips and nails
> Wise men kneel before thy bier
> . . . .
> Those who nail thee up to die
> Hoist thee nearer to thy throne.

(pp. 295–96)

In this pastiche hymn Bond is ridiculing the violent traditions of Christian sacrifice. Many of the hymns of Passiontide exhibit the same concern with the gory details of the crucifixion. Compare for example words and spirit of the dramatic song with the following traditional Passiontide hymn:

> On the Cross the Lamb is lifted,
>   There the Sacrifice to be.
>
> There the nails and spear he suffers,
>   Vinegar, and gall, and reed;
> From His sacred Body piercèd
>   Blood and Water both proceed;
> Precious flood, which all creation
>   From the stain of sin hath freed.[31]

Bond says, "There are some pretty horrible hymns in *Hymns Ancient and Modern*. . . . There are extraordinary lines of that sort which little kids are made to sing."

The words hint at what Scopey hoped he might find in Alen: a powerful

spiritual mentor whose death would cleanse his soul and give his life meaning. Alen's death in the play is foreshadowed in this song, but the reality of
his life undermines the faith of the hymn. Far from being King of Heaven
("nearer to thy throne"), Alen is not even a Christian hermit, only a miserable
dirty old man who cannot remember why he lives as he does. The fact that he
sings a hymn at a moment of crisis does not indicate any spiritual faith on his
part. The dramatist in this way exposes the sterility and emptiness of contemporary culture.

Still another layer of irony in the song is revealed when we consider the
playwright's attitude towards the entire tradition of Christianity:

> The whole Christian idea to me is so absurd. The idea that a God could kill his son
> because it was demanded by some eternal law and order, is absolute nonsense.[32]

In his view, Christianity is just another form of repression and violence. It is
significant that the dramatist has created a hymn that portrays Christ crucified as a child. Children, throughout Bond's work, are not only the most
helpless victims of social violence, but also symbolic figures of hope for the
future. A crucified child is thus symbol of the ultimate dead end for any
society. Even if Alen had lived a life of Christian faith, this would not have
provided a viable alternative to modern cultural degradation. Thus the singing of this hymn at a moment of dramatic climax, which might at first glance
indicate a shimmer of spiritual hope, reveals in the end quite the opposite: the
hollowness of Alen's personal life and the absurdity of the entire western
Christian tradition. The dramatic climax is in reality an anticlimax, a void,
and the message for Scopey is nonexistent.

In spite of this almost tragic conclusion, Bond nevertheless wants Scopey's
curiosity and his search for enlightenment to be understood as a positive,
analytical element in the play:

> What I was doing there was two things: One is to say that the means of expression
> are inappropriate, . . . the other thing is to say but there *is* a meaning which he or
> she wishes to grasp, and that's why they're pushed into song. In other words I
> cannot say this but if I can sing it then at least I will have some emotional
> identification. . . . I think Scopey has the right to his hymn. . . . In actual fact,
> . . . he's listening to a lie, he's listening to a further mystification. But the right to
> sing, or the right to express, the need for clarification, that would be his, . . . that's
> one of the fundamental uses of communication, . . . a sign of what human beings
> are. So that there, although the songs were lying, they would also be moments of
> truth, in that he was consulting himself as an oracle.

The object of Scopey's search is the wrong one, as indicated by Alen's
Christian hymn. Scopey's solution (murder) can bring him no further, but his
search will be carried on by his counterparts in two subsequent plays, Len in
Saved and Arthur in *Early Morning*.

Saved (1965) contains only two songs, but both are introduced at very important moments. "Rock a bye Baby" occurs in the crucial scene 6, the stoning scene, as the frustrations and aggressions of the gang are gradually working up to open violence. Again, one finds a mixture of song, joking, and violence as expressive of the gang mentality. The original text of the lullaby, one of the most familiar in the English-speaking world, already contains a hint of disaster and violence:

> When the bough breaks the cradle will fall,
> Down will come baby, cradle, and all.[33]

Although this text has much puzzled the scholars,[34] and possibly contains political implications, it is surely understood by most singers and listeners as a harmless and playful threat: when baby falls, mother or nurse is at hand to comfort any minor hurt. Barry, in *Saved*, however, alters and extends the final line of the rhyme to include explicit although joking mention of violence:

> And down will come baby and cradle and tree
> an' bash its little brains out an' dad'll scoop
> 'em up and use 'em for bait.
> *They laugh.*
> *Fred.* Save money.[35]

The words foreshadow the baby's violent death later in this scene. In addition, Bond has subtly turned a familiar nursery tune into a piece about the victimization of the child and the emotional indifference of parents, both major themes in this drama. The song is ironic in function in that it is intended not to comfort and lull to sleep but to incite to violence. At the same time it serves as an oblique commentary on the cultural and social consciousness of the gang.

The other song, a pop tune, is played on the juke box in the café scene. In the original production a pop number was composed and taped for this purpose. The title, "My 'Eart is Broken," (p. 113) speaks for the whole lyric. Bond refers to the use of song in this scene as "quasi-ironic." On the one hand the text of the song is utterly trivial; on the other hand it points to an inarticulate need to feel "that there is meaning to life." He says about the device of introducing music at these crucial moments in the early plays and his own consciousness of what he was doing:

> I was in a certain sense totally unconscious, but it came to hand as being necessary. In other words in order to get through certain dramatic moments. . . . I had to use music there, or there would be no way of getting through into what follows.

One can see here an almost instinctive understanding on the dramatist's part of the emotional and dramaturgical expressiveness of song. The tunes in these plays reveal information about social relationships, thus serving as indirect commentary on the wider issues of the dramas. They help to isolate the themes of the violence of Christianity and the victimization of children in modern society.

Early Morning (1968) contains only one song, a parody of the popular little snatch tune, "Lloyd George Knew My Father." It comes at the height of the trial scene and is, as Bond says, "satire on top of satire. . . . It's . . . sending up the idea of reverence for these Victorian traditions." The following plays in this first cycle significantly extend the function of song in Bond's work. New and central to the comedies *Narrow Road to the Deep North* and *The Sea* is a satiric use to expose the hypocrisy and inherent contradictions of Western society. The songs in these two plays are prominent, and in contrast with the earlier more sombre works, the dramatist here introduces them in outrageously incongruous contexts, thus contributing to the comic effect. It is partly through music that Bond analyzes our cultural heritage. Because he clearly expects his audience to recognize and still be familiar with these melodies, he is at the same time implicating the contemporary audience in his criticism of cultural traditions and standards.

NARROW ROAD TO THE DEEP NORTH

Narrow Road to the Deep North (1968) is the first drama to be subtitled a comedy, and it is the first to employ traditional songs in distinctly satiric fashions. Here the Christian hymns, all associated with Georgina, expose discrepancies between the ideals of Western society and its actions. To make the absurdities and inconsistencies more blatantly obvious, Bond has created in Georgina an exaggerated figure of narrow-minded fanaticism, a missionary for the worst aspects of English culture and Christian religion. The entire play, built as it is upon the contrasts between East and West, of course demonstrates that our norms of Western civilization and morality are just as repressive and brutal as Shogo's more open form of barbarism.

In Georgina, incongruous attitudes are expressed in musical terms. The development of her consciousness, and also of her sanity, is conveyed through tambourine playing and through song. In scene 5, her first appearance, Georgina embodies repressive and perverted aspects of Western education (and implicitly also of her music). Care of children is associated with violence, just as religion is associated with violence. Speaking of the infant emperor she exclaims: "Another soul for Jesus. (*She bangs her tambourine in the baby's face*)."[36] In Bond's own adaptation of this play for radio[37] the baby begins to cry at this moment, a clear indictment of Georgina's behavior. In the perception of Basho and the Prime Minister her performance is evaluated as that of a madwoman. Georgina's tambourine fanaticism seems to them insane. Later, the beginning of Georgina's real insanity is heralded by the distraught singing of a fragmented Christian hymn for the murdered children. By means of musical elements and song Bond demonstrates that Western traditions are actually irrational and repressive, whereas Georgina's moment of truest humanity occurs when her hymns are sung in a state of incipient insanity.

This satiric function of song is particularly marked in scene 6, in which Shogo's city is bombarded and destroyed to the accompaniment of a British patriotic tune and a Christian hymn. Kiro evaluates these sanctified traditions of English civilization as the "devil's music" of "barbarians" (p. 199). Although Bond does not call for the text of "The British Grenadiers" to be sung—it is played by a military band—he was surely aware of the song's proud avowal of violence in the name of patriotism:

> Whene'er we are commanded to storm the palisades,
> Our leaders march with fusees, and we with hand grenades;
> We throw them from the glacis about the enemies' ears,
> Sing tow, row, row, row, row, row, for the British Grenadiers.[38]

The nonsensical refrain line ("sing tow, row, row . . .") is consistent with the fanaticism of the bombardment. This is quite an old tune, the original words dating from the end of the seventeenth century.

In the case of Georgina's hymn, "Abide With Me," sung as she fires the opening shot of the cannon, the ironies are even more complex. The entire scene is clearly satiric in its juxtaposition of exaggerated religious fervor and violence:

> *Georgina.* Two lines of Abide With Me. (*Sings.*) Abide with me, fast falls the evening light. Three cheers for Jesus! Hip hip! (*Shouts and tambourine:* 'Hoorah!' . . . *She drops a light on the cannon. There is a flash and a roar. The men cheer.*) I saw an angel hovering over it with a Union Jack! (p. 201)

Georgina, in the name of Western civilization, manipulates through music the religious and patriotic feelings of the men to engender the necessary enthusiasm for the military attack. Bond's conscious exaggeration is obvious in her vision of an angel with a Union Jack and the rabble-rousing "three cheers for Jesus."

In addition, the playwright has chosen a hymn that carries ironic overtones in the circumstances. Although Georgina's singing of only the first two lines might lead the uninitiated to believe that this is a hymn of the church militant calling for God's aid in war, quite the opposite is the case. The text was written in 1847 by Henry Francis Lyte shortly before his death.[39] The words, based on Luke 24:29 but used metaphorically, reflect clearly the appeal of a dying man to his God not to desert him in his last hour:

> Abide with me; fast falls the eventide;
> The darkness deepens; Lord, with me abide;
> When other helpers fail, and comforts flee,
> Help of the helpless, O abide with me.
>
> Swift to its close ebbs out life's little day;
> Earth's joys grow dim, its glories pass away;
> Change and decay in all around I see;
> O thou, who changest not, abide with me.[40]

Georgina and her army in this scene are neither "helpless," nor do they wish to call attention to "change and decay." Bond is in effect demonstrating a perversion and misuse of the Christian tradition in the name of patriotism. Both the scene and the musical satire find their finale in the sung amen:

> *Georgina.* The city's taken and now I can begin my mission. Amen.
> All. (*Sung.*) A-a-a-men. (p. 204)

The communal singing of the amen emphasizes the complicity of all present. These ironies and inconsistencies combine to make this scene the comic climax of the play. Through the discrepancy between song and action Bond has significantly added to the effect.

In part 1 Georgina is portrayed as a religious fanatic, thoroughly convinced of the truth and righteousness of her beliefs. When she reveals in part 2 that she has been aware all along of the repressive and manipulatory powers of her morality, and by implication of her music, Bond's satire is widened to include not just fanatic religion and patriotism but all conscious manipulations to maintain power and status quo. For him, morality so used is a form of repression and violence: "In western society morality is a form of violence and not, as it should be, of creativity. It is used to coerce people."[41] Because Georgina uses music to persuade and to enforce her morality, her music becomes an accomplice in repression. We are here quite close to Bond's later pronouncements on the evil capacities of manipulated music.

Basho's response to this revelation foreshadows Georgina's fate in the play: "people who raise ghosts become haunted" (p. 208). This development is expressed in musical terms. As the children are led out to be killed by Shogo's soldiers in part 2, scene 3, Georgina sings a line of "God Be With Us in Our Labour." Again, Bond has exploited the effects of ironic discrepancy. Speaking of the hymn he says,

> I used it because she's a virgin. It's the idea of childbirth labour, and that she wants children. . . . I used it because of the murder of the children, as opposed to the bearing of children.

After the children's bodies have been carried out, Georgina remains alone on stage and distractedly begins to play her tambourine and sing. The peasant explains to his wife that she is "haunted" (p. 218), echoing Basho's earlier words of warning.

> Georgina [. . .] (*Plays and sings* [. . .]) All things bright and . . . all creatures great and. . . . My little chicks all gone. . . . Hands together, eyes shut tight [. . .] (*She dances, plays the tambourine and sings.*) He gave them snow in winter . . . and lips that we might tell . . . all things bright and . . . dead . . . (p. 218)[42]

Spoken words and snatches of the hymn "All Things Bright and Beautiful" are here intermingled. In her suffering, Georgina cannot finish the lines of the hymn; she cannot sing the words *beautiful* and *small* because they remind her of the children. Toward the end of this passage she confuses the words and finally concludes by substituting *dead* for *beautiful*. The relevant verses of the hymn run:

> All things bright and beautiful,
>   All creatures great and small,
> All things wise and wonderful,
>   The Lord God made them all.
>
> . . . .
>
> The cold wind in the winter,
>   The pleasant summer sun,
> The ripe fruits in the garden,—
>   He made them every one;
>
> . . . .
>
> He gave us eyes to see them,
>   And lips that we might tell
> How great is God Almighty,
>   Who has made all things well.[43]

By singing "he gave *them* snow in winter,"[44] Georgina conveys to the audience that she is thinking of the little children playing rather than the totality of God's creation. The isolation of winter from this stanza about all the seasons implies her horror at Shogo's emotional coldness. The lines on winter are echoed in Georgina's words in the following scene "Snow. Snow. It's a cold winter that blows nobody any good" (p. 219). The singing of the line "And lips that we might tell" out of context from the last stanza gives it an entirely new meaning. Rather than praise of God's creation, Georgina's implication is that Shogo's atrocity must be revealed to the world.

"All Things Bright and Beautiful" is a hymn written for children to explain the article of the creed that God is the "maker of heaven and earth." The words are by Mrs. C. F. Alexander in her *Hymns for Little Children*, 1848. The playwright has chosen a hymn that is not inappropriate with respect to the singer, and whose direct emotional impact is due to its association with

For the Young.

Hymn 573. ALL THINGS BRIGHT AND BEAUTIFUL.—7 6 7 6.

♩ = 100.

Verse 1, and the Refrain after Verses 2, 3, 4, 5, 6, 7.

All things bright and beau‑ti‑ful, All crea‑tures great and small,

All things wise and won‑der‑ful, The LORD GOD made them all.

Verses 2, 3, 4, 5, 6, 7.

"The Lord made all things."

f ALL things bright and beautiful,
    All creatures great and small,
All things wise and wonderful,
    The LORD GOD made them all.

mf Each little flower that opens,
    Each little bird that sings,
He made their glowing colours,
    He made their tiny wings.

The rich man in his castle,
    The poor man at his gate,
God made them, high or lowly,
    And order'd their estate.

The purple‑headed mountain,
    The river running by,
The sunset and the morning,
    That brightens up the sky;—

The cold wind in the winter,
    The pleasant summer sun,
The ripe fruits in the garden,—
    He made them every one;

The tall trees in the greenwood,
    The meadows where we play,
The rushes by the water,
    We gather every day;—

He gave us eyes to see them,
    And lips that we might tell,
f How great is GOD Almighty,
    Who has made all things well.

"All Things Bright and Beautiful," by Mrs. C. F. Alexander, in *Hymns Ancient and Modern*, standard edition (London: Clowes, 1916), no. 573, p. 496.

children. He wishes to indicate that the distracted Georgina is no longer the dangerous, manipulating woman that she once was. Bond's criticism of Georgina as an instrument of the imperialist system gives way to a certain limited sympathy toward her as a victim of her own contradictions:

> I had sympathy with her as a person, because I thought that she was a person who was going to be very unhappy, because she had no understanding of herself and was so full of contradictions . . . so that she . . . must finally crack up in some way.[45]

His sympathy is conveyed in Georgina's song. Nevertheless, the quiet peace of the original hymn stands in stark contrast to the violent deaths of the children. The satire is directed at those who have created the situation, rather than at the singer.

One interesting minor revision Bond made in this drama for the edition of *Plays: Two* (1978) pertains to the choice of music to be played during the execution of Shogo in part 2, scene 4. The scene is vitally important, showing how violence inevitably overtakes its perpetrators. Shogo is mocked, pronounced guilty, and put to death publicly in a scene that is reminiscent of ritual mock crucifixion. The crowd mills about, shouting "Hallelujah" and playing tambourines. In the original edition (1968), the dramatist merely called for "a band playing out of tune" during the execution.[46] In the revised edition in *Plays: Two* he specifies in addition "a Sullivan medley or 'Sussex by the Sea'" (p. 222). One can discern the principle of ironic contrast in his thinking, since he has taken care to specify the most cheerful and innocuous melodies possible. Bond says that this was done to guard against the use of music that sounded meaningful and pompous: "I wanted it to be very satirical." In addition, this revision proves that he cared strongly enough about the effects of music and song in his plays to make such a comparatively minor alteration ten years after the original edition.

PASSION

Ironic and satiric functions are taken up again and developed in Bond's next major comedy, *The Sea*. Between these two comedies lie *Lear* (1971) and the two short agitprop pieces *Black Mass* (1970) and *Passion* (1971). Of these, only the latter contains songs, and in function they are very closely related to those in *Narrow Road to the Deep North*. *Black Mass* includes no songs. The sombre *Lear* uses music only in act 1, scene 2, where "marching, march music, and parade commands are heard during the scene."[47] This serves briefly to remind us of Bond's criticism of the repressive use of music in the hands of reactionary regimes, but it is heard no more. In the original Royal Court production of *Lear* (1971), William Gaskill decided to use "the official battle call of the British army,"[48] a scenic interpretation that is certainly not inconsistent with the intentions of Bond's cultural criticism. The playwright was, however, extremely dissatisfied with additional music, composed by Ilona Sekacz, in a later Royal Shakespeare Company production of 1982:

> I did complain about it, I wrote and told them they mustn't use it. It was a misuse of music. It's saying "We are being profound" and "There's this ungraspable problem here."

Passion, while dramatically a minor work, is visually very striking and contains larger-than-life cartoon style scenes.[49] The piece contains two songs and a version of the English national anthem, all in important satiric functions. The play's characters are intended "as types or even archetypes."[50] The Queen and the Prime Minister represent the superficiality and irresponsibility of established rulers in the face of war, death, and nuclear holocaust. This is conveyed by the exaggerated absurdity of their speech, their childish yo-yo playing, and by the songs they sing as they enter. The queen is given "The Camptown Races,"[51] the well-known tune by nineteenth-century composer Stephen C. Foster, who wrote many sentimental and comic songs of the American south, including "My Old Kentucky Home" and "Swanee River."

The choice of this song for the Queen illustrates that she is more interested in trivialities such as horse racing than in such vital national concerns as the bomb. The nonsensical elements of the lyrics coincide with the nonsensical character of the rest of the Queen's speeches. In this way Bond indicates that all our "pleasant and well-bred" (p. 241) formulas of social politeness have no more real meaning than "Oh! doo-dah-day!".

The Prime Minister also enters playing with a child's yo-yo and singing "A Life on the Ocean Waves."[52] Here too the principles of satiric and ironic contrast are at work. This mid-nineteenth-century song has been the official march of the Royal Marines since 1889. As in the case of "The Camptown Races" the song has come to England from the United States. The text by the New Englander Epes Sargent is full of breathless enthusiasm and romantic idealism. The Prime Minister is a man of cautious conformity. The dramatist's satiric purpose is, in part, to indicate that neither the absurd adaptability of the Prime Minister nor the romantic enthusings of the traditional song are adequate or rational responses to the problems of modern society.

The apotheosis of this perverted society is reached in the crucifixion of a pig with a soldier's helmet in place of Christ (who arrives too late) to the tune of the English national anthem, "Elgar version" (p. 247). For Bond, the composer Edward Elgar is the embodiment of Englishness. The crucified pig is unveiled as a national "monument." Bond thus expresses by acoustic and visual means the disastrous intermingling of religion and patriotism and the

DE CAMPTOWN RACES

This rollicking song, originally published as "Gwine to Run All Night," ranks with "Oh! Susanna" in popularity. It belongs to the period immediately following Foster's marriage in 1850.

Words and Music by Stephen Foster

"De Camptown Races," words and music by Stephen Foster, from *The Fireside Book of Folk Songs*, ed. Margaret Bradford Boni (New York: Simon and Schuster, 1947), pp. 64–65.

hollow depravity of both. The English national anthem has, in its little-known second stanza, words much in the spirit of the ironic scene:

> O Lord our God, arise,
> Scatter our enemies,
>   And make them fall;
> Confound their politics,
> Frustrate their knavish tricks;
> On thee our hopes we fix:
>   God save us all.[53]

Shortly afterward, the enemy bomb of reprisal explodes in the assembly. The playing of the tune in this context indicates the dangerous misuse to which music can be put in the name of national and spiritual values. In its employ-ment of song and music the short play *Passion* is most closely related to *Narrow Road to the Deep North*, which also exposes the degeneracy of religious and patriotic values through musical means. In its themes it is also related to *Early Morning* and *Black Mass* of the Sharpville sequence.

THE SEA

The final play in this first series of Bond's drama is again a comedy, *The Sea* (1973).[54] *The Sea* is influenced, at least structurally, by Shakespeare's *The Tempest*.[55] One can see a relationship in the music of these two dramas, but essential differences are also apparent. *The Tempest* is permeated by song and music. Central to the drama is the contrast between Ariel's magical music, which echoes the heavenly "music of the spheres," and the drunken, vulgar singing of the earthly Stephano, Trinculo, and Caliban. In *The Sea* we also find drunken singing by Evens; this is contrasted musically not with the divine sphere but with songs representing the perversion of religion and human emotion. *The Sea* thus presents only negative aspects of song. In Shakespeare, tempest and music are structural opposites, representing re-spectively chaos and harmony. In Bond's drama, the singing is part of the chaos, repression, and destruction. *The Sea* not only thematically forms the close of Bond's first series of plays; theatrically it also represents the climax of the playwright's use of traditional tunes.

Almost all of the songs in the drama belong to the high comedy world of Mrs. Rafi and are used to uncover the hollow pretensions and perverted values of upper-middle-class society. Scene 4 is devoted to the rehearsal of the ladies' play in benefit of the Coast Guard Fund, and exposes the false pretensions and hypocrisies of this small-town society, particularly its misuse of art, including song. Outrageous incongruities make the scene one of the comic highlights of the drama. The theme of the "play within the play" in itself embodies many comic discrepancies: the tragic story of Orpheus and

Eurydice is here incompetently acted by society ladies and the parson, the representatives of morality and social authority. A tale of passion and incomparable artistry is recreated by those who have no love, no passion and only mediocre artistry in their lives. Ironically, the dominant figure of repression and mediocrity, Mrs. Rafi, reserves the role of the great singer and poet Orpheus for herself. Mrs. Rafi as a singer can move her audience to tears only by middle-class sentimentality.

Bond introduces particularly incongruous songs into the Orpheus rehearsal to expose the hollow sentimentality and pressures of conformity in English upper-middle-class society and culture. Mrs. Rafi, alias Orpheus, arriving at the edge of the River Styx sings that embodiment of English conformity and sentimentality, "Home Sweet Home" (p. 123). In interview, Bond emphasized the overtones this song conveys to an English audience:

> Music is very useful, because it has often been used to capture, in a very easily accessible form, very large world views. "Home Sweet Home" is a song of the British Empire. You own the earth and you talk about "Home Sweet Home."

The text has only the most tenuous connection to the context in which it is sung: it is suggested by the idea of the exile from home. But in all other respects it has only ironic relevance. Instead of singing of the dangers of Hell and his passion for Eurydice, this comic female Orpheus sings that all the "pleasures and palaces" she encounters cannot soothe her longing for home:

> 'Mid pleasures and Palaces though we may roam,
> Be it ever so humble there's no place like home!
> . . . .
> An Exile from Home, Splendour dazzles in vain!
> Oh! give me my lowly thatch'd Cottage again!
> The Birds singing gaily that came at my call,
> Give me them with the peace of mind dearer than all!
>   Home! Home, sweet sweet Home!
> There's no place like Home! There's no place like Home![56]

Although in rehearsal Mrs. Rafi sings only a few lines of the song, she obviously in performance expects to sing the entire text and to wring all the sentimentality she can out of its gushing enthusiasm:

> My performance of 'There's no place like home' will be one of the highlights of the evening. . . . Moved by the atmosphere I have created, I cry—together with a large part of the audience, if things go as usual. (p. 123)

To understand fully all the ironies, more should be said about the creation and the reception of "Home Sweet Home." As explained in Michael Turner's notes to *The Parlour Song Book*, it was perhaps the most popular of all songs in nineteenth-century concert halls and parlors. Written originally in 1823 for

Home! Sweet Home!

Written by JOHN HOWARD PAYNE   Composed by SIR HENRY BISHOP

From "Home! Sweet Home!", text by John Howard Payne, tune by Sir Henry Bishop, in *The Parlour Song Book*, ed. Michael Turner (London: Michael Joseph, 1972), pp. 140–45.

the melodrama *Clari; or, the Maid of Milan,* it became an "undying favourite . . . the world over. . . . It certainly struck as no other composition has done a responsive chord in the human breast."[57] Turner also mentions that both text and melody have been "the subject of frequent critical scorn over the years," and suggests that the tune may be so successful precisely because it lacks distinction: "This is, one may hazard, a vacuum of a tune which nostalgia rushes to fill."[58] On the one hand, Mrs. Rafi majestically claims that it is the "task of art" (p. 124) to give light; on the other hand she calmly admits that she sings the song for the personal acclaim she will achieve with it and because "the town expects it of me" (p. 123). Her social pretensions are ridiculed in the elaborate accent: "Bait havver sah hoobull hahs noo-hoo place lake hoo . . . " (p. 123). Coult speaks of the "cheap exploitation of old cultural conditioning."[59] Through the introduction of this song, Bond points out Mrs. Rafi's personal selfishness and the desire for domination that lies behind her artistic facade. He also notes the pressures for conformity within her society. By implication, the hollowness and conventionality of the emotions conveyed in the song are also criticized. Mrs. Rafi is in fact aware that the song is not appropriate, but she is indifferent to artistic integrity as long as she can achieve the desired effects socially. Such blatant unconcern with artistic truth also makes the ensuing efforts to achieve a realistic illusion all the more ludicrous.

Realism is immediately undermined by another song that is equally misplaced in the context. Orpheus is ferried across the river Styx in a punt while the cast hums the "Eton Boating Song." Here again, the only connection with the Orpheus action is the idea of rowing—in all other respects the song is totally incongruous. Bond does not have the cast sing the words, but he obviously expects the audience to recognize the song. This nineteenth-century public school song praises the "old boy" spirit, with a specifically English upper and upper-middle-class consciousness. Rather than reflecting the atmosphere of the tragic legend, in which the Styx is "made from the tears of the penitent and suffering," (p. 126) it is cheerful, confident song about a boating competition. Bond deliberately exploits the effects of these incongruities.

> The "Eton Boating Song" . . . is . . . traditionally associated with Elgarian England. And there's a lady talking about singing this song as she goes into Hell. That is one dislocation. The other is what sort of woman does this, anyway? And what is her purpose . . . ? If one is destroying the comfortable world of the song, one is also destroying her world, the world which uses it. . . . That is one of the general uses of satire.

This song, more than any other in the play, serves to satirize the class consciousness of English tradition.

The artificiality of the performance is brought out sharply as the sound of guns interrupt the rehearsal. The "art" of the town is abruptly confronted with the realities of armies and potential war. The action is set in the year 1907, shortly before the First World War, so this comic confrontation also implies serious political commentary. The sea, as Bond says in his author's note to the 1975 edition, symbolizes, among other things, our moral involvement with other people.[60] Mrs. Rafi has attempted to shut out awareness of the sea during the rehearsal; now the guns force reality into consciousness:

> Open the curtains. . . . The mood of art has been pounded away. If I were doing Lear I could rise to it. But one can't play lutes to the sound of gunfire. (p. 130)

For the time being, reality has won out over artifice.

Another episode in *The Sea* to make use of song is the funeral scene (scene 7), and it is the second comic highlight of the drama. In Bond's view any funeral service represents a misuse of music:

> It's the misuse of things that worries me. Music is used at birth and death. . . . And it's used always to mystify those things. . . . The funeral service is a desecration of the dead and of the living.

Here he creates a grotesque parody of the funeral service; it is Mrs. Rafi's personal misuse of a misused tradition. The histrionic funeral is arranged, directed and performed—in a clear parallel with the rehearsal scene—on a clifftop near the town. It has been carefully planned as a quasi-theatrical performance in which Mrs. Rafi can star, her recitation being intended as the climax. The rivalries and pent up aggressions of this small town society, the result of Mrs. Rafi's social repression, erupt, however, to spoil the performance. The "hymns turn out to be the battleground over which Mrs. Rafi and Tilehouse struggle for power."[61] The musical rivalry leads into a full-fledged physical melee.

The first hymn chosen for the funeral service is, on the surface, appropriate. "Eternal Father, Strong to Save" (pp. 152–53) was written by William Whiting in 1860 and is included in the first edition of the classical *Hymns Ancient and Modern* (1861). Bond quotes two stanzas of the original version, which was subsequently revised in minor points. It is a hymn suitable to a seafaring or a seaside community as in *The Sea*, calling as it does on God to calm the fury of ocean storms and protect those at sea. It is less the text of the song than the manner in which it is performed that draws the audience's attention to Bond's satiric purpose:

> *As they sing a rivalry for the most elaborate descant develops between Mrs Rafi and Mrs Tilehouse. Mrs Tilehouse becomes operatic. Mafanwy stamps out the proper rhythm at the piano. (p. 152)*

As in the farcical rehearsal scene, two influential members of the community are jostling for social and artistic position in utter disregard of the circumstances. Mafanwy at the piano represents the voice of embarrassed conventionality trying to keep up a dignified appearance as she pounds out the rhythm. Mrs. Rafi, the domineering head of local society, sets a decided close to this phase of genteel rivalry with her emphatic sung "A-a-a-a-*men*" (p. 153).

Shortly afterward, the world of artistic pretensions is confronted, as it was in the rehearsal scene, with the world of brutal realities: in the pause between the two hymns the vicar's words are interrupted by the sound of the battery guns firing. The vicar misuses both prayer and song as a means to soothe and pacify and to preserve order and respectability, while the ladies continue their squabbling:

> *Jilly faints and drops the ashes on the ground.*
> . . . .
>
> *Vicar.* Miss Price, the next hymn.
>
> *Mafanwy starts to play 'Eternal Father'. She switches to 'All People'. She stops in confusion and starts to cry. Mrs Tilehouse is trying to sweep up the ashes in her handkerchief.*
> . . . .
> *Rachel starts to beat Hollarcut with the sheet music.*
> *Ladies surround Hollarcut and Hatch and hit them. The Vicar kneels.*
>
> *Vicar.* . . . A prayer in time of war and tumult. (pp. 156–57)

Behind the ludicrous juxtaposition of descant rivalry and scattered ashes, Bond's serious criticism of the misuse of cultural traditions must not be forgotten. Tony Coult observes:

> The whole funeral scene criticizes the use of art and imagination to smother thought, to mystify reality, and so evade responsibility for the life of the community. . . . The scene is part of a socially-correct death-rhythm opposed to the struggling life-rhythm of the growing consciousness within Willy and Rose.[62]

Narrow Road to the Deep North and *The Sea* represent two excellent examples of Bond's exploitation of traditional English song in ironic and satiric functions. Whereas in *Narrow Road* and *Passion* the emphasis is more on satire of political hypocrisy and on political manipulation, the focus in *The Sea* is more on social hypocrisy and moral manipulation. In all of these plays, however, song is seen primarily in negative functions. It is employed to support a repressive system and to preserve a hypocritical status quo.

A-A-AMERICA!

Of Bond's later plays, only the short piece *The Swing* (1976) employs familiar tunes in ironic uses similar to those of the earlier dramas. *The Fool*

(1975) includes two traditional melodies, but in function they differ considerably from the songs in the earlier series of dramas. I intend to treat them together with other works of Bond's second cycle dealing with cultural tradition and the past. Of the double bill *A-A-America!*, the burlesque *Grandma Faust* is the more fantastic and exaggerated. Malcolm Hay and Philip Roberts call it "a comic parable in which caricature and parody are used in an onslaught on slavery, racism and the capitalist ethic."[63] Bond uses new song lyrics of his own composition. As Hay and Roberts point out, the years 1974–77 were years of experiment and investigation for the playwright.[64] The two works that were produced earlier in the same year, *Stone* (June 1976) and the opera *We Come to the River* (July 1976), both began to use primarily original songs, partly—but not exclusively—in commentary functions. The same is also true of the unperformed *Text for a Ballet*, which also was written in 1976. *Grandma Faust* points forward, then, in the direction to which Bond's use of music in drama develops in the future. *The Swing*, on the other hand, subtitled a documentary, is reminiscent of the earlier work. For the last time, Bond employs three traditional tunes in strongly ironic functions. In the order in which they are performed, the more experimental *Grandma Faust* comes first, while the more traditional *The Swing* follows as the second part of *A-A-America!*[65]

Grandma Faust contains two pieces sung by the black man Paul. The first is a spiritual, expressing all the suffering and deprivation of the Negro in the United States. The dramatist remarks, "Paul's spiritual is a legitimate expression of slave feeling." Paul's second song closes the play. Here he sings with a new confidence and a new awareness. He has outwitted his oppressors and sings of freedom in a joyful tone and with a tongue-in-cheek humor:

> Little silver fish for my soul an me
> Dancin t'gether in the bright blue sea
> A golden apple bouncin on the tree
> Pick it an eat it an you will be free.

(p. 29)

This stanza contains the idea of the "Tree of Liberty" that will be developed more fully in some of Bond's later metaphorical pieces. It is the opposite of the tree of sinful knowledge in Christian tradition. The second stanza envisions a fantasy tidal wave of change that will not only destroy the Devil, but also his (or rather her) counterpart, the Lord, in other words the entire repressive morality of Christian tradition:

> When the river's as wide as it is long
> It'll be a sea for ships to sail on
> When waves are as high as the sea is broad

They'll flush out the devil and drown the lawd.

(p. 29)

Originally the final song ended here.[66] In the revised version printed in *Theatre Poems and Songs*, and then in the new Eyre Methuen edition of 1981, Bond has added a new stanza of a strongly didactic nature that confirms this interpretation of the symbolism:

> Now here's the moral of this here show
> Wise man said long time ago
> No man step in the same river twice
> Why the fish his world just flow away!
> Ain no knowed way of making it stay
> How's your world folks? You snug in bed?
> Once every day your world stand on its head.

(p. 29)

Referring here to an axiom of Heraclitus, it is asserted that change is as inevitable as the flowing of the river and cannot be stopped. Bond now ends with a direct appeal to the audience to compare its condition with the situations of rebellion and change portrayed in the drama. The addition of this final stanza is an indication that Bond felt that the social commentary had not been strong enough. It shows the direction in which his work as a whole develops later in his career. "Spirituals are songs of protest, but they're also songs of solace, and I wanted to guard against the emphasis being too much on solace, . . . make it a more active use of music."

The Swing differs musically from *Grandma Faust* in its use of traditional tunes.[67] In its extreme violence, it approaches *Lear* in horror. Although it is a minor piece, written for a specific occasion, its ending is one of Bond's most savage. Its music, by contrast, is deliberately lighthearted. Bond, basing his documentary on a historical incident, is examining the influence of cultural heritage. Part of the purpose in employing familiar songs is to point out the discrepancy between traditional culture and the actual social situation portrayed. By inviting the audience to sing along, the playwright challenges cultural assumptions and indicates complicity. The modern musical fashion in the play—vaudeville—is a superficial and frivolous form of entertainment, inadequate for expressing the horror and decadence of reality.

Mrs. Kroll's song "Life is a Milliner's Show" (also known as "I Wore a Little Grey Bonnet") is an inane piece of superficial flirtation. Life is determined by fashion and outward appearances. The Quaker girl, pretending to be innocent and demure, supposedly does not notice the advances of a young man until he is kissing her under her plain little grey bonnet. It is from the show *The Quaker Girl* (1911), written by Lionel Monckton, who was a successful composer of musical comedy and operetta such as the *Country Girl*

(1902) and *The Dancing Mistress* (1912). The tune is contemporary with the setting of the play; the newest of the current hits, as it were. The lyrics are coy and pert, the melody is a cheerful one in quick waltz time. It creates a mood of discrepancy with the shooting:

> This is a typical music-hall number, with a music-hall orchestra backing it. . . . I chose it because the idea of life being a hat show contrasts so strongly with the reality shown in the play and shows the failure of most of the people in the play to understand their society. . . . It's very important that this is got right because it affects the whole atmosphere of the lynching.[68]

Bond describes the style of scene 3 as "the farcical-tragedy of the ordinary,"[69] indicating the inability of the audience to grasp the seriousness of the situation.

When the second song sung during the shooting scene, "The Daring Young Man on the Flying Trapeze" (p. 74), begins it is important that the live audience be invited to join in on this familiar music-hall and circus tune. As Bond remarks, "When anyone is swinging in a comical way in England it's almost an automatic response for spectators to sing it! It's a very corny reaction."[70] Writing to the German translator of *The Swing*, he cautions her to choose some well-known comic song here "so that the audience can sing a snatch of it."[71] In the play it is sung by the (invisible) theater audience, implying their collective guilt. If the live audience joins in during performance, it becomes, by analogy, an accomplice. The audience in the play is in an almost hysterical state of exhilaration—screaming, laughing and singing—an image of society out of control. Yet the song sung is corny, light and comic in nature. Here again Bond intended a brutally ironic contrast with the real situation: "The song is terribly inappropriate to Fred's condition, and so the effect is very cruel."[72] It serves as a satiric exposure of the society's lack of moral responsibility.

At the climax of the violence the scene ends with yet another song, the American national anthem:

> *Last volley. Audience noise explodes. Fred has keeled over. He swings slowly and silently upside down. Blood falls and swishes over the stage. . . . Skinner starts to sing the American national anthem. The vaudeville orchestra joins in, in full, sonorous orchestration, and then the audience. Skinner raises his hat and waves it like a venerable senator. The lights go. The music plays on.* (p. 76)

This brutal juxtaposition of violence and patriotism exposes the American nation as a society of violent repression and hypocrisy. The public (the audience) and those in positions of responsibility (Skinner as senator) are satirically revealed as equally guilty of the social ills of the nation.

A-A-America! represents an interesting transitional phase in the use of song in Bond's work. *Grandma Faust* looks forward to later works, as it introduces

American national anthem and violent death in Edward Bond's *The Swing*; photograph from Malcolm Hay and Philip Roberts, *Edward Bond: A Companion to the Plays* (London: Theatre Quarterly Publications, 1978), p. 71. Photo by Alex Levac.

lyrics that express limited social commentary and the hope for change. *The Swing* forms the conclusion of the development of the earlier phase, using familiar tunes for ironic contrast and satiric exposure. The singing of the American national anthem at the moment of Fred's violent death is one of the most brutally ironic situations in all of Bond's work. Even the singing of "Abide With Me" as Shogo's city is stormed in *Narrow Road to the Deep North* or the playing of the English national anthem at the crucifixion of the pig in *Passion* cannot quite compare with this effect.

3. Song as Celebration in a Rural Folk Culture

Bond's dramas *The Fool* (1975) and *The Woman* (1978)—both belonging to the series of plays on cultural heritage and the past—form a category of their own. These dramas use music in a function not occurring elsewhere: it incorporates the spirit and cohesion of relatively simple rural communities of the past at the moment when they are threatened by forces of change. As such, they offer a contrast to the early plays that employed song as expression of the solidarity of degenerate modern youth gangs. *Bingo* (1973), which also belongs to this series of history plays, contains no tunes at all.

THE FOOL

At the beginning of *The Fool*, an early nineteenth-century rural English community is portrayed as outwardly intact but imperiled. Traditional social relationships and class hierarchies function, but social repression and the roots of rebellion are obvious. The village lads have arrived at Lord Milton's to present the traditional Christmas mummers' play. The play takes place as usual: portrayed is the final phase of a traditional culture at the point of breaking up. The year is 1815, the Napoleonic wars are over, and prices and wages are beginning to fall. The ensuing social disruptions are not only a result of the wars, they are also a consequence of the upheavals of the industrial revolution. These changes will mark the end of much of traditional English folk culture, including the mummers' play.

The mummers' plays were old rural folk plays that endured into the middle of the nineteenth century, until "the advance of enclosures . . . brought about the ultimate degeneration of the agricultural labourer."[73] They are part of a very old heritage; indeed, the mock death and resurrection are derived from pagan rituals. They are "survivals of ceremonies intended to promote agricultural fertility."[74] "Their central incident symbolizes . . . the annual death of the year or the fertilization spirit and its annual resurrection in spring."[75] Bond's mummers sing a piece that clearly reflects the ritual origins of their performance as a fertility ceremony:

> Hal-an-tow jolly rumble-o
> For we were up as soon as any day-o
> An for to sing for summer come
> The summer an the may-o
> For summer will a-come-o
> The winter will a-goo-o.[76]

"Hal-an-Tow" is traditionally associated with May rituals in Helston, Cornwall. Bond has altered a few words to suit his winter context: instead of "For summer *is* a-come-o / And winter *is* a-gone-o," Bond writes *will*. Otherwise, the text is traditional.[77]

The second song of the mummers, "Hunting the Wren," is also appropriate to a mummers' play.[78]

> How'll we eat him? says Robin the bobbin,
> . . . .
> With knives an' forks says Robin the bobbin,
> . . . .
> Eyes to the blind says Robin the bobbin,

HELG YN DREEAN
HUNT THE WREN

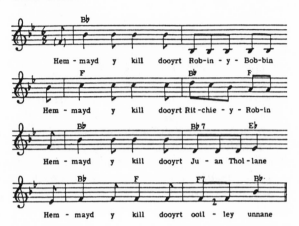

Hem - mayd y kill dooyrt Rob-in - y - Bob-bin

Hem - mayd y kill dooyrt Rit -chie - y - Rob-in

Hem - mayd y kill dooyrt Ju - an Thol-lane

Hem - mayd y kill dooyrt ooil - ley unnane

1 Hemmayd y kill *dooyrt Robin-y-Bobbin*
   Hemmayd y kill *dooyrt Ritchie-y-Robin*
   Hemmayd y kill *dooyrt Juan Thollane*
   Hemmayd y kill *dooyrt ooilley unnane*

2 Cre'n fa shen? *dooyrt Robin-y-Bobbin*
   (*etc.*)

3 Dy helg y dreean

4 C'raad t'eh? C'raad t'eh?

5 Soie ayns y crouw

6 Kys yiowmayd geddyn?

7 Ceau clagh, ceau clagh

8 Nish t'eh marroo

9 Crenaght ymmyrk eh?

10 Ayns sleod ymleyder

11 Crenaght coagyr eh?

12 Harrish y voain

13 Crenaght neemayd g'ee eh?

14 Lesh meir ain

15 Quoi hig yinnair?

16 Yn Ree as Ven-rein

17 Sooillyn y doal, *dooyrt Robin-y-Bobbin*
   Lurgyn y croobagh, *dooyrt Ritchie-y-Robin*
   Scrobbag ny moght, *dooyrt Juan Thollane*
   Crauyn y moddee, *dooyrt ooilley unnane*

18 Dreean, dreean, Ree n'eeanlee
   Laa'll Steoain marroo ayns y connee
   Ga t'eh beg e cleinney mooar
   Cur dooin jough, ven-thie, dy liooar'

1 Let's go to the wood, *said Robin-the-Bobbin*
   Let's go to the wood, *said Ritchie-the-Robin*
   Let's go to the wood, *said Juan Thollane*
   Let's go to the wood, *said everyone*

2 Why do we go there? *said Robin-the-Bobbin*
   (*etc.*)

3 To hunt the wren

4 Where is he? Where is he?

5 Sitting in the bush

6 How'll we get him?

7 Throw a stone, throw a stone

8 Now he is dead

9 How to carry him?

10 In the brewer's sledge

11 How to cook him?

12 Over the turf

13 How'll we eat him?

14 With our fingers

15 Who'll come to dinner?

16 The King and the Queen

17 Eyes to the blind, *says Robin-the-Bobbin*
   Legs to the lame, *says Ritchie-the-Robin*
   Crop to the poor, *says Juan Thollane*
   Bones to the dogs, *says everyone*

18 The wren, the wren, the king of the birds
   St. Stephen's day he's caught in the furze
   Although he is small, his family's great
   Give us plenty of drink, woman, plenty to eat

"Hunt the Wren," in *Folksongs of Britain and Ireland,* ed. Peter Kennedy (London: Cassell, 1975), p. 188.

Legs to the lame says Richie the robin,
Scraps to the poor says Jack a the land,
Bones to the dogs says everyone.

The wren the wren is king a the birds,
Saint Stephen's Day he's caught in the furze,
Although he is little his family is great,
We pray yoo good people to give us a treat.

(p. 5)

This melody, too, has its origins in ancient ritual. As A. L. Lloyd explains in *Folk Song in England*, "We know that the wren-hunting song was attached to a pagan midwinter ritual of the kind that Church and authority fulminated vainly against."[79] The strange lines about the partition and devouring of this tiny bird ("How'll we eat him? . . . With knives an' forks") are part of an ancient sacrificial rite,

> that central agrarian rite involving a sacrifice, human or other, at some critical time of the farming calendar, aimed at the regeneration of natural forces.[80]

The human sacrifice was gradually "replaced by a symbolic deputy such as the wren 'king of the birds' or the herring 'king of the sea.'"[81] Lloyd continues, "His various parts were distributed and eaten as a charm that passed on his divine qualities."[82] "Hunting the Wren" is often thought of as a harmless children's piece, because its ritual origins have largely been forgotten. The lads of the village in *The Fool* are in all probability no longer aware of the significance of the song they sing. Nor can it be assumed that they still believe their seasonal performance of the mummers' play will help to ensure agricultural fertility.

A version of this ancient song known as "The Cutty Wren" has for many centuries been associated with the idea of rebellion against injustice and oppression. As early as the Peasants' Revolt of 1381, it was sung as expression of defiance and hope, "the little wren symbolising power and property."[83] In the words of John McDonnell, "The wariness cloaking a mounting anger comes across clearly in *The Cutty Wren* . . . where the oppressive enemy is symbolised by the Wren, the King of all Birds."[84] Bond, well acquainted with contemporary English drama, surely knew that Arnold Wesker had introduced "The Cutty Wren" into his play *Chips With Everything* (1962) as a symbol of class rebellion.[85] Here, to emphasize traditional cultural roots the playwright deliberately chose the more ritualistic, rather than the more militant version. "At that stage in the play I didn't need that. I wanted that to come out in the process of the play. At that stage I wanted it to be a traditional culture which was going to be broken up," he says.

The primary function of the mummers' play and of both songs is to portray a state of folk culture in which ancient customs, although perhaps no longer fully understood, are still observed with a natural self-assurance. Bond writes:

> The 'Mummers' play shouldn't be gauche—like the rustics' play in *Midsummer Night's Dream*. We should feel they have their own expertise, that their clothes have a real eye for colour and design—they aren't at all Walt Disneyish. They should be very competent dancers and singers: it is their culture, and they can still express themselves in it.[86]

As the rest of the drama portrays the destruction not only of village society but also of its culture, it is perhaps logical that Bond introduces no further songs. What remains after the execution of Darkie is a disintegrating Clare who cannot reconcile the world of his imagination and his social conscience with the realities of changing society, and who, like the General in *We Come to the River*, is exiled to a madhouse until he really does lose his sanity. The working-class characters of the drama have a kind of resilience, but they are still groping for direction. Their rebellion has no cohesion as did the traditional folk culture. On the other hand, the urban culture shown in the second half of the play is revealed as hollow and superficial, even inhuman. It presents no alternative to a lost folk culture.

THE WOMAN

The Woman (1978), the last in Bond's series of plays about the past, uses music primarily in functions similar to those of *The Fool*. Song here indicates the intact spirit of a rural community of the past. In this case, however, the community also contains elements of a utopian future. In contrast with *The Fool*, which portrays an English village by means of traditional English folk tunes, *The Woman* employs new texts by Bond set to music by Hans Werner Henze, the composer who had written the music to *We Come to the River* two years earlier. Bond wanted to connect Greek heritage and contemporary Western society. Newly composed melodies seemed the best way of doing this: contemporary music best comprises the fusion of idyllic past and utopian future as threatened by a discordant present. Although Bond was not wholly satisfied with the tunes composed by Henze, he finds it hard to envision a better kind of music:

> I think that's a very, very difficult problem, because in some sense one says it's got to be ethnic music, or ancient music, but one can't do that. They are songs of a historical festival . . . something equivalent to "Hunting the Wren" for that society. . . . But the trouble is that modern realizations of that sort of music always sound like reconstructions of Egyptian music by Cecil B. de Mille.

In this respect Henze's score, inspired by Sicilian and southern Italian folk music, presents a good solution.

In part 1, as the Greeks and Trojans are in the throes of war, Bond does not yet use song as expression of harmony; it does, however, denote common purpose. The only mention of singing in part 1 occurs in scene 12 when the crowd of Trojan beggars storms the temple and removes the statue of the goddess of fortune. These are "the poor, starved, wounded, sick, lame, crazed"[87]—the victims of this irrational war—and they are desperately resolved. The violence of their actions and reactions as they carry out the goddess must be understood as a direct consequence of their deep sufferings:

> Out! Out! Out! Throw her out! Chuck her out! Get rid of her!
> Out Out! Out! Bitch! Bitch! Bitch! No more bitch! Out!
> *The Beggars spin, stamp, shout, chant, laugh, cry—but above all dance and sing.* (p. 49)

No text is given for the song they sing, because their united actions are more important than their words. The song is an indication of almost hysterical tension, repressed hatred, and the joy of release, but Bond wants attention focused on the common purpose of the crowd: the return of the statue to the Greeks. For this reason he emphasizes that the crowd should have no individuality,[88] and for the same reason their song has no words. The scene is crucial, because the revolt of the Trojan poor seals the doom of Troy.

At the beginning of part 2 the contrast with part 1 is worked out. According to Hay and Roberts:

> After the intensity of this scene [part 1, scene 14], the opening of Part Two shows a calmer, less inhuman world. The village festival—the song, the dance and the start of the footrace—at once establishes a feeling of natural community life.[89]

It is, however, not an idyll, but rather a historical community, subject to tensions from within and without. The effect that Bond intends through song and ceremony is twofold: the contrast between this primitive but harmonious island and the war-ravaged, hate-torn urban society of Troy illustrates both what civilized Troy has lost and what the earlier form of culture on the island is threatened with. On the other hand, the ceremony tells us a great deal about the social relationships on the island itself. The song is expression of a culture that is based on mutual trust and understanding, the prerequisites of peace. The contrast between the tunes sung in parts 1 and 2 thus illustrates the organization of the societies.

The rural island population still uses ritual and dance to ensure fertility. Men are closely bound up with the soil and the sea; the mummers' play and the songs sung in *The Fool* were also originally connected with fertility rites. Here, as in *The Fool*, rural society is endangered, but as yet its cohesion is embodied in its songs and its culture. Part 2 is framed at beginning and end by community rituals to assure a bountiful catch for this fishing village. The first sound of part 2 is music, the first action a sacrifice for the spring. As symbolical loaves of bread and a platter of fish are publicly paraded in procession as an offering to the gods, the boys of the village sing a traditional song. The village girls dance to the tune. Their ceremony reminds us in some of its details—especially the wearing of goat-skin costume or mask—of the fertility rites from the southern Balkans and Greece that Chambers sees as congeners of the English mummers' plays.[90] Bond certainly intends a symbolical connection between the fertility ritual in *The Woman* and the mummers' play ritual in *The Fool*. Both are a form of comment on the nature of social relationships in their respective communities.

The effect the modern music has in this scene is not at all folksy:

> The dance is a simple folk dance, but Hans Werner Henze's music for the song that accompanies it is atonal in style. . . . Bond does not want to allow the audience to relax completely.[91]

The tune is strongly rhythmic, underlined by percussion and clapping, and slightly syncopated, but it is not unharmonious. The overall effect is that of controlled joy and exuberance. The exclamation "To fish! Fish! Fish!" at the end is almost shouted. The dance that follows is accompanied by strong, rhythmic stamping and clapping.[92] Hay and Roberts quote in this context from an unpublished interview with Bond in which he explains that his primary intention in presenting such ritual songs on stage is not to create atmosphere but to comment and to incite analysis:

> I don't want to record. I want to comment. So I only record as much as is necessary for people to recognise, then I start analysing in order for them not to recognise but to think, to resituate the situation that I show. I didn't want the audience to be able to say: "Oh yes, we know where we are."[93]

At the end of part 2 the situation is far more dangerous. The Greeks have traced Hecuba and Ismene, and their search for the goddess threatens to destroy the entire island community. The storm at the end is not only a herald of the winter season; it also symbolizes the force of history and the possibility of change. The concluding song takes up the image of the storm. In a kind of ritual incantation, the elementary powers of nature are harnessed so that they appear conciliatory towards and helpful to man. The girls' dance this time physically imitates the wind, while the boys' singing aurally evokes the noise of thunder, wind and storm. The tone sounds not only energetic but also gleeful: the music is not menacing but cheerful, with a reed instrument playfully imitating the rising and falling wind.

> *The Girls dance, imitating the wind.*
> Girls. Wheeeeeeeeee!
> *Boys. (Imitating thunder.)*
> Boom! Boom! Boom!

> Sea rocks the boat
> Big man's cradle
> *Girls.* Wheeeeeeeeee!
> *Boys. (Sing.)*
> Boom! Boom! Boom!
> Wind blows wheeeee!
> God panting on his woman
>
> Crack bang! Crack bang!
> Old man thunder
> Broke his walking stick
> And fell down in the sea!

(p. 101)

The boat rocked in the storm is associated in the first stanza with a baby's cradle and is seen in a context of mothering and care. In the second stanza the fury of the storm is related to the energy of human sexuality: "God panting on his woman." And in the third stanza the power of the thunder is rendered harmless by personification as an old man, "Old man thunder." The movement of the storm in the three stanzas is patterned according to the rhythms of human life, from childhood via mature sexuality to old age. Nature is seen in human terms and thus rendered less dangerous, more of a companion. The storm as image of change does not seem threatening but promising. The real storm at the end of the play may cost Hecuba's life, but it also heralds transition to a new era of peace and harmony.

The juxtaposition of this ritual song with the footrace that is to determine the fate of the village makes the vital importance of the ceremony all the more clear. From the outsiders Hecuba and the Dark Man come the experience of suffering and the determination to take revolutionary action. But it is from the community itself, held together by the acceptance of such ritual, that these outsiders derive much of their strength to resist the Greeks. And it is significant that the play ends on a note of strength and continuity with the performance of yet another rite, the young men's race as part of the funeral games. These rituals are worth preserving, but it is only through revolutionary action that such traditional values can be maintained.

Bond's setting of part 2 on an island creates symbolic connections to the traditions of literary utopia, which often has an island setting, and to the Arcadian pastoral, which frequently takes the form of "piscatory eclogue" in a fishing society.[94] Certainly the harmony of this island, as expressed in its ritual songs—harmony of man with man and of man with nature—is closely related to other utopian visions of the future in Bond's work: for example, that of the closing scene of *The Bundle* and the vision projected in Rose's "Dream" song in *Restoration*.

Both *The Fool* and *The Woman* introduce song as embodiment of a cohesive village society and intact rural folk culture. Both dramas employ songs with ritualistic function. In *The Woman* the people still believe in the efficacy of the ritual, whereas *The Fool* represents a late and degenerate form of ritual in which the original significance has largely been forgotten. Bond does not, however, intend to present an idyll: in both cases the negative forces of change menace the communities and the negative consequences of progress and civilization are clearly presented. The positive forces of change may indeed be incorporated in a society of the future. The belief in the subtle connection between natural seasons and human life lends the community of *The Woman* courage and resilience and gives the lives of its inhabitants a deeper meaning.

4. Political Commentary, Parable, and Metaphor in Original Song

From about 1976 or a little earlier, music in Bond's drama undergoes a major shift in focus. The first series of plays through *The Sea* tends to employ song in ironic and satiric functions. Most are traditional English melodies. Certainly they are intended as a kind of comment on society, but this comment is primarily indirect. The familiar lyrics do not state a moral; the implied judgment is instead left up to the audience. The same is true of the tunes in *The Fool* and *The Woman*: these are no longer satirical, but the meaning must still be inferred from the context in which they are sung.

In Bond's work after about 1976, direct commentary gains in importance. Many of the songs in his later works draw a moral, or state the theme in an outspoken manner. Others function indirectly, often making use of metaphor or parable to convey a lesson. These new pieces almost invariably have original lyrics written by Bond. After 1976 the playwright employs very few traditional melodies in his work. As the morals of his parable plays become more and more explicit, so also do the moral lessons of his commentary or parable songs.

This experimentation with commentary is apparently not entirely a late development in Bond's work. Hay and Roberts describe the unpublished *The Golden Age*, written for the Royal Court writers' group in 1959–60, as "a parable play with songs (similar in style to those in *Stone*), retelling the story of the Good Samaritan."[95] It was not until about 1976, however, that these early attempts were taken up again and reworked in a mature context.

WE COME TO THE RIVER

We Come to the River was first performed one month after *Stone* in July 1976, but was written two years earlier. The piece was designed from the beginning as an opera libretto for the composer Hans Werner Henze and not as a drama with songs. The music plays a far more integral role than in any other Bond work (with the exception of his other opera libretto *The Cat*). Sung passages have a different total effect in opera than they do in a spoken stage play; they are not set off from the rest of the text by the musical medium, but are part of the total musical conception. Despite the fact that Bond has isolated certain lyrical passages from the opera and printed them as songs in *Theatre Poems and Songs*, such pieces cannot be directly compared to the songs in his other work. They correspond more closely in function to the lyrical sections of traditional opera, whether aria, duet, or chorus. They are indeed set off from the surrounding prose dialogue by their lyrical verse form. But they are not set off by the musical medium from a spoken surrounding. For these reasons the opera is only partially comparable to Bond's other work and thus only conditionally relevant to the theme of song in drama.

On the other hand, *We Come to the River* is very much an integral part of the canon. The action of the opera displays the same concern with social and political reality, with repression and freedom as Bond's other work of this period, and the ending is as optimistic—or more so—than that of *Stone*. The technique of simultaneous staging is used to highlight a concern that is particularly vital to Bond's artistic work: the demonstration of political causes and effects. Above all, two major aspects of the opera are especially relevant: the theme of the corruptibility of music under a reactionary government and the idea of a new music for a new society.

One cannot fail to recognize the irony that two such committed left-wing artists as Bond and Henze are using opera, that archetype of bourgeois conservative state-subsidized theater, for their ends. Such other dramatists of similar convictions as John McGrath would not want a play to be put on in the National Theatre, to say nothing of Covent Garden or the West Berlin Opera where *We Come to the River* was presented. Bond, however, believes in using all means available:

> The NT . . . has resources of space, time, skill and technology that we can use to strengthen our work and relate it more closely to our age. . . . We must not merely occupy the fringe but the centre.[96]

When asked about his awareness of writing for a typically bourgeois opera audience, the dramatist replied cautiously:

> I felt there would be no point in going through the game of producing something that was a piece of agit-prop and that they wouldn't like. They would all have the great pleasure of being able to get up and walk out and slam doors. I didn't see any point in doing all that. Why get all these people involved—because an opera is a big job. So I wanted to say, given a large modern orchestra, how can one use these things for one's own purpose, taking over what opera singers can do . . . try to use their skills.

The interrelationship between text and music in this opera will be summarized, then a few selected song examples will be analyzed, primarily from the textual standpoint.[97]

Words and music in *We Come to the River* have been fused into a new entity differing greatly from a drama with songs. In his volume of essays entitled *Musik und Politik* (translated with a slightly different selection of essays as *Music and Politics*), Henze emphasizes the new unity of text and music in this work:

> Edward Bond hat das Libretto 'Actions for music' genannt, und in der Tat sind sein Libretto und die Handlungen, die es enthält, in vielfacher Hinsicht undenkbar als Schauspiel: alles, was darin vor sich geht—und die Art und Weise, in der es vor sich geht—, ist auf Musik gerichtet und an die Musik. Man muss noch einen Schritt weitergehen und sagen: an meine Musik.

> [Edward Bond described his libretto as 'Actions for Music', and in fact his libretto and the actions it contains are in many respects inconceivable as a stage-play: everything that takes place—and the way in which it takes place—is aimed at music. You have to go a step further and say aimed at *my* music.][98]

Bond expresses himself in much the same way when he writes of his libretto:

> I found that when I wrote the libretto for the opera . . . I was not merely providing language to be set to music, in the way a nineteenth century libretto would be set, but that I was throwing language into a cauldron; that its meaning would have to be recreated by the music; that the music would not merely colour it or comment on it. . . . The sound world Henze created . . . was . . . an analysis of the various events.[99]

In this view, Bond is very much in accordance with the newer agonistic theories of song and theatrical performance outlined in the introduction. Meaning is recreated in performance through the creative interaction of elements. It also means that the libretto is shorter and more concentrated than the text of any other major drama. After a substantial revision in 1974 Henze writes:

> Jetzt ist alles geraffter, klarer. Man muss sich vorstellen, wieviel länger ein gesungener Satz ist gegenüber einem gesprochenen, wieviel Zeit Musik braucht, um einen Satz "über die Rampe" zu bringen. . . . Bond . . . ist . . . ein "Handwerker," der es vorzüglich versteht, sich auf die musikalischen Gegebenheiten einzustellen.

> [Everything is now much more concise, much clearer. You must remember how much longer it takes to sing a sentence than to speak it, how much time music needs to get a sentence "across the footlights." Bond is a "craftsman" who is an expert in adapting himself to the necessities of the music.][100]

Aesthetically, one can note a similarity in the positions of composer and dramatist, for while Bond emphasizes that his theater language is becoming more musical, to the point where he says "speech is a form of music,"[101] Henze is increasingly concerned with creating music that approaches speech: "Was ich möchte, ist, zu erreichen, dass Musik Sprache wird." ["What I hope to achieve is that music becomes language."][102] Bond and Henze appreciate each other not just on an artistic but also on a political level. Indeed, for both of them political and aesthetic considerations are inseparable. Henze, in his more recent work after 1968, is trying to develop a modern form of musical realism that makes extensive use of traditional musical expression to shed light on contemporary political and social reality. This has been called a "humanist" conception of music,[103] much as Bond has called his theater "humanist" theater.[104] Bond says of Henze:

> He's a man I admire immensely because he understands the social responsibilities of music, and wishes to explore musical forms in relation to people's needs, rather than just the formal needs of music.

Henze's music in *We Come to the River* is not abstract; it is closely adapted to the text, but it tries to analyze rather than illustrate the meaning. In the opera, Henze distinguishes between the music of those in power, the "music of violence," (Musik der Gewalt) and the music of the victims.[105] In part 1, the music of the oppressors dominates. But rather than choosing to illustrate violence and repression directly by such means as dissonant or harsh music, Henze's technique in this part is based primarily on the principle of parody and musical satire. He uses old-fashioned musical traditions of middle-class society to represent the banal, frivolous nature of this world: military marches, dance music, waltzes, and coloratura arias, for example. The music of those in power is loud, brassy, and vulgar. Henze divides the musicians into three separate orchestras, corresponding to Bond's actions played on three different stages. Most of the music of those in power is played by orchestra 3; it is composed of stringed instruments amplified by microphones, brass, and woodwinds.[106] In this way the composer wishes to indicate that the world of the oppressors is old-fashioned, indeed already dying, although its representatives do not realize this.

The music of the victims, on the other hand, is played by instruments not traditional in opera or concert hall, but that have long been associated with popular and folk music. The music of the victims is played mostly by orchestra 1, which consists of two viola da gamba, a guitar, a mouth organ, a piano, and percussion, such as cow bells, gong, tambourine and log drums.[107] In part 1 this music still sounds weak, endangered, helpless, tender, and fragile. It can scarcely make itself heard against the music of the oppressors. In part 2, the music of the victims becomes stronger and stronger, while the music of violence slowly becomes petrified and dies away. Finally, the music of the victims takes over completely, symbolizing the hope in a new music for a new society. As the author and composer say in their collaborative program note:

> The first half of this opera is dramatic. The second half is closer to ritual . . . Our ritual celebrates man's responsibility to man . . . we are interested in the new consciousness that men create for themselves when they begin to change their society.[108]

The final sections of Bond's "Orpheus and the Wire," written later, seem to represent the feeling at the end of the opera exactly:

> . . . I have seen fools lose power
> And learned how they lose it
> . . . .
> And therefore I praise this world
> In music.[109]

One of the most striking features of the opera is the simultaneous staging of as many as three scenes on three different stages, each with its own orchestra fully visible. Bond sees this experiment as a logical continuation of his earlier efforts to create a new epic theater, a theater that emphasizes analysis of causes and effects as portrayed in contrasting scenes. But he also stresses the aid that the musical medium gives to this principle of simultaneity:

> Well, it's a continuation of some of those things. What I wanted to do is put on the stage scenes happening at the one and the same time and it seemed to me a very good idea to do this with music, because music is contrapuntal anyway, so that one could counterpoint these visual and action elements as well, at the same time.[110]

Bond uses the simultaneous staging to contrast the worlds of the rulers and their victims, thus pointing out responsibility and consequences.

Henze often exploits this technique of simultaneity to suggest contrasts and contradictions musically. In this way he illustrates particularly vividly the corruptibility of music, because music is heard in totally inappropriate contexts, indicating perversion. An excellent example is found in scenes 4 through 7. The dominant music of scene 4 is dance music: mazurkas and waltzes. While this music is suitable to the celebration and dance in the assembly rooms, the simultaneous staging of scenes 4, 5 and 6 means that this music is also heard together with the scene in which the General learns he is going blind (scene 5) and the scene in which the condemned Deserter speaks of the hardships of his early life (scene 6). Fragments of this waltz music are then—as it were carelessly—carried over into scene 7 in which the Deserter is shot (most audible just after the shooting), so that we have a deliberate evocation of the misuse of music in fascist Germany. Both Henze and Bond have made the intended parallel to Auschwitz explicit. Bond writes in his poem "On Music" that accompanies *We Come to the River:* "At Auschwitz they hanged men to waltzes."[111] Henze comments on the effect of the music in these scenes:

> So drückt sich Ohnmacht aus, und gleichzeitig wird Anklage erhoben, und gleichzeitig wird eine Assoziation geschaffen zu dem entsetzlichen Bild der Lagerkapelle von Auschwitz, die auf Anordnung der Lagerleitung zu Hinrichtungen aufspielen musste. . . . Hier wird Gewalt selbst durch einen Akt von Gewaltanwendung dargestellt.

> [Thus a feeling of powerlessness is expressed at the same time as an accusation is made, and also an association with that horrifying image of the camp orchestra at Auschwitz, which by order of the commandant had to play at executions. . . . Here violence is itself portrayed by means of an act of violence.][112]

The effect is equally jarring when the regimental band for scene 10 begins its music while the battlefield scene (scene 9) continues. The juxtaposition of the anguished cries of the wounded with the cheerful band music makes the latter appear callous and brutal.

Among the sung lyrical passages, the arias, or songs, of this opera, one of the most interesting instances of the music of the oppressors is the "Ladies' Anthem" in scene 4. It also provides an excellent illustration of Henze's technique of musical parody. The text, the style of the song, and its music all serve to expose the perverted norms of society. The combination of religion, patriotism and the violence of war shows the misuse made of these values by a repressive regime:

> Clouds sweep over the battlefield
> Over the sacrifice
> It is an altar for the fatherland

> God has granted the prayer
> Uttered by the gun
> He gives peace to the fatherland.

(p. 86)

The gun is personified and associated with human piety and patriotism. The language is stilted and conventional. In the Schott edition the stage direction to sing reads "sing with cold white voices,"[113] exemplifying sterility and artificiality.

Henze's music for this song also aims at ridiculing the cultural values of established society, thus underlining Bond's intention without directly illustrating the text. The ladies begin with an exalted, sweetly harmonious choral passage. Henze has then composed a coloratura aria for Rachel with

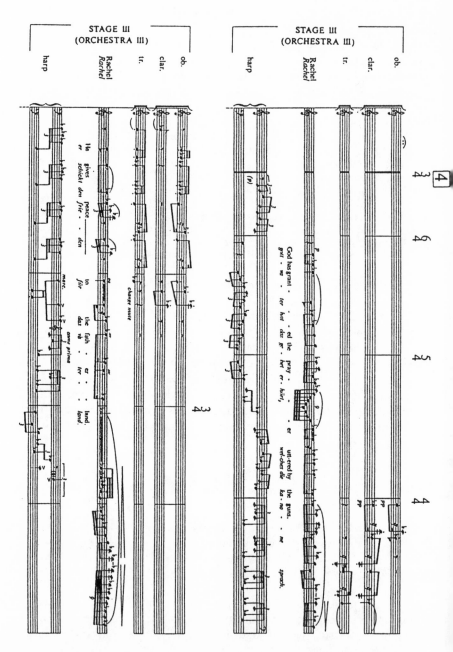

From "Ladies' Anthem," in *We Come to the River*, text by Edward Bond, music by Hans Werner Henze, Studienpartitur (score) (Mainz, W. Germany: B. Schott's Söhne, n.d.), p. 47. © B. Schott's Söhne, Mainz, 1976. All rights reserved. Used by permission of European American Music Distributors Corporation, sole U.S. and Canadian agent for B. Schott's Söhne.

harp accompaniment that would be appropriate in traditional opera. Here, however, the elaborate ornamentation of coloratura seems artificial, a pompous society praising itself in a pretentious style. The most elaborate ornamentation falls on or immediately after the end of the lines, emphasizing words such as "sacrifice," "fatherland," "prayer," and "guns." Becker and Müller comment:

> Die Aria, die Tochter Rachel dem Sieger dichtete, von traditioneller Koloratur-schwierigkeiten, wie sie in allen Opernhäusern dieser Welt tausendmal goutiert . . . wird, hält diesem Kulturbetrieb seinen Spiegel vor, verweist auf die Kompromittierbarkeit der Musik.

> [The aria which the daughter Rachel has composed for the victor is full of the difficult coloratura which delights audiences in all opera houses of the world; this aria satirizes the culture market and shows that music is corruptible.][114]

Henze is not only ridiculing middle-class society through his choice of musical style, he is also making a serious comment on the misuse of traditional culture in the interests of war and oppression.

As mentioned, the music of the victims gains strength very gradually during the second half of the opera. Part 2 opens with the music of a single viola da gamba, alternating with the percussion of a Madman who is dressed from head to toe in an assortment of bells and cymbals.[115] The fragility and remoteness of the Mad People's world are incorporated in the music. The first two songs in part 2 are songs of the Mad People and represent a phase in the music of the victims in which they have not yet achieved a positive consciousness. The songs in scene 13 express a desire for escape from the fears and repressions of the society that has driven them mad. But for Bond there can be no escape into an imaginary world of harmony: the solution must be fought out in the real world. The Mad People "are quiet, slow and withdrawn. They move like clouds on the tops of mountains" (p. 105). As they sail off to their imaginary island refuge, they sing of escape, but also of fear:

> The boat goes over the water
> Birds fly from the broken sea
> The iron chain drops to the deep
> Like a silent killer.
>
> (p. 106)

The words "like a silent killer" are emphasized in performance, sung threateningly in staccato and piano by the voices of the lower registers. "Killer" is almost whispered. The Mad People sing of "tears" and of their vulnerability. Their hands are weak and small as a child's. In this song an association is established between the Mad People and children, the weakest of the victims.

The last three songs in the opera also belong to the world of the victims. By

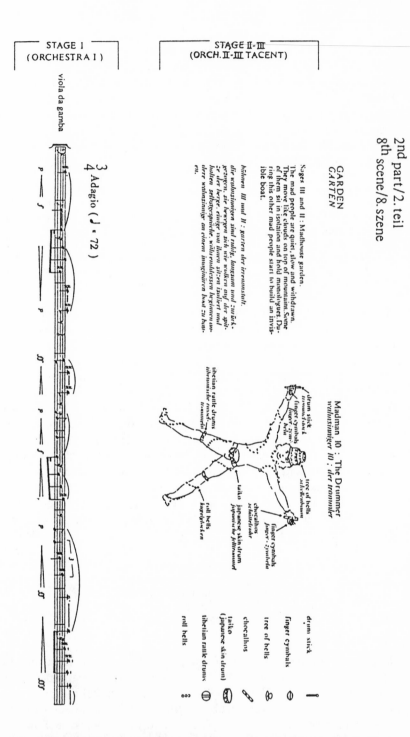

From Bond/Henze, *We Come to the River*, part two, scene 13 (Madhouse Garden), music by Hans Werner Henze, Studienpartitur (score) (Mainz, W. Germany: B. Schott's Söhne, n.d.), p. 286. © B. Schott's Söhne, Mainz, 1976. All rights reserved. Used by permission of European American Music Distributors Corporation, sole U.S. and Canadian agent for B. Schott's Söhne.

now the music of the oppressed has become dominant, just as the oppressed will lead the new society. These songs are metaphorical, but at the same time contain the most open statement of hope in the entire work. As the blinded General comes to "see" in a visionary sense, his dead victims reappear before his mind's eye. First the Old Woman, then the Victims, and three dead children sing their songs to the child who was shot at the end of part 1. The "Song of the Old Woman" is a powerful statement of faith in the future and proclaims confidence in the real power of the weakest of the victims:

> Shall I tell you who is strong?
> Child, you are strong.
>
> (p. 119)

The "Song of the Victims" is also sung to the Child. Here the association of the child, symbol of hope, and the river, symbol of renewal, is made explicit: "Child from the river" (p. 120). This song begins as a lullaby. In contrast with the lullaby of deprivation at the end of part 1 (p. 99), the child's needs are fulfilled by nature and the child is at peace:

> Child from the river
> The water has rocked you
> The reeds kept the wind from your head
> The wind has sung to you
>
> Child you have slept so still by the river
> The earth was a pillow under your head.
>
> (p. 120)

Still, the vigil of men is necessary for a just society: "And man stood watch over your bed" (p. 120). Primarily, the renewal of society is symbolized in terms of natural phenomena. Oppression is overcome as inevitably as ice melts in the sun, and social regeneration is implied in the fertility of spring:

> The dark ice melts in the sun
> The rain runs into the river
> Spring has begun.
>
> (p. 120)

The music picks up the rising chain of intervals ("Intervallkette") from the previous song. The accumulation of voices here, with all the victims singing simultaneously, underlines the feeling of solidarity and community. The line "Spring has begun" is resolved in unexpected harmony, emphasizing its function as metaphorical image of a more harmonious future. Here, the condensed lyricism so typical of Bond's later song lyrics is already apparent. Linguistically, metaphorically, and symbolically this complex poem retains the simplicity of a lullaby.

The "Song of the Victims" then modulates from lullaby to prophecy. In metaphorical form the Victims sing of the end of the old order and the beginning of the new. The "white horse" and "silk cradle" would seem to symbolize the new peace.[116] Military orders and the sound of guns have faded away out at sea, the great sea of change. Symbols of oppression are transformed into peaceful objects: "The chains of prisoners are turned into chains for anchors" (p. 122). This is reminiscent of the menacing words of the "First Mad Song" ("The iron chain drops to the deep/ Like a silent killer"), and at the same time illustrates a positive transformation. Other lines symbolize the hope of fertility: "Where the earth was trod to dry circles they heap flowers" (p. 122).

The last stanza, which closes the opera, is openly programmatic but still employs the image of the river to symbolize decision and change:

> We stand by the river
> If there is a bridge we will walk over
> If there is no bridge we will wade
> If the water is deep we will swim
> If it is too fast we will build boats
> We will stand on the other side
> We have learned to march so well that we cannot drown.
>
> (p. 122)

The tone is determined, the words are about both the present and the future. The song is contemporary and prophetic. In part, the function of this song is that of ritual celebration, and as such it is clearly related to the ritual songs in *The Woman*. In part, it is a kind of rallying song to strengthen solidarity.

The accompaniment changes for the final stanza and begins a rhythmic pulsation suggesting a marching beat. An accumulation of staccato notes brings out the hesitant nature of the steps into a new world. Immediately before the final two lines, the rhythm accelerates and all the voices join together. The last lines are sung in a confident, even joyous, manner. The closing instrumental phrases, in contrast, are extremely soft and are played "very tenderly."[117] Henze comments that this final song of hope combines all the elements of the music of the victims, but finds a new tone, free from all inhibitions and fears:

Ganz am Schluss, zum Gesang an die Hoffnung, werden die wichtigsten Motive der Unterdrückten in eine Intervall-Kette geordnet, zu einer Bildhaftigkeit, wie sie im ganzen Stück nicht möglich war. Alle Angst und Beklemmung ist von der Musik abgefallen, und es ist wie ein Neubeginn in einer von allen Schrecknissen, allem Unrecht befreiten Welt.

[At the very end the most telling motifs from the world of the oppressed reappear. They form a chain of intervals which is a metaphor for hope, a hope for love and peace that is possible only now at the end of the opera. All fear and anxiety have left the music; the end is like a new beginning in a world freed from terror and injustice.][118]

This music is not in the manner of a grand operatic finale:

> We tried not to make a grand affirmative statement—not like *Fidelio:* like a flower in winter, like the child as a lone figure of hope; the music becomes very quiet and tender, almost like a folksong.[119]

In *We Come to the River* Bond's libretto satirizes society and culture of a repressive regime. A political parable, set in the "nineteenth century and later" (p. 82), it contains reflections on other military dictatorships such as Nazi Germany and Chile after Allende.[120] In part 1 the element of song is used particularly to strengthen the satire. Henze's music here uses the techniques of musical quotation and parody to underline the satire musically. In part 2 the helpless, fragile music of the victims is strengthened until it dominates in a choral passage as finale. The text of the final chorus is a symbolical prophecy of hope and determination: the victims will cross the river of death and renewal and begin to create a new and just society.

STONE

Stone (1976) is also a parable play about oppression and capitalist exploitation, although it is a much lesser work than *We Come to the River*. The original printed version contains songs with music composed by Robert Campbell.[121] In *Theatre Poems and Songs*, Bond alters the titles of all except one ("Song of the Seven Deadly Veils") and includes a passage which in the original was not sung but recited. In the revised Methuen edition of 1981, the playwright uses double titles (original and altered title) throughout.[122] In several cases the change had a didactic intention, and Bond retains this effect in his subtitles. For example, "David and Goliath," a piece which is possibly open to misinterpretation in the original, is now unmistakably entitled "David and Goliath, or Song of False Optimism."

The music by Robert Campbell is not printed with the text, as Bond recalls, for economic reasons. This is unfortunate, as the dramatist retains a positive recollection of its effect:

> I thought it was good music. It was very busy music, very city music, which I liked. It was much busier than the play itself, and I thought that was good. The fact that the music was busy, I thought was very helpful for the audience. It made the audience not rest with the simplicities, in other words you had to keep falling back into a problematic context. In that play this was very useful.

The contrast between the style of the music and the nature of the text helped to bring out the complexities of the piece in spite of its surface simplicity.

Also, the contemporary music emphasized the relevance of this timeless parable for the present. It was, after all, written at the request of homosexual men.

The opening chorus, "Stone," strikes a general note of commentary before the action begins. The audience is led to expect a drama about exploitation, self-deception, and spiritual imprisonment. The protagonist of *Stone*, the naïve young Man, has a long journey to make, physically and mentally, before he arrives at the self-recognition and active rebellion suggested in this prologue. Three of the songs are placed at the end of the scenes in which they occur. This positioning not only gives them prominence, but also points to their function as summary and moral. The first two of these, in scenes 1 and 2, are parables in form, using first a biblical story (David and Goliath) and then a legendary one (Merlin and Arthur) to illustrate the moral.

The biblical parable teaches that the weak can achieve victory over the strong. But the conclusions that the young Man draws from this story are wrong. He associates himself with David, feels that he has already won a kind of victory in his encounter with the Mason. The song recounts how David continuously manages to avoid disaster in the nick of time by side-stepping. By using similes to describe the dangers, Bond suggests a connection to modern warfare. Bond's implication is that because mere avoidance of evil and danger does not eradicate their causes, the threat may recur at any time. If an individual has the luck to avoid calamity, nothing changes concerning the root causes of war. For this reason, David's sense of optimism is false, and is in reality a form of escapism. The song reflects on the action of the scene which it ends. With the help of this indirect commentary we can recognize that the decision of the Man to carry the Mason's stone has been a false decision, and that his words "It can't do any harm" (p. 91) are dangerously naïve.

In contrast with these two parables of the naïve Man, the song at the beginning of scene 3 sung by the Girl, "Song of the Seven Deadly Veils," is an extensive direct commentary on social organization and exploitation. It begins with provocative questions, and the refrain openly criticizes the perversions of capitalist society: "Evil creates its own remedy," and violence perpetuates violence. In each stanza a vision of justice is presented. The Girl sings outside of the action in a kind of public soliloquy. Bond did not define his concept of the public soliloquy, the general political commentary spoken or sung on a different level from the dramatic action, until *The Worlds*. Here, however, he is, in effect, already exploring the related technique of the public song, which he would expand so significantly in *Restoration*.

Scene 5 portrays the Man as old and broken. But he finally has a first glimmer of self-recognition. The last song in the play, originally called "Help," was renamed "Help, or Song of Experience" to indicate his dawning understanding. For the first time, the Man encounters not representatives of exploitation but another potential victim. The Boy offers the Man help in his

meaningless task, a help which the youngster would be incapable of rendering. Here, the Man shows a clear sense of perspective, an understanding of
the mechanisms of oppression, and above all, a realization of the need for
active resistance:

> You come smiling to offer service
>
> . . . .
>
> But you find you are too weak to help
> The grain you wanted to take to the farmers
> Is in a tower—with guards at the door
>
> You haven't even got the things that are yours
> To get them you have to fight
> The steps of your journey measure out a duel
> And the weapons are chosen by your enemy.

(p. 111)

From this recognition of allies and enemies it is not far to the deeds that
reflect this consciousness. The final two scenes of *Stone* at the Mason's house
contain no singing, but show the action that the last song implies and
anticipates. Finally understanding that the exploiting Mason is not simply his
personal enemy but the enemy of all oppressed victims, the Man kills him.
The Man has overcome the passive, fatalistic attitude of the tool that was
criticized in the first chorus. The songs in *Stone* thus help to "clarify the
process the Man goes through."[123] In "Help, or Song of Experience" the
Man has finally achieved the awareness that is appropriate to his suffering and
exploitation. As long as the Man has not reached this state of consciousness
his tunes are parabolical or metaphorical. But his final piece is openly
commentary.

Another work begun in the year 1976 and completed in 1977, the unfinished *Text for a Ballet*, was written for the composer Hans Werner Henze.
This shows how intently Bond was continuing to think in terms of theater
and song. In the end Henze did not write the music for this text, but the
collaboration of dramatist and composer has continued to be fruitful. The
Text for a Ballet will not be analyzed in detail, as the script has not been
published. It is, however, described in some detail by Hay and Roberts[124]
and the lyrics of nine of the fourteen songs have been printed in *Theatre
Poems and Songs*.[125] Because these texts are of considerable importance in the
light of the emergence of commentary in Bond's work, a few of them will be
treated briefly from the textual standpoint. They are for chorus, and contain
the only words in the script, for the ballet otherwise has no dialogue. The
choruses are generally placed at the beginning of the scenes, and most are
strongly didactic in function, although they retain parable and metaphor as
means of expression.

"The Shepherd" evokes the biblical parables of the Good Shepherd (John 10) and of the Lost Sheep (Luke 15), but ironically transforms the traditional Christian morals into anticapitalist lessons. The shepherd only protects his property because it brings him profit:

> The good shepherd protects the sheep from the wolf
> And delivers them up to the butcher
> . . . .
> When you are lost
> He will go back over the road
> Like a man who has dropped
> His purse.
>
> (pp. 125–26)

The sheep in Bond's parable are not erring souls but victims of social violence. The song contains an appeal for changed conditions, but it is addressed directly to the sheep themselves, the victims; the speaker urges them to undertake active resistance.

> Sheep! take pity on yourselves
> Savage the shepherd when he comes.
>
> (p. 126)

This revision of biblical parables exemplifies Bond's rejection of the Christian heritage in favor of a new revolutionary morality.

In "A Song of Tactics" an omniscient speaker didactically points out to the workers and their comrades, with illustrative examples, that it might be worth giving up one tactical victory for the sake of wider aims. Hay and Roberts sum up the moral of this song: "isolated local victories are not the answer, society as a whole must be changed."[126] The second stanza points forward directly to the moral dilemmas and the political answers of *The Bundle* by asking the same provocative questions that are embodied in the dramatic action of the later play:

> Who can pass the child left to drown by the river?
> But who feeds the tenth child? Or shelters the hundredth?
> Who owns the river? Whose fields
> Does its water make fertile?
>
> . . . .
> While you are asking the landlord these questions
> For the sake of the child—the child might drown
> But ask and be answered.
>
> (p. 130)

The final "Chorus to Peace" evokes the vision of a world of peace in which social justice reigns and pity is no longer necessary:

In those days fathers will take their sons to the hills
Where battles were fought

. . . .

And their sons will not be sent to kill families

. . . .

And children will play on the hill
And pity will smile.

(p. 132)

This unfinished ballet contains some of the first lyrics in Bond's work that call
for active resistance or revolutionary action. In other respects they are similar
to the songs of *Stone* or *We Come to the River*. The choruses of the ballet
contain strong political commentary, indirect social commentary through
parable ("The Shepherd") and satire that exposes the hypocrisies of ruling
society.

Neither of Bond's following two plays, *The Bundle* (1978) or *The Worlds*
(1979) includes any melodies. Nevertheless there are aspects of these works
that indicate their close connection with the other plays. Several of the poems
accompanying *The Bundle* reflect the same concerns as earlier songs, indicating that Bond was thinking along the same general lines. Many, for example,
are concerned with the issues of pity and justice as were several of the
choruses for the unfinished ballet.

The Worlds (1979) is songless, perhaps because it portrays a ruthless contemporary world where all natural use of music has been driven out by
capitalism. But in *The Worlds*, Bond's experimentation with the technique of
the public soliloquy prepares directly for the songs in his following play
Restoration. Public soliloquies enable a character to step out of the action and
speak "with historical hindsight, with greater political consciousness and
stronger political presence than he yet has."[127] They provide a kind of
"politically informed commentary,"[128] broader than the point of view of the
individual character. These words could well summarize the function of
many of the pieces in *Restoration*.

RESTORATION

Restoration (1981), subtitled a pastoral, is a parody of a Restoration comedy
in which the tragic (or tragicomic) main plot is concerned with the low-bred
servants, while the comic, (or farcical) subplot revolves around the foppish
aristocrat and his wealthy but naïve country wife. "If, as Bond once said, *The
Sea* dealt with tragedy but was a comedy, then *Restoration* deals with comedy
but is a tragedy."[129] It is Bond's first—and to date only—work with a strongly
comic effect which uses didactic, even revolutionary, songs. These are sung
exclusively by the servants, the victims of the ruling and merchant classes,

and they contain a detached, informed commentary on this society and the servants' role in it. Many of the songs in *Restoration* work in the same way as the public soliloquies in *The Worlds:* they place the action of the play in historical perspective; they articulate a political consciousness that the character in his or her role in the play does not yet possess; and they present a politically informed commentary that helps the audience to relate the conditions in the drama to those of contemporary society. They are, in effect, public soliloquies in the form of song. They also serve to relieve the tensions as the action moves inexorably towards its tragic close. As Katharine Worth relates:

> The moments when they step forward and sing directly out to the audience are moments of intoxicating release. Only the servants are allowed the privilege of song. . . . It also makes them the forward-looking ones, singing in the rock-music style of the present which for them is the future. . . . They gain the articulacy they lack in that world.[130]

The tunes help to bridge the gap between historical tale and present reality for the audience. Bond says,

> In *Restoration* there's a discordancy between what they are seeing on stage and what the songs are about. The songs are about factories and atom bombs and so on, and the play is about the eighteenth and nineteenth century.

Elsewhere the dramatist summarizes his overall intention in *Restoration:*

> I wanted to write a play which would demonstrate the way in which working-class attitudes were manipulated by the rulers of our society . . . so . . . I took a very simple story from the past which is about an innocent man who allows himself to be misled into accepting guilt, and then all the while I cut into it songs which refer to accidents in factories, to strikes, to H bombs, to various things that have to do with our modern world, so that you could then get a connection—you would be able to see the simple story saying this man is behaving in an absurd way, but then the songs would keep saying aren't you doing the same thing? That's the way the play works I think.[131]

The playwright here emphasizes the function of commentary. Many of the songs in *Restoration* also embody a powerful lyricism; this element is equally important to Bond in his creation of a new epic-lyric theater. Some songs make their point by means of metaphor or parable, as did those of *Stone* or the unfinished *Text for a Ballet*. Several also approach folk song in their concentration and simplicity. Throughout the lyrics of *Restoration* the dramatist regularly employs rhyme—not a usual feature of his poetry or songs—perhaps as an implication of folk consciousness.

One of the play's 16 songs is a traditional folk tune. The fifteen others have original texts by Bond.[132] Fourteen have been set to music by the young composer Nick Bicât; his melodies are printed at the back of the revised Methuen edition. Nick Bicât has collaborated on productions in alternative theater such as *England's Ireland* with Portable Theatre; he has worked with the Royal Shakespeare Company composing music for productions of Shakespeare's plays; and he has also written the music for David Hare's drama about a disintegrating rock band, *Teeth'n'Smiles*. Bicât, who left Oxford to join a rock band, is excited by the idea of a rock musical. In his work for *Restoration*, he was enthusiastic about the texts for the songs, but apparently did not fully appreciate Bond's intentions concerning their placing and functions. As he says,

> The songs in *Restoration* were magnificently telling poetry, thrilling to set, and the actors loved doing them. But of course they were self-contained, punctuating the scenes.[133]

In contrast with many musicals, where the songs blend into the action and flow out of the dialogue almost without transition, Bond's songs must be clearly set apart because they are comments on the action from a different angle. They are isolated in form and presentation, but intricately interwoven in meaning. In the first performance at the Royal Court Theatre, the songs were produced in a way that emphasized their separation from the dramatic action. Here, one could literally say that they were foregrounded. The lighting changed, the band was rolled forward on a bridge, microphones came up at the front of the stage, and the characters stepped forward to sing directly to the audience. In this way the intention of bridging the gap between fictional past and present reality was brought out quite well.

Bicât's tunes are powerful in effect, but are perhaps too pleasing to the ear to convey fully Bond's revolutionary content. The music generally illustrates moods and statements, rather than analyzing as Henze's music does. It is on the whole far more conventional than Henze's. The tunes are tonal throughout, and the key modulations are generally those that would be expected between related keys, especially relative major and minor. Bicât's music tends to strengthen the emotional rather than the intellectual impact of Bond's lyrics. To be sure, the dramatist's texts combine lyricism and folk simplicity with strong emotional impact, but his ultimate purpose is to create critical detachment in the audience, to disturb and to challenge. Bicât's music, on the other hand, is close to the popular idiom; his primary aim is to please rather than to upset the listener. For this reason, it is conceivable that music by a different composer might have conveyed Bond's intentions more adequately.[134] Bond himself is cautious in his evaluation:

> As to Nick Bicât's music, it's an area that one wants to explore. There aren't any immediate aesthetic answers. . . . The only way you can find solutions . . . is by creating new problems for a musician, presenting new difficulties. I've got a feeling

that in that sense I interfered with the music too much. He would say to me 'What's this song about,' and I would tell him. I think perhaps this is not a good way of working. I find the more I work in theatre, the more I want to create problems for other people.

Most of the songs close scenes; only two of the 12 scenes do not end in this manner. The melodies are thus given a strong summarizing role, providing a direct or an oblique comment on the action, placing it in a wider perspective. Some are so general in their analysis that they could conceivably be transposed to another position without distorting or altering the meaning. In the rehearsal edition of *Restoration*, for example, "Suddenly" is placed at the end of scene 6 and the "Song of Talking" at the end of scene 10. In the revised Methuen edition of 1982 these positions are reversed.[135] In the latter edition, Bond further notes that "Drum Song" could be placed at the end of scene 10 and "Suddenly" cut altogether. He also adds that in the first production, "Hurrah" was eliminated from scene 8.

The opening scenes of *Restoration* contrast the cynical, loveless marriage of money and ambition between Lord Are and Ann Hardache with the incipient love between the servant Bob and the black woman Rose. "Roses," which closes scene 1, contrasts the artificial pastoral ideal with real feeling.[136] The "Song of Learning" at the end of scene 2 differs sharply from "Roses." At his first appearance the singer, Frank, is shown as a cheeky, self-assured young town servant: "smart lad down from London, good looker, spin a yarn, knocked about a bit—what? Answer to a maiden's prayer" (p. 18). In his song, Frank's consciousness is enormously expanded; in effect, he represents the experience of all serving and working men in the history of the human race:

> For fifty thousand years I hammered and toiled
> All that I made was taken away from my hands.
>
> (p. 19)

The learning process is a result of centuries of pain and deprivation and also a product of the understanding of the mechanisms of exploitation:

> For fifty thousand years I fought battles to save their wealth
> That's how I learned to know the enemy myself.
>
> (p. 20)

Recognition of the enemy also was the first sign of the Man's learning process in *Stone* ("Song of Experience"). The awareness of the singer here, however, goes far beyond that of the Man in *Stone,* and calls for active resistance, destruction of the unjust society and creation of a new.

> From now on the food is gonna be mine
> . . . .

From "Song of Learning," and the coda to "Dream," Edward Bond, *Restoration*, text by Edward Bond, tune by Nick Bicât. (Unpublished piano score, arranged by Terry Davies.)

> For fifty thousand years I was governed by men of wealth
> Now I have learned to make the laws I need for myself.

(pp. 19–20)

The final stanza changes in both rhythm and rhyme, switching to rhymed couplets. It sums up the experience of learning from the rest of the song, and ends with a quiet, but deadly serious threat:

> I have known pain and bowed before beauty
> Shared in joy and died in duty
> Fifty thousand years I lived well
> I learned how to blow up your hell.

(p. 20)

Bicât's tune is composed in major keys, giving musical expression to the confidence and aggressiveness of the text; the melody is then altered for the last stanza. The final line ends on a monotonous but threatening series of low D's. Here, the words are sung unaccompanied, drawing attention to their meaning.

Frank's "Song of Learning" not only creates a contrast to Bob's personal love song, it is also intended as expansion of Frank's own role in the drama. When he sings he steps out of his own time, and he gains historical perspective and a critical consciousness. In the play Frank is defiant and resentfully aware of class differences, but he is shown to lack wider perspective. He cannot find the right form of rebellion, and dies for a petty theft. As singer, he has not stepped out of character, "but the audience sees the character's potential self, sees him as he could be"—Bond's words to describe the function of the public soliloquy.[137] This is a good example of a song that has a function very similar to that of the public soliloquy. As Bond says, "The author becomes the spokesman of his character."[138] Here, Frank has found what Bond would consider to be the right form of universal solidarity and revolutionary awareness.

Scene 3 begins with a hilarious marital squabble about petty details of fashion and frivolity, resulting in Ann's comic plan of revenge on her husband. The conversation at the end of the scene between Ann and Rose, in contrast, touches on some of the serious realities in the life of a personal servant: it is clear that Rose was hired for reasons of snobbish pretension, as a black-skinned "novelty" (p. 25), and that her mistress has no desire at all to understand the real woman. Rose's song, "Dream," is one of the most impressive in the entire drama. It conveys pent-up anger at centuries of injustice and discrimination. It is fiercely intense and at the same time metaphorical. Here once again, as so often in Bond's work, the river is used as a metaphor for revolutionary change. Fire is employed as a metaphor for wrath. Both river and fire are the vehicles for black anger that will destroy the white man's world:

> I sit in a boat and float down a river of fire
>
> . . . .
> The boat sails safely on
>
> . . . .
> The whitemen run and the fire comes out
> The river of fire chases them till they fall
> To their knees and crawl about in the flames
> The river burns everything that stands in its path
> Forests and men are all consumed in its wrath.
>
> (p. 25)

The chorus manifests the singer's black consciousness and awareness of her strength, and also her revolutionary menace:

> I am black
> At night I press through the land unseen
> Though you lie awake
> My smile is as sharp as the blade in my hand.
>
> (p. 25)

The second stanza creates a vision of a new world in which justice and peace reign. Here, the positions of black and white have been reversed. The river of fire has annihilated the white man and his sphere of violence ("tanks"), but not the natural world, which has remained intact for a new society:

> The land is green in the morning dew
> The cattle passed through the flames yet are not dead
> Only the whiteman's bones are black
> Lying by his burned out tanks
> Now cattle graze the river banks
> Men and women work in the fields
> All that they grow they own
> To be shared by old and young
> In the evening they rest
> And the song of freedom is sung.
>
> (p. 26)

The final chorus adds one new line that summarizes the singer's consciousness of her revolutionary strength: "The venom does not kill the snake" (p. 26). Rose's "Dream" could be said to be a visionary song, producing a prophetic picture of what freedom and justice might mean. Rose possesses more class consciousness and more black consciousness than any other character in the play, but she is still trapped in the constraints and contradictions of her age. Even she makes the mistake of trusting a class enemy, Hardache. Here too, as in Frank's previous piece, the song shows the person she might be under different circumstances and in a different time.

The tune is powerful, but one could not call it lyrical. The entire first stanza is composed in D minor, the combined horror and promise of the text thus held in balance musically. At the beginning of the second stanza, when a new dawn breaks over a visionary world ("But when the fire is spent"), the tune modulates to the relative major and sounds in contrast radiant and liberated. At the words "Only the whiteman's bones" the melody modulates back to D minor again and returns to the melodic line of the beginning, but in the new context the minor key seems to correspond to the quiet peace of this harmonious world. The additional last line of the refrain ("The venom does not kill the snake") is set apart musically. It uses the same ominously threatening series of low D's as did the final line of Frank's "Song of Learning," although the two differ rhythmically.

The "thieving scene" (scene 4) is crucial to the action of the drama, and is distinguished musically by the fact that it contains three songs. Here for the first time the audience becomes fully aware of Mother's (and her son Bob's) unconditional subservience to authority. Neither has any awareness of class solidarity. They are examples of mental conditioning in the interests of the ruling class. The first eleven lines of Mother's "Wood Song" imply this unquestioning acceptance of the fated course of life. It is not until the final couplet that this attitude is challenged. Indeed, the first six lines use repetition to the point of monotony as a linguistic equivalent to this fatalistic mentality:

> The wooden cradle the wooden spoon
> . . . .
> The wooden gallows the wooden box.
>
> (p. 28)

From cradle to grave man's fate is predestined, it is useless to struggle against it. The following lines alleviate the monotony but are even stronger in their belief in a preordained pattern of life:

> The human toil the earthly span
> These are the lot of everyman
> The winds that drive the storms that blast
> For everyman the die is cast.
>
> (p. 28)

The simple, repetitive wording, the dominance of regular iambic tetrameter in many of the lines, and the use of rhymed couplets in the second half all give the lyrics a diction close to that of the folk idiom. The simple melody, too, is reminiscent of a folk tune, and is kept low and quiet; indeed it is almost monotonous. The voice line is accompanied only by a harpsichord following the melody at an octave. The first eleven lines are, both in wording and in mentality, very close to the mentality of Mother.

In the final couplet the singing persona moves out of her time and warns against acceptance of this attitude:

> All you who would resist your fate
> Strike now it is already late.

(p. 28)

In these two lines the singer incorporates a consciousness that is far more advanced. The harpsichord stops at this point, so that the human voice alone is highlighted. Harmonically, the cadence is unresolved; in other words, the final couplet is left musically open. Textually and musically the challenge is passed on, as it were, to the audience without a solution.

Due to its predominantly pessimistic attitude the piece has ironic and foreshadowing rather than commentary functions. The "wooden gallows" of the text foreshadow both Frank's and Bob's fate: death by hanging. It is precisely this kind of fatalistic attitude that makes the hangings possible and inevitable. In particular, it is Mother's unerring obedience to authority that will allow her to unwittingly burn her own son's pardon, thus sealing his fate. The final lines are thus an ironic challenge to Mother herself.

Bob's "Song of the Calf" is like his Mother's "Wood Song" in its determinism. It tells of the inevitability with which the calf is led to slaughter. Although Bob will lead the chase after Frank in this scene, ultimately he himself will be a victim of this unjust society: he will be sacrificed, slaughtered like the calf, to protect the reputation of his master. The song thus has a foreshadowing function as did Mother's tune.

The scene in Peterborough Gaol that opens part 2 elaborates on the mechanism of injustice in that earlier age. Lord Are at first plays the friendly patriarch, then threatens the prisoner with the full weight of his authority and his power to control the law. Finally, he appeals to Bob's deference to authority, instilled in him since childhood. While he withdraws to leave Bob time to consider, Bob and Rose together sing "The Gentleman." The song begins by relating the historical scene of oppression to a modern example of social and political violence. Just as Lord Are pretends to play the role of genial, patriarchal authority, the S.S. guard in the concentration camp acts the gentleman at the door to the gas chamber, gallantly helping the woman with the child. The text employs heavy irony:

> What politeness he shows the stranger!
> In his hand there's a rifle
> At the door to the gas chamber
> He hands the child back to her arms.

(p. 57)

This juxtaposition of gallantry and brutality and the misuse of music in a violent context are also communicated in the melody. In the first part Bicât makes use of musical irony; in contrast with the gruesome text, the tune here is pleasant, even lyrical in the manner of a love song.

The second part of "The Gentleman" is strongly didactic and commentary, pointing out that there are numerous forms of violence other than bodily assault:

> Who would raise a whip when an order is obeyed?
> . . . .
> Why use a knife when a smile makes cuts that bleed?
> When you have the mind why bother to chop off the head?
> When white hands will do the work why make your hands red?
>
> (p. 57)

On the one hand this chorus points out the partial complicity of the victims: Bob's deference to authority and obedience to orders make it possible to exploit him. It also exposes indirect and insidious forms of social injustice— violence achieved through superior social position or superior education. Once again, as in Mother's "Wood Song" and "Song of the Calf," the ending is unresolved harmonically as if it ought to continue. This underlines the provocation of the text; questions are asked that the audience should take away with them to ponder.

Scene 7 depicts how even the most class-conscious character of the drama, Rose, makes a mistake in trusting a class enemy, Hardache. It contains her words of false optimism: "Mr. Hardache you're our only friend" (p. 66). The song which concludes this scene, "Legend of Good Fortune," presents a simple moral lesson. Using the story of a god as robber, the listeners are warned never to trust the "gods," the powerful of this earth, and to actively defend themselves against exploitation. The story portrays a learning process, for it is not until the god comes to rob them for the second time that the people learn to resist. So too, Rose learns from her mistake, although too late to save Bob, and emerges at the end of the play as a stronger, wiser, and more determined woman. The singer in this case, however, is Mother, the character who learns least from her experiences. The song demonstrates what Mother might have become under different circumstances. Within her lifetime, however, she cannot learn. The diction is in keeping with Mother's character: simple and unsophisticated. In form and language the "Legend of Good Fortune" is comparable to Mother's earlier "Wood Song," but the parable form and the didactic message help to convey a much more positive attitude. Bicât's tune remains throughout in an extremely simple folk style. Composed in the major, it is lyrical in nature. The accompaniment is harmonically uncomplicated, consisting predominantly of a four-part arrangement remi- niscent of a nineteenth-century carol, leaving the listener with a feeling of satisfaction and confidence.

"The Fair Tree of Liberty," sung by Rose and Frank in scene 9, has no

TREE OF LIBERTY (ROSE AND FRANK)

From "The Fair Tree of Liberty," text by Edward Bond, tune by Nick Bicât, in Edward Bond, *Restoration and the Cat* (London: Methuen, rev. ed., 1982), [p. 188–89].

direct connection to the action, but a strong link to the themes of the play as a whole. It is a lyrical, metaphorical piece that tells of the power of the Tree of Liberty to defend its fruit and to repulse those who wish to harm it. It contrasts the scene it concludes: the superficiality and irresponsibility of those in power (here, Old Lady Are) are compared with the solidarity and confidence of those whose liberty is endangered. The former are made to appear petty and insignificant, but we know for all that how dangerous they are. The song thus offsets the pessimistic scene, in which Rose has to admit defeat, with a note of optimism. The tune sounds confident, even radiant. The verses are sung alternately by Rose and Frank. In its last two stanzas the rhythm changes and becomes intensely lyrical. Striking is the use of dactyls at the beginning of three consecutive lines:

> Deep in the trunk bees murmer like thunder
> High in the crown birds call
> Telling the names of the passers-by.
>
> (p. 84)

Here the singers' voices join together to form a chorus of mysterious joy. The music becomes almost intoxicating in its harmonic sweetness. The song ends on a strong note of faith in the future and implies a bond of continuity between past and present:

> And so the fair tree grows
> As tall as the pine and strong as the oak
>
> . . . .
> As our forefathers spoke.
>
> (p. 84)

A rise in the melody from D major to E major at the second repetition of this chorus helps to underscore the confident mood. The lyrics' combination of nature imagery with the human sphere symbolizes the harmony in which the two will live in the future. Thus the song functions as prophecy.

The final scene of the drama is also prophetic and symbolical. Standing on London Bridge, Rose speaks a soliloquy that embodies a vision of destruction and oppression. Bond calls this an "emotional photograph" of what she sees in the city:

> Bodies float in the sky . . . Crocodiles drift in the Thames . . .
> Men walk the streets with chains hanging from their mouths . . .
> The stars will come out like scabs on the sky.
>
> (p. 99)

She calls on the audience to consider with her what she has learned from her experiences, and sings her song of learning, "Man is What He Knows," which concludes the drama. After three stanzas exemplifying the lesson that the rulers of this earth pursue their exploitation with bitter consequences, the piece suggests the moral of this play, that exploitation and oppression are often accomplished by means of conditioning the mind of the victim:

> Once Satan roamed the earth to find
> Souls that money could buy
> Now he comes to steal your mind
> He doesn't wait till you die.[139]

(p. 99)

The following stanzas pick up the title and sum up the vital importance of the learning process: "Man is what he knows—or doesn't know" (p. 100).

The final stanza is one of condensed lyricism. Images from nature are used to illustrate natural beauty and energy, and these are contrasted with human determination and capacity for recognition and direction:

> Geese fly over the moon and do not know
> That for a moment they fill the world with
> beauty
> Flakes do not know where they drive in
> the storm
> But each flake falls to the earth
> below
> And in the morning shines in the
> world of snow
> Wind and rain cannot tell where
> they blow
> But we may know who we
> are and where we go.

(p. 100)

The first part is thus didactic, the second part characterized by lyrical vision. Rose's last words in the drama make the symbolical nature of the setting and of her vision clear: "I cross the bridge and go into the streets" (p. 100). The bridge thus becomes the means of carrying the moral of the play into the real world of the audience. This song, like all those in *Restoration*, makes extensive use of rhyme, ending on a fourfold rhyme. But its diction is not as simple and folk-like as that in several of Mother's or Bob's tunes. It concludes the work with a strongly didactical—yet complex and lyrical—commentary.

Bicât has written a difficult melody for "Man is What He Knows," with frequent changes of key. Many incidental sharps and flats (even double sharps) add to the unusual, even disturbing quality of the tune. The last stanza is sung more slowly and is accompanied only by a solo piano, emphasizing the shift from didacticism to delicate lyricism in the closing passage. The tune ends, as so often when a provocation or challenge is intended, with an unresolved harmony.

The songs in *Restoration* exhibit a wide variety of functions and of diction. Most of them are set apart, usually ending the scenes with direct or indirect commentary. A marked contrast to the historical action is provided by those that contain didactic commentary, such as "Song of Learning" or "Man Groans." Here particularly the characters step entirely out of their time and analyze the dramatic events with a balanced but provocative hindsight. Typical for Bond's creations are also those pieces which use parable or metaphor to convey a social or political moral; for example, "Song of the Calf," "Legend of Good Fortune" or "Song of the Conjuror." One is distinctly contemporary and colloquial in diction, the "Song of Talking." More traditional uses of song are to be found in various foreshadowing functions. Irony and satire, so important in Bond's earlier work, are still present but no longer predominant. Those songs that are close to the mentality of the singers are usually ironic, including Mother's "Wood Song," Bob's "Song of the Calf" and "Suddenly."

Many of the lyrics in *Restoration* are of folk character; the rhyme scheme and rhythm are often ballad-like, and the diction of several is of a simple folk variety. Even those that do not approximate folk style but are more sophisticated in vocabulary and tone make consistent use of rhyme. In Bond's other works in which didactic and commentary songs prevailed, *Stone*, *Text for a Ballet* and *We Come to the River*, little or no use of rhyme was made. The songs of *Restoration* thus suggest a folk flavor while retaining a highly serious overall political and social purpose in their commentary. The most striking— and to my mind the most successful—pieces are those which combine informed political commentary with intense lyricism and a sense of visionary truth, for example "Dream," "Fair Tree of Liberty" or "Man is What He Knows." Such songs are crucial in helping to create the new type of drama Bond envisions; they epitomize in effect both the rational political analysis and the lyrical concentration of the epic-lyric theater of his later career. They have both intellectual and emotional force. Because of its songs, *Restoration* achieves a unique position in Bond's creative canon: it is a musical tragicomedy that tells its story in an entertaining fashion, using popular music, but that incorporates the same seriousness and urgency in its political aims as the more sombre of his plays.

5. Later Works

Restoration is the most important musical stage play among Bond's later works. It achieves a delicate balance between spoken dialogue and songs— neither would be complete without the other, and the songs add considerably to the intellectual and emotional dimensions of the drama. Among the works produced after 1982, none is of equal significance with respect to the theme of song in drama, but in most, Bond continues to employ music, and one, *The Cat*, is again a libretto for Hans Werner Henze.

Derek (performed in 1982 and published in 1983) is a brief piece in seven scenes with seven songs. Their placing is not as predictable as this sounds: one opens a scene, several come in the middle and several are used as closing pieces. The play is described by Bond as based in social realism, but it "should be performed with farcical energy."[140] The songs, too, combine didacticism, energy and the extremes of farce. Many are exaggeratedly simple in both text and tune. The only character in the drama with political awareness is Julie, and hers is the only musically sophisticated song. The "Last Song" ends the short piece with a horrible vision; it is concerned with the H-bomb and hence related to "Suddenly" in *Restoration:*

> And the tempest when the bomb was dropped
> Blew my whistle to the edge of the world
> And there it will shriek till the end of time.
>
> (p. 17)

The melody, however, remains naïvely childlike, ending in quiet resignation. In the first production the music was by David Shaw-Parker, and it is his music which is printed at the back of the published edition. In a later staging, a different director wanted another composer to be part of the team, and Bond agreed to allow new music to be introduced by Ilona Sekacz. As he says, he is happy to experiment, although he would normally insist on the use of music that has been especially written for his songs and which he has found suitable. *After the Assassinations* (performed in 1983) contains spoken choruses (printed together with *Derek*), an experiment in poetical public soliloquies.

Human Cannon (published in 1985, but finished several years earlier)[141] introduces a number of songs and choruses. "They are, with one or two exceptions, interlude songs. They occur in between the scenes. . . . Some of them tell the story, and some of them comment," Bond says. The drama is about human resourcefulness, strength, and capacity for learning; it is set in Spain from the late 1920s to 1940. Several of the choruses are strongly didactic ("You who . . . "). In the manner of the best songs in *Restoration*, some of the pieces combine metaphorical, lyrical, or emotional intensity with didactic commentary. Agustina's "The Curse," for example, begins with analysis and modulates to an anguished personal cry at the end: "May the stone lie heavy on your head!" (p. 26). A later song by Agustina starts metaphorically and leads to prophecy:

> The fire will consume itself
> The tempest will exhaust itself
> The flood will return to the still deeps of the sea
> But I will ride the world with my two talking horses

Till the generations of the earth are free

.   .   .   .

And you'll never never never conquer me.

(p. 37)

Here, Bond's natural metaphors for revolution (fire, tempest, and flood) are surpassed by the human determination to achieve justice and change.

The narrative songs are a new development in Bond's drama. In a manner reminiscent of the mature Brecht, or the later Arden and D'Arcy, such pieces cover epic developments difficult to stage:

> For three years the people's militia slowly retreated before Hitler Mussolini and
>   Franco
> In December nineteen thirty-eight Barcelona fell
> Soon Madrid would fall
> And on the first of April nineteen thirty-nine the Republic would fall.

(p. 13)

Presumably they should be set in a recitative rather than lyrical manner. A remarkable fusion of the lyrical and epic manner can also be observed in Agustina's impassioned praise of Spain:

> It is my Spain!
> Mine!
> The fertile coasts and the rocky enduring heart are mine!
> The red earth and apple orchards of Asturias
> .   .   .   .
> Scented deserts of thyme and tarragon
> Roadsides thick with Prometheus' fennel
> Bay and wattle
> The rockrose from which came myrrh
> The dark sweet myrtle and mandragora, the plant that shrieks
> Pines and junipers and Spanish oaks
> All mine!

(p. 34)

Here the language is lyrical, but the texts are composed in a looser verse than Bond's other songs, which are often condensed and patterned in stanzas. Again, one could imagine a fast and driving rhythm rather than a melodically beautiful tune. *Human Cannon* shows interesting innovations in the combination of didacticism, commentary, narrative and epic-lyric texts.

Red Black and Ignorant, performed in 1984 and published in 1985, forms the first part of the trilogy *The War Plays*. It employs only one song, but illustrates again the playwright's exact conception—musically and dramatically—of the ways in which music can work. Of the piece, Bond says,

> The one song comes out of nowhere. . . . It's just there I think for its shock impact, the idea that music could work in that way. And because it's a soldier who sings it, it

makes the audience see him differently as well as at the same time making them understand more the way music works. . . . I didn't want it to be set like traditional army music. . . . We want something highly technological, to do with computers and modern machines and that sort of thing. So that next time the audience hear a military brass band they will think something else about the music they're hearing. . . . I suppose that what one wants to do is to make people conscious of the language they're using.

The music to this song is again by David Shaw-Parker. *Red Black and Ignorant* contrasts with many of Bond's earlier works in that the spoken text, too, is lyrical and nonrealistic. The dramatist sums up the general direction of music and language in his later plays in the words:

Oddly enough what's happened in the two plays I've written since then [since *Human Cannon*] . . . *Red Black and Ignorant* has only one song, the soldier's song, and the other one, *The Tin Can People*, doesn't have any song in it, but the language has become more "song-ful," more what is traditionally understood as poetry.

In *The Tin Can People* (1985) several general commentary choruses introduce the scenes; *Great Peace* (1985) employs both verse dialogue and verse soliloquy. These form the second and third parts respectively of *The War Plays* trilogy.

Bond's continuing concern with the combination of drama and music is also exemplified by his second opera libretto for Hans Werner Henze, *The Cat* (printed in the revised edition of *Restoration* in 1982 and performed at Schwetzingen, West Germany, in 1983). The libretto will be treated only briefly. I have not been able to consult score or recording, but Henze has written a book documenting the stages of the collaboration in detail, including reproductions of several of Bond's letters to him.[142] The opera was inspired by Geneviève Serrault's adaptation of Balzac's tale *Peines de Coeur d'une Chatte anglaise*. The idea for the collaboration came from Henze. As in the case of the earlier opera, the cooperation was intense and included frequent telephone calls, letters, and some personal consultations. But the results were perhaps not as satisfactory for Bond as *We Come to the River*. Henze seems to have treated this comic and satirical animal fable in somewhat the same way as his children's opera *Pollicino*, and Bond thinks that the naïve seriousness of a fairy tale approach does not work well given the nature of his text:

I think that various things that I regarded as satire and comedy have been set for seriousness. I don't see how an audience knows how they should approach it.

Nevertheless the collaboration on this *opera buffa* illustrates Bond's sensitivity to the interaction of text and music. He emphasizes the task of the librettist to inspire the composer, draw the music out of him,[143] and their goal of creating a kind of music which can encompass joy and sadness without changing its aesthetic style.[144] Henze writes after a meeting with Bond in Great Wilbraham:

> Edward hat ganz genaue Vorstellungen von dem musikalischen Gesamtstil und weiss auch, wie es *nicht* klingen soll, z.B. nicht wie Gilbert & Sullivan.

> [Edward has a very precise idea of what the musical style as a whole should be like, and he knows exactly how he does *not* want it to sound, e.g. not like Gilbert and Sullivan.][145]

Rather than Gilbert and Sullivan, the Mozart ideal was at the back of Bond's mind.

The dramatist not only has an idea of the general musical style he wants; he can also imagine precise details of specific arias, including type of instrumentation, style, rhythm and mood. Especially illuminating is a letter to Henze of 3 October 1979 in which Bond goes into details of rhythm and pattern, even making a sketch of the way in which he envisions the melody. Describing the farewell scene between Minette, Tom, and Babette (part 2, scene 6) he writes:

> Then the rhythm should signal an important moment. The rhythm increases for "O little sister"—and it's really strongly reinforced by Bab at "His touch is gentle"—though her voice keeps it light: and then the rhythm should really pound (the music descending in straight lines) [note referring to sketch] at "What strange ideas are in my head." The rhythm remains strong till the end of the ensemble but Min's "With this good deed" rises and floats above it [Second note referring to sketch].[146]

Although on the surface this animal opera is light and comic, its deeper occupations are related to Bond's other work. He sums up his intentions:

> The play is about good luck, chance, hope, charity, opportunism—as opposed to understanding what you are doing and not relying on fortune or accidents (fascism v. socialism).[147]

Some of the arias retain a superficial naïvety and achieve their effect through the context in which they are placed. Some combine a psychological awareness which goes beyond that of the character with satire on conventional romanticism. Others, in their lyrics and dramatic function, are closer to the public soliloquy songs of *Restoration:*

> O moon you pass so calmly in the sky
> What acts of folly you have seen!
> The madman's cry, the killer's rage
> The clown laugh on his little stage

then the rythmn should signal an important moment. The rythmn increases
for "O little sister" - and its really strongly reinforced by Bab at "His touch
is gentle ⹀ though her voice keeps it light: and then the rythmn should
really pound (the music descending in straight lines) at "what strange ideas
are in my head. The rythmn remains strong till the end of the ensemble but
Min's "With this good deed" rises and floats above it. *Opportunism*

In sc 7 Tom's If every creature. This may seem a bit long but I think its
important. The play is about good luck, chance, hope, charity, opportunism -
as opposed to understanding what you are doing and not relying on fortune
or accidents. One should feel that after all his ups and downs - and sudden
reversals - Tom begins to ask himself what's the point of it. It should be
quite a light aria - but an intellectual aria (though not cold but very
human) music in the head (calmly) and not just in the voice ! Gentle,
slightly greyish orchestration - and it shouldnt last long: he has come to
this conslusion on the way to the Lawyers Office - he doesnt have to
struggle to think it out as he sings it. The Temple - by the way - is
just the old, stately area by the Thames where lawyers have their offices
(they call them chambers) - Dickensian place.

I dont think Lucian can be a rat - its confusing. What about a fox ?

At the end of the court scene Tom sits down and has a rather bleak sad
song. I like this because its well written and rather "folksy" - but it
needs gentle, despairing (violas ?) colouring - and into this (after the
mood is well established) could suddenly cut strange trills (say on wind:
trills, but I really mean a shape or semi-tune like a trill.
This portrays the increasing attention and excitment of the Prosecutor (but
the actor mustnt over-act this). Now, when the Pros starts to describe the
ship wreck this strange, dramatic shape could be played on other instruments
- perhaps the basses - and become the dangerous rythmn of the water and the
storm: and perhaps part of the tune or shape could be used once or twice to
suggest lightening and fireballs. The last two lines of this (about the
chaconne) could be cut. If you use them the last "e" of chaconne isnt sounded
in English - it rymes with 'gone'.

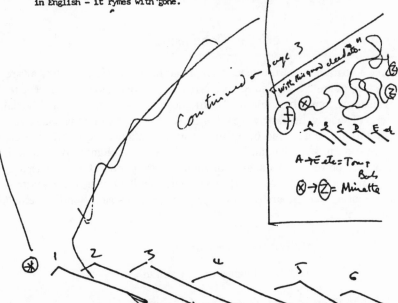

Continued on page 3

From Edward Bond, letter to Hans Werner Henze (3 October 1979), in Hans
Werner Henze, *Die englische Katze: Ein Arbeitstagebuch 1978–1982* (Frankfurt
am Main: S. Fischer, 1983), p. 45.

And men with power for a day destroy an age
And send their sons to die.[148]

The satire is most obvious in the pieces sung by judge, jury, or members of
the reactionary Royal Society for the Protection of Rats; for example, the
chorus of the jury of doves and geese at the divorce trial:

> We quietly sit in his jury box
> We do not ask him if the law
> Defends the rich to rob the poor
> That's not what he summoned us for
> We do our humble duty
> As citizens quack quack!

(p. 145)

Henze has continued the satire musically by combining elements of aggressive street ballad and pious hymn in the melody.[149] He thus captures
musically the fusion of vulgarity, subservience, bigotry, and hypocrisy in the
text. The opera concludes with a song of rebellion by the weakest of the
characters, the mouse Louise, another bridge to the optimistic or revolutionary conclusions of the dramatist's later work.

6. Conclusion

Bond's attitude toward music is deeply ambivalent. He is acutely aware of
the power of music and song to startle and to persuade, to rouse and to
convince, particularly emotionally. In the context of his rational socialist
analysis of society, he clearly sees that these capacities can either be misused,
to support the status quo of an unjust and reactionary system, or used in
positive ways to stimulate and celebrate the forces of change. Bond's evaluation of the powers and dangers of music corresponds closely to that of a
playwright such as John McGrath, who shares similar political convictions. It
is illuminating to compare statements by these dramatists. Bond's poem "On
Music" maintains:

> Music is very dangerous
> . . . .
> At Auschwitz they hanged men to waltzes.[150]

McGrath in interview says almost the same thing:

> Music is dangerous because it can be so effective, even if its basic intellectual
> position is wrong. It worked in Nazi Germany very well.[151]

Both playwrights emphasize that a major aim behind their introduction of music into stage plays is to make an audience aware of the ways in which it is working, to convey their critical consciousness to the listener. Bond says:

> You should use music with great care, because it's a humanizing activity. . . . One has to say [to an audience] you've got to learn a new way of listening. Because then you will understand new things.

McGrath speaks in a similar vein:

> You have to be very responsible about music, you have to let people know what you are doing. . . . You've just got to use music critically.[152]

One can say that in Bond's earlier work the negative aspects of music and song predominate, whereas in the course of his career he develops the more positive functions. This corresponds to the general trend in his plays toward more openly optimistic endings. In his early series from *The Pope's Wedding* to *The Sea* the dramatist employs song primarily in ironic and satiric roles to expose Western society and culture. To do this, he introduces traditional songs from both the English and American heritage. In the earliest plays the ironic function prevails. The gang songs, in which sex and violence are linked, expose the degeneracy of modern culture. The hymns point to multiple ironies and contradictions in Christian tradition. In the dramas that follow, Bond shows increasing awareness of the satiric possibilities of traditional song. Patriotic and religious tunes and melodies from the popular cultural sphere take precedence. In sharp contrast with John Arden, Bond employs very few folk songs in his work. Patriotic airs, placed in deliberately exaggerated comic situations, help to underline dangerous aberrations. The juxtaposition of patriotism with violent death exposes the perversions of a repressive society. The Christian hymns illustrate the playwright's view of Christian morality as a form of social violence. From the sphere of popular culture, Bond includes familiar songs from nineteenth-century parlor, music hall, and black-face minstrel shows. Social snobbery, self-deception and cultural hypocrisy are satirized through the use of such pieces. The choice of light and frivolous music ridicules the irresponsibility of the rulers of the Western world and satirically unmasks the superficiality and subterfuge of social leaders. Particularly in the plays from *Narrow Road to the Deep North* to *The Sea*, a resemblance to the grotesque satire in the work of Peter Barnes can be observed. Both playwrights deliberately insert trivial songs in outrageously inappropriate situations in order to ridicule dangerous pomposity, pretentiousness and political reaction. Both combine a bizarre visual imagination with a sensitivity to the comic and satiric effects of music.[153]

A phase of transition to the later, more positive function of song in Bond's drama is represented by the two plays *The Fool* and *The Woman* which employ music as expression of a community spirit that is worth preserving. The former uses traditional English folk song, whereas the latter introduces original texts written by Bond and set to music by the composer Hans Werner Henze. These plays illustrate the important shift in Bond's work from traditional to original song. In contrast with the earliest plays in which a choral function indicated the aggressive tendencies of modern urban gang mentality, the songs of these dramas embody the collective spirit of small rural communities still at peace with their natural surroundings. The tunes indicate a communal faith in renewal and regeneration in close harmony with nature.

These works, which were completed in roughly the first fifteen years of Bond's career as a dramatist, contain few songs, and ones that do not dominate the action. These tunes are, however, strategically placed and functionally important and are incorporated into the dramatic action with subtlety. Even here they are always integral to theme and style of the play, never incidental or merely ornamental. Very seldom does the dramatist use a song for its emotional effect only; he almost always has a satirical or intellectual purpose behind the singing. In this early period one cannot speak of a musical style as in Arden. Indeed, several of the most important dramas in this period—for example, *Lear* and *Bingo*—contain no songs at all.

In the later phase of his career the playwright experiments more extensively with music and song in drama. As his theater language becomes more condensed, metaphorical, and lyrical, his tendency increases to include songs in his drama. Here for the first time we can find works that are predominantly musical, conceived from the beginning from the standpoint of the interaction of drama and music. The nature of the fusion of song and text shows considerable variety in the later works. The operas *We Come to the River* and *The Cat* and the ballet *Orpheus*, all with music by Hans Werner Henze, are permeated by music. The short parable play *Stone* has choruses and songs set to music by Robert Campbell. In the pastoral, *Restoration*, the collaboration with the young composer Nick Bicât, who has been associated with rock music, gives the piece an entirely different musical flavor than the more complex and sophisticated operas. The dominant tendency in Bond's work from about 1976 on is toward original songs. Only occasionally does he use traditional tunes. In this period, some works are still without music.

Particularly important in this later stage of Bond's career is the development of new functions. The most stimulating and effective songs in the later work develop various commentary, metaphorical, and visionary aspects of the theme. Characteristic of the original texts are those that embody direct didactic commentary. The placing of such tunes at the end of scenes and their detachment from the dramatic action emphasizes their role as commentary or public soliloquy. Typical are also the parable songs; these combine a fictitious story with a moral lesson. Sometimes Bond uses a traditional tale as starting point for his parable, but ironically reverses the original meaning. This is especially evident in those of biblical origins, another indication of his rejection of Christianity.

One of the most interesting features of the later work is the extended use of metaphor and symbol. These can be found throughout the plays, but they are especially concentrated in the songs. The image of animals prepared for slaughter is used to suggest human victims of social or political oppression. Typical of the dramatist's method are songs in which comparisons are made or implied between the historical or parabolic settings and contemporary reality. Similes are drawn from modern warfare, the lyrics evoke atomic holocaust, present-day industrial accidents or concentration camps. On the more positive side, the abstract ideal of Liberty is sung of in terms of a living, even humanized, tree. Little silver fish symbolize natural abundance. The river may be a force that brings about change, as it inexorably flows to join the sea, and especially when it floods. The river can also be a boundary line between life and death, or simply a place of decision and change. The metaphor of the bridge occurs as an image for the transition into a new world of peace and justice.[154] From here it is not far to totally visionary lyrics. I would not say, however, that it is possible to distinguish neatly between the didactic and the metaphorical or visionary songs in Bond's work. On the contrary, some of the most successful in this later phase are those combining and balancing rational, lyrical, and emotional elements. One can say that such songs epitomize Bond's new epic-lyric theater.

Bond is indeed a dramatist who, without being spontaneously musical like John Arden, shows great sensitivity to the subtleties of song, whether poetic or didactic, and to the varieties of interaction between dramatic text and musical medium. He will almost certainly continue to experiment. A recent development is the emergence of epic narrative songs in *Human Cannon*, in which offstage battles and events are recounted. Here, a certain resemblance to the later work of Arden and D'Arcy can be observed. Both also employ songs of political commentary. Whereas Arden and D'Arcy are primarily influenced by traditional airs, setting new texts to well-known tunes or to improvised rhythms, Bond is more flexible and experimental with regard to the type of music he chooses—it may be anything from rock to contemporary operatic composition. In contrast with Arden and D'Arcy, Bond's texts are more concentrated and poetical. He has created some of the most powerful original song lyrics in all of modern drama.

4

The Dominance of Popular Song:
Music Hall to Rock

The detailed examination of song in the works of John Arden/Margaretta D'Arcy and Edward Bond illustrates the diversity of functions in the hands of playwrights who pay close attention to the role of music in their drama. Few other contemporary dramatists have so consistently and so extensively introduced song with so serious a purpose. Most notable among those who do are Peter Barnes, who uses a wealth of tunes, mostly from the popular sphere, as an integral element in his social satire, and John McGrath, working within alternative theater, who considers song an essential factor in the creation of a new popular theater with political intent. Although song is employed by other contemporary dramatists, it is not so consistently used throughout their work. Where it is introduced, however, its function can be complex. For example, nostalgic immersion in the past may have many-faceted ironic overtones. And tunes employed for their show-business effect may also have structural or thematic implications. Frequently the ambivalence of the playwright's attitude toward popular culture is reflected in song.

To determine whether general patterns are discernable in contemporary drama as a whole, it is necessary to examine less the careers of individual dramatists, and more the overall functions and origins of song. Certainly, one can say at this point that by far the largest number of songs in contemporary drama is derived from the popular sphere. Beyond this it does not seem meaningful to categorize according to period, as many dramatists draw on a wide range of popular song, from music hall or parlor favorites of the nineteenth century to pop and rock tunes of today.

No attempt has been made to mention every play with songs in the post-war period. I have chosen instead to concentrate on those plays whose songs exemplify particularly distinctive functions. Within the plays, only the most exemplary songs have been examined.

1. Satire and Theatrical Alienation Through Popular Song

PETER BARNES

Peter Barnes (born in 1931), although perhaps more controversial than other dramatists of his generation, is, I believe, a writer of great originality.

The fertility of his visual and verbal imagination creates a drama that could be characterized as total theater. The epithets applied to his playwriting (by himself and by critics) range from surrealistic and gothic to Jacobean and baroque. Some of the most memorable features of Barnes's theatrical technique are the use of quotation and literary parody, deliberate anachronism, stylized rhetoric, and grotesque visual imagery. Particularly striking as well is his tendency to scatter songs, or snatches of song, throughout his plays. They may seem on the surface jarringly incongruous, but they almost always reveal themselves on closer examination as subtly integrated into context and dramatic purpose.

Barnes introduces his aims as a playwright in terms of excitement, contrast, and contradiction:

> I wanted to write a roller-coaster drama of hairpin bends; a drama of expertise and ecstasy balanced on a tight-rope between the comic and tragic.[1]

> The aim is to create, by means of soliloquy, rhetoric, formalized ritual, slapstick, songs and dances, a comic theatre of contrasting moods and opposites, where everything is simultaneously tragic and ridiculous.[2]

Barnes wants to produce an unsettling theater that rouses and disturbs an audience. Behind any momentary disorientation, however, his ultimate goal is not confusion or anarchy but rather—in a manner similar to the Brechtian aim—the establishment of a discriminating political consciousness in the spectator:

> I want to help create a people who are sceptical, rational, critical, not impressed or fooled. In a word, free, and in the literal sense, ungovernable.[3]

Barnes is profoundly censorious of class differences, hierarchies, and the repression of feeling both in both English society and Western society. His goal is to write plays full of passion,

> glorifying differences, condemning hierarchies, that would rouse the dead to fight, . . . an anti-boss drama for the shorn not the shearers.[4]

Thus although he works within a "comedic vein," Barnes describes his intention as "intensely serious."[5] Likening his satiric technique to that in *Volpone* and *Measure for Measure,* he says that he is "using the theatre as a moral platform."[6] Barnes characterizes himself as both a comic writer and a political writer.

When asked about his basic principles in the integration of song into drama, Barnes replies:

> The theatre is an eclectic form, and . . . you must use everything to hand in order to convey what you wish to convey. . . . Prose, blank verse, music, dance, mime

. . . are part of the theatre, part of drama. . . . What one is after is total theatre, and popular songs are part of that total theatre.[7]

Barnes's reasons for the use of song in his dramatic work are closely related to his aims as a playwright. For him, music is never decorative or incidental. It is always intimately bound up with the meaning of the whole. As he puts it, the tunes are "part of the very tapestry of the work." It is significant, for example, that Barnes says he has never added a song during rehearsals as other dramatists sometimes do. Structure and technique have been too carefully worked out beforehand: "They are so integrated into it that you can't just add a song."

Barnes's techniques are derived from his unique sense of theatrical style. Songs are not used realistically but for stylistic effect. Since Barnes's theater is essentially nonrealistic, "created," "artificial," or "mannered," as he says, the melodies prove an essential element in establishing the unreality of the stage performance. Particularly, his use of incongruous airs—incongruous in character, situation or period—at inappropriate moments helps to create Barnes's particular type of "theatrical alienation."

> My ideal situation would be a situation as intense as *Oedipus Rex*, where a man seduces his mother and kills his father and then blinds himself, and he'll still be able to sing a song and yet not devalue the tragic framework when that song is actually delivered.

The songs often undercut the immediate mood or atmosphere, but they never diminish the intensity of the whole. Barnes is thus using the term alienation in a theatrical rather than a political sense: "I don't use it like Brecht uses it, not at all."

Barnes sometimes employs tunes with the traditional words, sometimes texts that he has satirically altered, and—particularly in the later work—original lyrics. Most of the familiar pieces come from the popular sphere, primarily from the American musical and secondarily from English music hall and parlor. But the dramatist also uses many other types of traditional melodies: Christian hymns, motets, madrigals, Negro spirituals, lullabies and nursery songs, political, patriotic tunes, and operatic airs. His satiric parodies given new words are most often derived from popular pieces, and his original lyrics also remain inspired by the popular idiom. Barnes understands himself as a pioneer in the use of popular song in modern drama:

> I can't think of another playwright who has used popular songs as part of the very tapestry of the work. I mean not used them naturalistically but stylistically.

A brief glimpse at the sources of Barnes' theatrical imagination reveals both literary and popular influences. Elizabethan and Jacobean drama, in which the playwright is widely read, have influenced particularly the rich texture of his language. Barnes readily acknowledges the inspiration of Artaud's Theatre of Cruelty, which may be seen both in his tendency to express passion through inarticulate sound and screams, and in the constant use of music, song, pantomime, dance, and grotesque visual effects.[8] Barnes refers frequently to surrealistic techniques, by which he loosely means his use of dreamlike and fantastic elements. On the other hand, the general similarity in aims to Brecht's critical, political theater has been noted.[9] Barnes says,

> I very consciously try to incorporate the two opposing poles of modern drama, which is Artaud and Brecht. They are the opposite sides of the coin. I try to actually use both of them.

The playwright emphasizes, however, that his songs do not state his purpose directly in the way that many of Brecht's do:

> His [Brecht's] are overtly political songs in the sense that they affirm a socialist message in the most . . . blatant way. I hope my plays do that, but I don't think the actual songs do.

Especially prevalent in Barnes's drama is popular culture of all sorts. This includes popular theater, particularly American musicals, but also English music hall, films, comic strips, farce, detective thrillers, and the like.[10] Barnes, who has worked for a film company and written film scripts, has been steeped in popular film culture. It is not surprising then that many of the tunes he uses come from films. "I started off, really, with film musicals. I have a vast knowledge of film, . . . particularly of the great MGM period . . . then the American stage musicals." He sees the primary influence of film on his work in his tendency to speed of dramatic timing. This is a "legacy of the films. We make rapid shifts now from thought to thought, feeling to feeling."[11] With respect to English popular theater Barnes says: "I'm steeped in music hall. I adore comics and comedians."[12] It was another tradition he grew up with from boyhood: "That again is something I was soaked in." His mother knew a wide range of music-hall favorites that she would gladly sing on request, and Barnes regularly attended live music hall performances until most of the halls he frequented were finally demolished in the late 1950s. One of his earliest unpublished plays contained many music-hall numbers. In his more mature work, however, American popular music prevails over English music hall. He explains his reasons for the use of music hall in somewhat the same terms as his use of film techniques; in effect, his words apply to the whole range of popular song:

> Their speed and immediacy of impact, and also change of mood, but particularly they're a shorthand. I think there's nothing so evocative as popular songs. They not only evoke certain feelings, but they evoke whole decades.[13]

The songs in Barnes's work have a variety of different, even contrasting functions. The playwright may use them to evoke feelings, or to create atmosphere or period. They can be "part of almost a folk memory," he says. But he also emphasizes their effectiveness for contrast and theatrical alienation. Frequently they break or undercut the mood of the scene in which they are embedded and contribute to a swift change of atmosphere:

> I usually use them . . . for an alienating effect, to jolt the audience, and to create a mood, usually a mood that is totally different from the mood that's created preceding.

In the sense that the songs are often deliberately anachronistic or inappropriate to context, they counteract any sense of realism in drama: "People must not get too immersed in the thing, you've got to bring them out from time to time."[14] Connected with the alienation effect are ironic and satiric functions. Such tunes provide impulses which lead to the formation of a critical attitude in the spectator. He says, "Most of the songs sum up something, have some sort of a message, either ironic or affirmative." As Barnes continues in his career, he is exploring new functions of music. One such experimental technique emerging, especially in the later work, is the continuation of a mood or a scene in the heightened form of singing at a point of emotional climax:

> When the pressure of a situation or the emotion of the characters within a play reach such a pressure point that language breaks down, and there is nothing for them to do except sing.

Despite the fact that the songs in Barnes's drama are entertaining, they are never merely ornamental; their function is always primarily critical: "Whatever forms I use, whether it is the drama or the song lyric it is still, above all, *information*."[15] The most important element, Barnes says, whether he is choosing a familiar popular song, parodying a text, or writing new and original lyrics, is always the meaning: "It's always the text, the lyrics, is the reason for it, not the musical setting ever. . . . It's the meaning every time." The entertainment effect is never allowed to overwhelm the more serious aims, whether these are primarily satiric, as in the earlier work, or epic, as in the later work.

The Ruling Class (1968) is a satire not simply on the English aristocracy, but more generally on human obsequiousness and deference to hierarchies, on human "ruthlessness, and inability to love, and to feel," and the "specifically English vice, this embarrassment about feeling."[16] The satire is characterized by incongruities, ludicrously ignored with English aristocratic good breeding. Some of the tunes are audaciously provocative; most are allotted either to Tucker, the manservant, or to Jack, the insane fourteenth Earl of Gurney. Tucker and Jack are the entertainers of this play, and they achieve their effect against the background of genteel nonreaction on the part of most of the others. At the beginning of the drama Tucker, having been bequeathed twenty thousand pounds by his dead master, unexpectedly goes into a wild caper and song:

> *Tucker.* Yippee! (*Shoots off the chair.*) *Twenty thousand! Twenty thousand smackers! Yawee!*
>
> *Jumping clumsily into the air, and clicking his heels together, he . . . gleefully capers forward.* (*Singing in a croak.*) 'I'm Gilbert the Filbert the Knut with a "K". (*Gives gouty high kick.*) The pride of Piccadilly, the blase roué. Oh Hades! The Ladies (*ogles Claire*) who leave their wooden huts, For Gilbert the Filbert, the Colonel of the Knuts.' Yah![17]

Scarcely raising an eyebrow, the family continues to read the will. In addition to the comic effects achieved by the exuberant performance of the usually-deferent Tucker, the incongruity of the lyrics, and the deliberate refusal by the family to react, the text can also be seen to have ironic implications arising from the dramatic situation. A comic music-hall patter song, it parodies the airs of the title-proud aristocracy, and in its horrible puns on "kernel" and "nuts" it also alludes to Tucker, who is "mad" with joy, and satirizes the family dilemma concerning the insane heir to the family title and fortune. "The family are all mad, but also he's mad with joy, so it works both ways," Barnes explains.

This element of theatrical performance characterizes the role of the rebellious Tucker until the end when, accused of murder, he makes his final exit, bawling an incongruous medley of the "Internationale" and "I'm only a Strolling Vagabond," the signature tune of a romantic gypsy-type balladeer O'Connor (p. 107). Grace's following remark, "What an exit" (p. 108), calls attention to the deliberate theatricality of the moment. Tucker's role as a whole is ambivalent and characterized by self-delusion: his pose as rebel is undermined by his deference to the family he now voluntarily serves. Likewise incongruous juxtaposition is typical of Tucker's songs. Throughout the play he sings both revolutionary hymns such as "The Red Flag" (p. 31) in his role as a one-man Communist cell, and romantic tunes such as the parlor ballad "Come into the Garden Maude" (p. 99), with text by Tennyson and melody by Balfe. As Barnes describes Tucker:

> He's got this image of himself as being rather gallant. . . . The delusion runs the whole gamut from being a Trotsky revolutionary to being a ladies' man and lady killer, and romantic hero.

His songs are incongruous both with respect to the character and to the situation in which they are sung. "Come into the Garden Maude," for example, is sung by the incoherently drunken Tucker just after the murder of Claire, making the contrast powerful. On the other hand, this piece, with all its connotations of nineteenth-century Victorian sentimentality, helps to achieve the transition from the Jack the Ripper scene of the 1880s to the present-day reality.

Jack, the fourteenth Earl of Gurney embodies one of the satiric points of the play in his person as he regresses from the insane and socially unacceptable God of Love in act 1 to the equally insane but better adapted God of Vengeance in act 2. Much of this development is reflected in his music. In three scenes, Jack unrealistically draws staid and proper spectators into song and dance routines that contradict their appearance of reserved good breeding. In act 1, scene 6, Jack is already exuberantly singing and dancing the "Varsity Drag," a popular dance melody from the American musical *Good News* (1927), when his conservative neighbors enter:

> *Suddenly, despite themselves, Mrs. Piggot-Jones, Mrs. Treadwell and Tucker sweep irresistibly Down Stage with the Earl, in an all-singing, all-dancing chorus line.* (p. 34)

The absurdity of these "solid, middle-aged WOMEN in grotesque hats" (p. 34) aping an American collegiate chorus line ridicules the artificiality of their good manners and the extremes to which their deference to the aristocracy will take them. The type of tune chosen embodies Jack's amiable and harmless high spirits.

In comparison, Jack's routine in act 2 appears much more calculating. To convince the Master in Lunacy that he is no longer insane, he unexpectedly launches into the "Eton Boating Song," and Truscott "without warning joins in, in a barber-shop duet" (p. 86). The success of this ruse mocks the spirit of "Old Boy" collusion among the upper classes. Barnes calls this song "a good example of shorthand. . . . It . . . evokes a whole upperclass world, . . . that whole attitude towards education and living and money and power." The style of the barbershop quartet, although inappropriate for that melody, was deliberately chosen to symbolize the sense of cohesion among the ruling classes. The singers in a barber shop quartet, Barnes explains, are

> usually . . . very much in tune. They sing without accompaniment, and there is a great closeness. So that's a very good example of using a song not only for comic effect, but also to evoke a whole relationship with all of its many ramifications.

The third episode contains black humor and irony as well as satire. Jack, having now adapted to upper-class norms, elaborates on the necessity for the death penalty. He then raves on sadistically about the pleasures of torture, imagining how the bones of a sinner are broken one by one on the wheel. The

From "The Eton Boating Song," words by William Johnson Cory, music by Algernon Drummond and Evelyn Wodehouse (London: Keith Prowse Music Publishing, n.d.).

Dry bones

Arranged by H.A.C.

From "Dry Bones," in *The Treasury of Negro Spirituals*, 4th impression, ed. H. A. Chambers (1953; Poole, Dorset: Blandford Press, 1982), pp. 26–30.

ensuing Negro spiritual, "Dry Bones," which the same conservative ladies join in "irresistibly," again questions the value of their breeding: "We understand each other perfectly. . . . Breeding speaks to breeding" (p. 94). At the same time, the episode satirizes Jack's development, his adoption of the vengeful norms of the ruling class, and ridicules the prevailing values of the upper classes, "the attitude of revenge and retribution and of backbreaking." For the meaning of the spiritual has been ironically reversed. Derived from the Old Testament book of Ezekiel, the original biblical text envisions a valley of dry bones resurrected and reassembled into an "exceeding great army" (Ezekiel 37 : 10), as symbol of the revival of hope for the Israelites. The spiritual, firm in its belief in this miracle, playfully enumerates the connection and disconnection of the bones as God's work. Jack, however, sadistically emphasizes only the disconnection of the bones, because the ruling class, to which he now belongs, systematically destroys others in a deadly assertion of its power and authority. It is relevant to mention that T. S. Eliot in "The Hollow Men" also reverses the implications of this biblical passage from Ezekiel in his negative vision of the hopelessness and sterility of modern civilization.

Other songs in *The Ruling Class* illustrate yet other possibilities of satire. The Victorian children's hymn "All Things Bright and Beautiful" is sung by the Gurney family at the beginning of the play as part of the funeral service for the late thirteenth Earl (p. 15). The effect is achieved simply through the inclusion of the seldom-used third stanza, usually omitted from modern hymn books:

> The rich man in his castle,
>   The poor man at his gate,
> God made them, high or lowly,
>   And order'd their estate.[18]

The spectacle of a family of the ruling class solemnly singing in praise of their own divinely-ordained privilege creates a critical distance in the modern audience. Edward Bond used the same hymn in *Narrow Road to the Deep North*. The effect there was more immediate and emotional, but Bond also achieved alienation through the situation in which it was sung.

The *La Traviata* episode in act 1, in which Grace is pawned off on Jack as an operatic "Lady of the Camelias" (p. 44), shows the desperation of Sir Charles to marry off his nephew, and the lengths to which he will go to achieve this end. When Grace and Jack, during their eccentric courtship, launch into the popular tune "My Blue Heaven" from 1927 (pp. 49–50), Barnes intended a "light, balloon effect." "If I could have had them in a hot air balloon I would have," he says. The song is an example of what Barnes calls an affirmative song. Although the playwright says he is not using it satirically, to my mind this sentimental piece about marital bliss does convey satirical overtones about the manipulations and perversions surrounding the planned marriage.

The final scene of act 2 (scene 11) expands the idea of death and destruction already illustrated by Jack's distorted spiritual "Dry Bones." Here the idea of physical and mental decay is brought to the fore and equated with the state of the ruling class. Visual imagery is crucial. The House of Lords is portrayed as consisting of "mouldering dummies . . . covered with cobwebs" and "goitred LORDS with bloated stomachs and skulllike faces" (p. 117). These skulls, and the skeleton one of them drags in, remind us of Jack's apocalyptic spiritual, but also recall the proverbial skeleton in the closet. When Barnes closes his scene with the song "Let Us Now Praise Famous Men," sung "exultantly" (p. 118) by this decaying company, the effect is grotesque. This late nineteenth-century imperialist hymn epitomizes the far-reaching power of tradition. In spite of their decadence, we know that these "men renowned for their power" (p. 118) have a very insidious and continuing influence.

The epilogue is a reminder of this fact. It consists exclusively of pantomimed action and Grace's song. The text, derived from Jerome Kern's ballad "Bill" from the musical *Show Boat* (1928), is a love ballad, but the effect in the context is foreboding, even gruesome. Jack, as the aristocratic Jack the Ripper, is systematically destroying the remnants of his earlier erotic love. The erotic impulse of the song provokes a murder we suspect will not be brought to justice, due to the class and privilege of its perpetrator.

The Ruling Class offers numerous variations on comic, ironic, and satiric functions of song. Memorable is the jolting incongruity of such numbers as "Varsity Drag" or "Dry Bones," but all of the melodies are carefully woven into the fabric of the play and all have subtly ironic overtones of meaning. On a deeper level, not one of them is superfluous or inappropriate.

Barnes's next play, *Leonardo's Last Supper* (1969), continues to explore similar contrastive, ironic, and satiric modes. An excellent film version of this short drama, directed by Peter Barnes (1977), conveys quite a faithful impression of the intentions of the stage play.[19] At the core of the drama lies the ironic contrast between spiritual and material values. The objective Lecturer at the beginning expounds on the spiritual and intellectual significance of the Renaissance, "a new birth: revival: resurrection" (p. 126); the drama concerns the grotesque and comic resurrection of Leonardo da Vinci and ends in a gory and violent second death. The songs underscore this contrast of values. When the supposedly dead Leonardo is delivered to their sixteenth-century Charnel House, the Lascas celebrate with an anachronistic song. A variant of the Negro spiritual "Didn't my Lord deliver Daniel?," the tune was originally intended as celebration of spiritual deliverance and as expression of faith in religious salvation. The Lascas, however, employ it to convey their hope of material profit and deliverance from material poverty. In the film version the anachronisms are underlined by the fact that husband

and wife go into an American musical-style soft-shoe dance to accompany their singing.

The final scene and closing song of this play exhibit parallels to the end of *The Ruling Class*. Again, Barnes has chosen an anachronistic American tune, "Mona Lisa," (by Jay Livingston and Ray Evans) popularized by Nat King Cole in the early 1950s. And again, as in the earlier play, the dramatist has embedded this light popular air in a context of murder and grotesque action:

> *Alphonso and Lasca . . . savagely descend on the corpse, hacking and cutting to drain off the blood.*
> *Maria crosses slowly to them with a knife, singing in a beery, maudlin voice . . .*
> *Maria. (Singing.)* 'Mona Lisa, Mona Lisa, men have named you.
> You're that lady with the mystic smile. . . .
> *All. (singing.)* 'Are you warm, are you real, Mona Lisa.
> Or just a cold and lonely, lovely work of art.' (pp. 151–52)

In the film version, Maria is polishing a saw as she begins to sing. During the final stanza the camera closes in on the faces of all three family members as they sing with harsh, triumphant, almost devilish expression on their faces.

Barnes intends this to be funny, cruel, disturbing and satiric all at the same time:

> That of course was a total satiric use of a popular song. In the sense of debasement of artistic values. It evokes a dreadful debasement of all civilized values.

It also establishes a connection between the physical action on stage and this idea of debasement of values, Barnes says:

> Actually what it is is the cutting up of Leonardo da Vinci. What they are doing, is what the song does as well. I mean the song cuts up . . . his one great completed painting, which is the Mona Lisa. The song debases the painting, and tears it to shreds, because of this rubbishy attitude towards art that . . . the people who wrote that song had. And what the Lascas do to Leonardo, the boys did to Leonardo's painting.

At the end of *Leonardo's Last Supper* the spectator is brought to consider critically the relationship between the mystery of artistic creation and mankind's animal nature, between aesthetic beauty and material profit. The song jolts us to laughter, while at the same time creating an awareness that this is not a laughing matter; this is indeed "a comic theatre of contrasting moods and opposites, where everything is simultaneously tragic and ridiculous."[20] The combination of twentieth-century popular tune and sixteenth-century setting draws our attention to the fact that civilization has not progressed markedly in the last three centuries.

The Bewitched (1974) explores new functions without abandoning the old. There is critical disagreement about whether the drama is a satire. Bryden sees in it a "scathing examination of the belief that any category of people, royal or not, is 'special'."[21] But Černy argues that it has no satirical message, and claims that it is essentially nihilistic or "absurd."[22] Barnes himself says that he would not call it a satire but instead a "tragic comic epic."

In accordance with the seventeenth-century Spanish setting, Barnes employs a large number of religious hymns in realistic contexts, evoking the Catholic ritual and historical atmosphere of seventeenth-century Spain. The piece resounds with "Te Deum," "Magnificat," "Gloria in Excelsis," "Miserere," as well as other hymns, plainsong, and old madrigals. Another feature connected with the theme of impotence and procreation is the use of lullabies and nursery songs. These have an emotional impact but also are alienated by the context. The German lullaby "Schlaf, Kinderl, schlaf!," for example, is sung at a moment of quiet happiness and hope (pp. 217–18). But the audience soon realizes that Ana's happiness is inspired by the prospect of worldly power, not motherhood: "My power grows wi' my belly. My happiness too; when the Queen Mother's finally banished 'twill be complete" (p. 218). In act 1, scene 8 when Carlos retreats from his worries into a fetal position, curled up in a cradle in the royal nursery, his deformed dwarf Rafael rocks him gently and sings "I Had a Little Nut Tree" (p. 234).[23] There is an element of comfort in this, but the emotion is soon exposed as regression into childhood, as irresponsible escape. Such ritual and atmospheric melodies represent the beginnings of a new function that becomes more important in Barnes's later work: "It's a different use of the song, in that it is an extension of the emotion or the situation in another form."

Barnes uses fewer popular songs in *The Bewitched* than in *The Ruling Class.* But certainly some of the most remarkable are derived from the popular sphere, and several are satirical. These include the "Sniffing Song," a grotesque parody of "Dig, Dig, Dig for Your Dinner" from the movie *Summer Stock;* a satiric variant of "Lucky in Love" from the musical *Good News* (1927); and Gershwin's "Clap Yo Hands" from the musical *Oh, Kay!* (1926). Barnes cites this latter, in which the dead and the living join together in a moment of contentment and unity (pp. 327–28), as an example of a song with a strongly affirmative (as compared to satirical) message. The dramatist says that he does not necessarily expect the audience to recognize the origins of his songs: "It's a bonus if they do, . . . and it's an extra laugh, but the laugh should be there anyway, because . . . it's the change in the medium."

One of the most interesting tunes of popular origins in the drama is sung in the torture chambers "to the painful, rhythmic cries of the PRISONERS" (p. 265). It is set to the melody of "John Brown's Body" or "The Battle Hymn of the Republic." Here Barnes switches, as in his other parodies, from a stylized seventeenth-century speech style to a more modern idiom:

> We'll sing a holy chorus when they're screaming on the rack.
> We try to make them Christians but they all get cardiacs.

We're rooting out the Devil and the other bric-a-brac.
God is marching on.

To keep the public happy is the object of the show.
They need the entertainment and it helps the status quo.
. . . .
The show is on the road!

(pp. 265–66)

The lyrics satirize the entertainment and distraction aspect of the gigantic Auto-da-fé. This purpose is even clearer in the original version, an adaption of "That's Entertainment." The original as quoted by Bernard Dukore contains a stronger element of the sadism that was also seen in Jack's rendition of "Dry Bones."[24] Barnes judges that the text as printed is not as funny as the original version, although the tune is better in the sense that it is "very stately." But the parody of "That's Entertainment" "was funnier, it . . . emphasized the show business aspect of the Auto-da-fé. . . . The incongruity of them all suddenly going into this American musical number was very funny." In either version the song is an exposure of the fact that power and authority inevitably lead to corruption.

In his later plays Barnes continues to explore new techniques. In *Laughter!* (1978), for example, a character conveys overwhelming emotional pressure by resorting to operatic singing. After the despot Ivan the Terrible has killed his own son, spoken words fail him, and he moves abruptly from inarticulate groans and cries to a sung passage from Gluck's *Orfeo and Eurydice:*

Ivan. Drown me, you tears, Suffering beyond the reach o' language. *KKK arrrxx ccrrrr aaaaakk AAAARRR*
He sings the air 'Men Tiranne' from Gluck's 'Orfeo and Eurydice'. (pp. 362–63)

Barnes chose this opera because, he says:

It's the only opera I could actually discover where somebody tries to bring back something, bring them back from the dead. Ivan has just killed his son, and instead of laments about it, he sings.

This scene provides an excellent example of a new technique Barnes is developing in his later work to heighten the existing mood and expand the emotional scope:

I have to find some other method, whereby I have to convey the emotional pressure that the character is under, or the characters are under, and the only way for them to go is either to dance or to sing.

Part 2 of *Laughter!* recalls to some extent the earlier plays. But in the epilogue, the contradictions between light-hearted song and dramatic situa-

From "On the Sunny Side of the Street," words by Dorothy Fields, music by Jimmy McHugh, in *The Thirties* (London: EMI Music Publishing, n.d.), pp. 32–34.

tion are so extreme that they no longer create comedy but rather almost unsupportable pain. As two concentration camp inmates die in the gas chamber of Auschwitz, they perform a dance and comic patter routine to the tune of "On the Sunny Side of the Street." Barnes's despairing conclusion in *Laughter!* is that comedy, even moralistic, satirical comedy, is of little or no use in bringing about change in this world. He says "I know it's not the answer. . . . Sometimes after seeing a comic I love, I'll say 'I loved it, but it didn't help'."[25]

Red Noses (1985) thematizes this problem of the role of entertainment in the creation of political consciousness. The play deals with reactions to sudden death and the breakdown of authority during the plague years of 1348–49, and examines the ways in which individuals and authorities cope with the unstable situation. In its epic scope and style, Barnes says, it resembles *The Bewitched:* "It's the end of a cycle, really. . . . In style . . . *The Bewitched* and *Red Noses* are oil paintings, in very thick oil with a pallet." In form, Barnes alternates popular lyrics with texts he has written himself. The attitude of Father Flote, head of The Red Noses, a band of clowns formed to distract people from their miseries, is well represented when he sings the popular song "Life is Just a Bowl of Cherries" (1931) to a group of people dying of the plague. Here popular music still is used satirically as in Barnes's earlier work.

A scene in which Pope Clement VI breaks into operatic-style song is more in the later manner of a play such as *Laughter!*, except the lyrics are now Barnes's own:

> *Clement VI.* A life which can't answer the question, "Why live?" isn't one. (*A distant choir sings the plainsong* Te lucis ante terminum.) Despair without bottom . . . Misery without meaning . . . (*Singing*) . . .
> "And when they write about these times.
> A hundred years of war and plague will get one line.
> And that will do.
> If they recall these days of death.
> They'll be asking Clement who?
> They won't care or even try to guess what men went through.
> And that's fine too.
> Because I've work to do . . ."
> And stop that pestilential howling. You call it singing, I call it neuralgia. Curtain![26]

The choice of colloquial idiom for the song lyrics and the self-conscious theatricality of the singer recall earlier techniques in Barnes. But the fact that the tune is highly stylized rather than popular, helps to convey the urgency of the emotion, Barnes says:

> The Pope . . . sings at certain climactic points in a very formal, operatic style . . . just a continuation of his own speech. He could have spoken the speech, but it has a resonance because he sings it.

Other of Barnes's original lyrics express the message of the play and the development of political consciousness in Father Flote and others. One song, "Join Together," recurs several times in the play, taking on more militancy as the characters gain awareness of their roles. It begins as a questioning of man's capacity for solidarity:

> Join together?
> Man's too frail.
> He's divided.
> It will fail.

(p. 40)

Under the influence of the rebellious Scarron this later becomes a fighting song, as the Red Noses join the Black Ravens and the Flagellants to resist the authorities:

> Join together
> Go, go, go
> Change conditions
> Here below.

(p. 80)

The melodies for both songs are composed by Stephen Deutsch, with whom Barnes has collaborated on several projects. Of this collaboration, Barnes says:

We have a little rule, in terms of the plays or the reviews. If there's a difference of opinion, the text wins every time. But, however, if he does what one would call art songs, which I have written, . . . there the music took preference over the lyrics. . . . But in terms of drama, it's the lyric every time, and the music has to fit.

Barnes may be characterized as a serious satirist with a grotesque verbal and visual imagination. In this respect, I see a certain limited similarity to the early plays of Edward Bond, particularly the period from *Early Morning* to *The Sea*. Both Barnes and Bond combine satire of English failings, especially of the repressive class structure, with wider satire on the abuses of power in Western civilization. Some aspects of their visual imagination appear similar. For example, the skeleton twin brother in *Early Morning* may be compared to the cobwebbed skeleton in Barnes's House of Lords. The heaven episodes of *Early Morning* are comparable to the grotesque resurrections in *Leonardo's Last Supper* and *The Bewitched*. The playwrights' use of satiric tunes in particular provides interesting parallels. The histrionic element in Mrs. Rafi's performance in *The Sea* is reminiscent of the entertainer aspects of Tucker's and Jack's roles. Both dramatists engender comedy by the introduction of song in inappropriate contexts. "Home Sweet Home" at the Orpheus and Eurydice rehearsal in *The Sea* is as startling as "Dry Bones" at an upper-class social tea in *The Ruling Class*. The Negro spiritual "Dry Bones" achieves social satire, whereas a secular Negro minstrel song "De Camptown Races" in Bond's *Passion* aims primarily at political satire. Both Bond and Barnes employ the "Eton Boating Song" as musical symbol satirizing rigid English class snobbery. Both have recourse to Christian hymns as technique of exposing the negative intermingling of religious and temporal power. "Abide With Me" is sung as the imperialists storm the colonial city in *Narrow Road to the Deep North*, while "All Things Bright and Beautiful" in *The Ruling Class* underlines the worldly might of those in power. Particularly interesting in both dramatists is the deliberate use of lighthearted popular songs in the context of murder or violent death. For example, "Life is a Milliner's Show" and "Daring Young Man on the Flying Trapeze" in *The Swing* were chosen by Bond for their ironic discrepancy to the cruelty of the action. "Mona Lisa" at the close of Barnes's *Leonardo's Last Supper* attains a similar effect. The irresponsibility and negative values of the singers are characterized in this way.

This comparison can only be of limited scope, for the two playwrights have developed in different directions. Whereas Bond has increasingly pared down his dramatic style and worked for honed precision, Barnes seems to become more and more extravagant in his dramatic language and his structural techniques. Bond has developed new commentary and metaphorical functions of song in his drama and tends to the creation of original lyrics carefully composed as dramatic poetry. Barnes has created new emotional and atmospheric functions in sung passages and remains inspired by the idiom of popular song. Both, however, in their earlier plays have significantly contributed to the creation of satiric song in twentieth-century drama.

In some respects Barnes's work is also comparable to that of John Arden. The two show similarities in the exploration of satire through song. Above all, their techniques of live theater—music, song, dance, mime—challenge both producers and audiences. The dramatists have encountered severe production difficulties, mainly because of the elements of stylization and the integration of music in their dramatic work. In *The Ruling Class*, as in Arden's *Live Like Pigs*, no one understood how to combine the singing with the dramatic action. Barnes says of *The Ruling Class* when it was first produced, that "it was looked upon as something very bizarre." In his later work Barnes seems to be moving closer to the later Arden/D'Arcy collaborative style in the integration of prose, blank verse, traditional, and newly written lyrics. The production difficulties, of course, remain. Barnes remarks of Arden: "It's very sad that he has had the same problems I had getting work on." Productions outside of the established theater, as in the case of Arden/D'Arcy, or long delays, as in the case of Barnes, are the typical results.

Peter Barnes is the most important pioneer in the introduction of popular song into postwar drama. Arden and D'Arcy are pioneers in the integration of the folk heritage into drama. All three share a strong sense of live theater. Barnes says: "I never consider a play finished until the curtain goes down on the opening night." And all three, through the music and song in their work, contribute to the creation of a modern form of total theater in England today. Speaking of the use of song in drama, Barnes says: "I just have a feeling that it's now accepted that you can do that if you wish. But when I did *The Ruling Class* it wasn't."

Despite the influence of such prewar playwrights as T. S. Eliot, Yeats, Auden, Isherwood and particularly Sean O'Casey, and the organizing theatrical and musical imagination of Joan Littlewood, it still remained to such postwar dramatists as Arden/D'Arcy, Barnes, and Bond to weave song and music into a dramatic stage play, making them an integral part of the whole in both structure and meaning. Because of the efforts of these playwrights it has become not only acceptable but almost imperative for certain types of plays (particularly those aimed at a popular audience) to contain song. In my opinion, however, the work of Arden/D'Arcy, Barnes, and Bond offers a far more imaginative and better integrated use of song than any other works in contemporary drama.

Other dramatists have profited from these pioneering efforts. Tom Stoppard uses techniques of jolting transitions and theatrical alienation that are reminiscent of Barnes. But his ultimate aims are quite different, and he does not concentrate as intensively as Barnes on the integration of song. Others may introduce some satirical tunes in their work, but they are not so consistently satirical as Bond, Barnes, Arden, and D'Arcy.

CECIL P. TAYLOR

Cecil P. Taylor (born in 1929) may serve as example of a playwright who does not so subtly integrate songs into the dramatic context, and who is not so consistently satirical. Taylor produced several dramas with songs and some musicals, including a historical documentary *Aa Went te the Blaydon Races* (1962, with his own music); an allegory *Who's Pinkus? Where's Chelm?* (1966, with music by Monty Norman); and the realistic *And A Nightingale Sang . . .* (1977, with popular tunes of the 1940s). His last play, *Good* (1981), represented "a radical departure" in his work, "a deadly serious play spiced throughout with an impish, almost daredevil humour."[27] It is a "tragedy which I have written as a comedy, or *musical-comedy*," as he put it.[28] I believe this was one of his best plays; unfortunately it was his last, as he died in December 1981.

In this drama, the humor with which he looks at developments in Nazi Germany never disguises his feeling of deep anguish and anger about this "trauma in recent history."[29] The major character, Halder, is a "good" German, a wavering academic who allows himself to be drawn into Nazi politics to the point where he becomes an adviser to the government, helping to organize and justify euthanasia and the extermination at Auschwitz. With his Jewish psychologist friend Maurice, Halder discusses his personal neurosis: crucial developments in his life are accompanied by music, most often by popular songs, playing in his imagination,

> bringing music into the dramatic moments of my life. But from '33, they became an addiction. Jazz bands . . . café bands . . . tenors . . . crooners . . . symphony orchestras . . . Depending on the particular situation and my mood.[30]

A strategy for survival? Turning the reality into fantasy?

(p. 1)

I can't lose myself in people or situations. Everything's acted out against this bloody musical background.

(p. 5)

Sometimes the tunes that come to his mind simply strengthen mood, atmosphere, or theme. At times, however, this technique enables Taylor to make satiric points. As Halder listens to the problems of his new friend Freddie, an SS major who is unable to have children, the song weaving through the scene is "My Blue Heaven":

> *Freddie.* [. . .] This regime. . . . It's obsessed with fucking breeding. I'm going to be stuck major [. . .] Till I breed some fucking kids [. . .]
> *Crooner.* [. . .] Just you and me
> And my baby makes three
> In my blue heaven.[31]

(p. 53)

This sentimental song of marital and parental happiness exposes the hollow ideals of the Nazi regime. The reader will recall that Barnes in *The Ruling Class* uses the same song to similar effect.

The end of the drama creates a mood of sardonic humor. As Halder arrives in Auschwitz, the prisoners' band is playing: "The significant thing: the band was *real*" (p. 69). Instead of the imaginary bands and singers of his mind which have turned "reality into fantasy" (p. 1) all his life, his fantasy has been transformed into a situation of gruesome reality. This dramatic constellation is reminiscent of similar moments of insight in Barnes and Bond. Barnes at the end of *Laughter!* confronts popular song and Auschwitz extermination policy; Bond warns "At Auschwitz they hanged men to waltzes."[32] Here, too, any laughter aroused by Taylor's musical juxtapositions dissolves in horror, so that the end result is critical consciousness.

The satirical use of song in contemporary drama is most prevalent among committed left-wing playwrights such as Arden and D'Arcy or Bond, socialists such as Barnes or C. P. Taylor, or political writers and companies in alternative theater such as John McGrath and the 7 : 84 Company—following the tradition of Theatre Workshop and Joan Littlewood. Such writers and companies often draw their satirical songs from the sphere of popular culture, although traditional folk song is also important. The use of popular culture is frequently political; such dramatists may wish to appeal to a nonelite audience, or they may wish to examine the relationship between society and popular culture. The playwrights' attitude towards popular culture is often ambivalent; they may love popular songs but be critical of them at the same time. Indeed, such songs are often introduced because of their negative connotations of superficiality and triviality.

2. The Ambivalence of Popular Culture

In their attitude toward popular music, many other dramatists of the modern period—not just the satirists—adopt a profoundly ambivalent stance. On the one hand, they are deeply uneasy with the manifestations of popular culture of the present day; on the other hand, they have a certain nostalgia for a past in which aspects of popular culture are subtly glorified. The dramas of the postwar period are often haunted by the melodies of earlier eras, particularly of the 1930s and 1940s when the playwrights were children and adolescents. Sometimes they look back nostalgically to even earlier periods; for example, to the Edwardian era. Many playwrights of the generation born around 1930 exhibit a "nostalgic affection for a fading environment. They preferred . . . music-hall songs to rock 'n' roll."[33] Even if a dramatist dislikes the forms of entertainment he sees today, there remains a longing; sometimes for that stage of personal development in which one was able to take popular tunes seriously, sometimes simply for an earlier era that seems at a distance less vulgar and more intact.

JOHN OSBORNE

The playwright who reflects this type of ambivalence most clearly in his dramatic work is John Osborne (born in 1929). The feeling both of cultural degeneracy and of cultural nostalgia is prominent in *The Entertainer*, a work that focuses on the decline of the English music hall at various levels. Aspects of music-hall nostalgia can be found elsewhere in Osborne's work, from *Look Back in Anger* (1956) to *A Sense of Detachment* (1972). *The End of Me Old Cigar* (1975) takes its title from a music-hall song with aggressive male sexual implications. Many of Osborne's plays depict central characters who are performers, entertainers, or more generally role-players, with all the ambivalences of such functions. The playwright typically is of several minds about the condition of popular culture. Along with his dissatisfaction with its contemporary state, there is a distinct nostalgia for an earlier period in which the music hall was supposedly "truly a folk art."[34]

Osborne's writings are not always consistent concerning his attitude towards mass culture, or even his self-conception as a dramatist. In "The Writer in His Age" (1957) he fulminates against the "cultural, emotional and spiritual rubbish"[35] that the mass media offer the common man, "the man on the street corner":[36]

> He is still sitting on the pile of rotting culture, the half-chewed bones of symbols and debased values that should have been washed away long ago.[37]

Here, Osborne sees his role as a dramatist quite clearly: He says he has

> got to start trying to clear away the rubbish . . . I believe a writer's job today is quite clear and staggeringly difficult. It is to try and get over to as many people as possible, to the ash-can.[38]

On the other hand, in his essay "That Awful Museum" (1961) Osborne could contradict this view: "It's not my job *as a dramatist* to worry about reaching a mass audience if there is one, to make the theatre less of a minority art."[39]

Osborne's dramatic creation is on the whole nonintellectual, and emotionally oriented; his words in "They Call it Cricket" (1958) are central to his playwriting: "I want to make people feel, to give them lessons in feeling. They can think afterwards."[40] He sums up his "present socialist attitude" as "an experimental attitude to feeling."[41] Osborne's approach to dramatic technique is similarly experimental but nonsystematic. An early statement yokes together the ideas of intimacy and enormity, remoteness and comfiness, without making it clear how this is to be realized:

> I think of a theatre that doesn't exist, one that combines the intimacy of the Court [Royal Court Theatre] with the grandeur of a circus. I'd love to write something for a circus, something enormous and immense, so that you might get a really big enlargement of life and people.[42]

In writing about the personal influences that contributed to his later dramatic creation, Osborne in his autobiography also reveals a certain ambivalence. The working-class music-hall tradition on his mother's side of the family remains in his memory as loud, vulgar, highly emotional, and excitingly vital, but personally he felt more comfortable among the quiet and genteel Osborne relatives. He recalls that his Grandfather Grove was a partial model for Billy Rice,[43] and that his own father knew a vast repertory of popular songs.[44] He recalls his mother's description of a music-hall sketch by John Lawson and points out:

Twenty years later it was this shaky fragment of theatrical memory that was to nudge me towards *The Entertainer;* not, as I was told authoritatively by others, the influence of Bertolt Brecht.[45]

Osborne's personal, firsthand memory is strong in the case of the music-hall comedian and singer Max Miller, "The Cheeky Chappie," who began as an army entertainer in World War I and became well known as a professional entertainer in the 1930s and 1940s. Miller has been suggested as a model for Archie Rice,[46] but Osborne appears to have loved and admired Miller as much for his flashiness and his audacious clothing as for any theatrical genius.[47] Whatever models he may have used, Osborne's insight into the appeal of music-hall technique and structure is significant and has certainly influenced the dramatic form of *The Entertainer.* As the dramatist says,

It is sometimes overlooked that the halls relied so much on undiluted drama, where laughter was interrupted perhaps for twenty minutes at a time by very simple appeals to emotions like jealousy, crude patriotism, lost love, poverty, death. . . . Even a nude backcloth with new actors every ten minutes or so provided the driving rhythm of dramatic "turns" and changes of mood and response.[48]

Although Osborne appears to have experienced a prewar and wartime exposure to cinema comparable to that of Peter Barnes, who at a similar age also went on virtual movie orgies,[49] the effect of film technique in Osborne's plays is much less apparent than in the drama of Barnes.

Osborne's work is permeated with the influence of music hall and popular song. *Look Back in Anger* (1956) contains a song and dance number after the manner of Bud Flanagan and Chesney Allen.[50] Flanagan and Allen were music-hall comedians and singers who teamed up in the early 1920s, and who were members of the "Crazy Gang" at the Palladium from 1935 to 1939. During the war they toured to entertain the troups, and then split up as a comedy team in 1946. They had their own special style of singing and popularized a number of music-hall songs, including "Underneath the Arches." The function of Jimmy and Cliff's routine in the drama is similar to that of their continuous sparring and bantering: the surface gaiety and activity cover a deep despair—at least on Jimmy's part. In this respect Jimmy is play-acting in somewhat the same manner as Archie in *The Entertainer;* the entertainer's facade of nonchalance may be seen as an attempt to hide a personal sense of hopelessness and desperation.

In *The Entertainer* (1957) music hall is reflected on at least four different levels, in structure, characterization, theme, and symbolism. The drama has original music by John Addison (who later composed the music to John Arden's *The Workhouse Donkey*):

The work is scored for viola, B♭ trumpet, trombone, percussion and piano. When all these instruments are not available it is desirable that at least a percussion player be used with a piano.[51]

John Addison has deliberately created music that sounds derivative and superficial. Osborne describes his intentions concerning the music: "The latest, the loudest, the worst" (p. 12). In keeping with the actual period of the setting and performance, the mid-1950s, the introductory music is rock and roll. This type of music seems to symbolize cultural degeneracy. In this respect there is an interesting parallel to the negative evaluation of rock and roll in another contemporary dramatist, Arnold Wesker.

The set designed by Alan Tagg at the Royal Court Theatre was intended to suggest tatty music-hall atmosphere, even in the family scenes. The music-hall numbers were played at the front of the stage with a microphone, while the gaudy gauze front-cloth with the naked lady separated this area from the Rice's living quarters. The film version (also directed by Tony Richardson) unfortunately dispenses with this effect, setting the entire drama in an extremely realistic manner and relating it to details of the outside world.[52] The stylistic and structural contrasts between the private family scenes and the public music-hall ones are thus lost. The realism of the film medium has destroyed the original structure.

The implications of music-hall technique for the form of the play are expounded by Osborne in his "Note" preceding the Faber edition:

> I have . . . used some of the techniques of the music hall . . . because I believe that these can solve some of the eternal problems of time and space that face the dramatist. . . . It cuts right across the restrictions of the so-called naturalistic stage. Its contact is immediate, vital, and direct. [p. 7]

It thus appears that a non-naturalistic approach to the play is essential for a realization of the possibilities that the drama offers and the author intends. Katharine Worth emphasizes this contrast in her evaluation of the production:

> It was that movement between the two stages—the cramped private one where sad events like the son's death occurred and the glaring, public one where they were translated into 'performance'—that made the play such an exhilarating as well as moving experience.[53]

Some reservations, however, appear necessary. Osborne's ideal of achieving music-hall immediacy and direct contact with the audience is effected only in the performance numbers, through the jokes and the songs. In the family scenes he has used a naturalistic technique without any audience contact and with causal links in both time and space.

At the level of characterization the major focus is on the figure of the singer and comedian Archie Rice, who is also allotted a majority of the music-hall songs. The role was played by Sir Laurence Olivier in both stage and film versions. In the family sphere Archie is characterized by egocentrism, patronizing arrogance, moral apathy, and a desire to avoid responsibility and emotional commitment. We are given to understand that his studied nonchalance is an assumed pose, a continuation of his public performance in private life (p. 34). Osborne warns against taking Archie's words at face value:

> Some believed Archie Rice when he said: 'I don't feel a thing'. . . . They were incapable of recognizing the texture of ordinary despair, the way it expresses itself in rhetoric and gestures.[54]

In his song numbers, Archie's attitudes are expanded and some new characteristics are added, such as superficial chauvinism and acceptance of the status-quo of English society in the mid-1950s. In other words, the primary function of the songs is not contrast but enlargement of characterization and creation of a period atmosphere and of music-hall feeling. But these songs are public performances themselves and cannot be taken as straightforward statements of Archie's beliefs.

"Why Should I Care" (pp. 24–25), his first piece, develops the idea of apathy, nonchalance. There is also a hint of a protective function: "If they see that you're blue, they'll—look down on you" (p. 25). John Addison's music to this song is light and jaunty, emphasizing the meaning of the text. In the film version, Archie accompanies his tune with a bit of indifferently executed tap dancing. In a reprise at the end of the drama, Archie is finally confronted with his failure, personal and professional. He falters in his singing, finally breaking off in mid-sentence (p. 89), no longer able to keep up a facade.

"We're All Out for Good Old Number One" (pp. 32–33) reflects the state of England at the end of the colonial era. Thematically, it carries on from Jean's ironic remark in the preceding family scene: "*We're* all right. God save the Queen!" (p. 31). It is a piece of the mid-1950s that reflects a resignative acceptance of the welfare state with mild jokes about "drab equality" and the National Health Service. And it is typical of the Suez era, with a sense of last-ditch chauvinism:

> Those bits of red still on the map
> We won't give up without a scrap.
> What we've got left back
> We'll keep—and blow you, Jack!
>
> (p. 33)

Addison's tune is strong, enthusiastic, and march-like. It trumpets the questionable assurance of the text. The melody is also sung in a reprise during Archie's final turn. Interrupting the rock and roll nude tableau (p. 86), Archie enters the limelight for a final time. But as "performance becomes a night-mare soliloquy,"[55] the hollowness of the sentiments becomes painfully appar-ent, and he does not finish.

Archie's third major number, "Thank God I'm Normal" (pp. 60–61) is at a surface level patriotic, but at a deeper level ironic. Again, it cannot be understood as a simple statement of Archie's beliefs but rather as perfor-mance. The audience already knows that the self-praise of the first stanza ("I'm . . . Not mad for women") is inappropriate in Archie's case. And the entire feeling of self-satisfaction of the normal, moderate, middle-of-the-road Englishman is caricatured not only by the repetition "normal, normal, nor-mal," but also by the use of Edward Elgar's "Land of Hope and Glory" from the *Coronation Ode* in combination with the "nude in Britannia's helmet . . . holding a bulldog and trident" (p. 61). The elevated, serious, patriotic sentiment of the ode is deflated by the vulgar show-business trappings, and the normalcy of the singer is revealed as hollow bombast.

These music-hall "turns" thus expand the idea of Archie as performer. Their function is not to create critical distance in the audience. Despite elements of irony and social satire, the songs involve the audience in the ambivalence of the position of the performer. Archie's technique of self-deprecation also makes the theater audience feel uncomfortable and thus draws it into his performance. As Peter Davison points out, this is the technique of traditional music hall rather than Brechtian alienation:

> The aim and the effect of breaking continuity in English music hall is quite different from the effect of Brechtian alienation. In the music hall . . . involvement is broken in the act . . . and a different kind of relationship is developed between the person of the performer and the audience rather than with his persona. But the detachment from the persona . . . is not at the expense of final, overall involve-ment; for the audience, though momentarily detached and alienated, becomes thereafter more deeply involved. Thus, despite John Osborne's attempt at *Verfrem-dungseffekt*, the audience of *The Entertainer* becomes not alienated but doubly involved, because his use of the technique is too closely associated with the technique of his subject matter, the music hall.[56]

In a later book Davison has come to understand that this is not a failing but precisely Osborne's intention.[57]

Osborne's primary purpose as dramatist is to create emotional involvement in the audience, and the music-hall turns achieve this effect. Nowhere is this clearer than in the melody that closes the play. Archie's final number concen-trates all its emotional intensity on the isolation of the individual in the face of defeat and death. The audience is thus left with a strong feeling of pity and involvement. *The Entertainer* works most strongly on an emotional level.

On the thematic level, music hall exemplifies the discussion about the decline of entertainment standards in contemporary England. "The music hall is dying" is Osborne's first statement in his "Note" accompanying the play. Old Billy Rice is the personification of earlier music-hall ideals. Not only Archie but Osborne also feels a deep admiration for Billy and a nostalgic longing for lost standards. To some extent this general theme of music-hall decay is also embodied in the tunes. In contrast with Archie's superficial, vulgar, and ambivalent numbers, Billy is characterized by the firm determination of his hymns, "Rock of Ages," "Nearer My God to Thee," and "Onward Christian Soldiers." When other characters in the play sing songs (in the realistic context of the party scene), they are significantly representative of great figures of an earlier era: for example, a Kipling ballad, "The Absent-Minded Beggar," (pp. 64–65) from the Boer War (1899),[58] set to music by Edward Elgar and sung on the halls; and "The Boy I Love Is Up in the Gallery" (p. 66), the song with which the famous music-hall singer Marie Lloyd achieved her first great success in the 1880s. Archie, too, at the only moment in the play when he expresses emotion openly, looks back to an earlier period of his life and to an earlier musical form of expression; he remembers a negress singing the blues and says "I wish to God I could feel like that old black bitch . . ., and sing" (p. 71).

There is general critical agreement that music-hall decay is also reflected on a symbolical level in the play. Most critics point out the correspondence between the decline of music hall and the political and social decline of England in the 1950s. Katharine Worth sees an interesting parallelism between *The Entertainer* and Shaw's *Heartbreak House:*

> The ship-like look of Shotover's house was a visual metaphor for England, the ship of state. . . . Archie Rice's music hall theatre stands for England too; a run-down version of the glorious halls of the past.[59]

Dying music hall has also been seen as a symbol for the disintegration of the family.[60]

Osborne's view of the decline of popular entertainment in *The Entertainer* leaves us with many questions. The nostalgia of this drama brings to mind the warning words of Raymond Williams, which seem especially applicable to Osborne:

> It is common to make a sentimental valuation of the music-halls as expressing the spirit of 'Old England' . . ., or as signs of great cultural vitality. In fact the music-hall was a very mixed institution, and there is a direct line from . . . the music-halls to the mass of material now on television and in the cinemas, which it is stupid to overlook. To complain of contemporary work of these kinds—from striptease shows to 'pop' singers—and to use the music-hall as an example of contrasting vitality or health, is to ignore the clear evidence that it was the illegitimate theatres and the music-halls which established these kinds of entertainment.[61]

The songs in Osborne's *A Sense of Detachment* (1972) are also tinged with nostalgia, but function within the play's framework of scathing criticism. In part a satire on experimental playwriting, this drama is a particularly difficult one to evaluate in the study. It demands performance, as does for example the related *Publikumsbeschimpfung* by Peter Handke. In the recording of the performance at the Royal Court,[62] the audience responded with laughter during the first half of the play, but grew restive and unresponsive later on. In this drama—without beginning and end and without plot—most of the songs are sung without motivation or reason. A majority is from the popular sphere, although there are also some hymns, patriotic tunes, excerpts from classical vocal music, some pieces by Robert Burns, and a few folk songs, including "Widdicombe Fair." The popular tunes represent the entire twentieth century, from "Yankee Doodle Boy" (1904) to "Jean" (1969), with a majority chosen from the 1930s.

Song in this play is treated as just one more "obvious overfamiliar theatrical device",[63] a technique used to persuade the audience that they are being entertained. Osborne caricatures the facile use of music in drama to cover over awkward or empty moments. Hymn singing is characterized as "scraping the barrel" (p. 22) in terms of entertainment. Music-hall technique is satirized by making the Chairman totally ineffectual. He can neither organize the chaos nor animate the others to sing.

Nevertheless, to the audience's and actors' surprise, songs do get sung. Act 1 ends with a self-consciously theatrical caricature of "Widdicombe Fair," which mentions several contemporary dramatic authors. The reaction of the (planted) Interrupter to the melodies that open Act 2 mocks the technique as outmoded: "Joan Littlewood did this years ago" (p. 28). One of the few tunes the actors actually seem to enjoy singing is "If You Were the Only Girl in the World" (from the 1930s); all end up joining in and holding hands (p. 30). In performance, this moment was one of the few the audience seemed to enjoy enthusiastically. In view of the aimlessness of the drama as a whole, it is scarcely surprising that it peters out without any sense of ending. Even the fact that the tune "Widdicombe Fair" is repeated and sung by the entire cast hand in hand with its right words (p. 59) does not create any sense of dramatic climax.

In this anti-drama, songs are a major device in expressing Osborne's criticism. But this criticism is too indiscriminate to be convincing. Since many of the tunes are popular ones from the 1930s there is a certain atmosphere of sentimental nostalgia evoked. Ahrends attempts to distinguish between *A Sense of Detachment* and Theater of the Absurd by asserting that in Osborne's drama all contradictions are experienced as meaningful.[64] I see the play, however, as a frustrating experiment in total caricature which negates everything and leaves nothing seeming meaningful or worthwhile. From here it is certainly not a large step to other contemporary authors who have been associated with the Theatre of the Absurd.

3. Variants of Musical Nostalgia

PETER NICHOLS

A play that is just as nostalgic as *The Entertainer* but more honest about its nostalgia is Peter Nichols's *Forget-me-not Lane* (1971). This is a partly bitter, partly longing dramatic memory about adolescence in the World War II era. It is more personal and more autobiographical than Osborne's drama. (Nichols was born in 1927.) Osborne, just two years younger than Nichols, looks back in *The Entertainer* not to his own adolescence during the war, nor to the adolescence of his father's—and Archie's—generation in the 1920s, but to that of his grandfathers' generation. The Edwardian era in which Billy Rice was young becomes the object of a nostalgia not based on personal experience. In *The Entertainer*, nostalgia is motivated less by the pleasure of personal memories than by a failure to cope with the present. In contrast, Nichols in *Forget-me-not Lane* limits himself to an experience similar to his own; his major character Frank was fourteen in 1941, as Nichols was himself. Frank's reminiscences are motivated by a desire to come to terms with himself and his own past.

What is interesting about this drama is that the nostalgia itself is thematized. Nichols examines the social reality of the 1940s unsparingly, but he also investigates the psychological needs that lead him to look back. To a large extent, this longing is expressed in terms of popular culture, particularly popular song. This is apparent not only in the title, which comes from a Flanagan and Allen number of the 1940s sung at the end of the play, but also in Nichols's choice of prologues. The first, a poem by Martin Bell entitled "The Songs," expresses the key idea of the drama:

> Continuous, a medley of old pop numbers—
> Our lives are like this . . .
>
> . . . .
> . . . We're dreaming while we work.
> Be careful, keep afloat, the past is lapping your chin.[65]

The second, from Philip Larkin's *All What Jazz*, introduces the theme of aging husbands and bitter wives, "deserted by everything that once made life sweet," reminiscing about the excitement of jazz. Nichols' play explores the importance of family heritage and of adolescent experience for the growth of the adult personality, and portrays the frustrations of adult life.

The songs in the play function almost entirely as evocation of the early 1940s. "The play is a hymn to the Forties," says John Russell Taylor.[66] Most of the melodies are not sung by the actors but played on a tape recorder. This stands in one of the six or eight doors of the set which represent access to facets of the memory. A majority of the musical numbers is concentrated in the medley of recorded pop songs and dance tunes that opens each of the two acts (p. 13 and p. 59). Act 1 begins with a "record recital for about twenty minutes" (p. 13), including tunes by Tommy Dorsey, Vera Lynn, the "Forces Sweetheart" of World War II, The Squadronnaires of the RAF, and others.

But the audience also is treated to one hilarious example of a wartime concert party in which young Frank, his best friend Ivor, and his mother Amy entertain the troops with an onstage rendition of "There'll Always Be an England," a song of 1939 (pp. 31–32). The performance includes a "young blonde wearing Union Jack satin briefs" (p. 31), who roller-skates and tap-dances to the tune. A comparison to the nude in Britannia's helmet in Osborne's *The Entertainer* is relevant, but the mood here is completely different. In both cases the attraction of the woman as sexual object is linked to the superficial patriotism of the song to form a tableau of supreme vulgarity. Osborne uses this tableau as example of the degeneracy of modern popular entertainment. Nichols, while not denying the frivolity, laughs indulgently and light-heartedly at his own adolescent fascination and excitement. Throughout the play the blonde reappears as an unreal symbol of temptation and of adventure that never materializes.

Treating nostalgia itself as a major theme in the play, Nichols on the one hand takes a hard and even bitter look at the realities of life in the early 1940s, with all its frustrations, embarrassments, and deprivations. The world of the parents and grandparents is treated with equal honesty. Frank's father Charles says of his own personal experience in the Edwardian era, in what he ironically calls the "Good Olde Days":

> My memories . . . may be summarized as the Three D's: dirt, drunkenness and disease. The twin stars of our tiny firmament were Big Jim, the fawning publican, and Ikey Stein the pawnbroker. (p. 78)

On the other hand, Nichols also admits to himself that adolescence produces memories which have a very special intensity and meaning for later life. Ursula and Frank reminisce:

> *Ursula.* We took what pleasure we could and hoped for more later . . .
> *Frank.* None the less there were pleasures, never to be equalled! Listening to jazz.
> Imitating our elders. (p. 44)

After military service in India at the end of the war, Frank and his friend Ivor try to resume their adolescent intimacy by playing their favorite old records of popular songs, but they no longer prove appropriate to adult experience. Frank has priggishly graduated to classical music, and the two former friends drift apart. In a long monologue Frank sums up:

> Somehow the time since nineteen-fifty seems unconvincing and goes too fast. The calendar pages fall away at silent film speed . . . the forties are my golden age, my

CHORUS

From "There'll Always Be an England," words and music by Ross Parker and Hughie Charles, in *I'll Be Seeing You . . . featuring the songs, the artists and the memories of the Second World War* (London: EMI Music Publishing, 1979), pp. 89–93. © 1939 by Gordon V. Thompson Music, a division of Canada Publishing Corporation, Toronto, Canada. Used by permission.

spiritual home [. . .] I know they were drab but austerity sounds so morally superior to affluence. (pp. 74–75)

The play ends with a rendition of the title song by all the actors.

In *Forget-me-not Lane* the sphere of popular culture is associated with adolescence, and pop songs are clearly seen as limited expressions of adolescent feelings. In spite of this, Nichols maintains—as Barnes did—that popular songs are extraordinarily evocative and have a magic and value all their own, perhaps because of the unreflected and undigested quality of promise associated with them.

Two other dramatists of the same generation who also introduce popular songs of the 1940s to evoke the atmosphere of the war years are David Mercer (born in 1928) and Cecil P. Taylor. Mercer in *Then and Now* (1979) follows the development of two young lovers from different social classes, Isabel and John, from 1945 to the 1970s. The atmosphere of VE day in London is created partly by offstage singing of a crowd in the streets, partly by the playing of a Vera Lynn record, "When the Lights Go on Again." The song, which closes act 1, also creates an ironic transition to the almost unchanged world of act 2:

Isabel. I think: thank God it's all over. Now we can get back to normal. . . .
John. I think: by Christ things are going to be different!
The room is nearly dark. He crosses to the gramophone, switching a lamp on . . . The record begins to play.[67]

Thirty years later the memory of Vera Lynn's singing takes the two back again: "Funny, how the end of the war seems just last week . . . The other day, really" (p. 122).

Taylor's comedy *And A Nightingale Sang* . . . (1977) makes more extensive use of music, but is on the whole a weaker play. The title is derived from a popular song of the war period, "A Nightingale Sang in Berkeley Square" (1940), and each of the scenes (set from 1939 to 1945) has the subtitle of a popular number sung in it. Most of the singing is done by the piano-playing father George, usually in a semi-realistic context, with others reacting to him and sometimes joining in. A majority of the melodies are structurally placed to open and close the scenes. The title song is sung when the young lovers first declare their love for each other, with "Berkeley Square" altered to suit the play's locale in Newcastle-upon-Tyne.[68]

Many of the tunes are straightforward expressions of the mood or theme of the scene. Others, however, are ironic in impact. For example, the one that closes act 1, "Yours," is sadly ironic: "Yours to the end of life's story" (p. 53), for Helen and Norman separate at the end of the war. And the tune that opens act 2, Vera Lynn's "That Lovely Weekend," is comically ironic, since Helen's sister Joyce, who helps to sing it, is in a comic panic about being pregnant by a lad who is not her husband. The numbers chosen were sung particularly by English entertainers, Vera Lynn and others, during the war years. They evoke a strong feeling of sentimental nostalgia, just as the drama as a whole is strongly tinged with sentimentality. Neither Mercer nor Taylor reflects critically on this nostalgia, as Nichols did in *Forget-me-not Lane*.

HAROLD PINTER

Harold Pinter's *Old Times* (1971) is also characterized by a diffuse nostalgia, especially for a phase of young adulthood in which the three characters of the drama experienced particularly intense personal relationships. The period of Pinter's play is not strongly fixed socially or historically, although the tunes he chooses are almost all from the 1930s. These are presumably the melodies that were new when Kate, Anna, and Deeley were about twenty. Anna reminisces:

> Ah, those songs. We used to play them, all of them, all the time, late at night, lying on the floor, lovely old things.[69]

But it is not entirely clear whether the "old" is from the perspective of the young woman or the forty-year-old. These and other uncertainties have led some critics to assume that the period the characters reminisce about is the 1930s, while others declare that they are recalling the 1950s.[70] Surely the vagueness of the setting is deliberate on Pinter's part. Just as one is not entirely sure where the truth lies in this three-cornered drama of emotion and possessiveness, so also the historical facts of the setting are immaterial in the face of shifting perspectives and memories. Colin Blakely, the actor who played Deeley, is closer to the essence of the drama when he says that *Old Times* is a play about early middle age, about people *in* their forties: "It's a time when you do begin to revaluate—when you stand still for a moment and think about old times."[71]

In contrast with other dramatists of roughly the same generation—for example, Osborne, Nichols, Mercer and Taylor—who often refer to singers and entertainers of their own adolescence in the early 1940s, Pinter has apparently not selected the songs in this drama because of the personal memories involved. (Pinter was born in 1930.) Indeed he says that he has forgotten almost entirely about his own childhood and adolescence and does not write about either: "Perhaps it's all too painful. Anyway I don't write about myself."[72] The very title of the play, *Old Times*, creates a vague nostalgia for an unspecified, not too recent past into which the familiar old melodies are perfectly fitted. Deeley's comment, "They don't make them like that any more" (p. 29), reveals a nostalgic enthusiasm for the old tunes of the old times; in addition, the phrase itself is the title of yet another popular song, this time from the 1960s. In contrast with Peter Nichols's *Forget-me-not Lane*, which places nostalgia for the old days in perspective to the social realities, Pinter's interest is directed more toward the role of memory in personal relationships and the connections between time past and individual identity.

Pinter's dramatic work has been compared to music, primarily on the basis of his taut, poetic language and rhythm.[73] But Pinter is not a musical dramatist in the sense that he often uses music or song in his plays. It is therefore interesting that he chooses to illuminate some of the aspects of the memory through the singing of popular tunes in *Old Times*. This combination of popular and poetic styles in *Old Times* has been compared to Eliot's *Sweeney Agonistes* and Beckett's *Waiting for Godot*. Worth evaluates the use of songs here as "a looking out to the audience which might be a move to ease the tightness of the closed form."[74] In performance, they do involve the audience directly, evoking a strong response of amused recognition.[75]

Old Times is partially about the workings of memory, and how relationships and personal conflicts emerge in contradictory perspectives. In much the same way as Nichols in *Forget-me-not Lane*, Pinter approaches the memory through the medium of popular song. The singers are Anna and Deeley; the more reticent Kate never joins in, indeed cannot recall some of the tunes (p. 27), and resists the others' interpretation of her. In act 1 Anna and Deeley, recalling Kate as a young woman, break into a medley of popular numbers, singing lines of various melodies in a comic stichomythic exchange (p. 27). In performance, this sung exchange is one of the comic highlights of the play. The stichomythia not only indicates a quick, playful rapport of their memories, but also, as Alan Hughes notes, hints at the underlying antagonistic battle of wits: "They are singing antiphonal snatches of songs, apparently with convivial nostalgia but actually in competition. The lines they sing are artfully chosen to illustrate their conflict."[76]

This first phase of confrontation is followed, after a slight pause, by a phase in which they pick up and finish the pieces which the other begins; for example, "I Get a Kick out of You" and "Smoke Gets in Your Eyes" (p. 28). Already in this scene memory plays slight tricks on them, and not all the familiar lines are quoted exactly. Thematically, these tunes range from love fulfilled ("Blue Moon" by Rodgers and Hart, 1934) to love lost ("Smoke Gets in Your Eyes" by Jerome Kern, 1933); from future promise ("All the Things You Are, Are Mine" by Jerome Kern, 1939) to memory of things past ("They Can't Take That Away From Me" by George Gershwin, 1937). The last sung line in this exchange emphasizes the haunting role of memory: "Oh, how the ghost of you clings . . ." (p. 29). At this point the antagonism between Deeley and Anna is still hidden beneath the surface, and the effect of the medley is primarily to evoke a spontaneous sentimental expression of praise for Kate. At the superficial, conventional level of popular music, where texts can be applied to almost any loved person, Anna and Deeley can agree in their memories while playfully sparring. But this area of shared memory is described by Pinter in an early essay as "quicksand":

> We are faced with the immense difficulty . . of verifying the past . . . . We will all interpret a common experience quite differently, though we prefer to subscribe to the view that there's a shared common ground, a known ground. I think there's a shared common ground all right, but that it's more like a quicksand.[77]

The sung exchange in act 2 (pp. 57–58) is different in mood and function. As Kate emerges from her bath, Deeley "begins to sing softly" (p. 57), almost as in a trance. Anna picks up the same melody "softly," and stichomythically they complete "They Can't Take That Away From Me." It is not until Kate comes down to confront them smiling that they become self-conscious and begin to "sing again, faster on cue, and more perfunctorily" (p. 58). This is a piece about memories of the lost loved one. In the first phase of the singing each seems absorbed in his or her own memory. In the second phase the confrontation of conflicting versions comes out more clearly. But each maintains—at first introspectively, then more aggressively—the value of the subjective memory for his or her present life. Arthur McGuinness comments:

> The songs foreshadow the major revelation in the play as the aggressive bravado of the two hunters is revealed to be the thinly-disguised cries of lonely and desperate people.[78]

Pinter has employed the tunes in *Old Times* in a variety of functions. They evoke a strongly nostalgic atmosphere of "old times." Their themes, centering as they do mostly around memories and lost love, serve to reinforce the central themes of the drama. The manner in which they are sung helps to illustrate the dramatic constellation of the characters: on the surface level the songs represent a store of shared memories, at the level of the subtext the singing clearly brings out the underlying antagonism between Deeley and Anna. Kate remains aloof, detached from the singing. The singing is also used by Pinter to add a surface lightness and comic effect to the dialogue, contributing to the overall musical pattern of the language.

Harold Pinter's early work has often been associated with theater of the absurd. In *Old Times*, however, as in many of Pinter's more recent plays, there is so much psychological realism, so detailed an investigation of meaningful personal relationships, that we cannot speak of the play as being absurd. Certainly, as in the earlier plays, we are not entirely sure at the end what is true or what really happened. But this uncertainty does not lead to a feeling that all human life is meaningless. A drama like John Osborne's *A Sense of Detachment*, with its destructive criticism of all values, I believe comes closer to the theater of the absurd than *Old Times*.

From "They Can't Take That Away From Me," by George Gershwin, in *Classic George Gershwin* (Ilford, Essex: International Music Publications, 1983), pp. 30–32.

4. Popular Song and the Absurd

In some dramas of the contemporary period, song is used as part of a strategy of total disorientation that may be seen in association with the absurd. A very interesting use of popular song in such dramas is to contrast and undermine endeavors that give human life higher meaning and purpose. This tendency is apparent in some of the works of Tom Stoppard.

By way of orientation, I will examine two classical dramas of the absurd, Samuel Beckett's *Waiting for Godot* (1955) and *Happy Days* (1961). In *Godot*, two songs are sung, a wordless lullaby and a children's tune that goes on endlessly. The lullaby is begun by Vladimir in a tone that is much too loud, thus rendering the function of the song meaningless.[79] Sung with the appropriate softness, however, it leads to one of the rare moments of tenderness and care in the play. Such moments enable mankind to go on living despite a lack of direction and perspective. Vladimir's second song, which opens act 2, symbolizes both theme and structure of the drama. The circular nature of the children's song "A Dog Came in the Kitchen,"[80] which endlessly repeats the same story of animal need and human violence, reflects the circular nature of the action. Just as the song may be sung *ad absurdum*, man repeats the same patterns, arriving nowhere. The childish tone corresponds to the slapstick play rituals that the child-like Gogo and Didi observe to cover the surface of their despair.

Happy Days, too, exploits a surface light-heartedness to bridge a chasm of frustration and hopelessness. Song here serves much the same general purpose as do Winnie's other physical activities, her story-telling and her memory recall; all help her to keep going, to get through the day in the face of a desperate personal situation. The music box that plays a tune from *The Merry Widow* is one of the treasures of her inexhaustible bag. It cheers her up at a moment in which she is close to breaking and provokes one of Willie's rare outbursts: "Brief burst of hoarse song without words—musical-box tune—from Willie."[81] At the end of act 2, Winnie sings the words: "I Love You So," the waltz from Franz Lehár's *The Merry Widow* (1905). This is comparable to the "old style" of speaking; both consist, in Andrew Kennedy's words, of "comforting clichés and fine but empty phrases."[82] Both are no longer relevant to Winnie's situation. Just as phrases about the passing of the day are inappropriate in her glaring desert of merciless light, the lyrics about the wordless understanding of young lovers contradict the desperation of her situation. It is significant that Beckett has chosen to end his play with a popular song. The light-hearted optimism of this tune presents the greatest possible contrast to the bleak and hopeless situation. The swinging movement of the waltz contrasts with Winnie's immobility. In this sense the song is bitterly ironic. At the same time, it is nostalgic and sentimental, and under the circumstances it seems touchingly cheerful. It leaves us with a sense of "sadness after song"[83] for a valiant but pathetic effort in a senseless and infernal universe. Beckett thus provides yet another example of ambivalent use of popular song.

TOM STOPPARD

Tom Stoppard (born in 1937) uses music as part of his dramatic strategy of total comic disorientation. Stoppard's drama is sometimes categorized as theater of the absurd. But his emphasis is really more on anarchic comedy, as C. W. E. Bigsby notes:

> His focus is less on the abandonment of man than the humour and perverse vitality which men generate even in despair: less on the absence of truth or its terrifying implications than its relativity.[84]

Stoppard admits that "the mixing up of ideas in farce is a source of confusion" in his plays and describes his dramatic technique as "seriousness compromised by frivolity."[85] Some critics see a development in the playwright's work away from absurdism. Michael Hinden calls Stoppard's theater "post-absurdism."[86] Victor Cahn in *Beyond Absurdity* contends that particularly in the later work Stoppard "creates characters who are not resigned to absurdity but are determined to battle against such a vision of the world."[87]

Stoppard emphasizes the influence of Beckett's technique of comic "dismantlement" in his work:

> I'm an enormous admirer of Beckett, but . . . I'd say that the Beckett novels show as much as the plays, because there's a Beckett joke which is the funniest joke in the world to me. It . . . consists of confident statement followed by immediate refutation by the same voice. It's a constant process of elaborate structure and sudden—and total—dismantlement.[88]

> I find Beckett deliciously funny in the way that he qualifies everything as he goes along; reduces, refines and dismantles.[89]

Stoppard loves, he says in a later interview, to let his characters "play a sort of infinite leap-frog" with conflicting ideas.[90] The songs in both *Jumpers* and *Travesties* are used by Stoppard structurally to achieve just this kind of comic effect of dismantlement and refutation that he has learned from Beckett. Particularly in *Jumpers*, they relativize more serious values until the latter often appear without meaning. In addition, this drama employs popular show business as a sphere of life to contrast and deflate academic seriousness.

Stoppard uses song, dance, and other music-hall and show-business elements in many of his works. He has even written a theater play that is to be accompanied by a full symphony orchestra: *Every Good Boy Deserves Favour.*

But the dramatist does not include song in drama for primarily musical reasons. He says of himself, "I simply have no musical ear."[91]

> I know nothing about composition. . . . I listen to pop music, and to some slightly better music than pop music sometimes, I don't buy records, I don't know one composer from another.[92]

On the other hand he is acutely aware of the show-business aspect of playwriting: "I like theatre, I like showbiz, and that's what I'm true to."[93] Of his earliest success he says:

> When I was writing *Rosencrantz* I was in no sense engaged in any sort of esoteric work. It was like music-hall if anything—a slightly literate music-hall perhaps.[94]

In *Jumpers* (1972) moral philosophy is reduced not only metaphorically to the level of mental gymnastics but literally to the level of physical gymnastics. George says of himself:

> The fact that I cut a ludicrous figure in the academic world is largely due to my aptitude for traducing a complex and logical thesis to a mysticism of staggering banality.[95]

Under these circumstances it becomes difficult to see any essential difference between the world of scholarship and the trivial world of popular entertainment. Dotty's apparently absurd comparison becomes logical: "Not only can I sing better than they can jump, I can probably jump higher than they can sing" (p. 19). Because Stoppard has already opened the drama with Dotty's failure to sing, even this statement has already been negated. We are thus confronted at the very beginning of the play with Stoppard's technique of comic refutation. Shortly afterwards he uses music again to achieve disorientation. Dotty's confused moon song sequence is both hilarious and pathetic:

> The musicians attempt to follow her but are thwarted by her inability to distinguish between one moon-song and another, and by her habit of singing the words of one to the tune of another. The music gamely keeps switching tracks, but DOTTY keeps double-crossing it. (p. 19)

This is very much a showbiz opening: we encounter a beautiful singer, a striptease act, a lot of physical action, and a mystery murder all within the first five minutes. One of the principal characters, Archie Jumper, is introduced as a music-hall chairman. In typical Stoppard manner, however, the function and meaning of show business seem to keep shifting, resisting definition.

Almost everyone in the play is involved with show business in some way or another, except George, Dotty's husband. Inspector Bones turns out to be

From "Shine On, Harvest Moon," words by Jack Norworth, music by Nora Bayes-Norworth, in *There Goes That Song Again*, compiled by Colin Walsh (London: Elm Tree Books, in association with EMI Music Publishing, 1977), pp. 29–32.

more interested in show business than in crime detection (p. 46) and is a fervent admirer of the singer Dorothy Moore. Dotty's seduction of Bones thus has a great deal to do with his enthusiasm for show business and song. The seduction scene is dominated toward its end by Dotty's "Sentimental Journey" (p. 55). This fades into the closing scene of act 1 that is also accompanied by the continuing strains of the same tune. But here it is the Jumpers who are associated with the music. With meticulous timing and choreography they remove McFee's dead body:

> The song dominates the whole scene. Nothing else can be heard, and its beat infects the business of removing the body, for DOTTY continues to sway and snap her fingers as she moves about welcoming the troops, . . . so that the effect is a little simple improvised choreography between the JUMPERS and DOTTY. (p. 56)

In this play one cannot expect any constellation to remain firm for long. And so it is George, the only character with no feeling for music or show business and no understanding of his wife, who comes closest to Dotty in spirit. Both have a "frail vision of a moral, romantic and intuitive world."[96] In the words of C. W. E. Bigsby:

> The anarchic energy of this embattled couple, alarmed as they are by the threatened collapse of their world but resisting with sporadic displays of affection, humour and faith, contrasts sharply with the crudely rational world.[97]

George is as nostalgic for the philosophy of forty years ago, as he is for "the irrational, the emotional, the whimsical" (p. 40). Similarly, Dotty longs nostalgically for an earlier age when "*things were in place*" (p. 41), the traumatic moon landing had not yet occurred and she could still believe in all the triviality she sang about. Stoppard judges the destruction by the moon landing of all the romantic and mythological associations of the moon as "a sort of minute lobotomy performed on the human race, like a tiny laser making dead some small part of the psyche."[98] Hinden calls George "one of the few authentic heroes of the modern stage," but he is "a comic hero, perhaps a sacred fool."[99] I believe that much the same can be said of Dotty as heroine. Stoppard gives this drama as hero and heroine a philosopher who cannot reason and a singer who cannot sing, both professional failures. They also fail to understand each other. But each embodies simultaneously triviality and truth, banality and morality. Show business and moral philosophy relativize each other, but do not negate human values.

The coda has inspired some very contradictory interpretations. It can be seen as a bizarre, climactic nightmare inquisition, or as an absurd circular return to the acrobats and murder mystery of the beginning. Dotty here once again functions as a performer and entertainer, making "her entrance on a spangled crescent moon" (p. 86). The fact that she has recovered her voice and can sing about mankind and heaven to the tune of "Sentimental Journey" does not seem to add any new message to the play. *Jumpers* creates comedy both by frustrating all audience expectations and by introducing the unexpected. The final song seems to function in the latter way. Just as Stoppard in this drama parodies the genres of the detective thriller and musical comedy, this aspect of his coda also parodies the conventional happy end of musical comedy.

Travesties (1974) also contains elements of music hall and musical comedy. Although it does not introduce as many songs as *Jumpers*, it employs musical bridges throughout. The James Joyce of the drama has been compared to "a music hall comedian,"[100] and at his first appearance he provocatively sings "Galway Bay" to annoy the disapproving librarian.[101] Scenes are constantly replayed in contrasting styles. Stoppard says of the stylistic shifting in *Travesties:*

> I . . . wanted to dislocate the audience's assumptions every now and again about what kind of style the play was going to be in. Dislocation of an audience's assumptions is an important part of what I like to write.[102]

Stoppard's use of song to create a structural effect of contrast, refutation, and dismantlement is clearest in the scene presented in the form of musical comedy as a "Gallagher and Shean" routine (pp. 89–93). Here, as elsewhere, it is the alternation of contrasting styles that is important. Stoppard has outlined his structural intentions in this play, emphasizing the element of contrast. First, he explains how both *Jumpers* and *Travesties* achieve comic disorientation by means of juxtaposition of opposites: "You have unexpected bits of music and dance, and at the same time people are playing ping-pong with various intellectual arguments."[103] Of the musical comedy scene in *Travesties*, he explains:

> What I was trying was this. What I'm always trying to say is 'Firstly, A. Secondly, minus A.'. . . . We have this rather frivolous nonsense going on, and then the Lenin section comes in and says, 'Life is too important. We can't afford the luxury of this artificial frivolity. . . . Then the play stands up and says, 'You thought *that* was frivolous? You ain't seen nothin' yet.' And you go into the Gallagher and Shean routine. That was the architectural thing I was after.[104]

In other words, in this sung passage Stoppard has deliberately aimed at a climax of superficiality. The literary source is the tea-party scene of *The Importance of Being Earnest*. The already absurdly stilted original is parodied in a style that is even more artificial and heightened by sung lyrics with rhyme. Ed Gallagher and Al Shean formed a comic team of one stage Irishman and one stage Jew. Their hit song "Mr. Gallagher and Mr. Shean" was a great success in the Ziegfeld Follies of 1922. This was a comic patter song of questions and answers that became their trademark and was often parodied.

Particularly important is also the wider context of this scene. Shortly before, Lenin has been passionately holding forth on the function of literature and art in a communist society. Following this, the "Appassionata" of Beethoven is heard, and Lenin reflects on the effect of Beethoven's music:

> I don't know of anything greater than the Appassionata. Amazing, superhuman music. It always makes me feel . . . proud of the miracles that human beings can perform. (p. 89)

Then Stoppard effects the abrupt switch to some of the most trivial music that human beings can perform: "The 'Appassionata' degenerates absurdly into 'Mr. Gallagher and Mr. Shean'" (p. 89).

Music and song are thus important instruments in Stoppard's dislocation technique. Abrupt changes in content and in presentation styles, from serious argument to sung passages or dance sequences, help to achieve his intended effect of total comic disruption and refutation. Starting with techniques derived from Beckett, Stoppard develops his own special brand of comic disorientation. Audience reliance on theatrical habit and consistency is undermined.

Every Good Boy Deserves Favour (1977) is an interesting musical and theatrical experiment. The title is musical; it is the phrase used to teach music pupils the names of the notes on the lines of the treble clef (EGBDF). The title also has ironic significance for the theme of the play, the struggle between dissidents and authorities in Soviet Russia. This "Play for Actors and Orchestra" combines stage drama with music for symphony orchestra composed by André Previn, who initiated the project. This piece belongs to a phase in Stoppard's work in which his plays are becoming more politically outspoken. It is concerned with political repression in general and specifically the treatment of dissidents in Soviet Russian society and their incarceration in insane asylums. Employing the orchestral metaphor, Stoppard compares the dissident to a "discordant note . . . in an orchestrated society."[105] At one point the title is menacingly varied, as the authorities put pressure on the dissident at his weakest point, his love for his young son:

> *Doctor.* What about your son? He is turning into a delinquent.
> (*Doctor plucks the violin EGBDF.*)
> He's a good boy. He deserves a father. (p. 29)

Every Good Boy Deserves Favour is basically "not . . . a piece for singers,"[106] and is of interest only marginally here. At the point of most intense emotional climax, however, Sacha, the son of the imprisoned dissident Alexander, breaks into a snatch of song. In an unreal and stylized sequence (pp. 34–35), the dying father speaks his farewell poems from prison while Sacha moves around the orchestra platform singing to a monotonous children's chant:

> Papa, don't be rigid!
> Everything can be all right!
>
> (p. 34)

The song here highlights the child's isolation, vulnerability and longing, and lends a special poignancy to his plea.[107] In typical Stoppard fashion, however, the drama ends with an unexpected comic reversal. When Sacha closes the piece with his song (p. 37), much of the earlier poignancy has been lost.

After the anarchic comic structure of the earlier dramas and the experimental play for orchestra, a later Stoppard drama such as *Night and Day* (1978) returns to a more conventional use of song. The title reflects the song of the same name (Cole Porter, 1932), although it is not actually sung. Stoppard distinguishes between the words of the character Ruth and her inner thoughts and feelings which he indicates by the designation 'Ruth.' Songs occasionally help to reflect 'Ruth's' moods. Thus a snatch of the Beatles' song "Help!" expresses a moment of inner panic.[108] The drama closes with 'Ruth' singing "The Lady is a Tramp" (Rodgers and Hart, 1937) (p. 95), which echoes her feeling of utter exhaustion after emotional turmoil. As atmospheric emphasis of moods or states of mind, the songs in this play fulfill mainly the function of psychological characterization.

Music in theater of the absurd (or postabsurd) thus also reflects a new variation of the ambivalence of popular culture. Popular songs in such plays are chosen for their implications of triviality and superficiality, and yet the mood of sentimental nostalgia which they evoke may represent a warmly human impulse in an otherwise harsh and desolate universe. Stoppard uses song as an important element in his technique of comic disorientation, while also exhibiting a sure sense of sheer showbusiness entertainment values.

5. "Musicals"?

The popular musical has been defined as theater of romance, in which emotion prevails over intellect; as a moral art, in which life is presented as it should be and the basic underlying attitude is optimistic; as popular theater with all its positive and negative connotations; and as presentational, in which all elements of total theater—spectacular staging, choreography, music and drama—combine to create a show of vigorous theatricality.[109] Musical comedy is generally understood as a sentimental, humorous play with light music. In this sense, most of the dramas examined in this study—even those their authors (with reservations) call musical comedy, for example, C. P. Taylor's *Good* or John McGrath's *Yobbo Nowt*—cannot seriously be equated with popular musicals. They are musicals only in the sense of being dramas with music and song. The basic interest of these plays is less romance and moral optimism than searching confrontation with emotions and ideas. Even those that come closest to musical comedy have a basic seriousness of purpose that distinguishes them from popular and conventional musical comedy.

By way of example, I will examine both plays that failed and that succeeded as West End entertainments. John Osborne's *The World of Paul Slickey* (1959) is called by the author "A Comedy of Manners with Music." It failed disastrously at the time and has been disparaged by critics since, with good reason. Apparently it began as a satire on modern journalism, but as often in Osborne the satire is diffuse and indiscriminate. Osborne chose the musical form in an effort to expand the formal experiments of *The Entertainer*, particularly by extending the functions of the songs. But the songs in *The World of Paul Slickey* are introduced arbitrarily and are often followed by equally arbitrary dances. Here, the surface appearance of the musical is adopted without any of the necessary enthusiasm for spectacle. Generally colloquial and repetitive in diction, the lyrics fail to create a contrast with the style of the surrounding dialogue, as they do, for example, in Eliot or Isherwood. Indeed, they are frequently appallingly trite. The music, by Christopher Whelen, has been called "unexceptionable."[110] Perhaps the songs might have saved *The World of Paul Slickey* had they been written with more lyrical intensity or satirical bite. As they stand, however, they neither contrast nor heighten the action and indeed contribute considerably to the failure of the play.

Nevertheless Osborne's goal was probably ambitious when he undertook the musical. Richard Findlater, in any case, gives him the benefit of the doubt:

> What Osborne meant to do, I took it, was to create a kind of *Threepenny Opera* of post-war England; to give teeth to the poor old English musical; to extend both its form and context; to break down, still further, the barrier between musical and non-musical theatre.[111]

In this case, then, the intention and the chosen form failed to cohere.

PETER NICHOLS

Quite a different problem is raised by Peter Nichols, another playwright who tends to use music, song, comedy, music-hall, or pantomime techniques while dealing with serious, even taboo, subjects. In contrast with Osborne's *The World of Paul Slickey* several of Nichols's dramas, most notably *Privates on Parade* and *Poppy*, have become smash hits in the West End. But Nichols is not entirely happy with the results: he can be self-critical about his own work and critical of productions that place too much emphasis on the spectacle and show-business elements. To some extent Nichols sees his tendency to use comedy and musical techniques as running counter to his political intentions. He admires writers who write in

> trenchant left-wing terms. I love plays and films that do it, but I can't. I write about characters in fusion. . . . I don't stick to my guns as Bond and Hare do.[112]

On the other hand he defends plays which offer entertainment without open didacticism:

> My aim is always to be an intelligent entertainer. I believe entertainment is good in itself, anything more is a bonus. I like the event of theatre. . . . I tend to prefer entertainers, the people who give way a bit like me. . . . Sometimes, I go to the more austere kinds of theatre and think they're a bit prim.[113]

In fact Peter Nichols, in contrast to Osborne, has an instinctive and profound enjoyment of all the facets of live entertainment. Mervyn Jones maintains:

> Nichols . . . is a true 'man of the theatre', eager to muster all available visual and aural resources to achieve a total impact on an audience. He draws with enthusiasm on forms broader than those of the verbal, naturalistic drama—on popular song and early jazz . . ., concert-party and cabaret . . ., music as dramatic comment . . ., and traditional pantomime.[114]

In contrast with Peter Barnes, who uses a similar love of popular entertainment to satiric effect, and who says that the meaning of his song lyrics is always more important than their music, in Nichols's drama the "showmanship tends at times to run away with the play,"[115] so that the surface gaiety smothers the political purpose. It is not difficult for directors and audiences to ignore the ironies and political nuances and to concentrate on the comic entertainment.

Privates on Parade (1977) is a good case in point. Nichols says that he originally conceived the drama as a rather "raw and Brechtian" war play.[116] But in the course of revision it gradually turned into a musical. It is his first play to use song and dance continuously, although he had employed elements of popular entertainment in such earlier dramas as *The National Health* (1969) and *Forget-me-not Lane* (1971). Certainly a core of serious themes is still present in the final version of the play; for example, the British imperial role in South East Asia during the cold war, exploitation, prostitution, and racial intermarriage. But given the context in which these themes are embedded it is fairly easy for an audience to focus elsewhere.

The play portrays a troup of military entertainers in the Entertainments National Services Association (ENSA; in soldiers' terms, Every Night Something Awful), Song and Dance Unit South East Asia (SADUSEA), in Malaya in 1948. Nichols gives their performance numbers (mostly songs, dances, and comic routines) ample scope, so that the general mood of the play builds into one of comical musical entertainment. Nichols recognizes in retrospect that "some of the songs soften the show"[117] and blunt the impact of his serious themes. Particularly, he feels that the last scene in performance is less bitter than he intended:

> It's pretty stark if you think about it . . ., but in performance, it changes. By that time, so much goodwill has been generated amongst the audience that it prevents them seeing what a trenchant scene it is.[118]

Many of the tunes are light entertainment and have little to do with plot or themes of the drama. Models are popular entertainers of the 1930s and 1940s; there are numbers in the style of Marlene Dietrich, Gene Kelly, Fred Astaire, and Flanagan and Allen (who also inspired Jimmy and Cliff's song routine in *Look Back in Anger*). Several, however, add comic, ironic or sentimental nuances to themes and character relationships of the drama. For example the number that opens act 2 is an interesting parody of various popular World War II melodies (all also used in Taylor's *And a Nightingale Sang . . .*):

> Throughout the war we soldiered on
> When almost every hope had gone
> And pinned our flagging faith to Vera Lynn.
>
> . . . .
> But when the lights went on we saw the vict'ry was a sham,
> The Lion's share turned out to be a smaller slice of Spam.
>   The bluebirds came one dreary day,
>   Looked at Dover and flew away
>
> . . . .
> And the nightingale in Berkeley Square can only sit and cry.[119]

Another piece is thematically linked to the love story between the innocent Steve and the half-Indian prostitute Sylvia, and comments on their relationship:

> Black Velvet had great allure
> For such a private, so young and pure.
> She took him well in hand
> And showed him the way to the Promised Land.
>
> . . . .
> *(The song is accompanied and lyrically arranged so that only the words are coarse.)*
>   (p. 52)

In the Royal Shakespeare Company performance this tune was sung with the harsh, grating intonation of the street singer, so that part of the coarseness of the words was reflected in the style of presentation.[120] The contrast between the traditional lyrical "Greensleeves" and the coarse words reflects the ambivalent mixture of naïvety and calculation in the relationship itself.

The title song, "Privates on Parade," is a smart number in modern musical

From "The White Cliffs of Dover," words and music by Nat Burton and Walter Kent, in *I'll Be Seeing You . . . featuring the songs, the artists and the memories of the Second World War* (London: EMI Music Publishing, 1979), pp. 12–13.

From "A Nightingale Sang in Berkeley Square," words by Eric Maschwitz, music by Manning Sherwin, in *I'll Be Seeing You . . . featuring the songs, the artists and the memories of the Second World War* (London: EMI Music Publishing, 1979), pp. 43–45.

comedy style in which the "theatre of war" (p. 82) is taken literally, and military drill becomes the subject matter of entertainment. In the film version of the play, Sylvia wears satin briefs with Union Jack design, reminiscent of the sexy blonde in the concert party of *Forget-me-not Lane*. In scene 9 of act 2 Charles and Len, who have become lovers and have decided to stay together, perform a Flanagan and Allen song (pp. 94–95), whereby Len impersonates the straight man of the team, Chesney Allen, and Charles the comic, Bud Flanagan:

> Through all the stormclouds we've been true
> To one another, just we two,
> . . . .
> Together we shall never more roam
> From the heart of home sweet home.
>
> (p. 95)

This number effectively underlines the real depth of the affection behind this relationship and ironically foreshadows the tragedy of Len's death far from home. With the exception of "Black Velvet," which is set to the traditional tune of "Greensleeves," the music was composed by Denis King. His score has been backhandedly praised as "faithflly pastiche."[121] The music is indeed unexceptional, but extremely effective in performance.

On the whole, most of the audience would probably agree with the reviewer who wrote of *Privates on Parade:* "To pretend that it is questioning the British presence in South East Asia or delving into the deeper issues of the emergency years is unadulterated bunkum."[122] When considered as a serious play *Privates on Parade* is a relative failure, when accepted as a musical comedy it was an unconditional success and indeed received the Comedy of the Year award from the Society of West End Theatre Awards for 1977. The problem is that Nichols intended it as *both* serious play and musical entertainment.

The film version of *Privates on Parade* (1983, with Michael Blakemore, director of the original RSC Aldwych production and many of the original cast) in part brings out the realities and the dangers of the political situation better, but in part also softens the conflicts of the original. The immediacy and realism of the film medium intensify the menace of the lurking communist intruders in act 2 and illustrate the brutalities of their attack more than the stage play. As a result, the light-hearted and frivolous songs of this act acquire a more clearly contrastive function and take on an artificial quality in this jungle setting. But the unsolved problem of racial intermarriage in the play is diminished by a change of plot and ending in the film. The film version is very effective and reflects much of the entertainment value of the original, if not all of its serious concerns.

Nichols's *Poppy* (1982) is also both a rousing musical, with music by Monty Norman, and potentially a thought-provoking serious play. By the standards of popular entertainment and commercial appeal, Terry Hands's Royal Shakespeare Company production at the Barbican was a rousing success, and it was subsequently transferred to the West End. But more than one critic was of the opinion that "by any other standard it is a catastrophic failure."[123] And Nichols was so dissatisfied that he announced his decision to cease writing for the theater altogether. It seems that the production was definitely not designed to emphasize the ironies and darker elements of the drama; on the other hand, it appears that once again Nichols's sense of showmanship has run away with him in writing the text.

Nichols's intention was surely to show the English-Chinese Opium War (1840–42) as a reprehensible mercantile manipulation in the interests of private profit. Yo-Yo's concluding statement almost certainly reflects Nichols' own opinion:

The plague you brought becomes an epidemic. For what? For gain. Whose gain? What's profit, after all? Your poet Blake said 'Man is not improved by the hurt of others; states are not improved at the expense of foreigners.'[124]

The form that Nichols chose for the presentation of this problem is a travesty of one of the most popular theatrical forms of the nineteenth century, the English pantomime. It is "a traditional English panto which gradually goes sour."[125] The loveable stage horse is slaughtered for food during a siege, and the principal girl degenerates into a wasted opium addict.

What role do the songs play in this drama? Do they once again seem to blunt the sharp edge of Nichols's intended criticism? On the whole I would say that they do, although again there are subtleties and ironies in them as in the tunes of *Privates on Parade* that might be brought out in performance. The music, composed by Monty Norman (who has also composed for C. P. Taylor and Wolf Mankowitz) is extremely effective but not remarkable; it is rousing and catchy, but with few surprises or interesting nuances.[126]

Many of the lyrics in act 1 have only very muted irony; often the irony can only be perceived in hindsight when one realizes the full destructiveness of the English opium trade in China. In keeping with the nineteenth-century setting, Nichols introduces Gilbert and Sullivan style songs (pp. 19–20 and pp. 27–28). They are associated with the merchant Obadiah Upward. Their cheerful, forceful tone emphasizes Upward's tale of social climbing and aggressive marketing:

> When I was a lad in Bromley, Kent,
> I worked as a grocer's assistant;
> . . . .
> I loved to buy and I loved to sell
> So I finally bought the grocer.
>
> (p. 20)

It is not until later in the play that the true ruthlessness of Upward becomes known, and the audience realizes that his profit is based on the addiction of others. The "Poppy" song that follows the transformation scene and closes act 1 is not designed to stimulate doubt or arouse critical alarm. The major characters are in an opium dream that causes peaceful and erotic visions with only faintly menacing overtones:

> How can I ever escape from the spell
> Of towering oceans heard in a shell
> Or flying with tigers half through the night,
> Cascading down forests of submarine light?
> . . . .
>
> *No pain in any of this, only gratification, the sense*
> *that life's all pleasure.* (p. 54)

The tune evokes the world of the modern rock musical. It is electronically amplified, at first dreamy and sublime, later modulating to a stronger, more aggressive beat.

The ironies become more apparent in act 2. The grimmest moment occurs when Jack sings a lullaby to his beloved horse Randy, "a costermonger song, Albert Chevalier style" (p. 90), shortly before the animal is to be slaughtered for food. The gentle and nostalgic sentiment of the song contrasts sharply with the macabre context in which it is sung. In words, style, and music it is moving, but the scene shocks the audience into an awareness of the costs of an exploitative war. One of the catchiest pieces in act 2 is a "rousing music-hall number" (p. 109), sung by Upward and the "Dame" Lady Dodo, with audience participation encouraged in the chorus. In performance, the song really does "take the roof off" (p. 109). The text, however, deals with the sacking of the Chinese Summer Palace and the barbarous destruction of invaluable works of art:

> Our officers' orders are to break
> Anything here we cannot take—
> The sound you hear's the fusiliers
> Shooting the crystal chandeliers—
> Rat-tat-tat-tat-tat-tat!
>
> (p. 108)

The irony lies in the contrast between the cheerful strident style of the song and the negative connotations of its lyrics.

Thus certain bitter ironies are apparent, especially in the songs of the second act when the traditional pantomime fun is disintegrating. The ironies, however, are not particularly strong, and to bring them out requires a subdued performance that emphasizes the distortions. Certainly the Royal Shakespeare Company's production did not do this. On the contrary, director Terry Hands "keeps the stage throbbing with so much complicated business and showy effect that our reactions are numbed to everything except the stunning showbiz professionalism."[127] The ironies can also only be perceived if the song lyrics are precisely understood, but here, too, the critic Mervyn Jones finds fault:

> It might have been different if the songs had been sung so that the words mattered—or indeed were distinguishable—instead of being belted out like reprises of 'Hello, Dolly'.[128]

Desmond Christy in *Plays and Players* concludes that Hands's extravagant production has not only distorted, but even reversed Nichols's intentions:

> *Poppy* has been inflated into a musical extravaganza. . . . It ends up not so much a broadside aimed at the ethics of Empire but a celebration of Britishness . . . selling Peter Nichols' soul to the Merchants of Extravaganza.[129]

Poppy may be judged as a commercially successful musical that "crucially failed to give expression to its purpose."[130] The fault is partly the comic exuberance of the text, partly the spectacular extravagance of the opulent performance.

PAM GEMS

Pam Gems's *Piaf* (1978) is another musical drama concerning a singer and performer. (Gems was born in 1925.) Its aims, however, are different from *The Entertainer* or *Privates on Parade*, which also have entertainment as their theme. Pam Gems's goal in this drama is to explore the emotional truth that underlies the songs of the chanteuse Edith Piaf and that endows them with their particular intensity. As the playwright remarks in her introductory note:

> In the world of popular music, there are two giants, and they are both women—Billie Holiday, and Edith Piaf. Piaf . . . became the supreme mistress of the chanson . . . For her, singing was ecstasy. She believed above all in love, physical love. . . . She sang of sexuality and, when the mood was sad, of betrayal: you believed her. She had been there. The accuracy and reality of her work is unique in a world usually characterised by the banal and the commercial. Miraculously, in a sentimental genre, Piaf found emotional truth. This was her genius.[131]

Looking at various exemplary stations in the protagonist's life, *Piaf* chronicles the personal experiences, the loves, the betrayals, the tragedies that lay behind her singing. The familiar melodies thus take on personal meaning. Above all, their intensity stands in direct correlation to the intensity of the singer's experience:

> *Marlene.* Piaf, you can't have an orgasm every single time you walk on a stage.
> *Piaf.* I can. (p. 59)

Nothing is glamorized or sentimentalized. The pettiness, bitterness, promiscuity and loneliness of Piaf's life are captured. "[Gems] shows a Piaf who is vulnerable to the values and pressures of her chosen milieu—drink, drugs, sexual patronage—but who continually bounces back."[132] Piaf never accepts the image of success, never allows herself to become exploited as an artificial, commercial product; she remains true to her working-class origins.

The raucous humor, the vulgarity and the vulnerability that characterized the legendary singer are superbly portrayed and give the play a warmth, vitality, and pathos that become emotionally intensified during the musical numbers. The primary function of the songs is to express emotional complexity and depth—quite an unusual undertaking in a musical. Although not properly speaking a popular musical, *Piaf* proved remarkably successful in the West End, on Broadway, and on the European continent.

Successful or unsuccessful, none of these musical plays can be identified with the theater of romance of the conventional musical. In varying ways these dramas make extensive use of entertainment values in order to explore social, political, or historical conflicts and express emotional truths.

6. The Rock Generation

Many playwrights of the generation born around 1930 tend to use as models or sources for songs in their plays entertainers and singers of the 1930s or 1940s. At times, they evoke even earlier periods in popular entertainment, Edwardian music hall (Osborne), nineteenth-century pantomime (Nichols), or the whole spectrum of popular song in the first half of the twentieth century (Barnes). In all the dramatists discussed until now, there are few, if any, references to rock music and to the revolution in popular entertainment from the mid-1950s on. In this respect a playwright such as Trevor Griffiths is an exception; although not of the rock generation (he was born in 1935), he has written a musical play, *Oi for England* (1982), about skinheads and their songs.

From two dramatists born in the mid 1940s, David Hare and Barrie Keeffe, come plays that are thematically concerned with rock bands and singers and the evolution of rock music in the 1960s. Both Hare and Keeffe belong to the generation that came of age with the student unrest of 1968. In *Teeth 'n' Smiles* and *Bastard Angel*, these playwrights look back to the Beatles decade of the 1960s, and to the generation in England for whom music was part of the class battle, helping to storm the institutions of higher learning and upset traditional standards. Both plays leave a sense of frustration and despair more than a decade later, with the realization that popular music has proved powerless to change class values. In this respect both are very English plays, a fact that can be seen clearly when compared with an American drama with a related theme, Sam Shepard's *The Tooth of Crime*.

DAVID HARE

David Hare (born in 1947) began theater work in political alternative theater. He was a founding member of Portable Theatre (1968) and of Joint Stock (1973). *Teeth 'n' Smiles* (1975) he says is "about 'the new man'; whether we have any chance of changing ourselves."[133] But the answer, both within the context of the play and for the writer Hare, is pessimistic:

We are living through a great, groaning, yawling festival of change. . . . In my view it is seen in the extraordinary intensity of peoples' personal despair, and it is to that despair that as a historical writer I choose to address myself time and time again: in *Teeth 'n' Smiles*, in *Knuckle*, in *Plenty*.[134]

Teeth 'n' Smiles is a "swan-song to the sixties,"[135] that looks back with nostalgia for the enthusiasm that has been lost, but also with open criticism of false ideals and misguided methods of reaching them. Hare does not necessarily identify himself personally with the nostalgia his play reflects; he sees himself rather as a chronicler of the moods and attitudes of the 1960s and 1970s. Speaking in a 1978 lecture, he says of the present university generation:

> I find a generation who are cowed, who seem to have given up on the possibility of change. . . . There is a demeaning nostalgia for the radicalism of the late sixties. . . . It would be sad if this historical period had no chroniclers.[136]

The viewpoint of the play is ambivalent. Hare, himself a Cambridge University man, lets us survey the epoch and what has become of it through the eyes of a lower-class lead singer, Maggie, and a middle-class ex-Cambridge man Arthur, the song writer for the group. Arthur, steeped in self-irony, sees the disintegration of the youth cult in personal terms: "I can see us all. Rolling down the highway into middle age. Complacency. Prurience. Sadism. Despair."[137] Maggie no longer believes in Arthur's songs (p. 52). Like Archie Rice in *The Entertainer* she embodies a cynicism and despair that can be understood not just in personal but also in political terms. Personal failure as an entertainer (both Maggie and Archie are shown in disastrous performance scenes) and a feeling that their form of entertainment is outdated both evoke parallels to the decline of postwar England. In *The Entertainer* dying music hall was symbolical of the death throes of the post-Suez Empire. In *Teeth 'n' Smiles* (set in 1969), Maggie's final song draws a general parallel between culture and the ship of state in the 1960s:

> Because the ship is sinking
> And time is running out
>
> . . . .
> The ship is sinking
> But the music remains the same.
>
> (p. 92)

As Catherine Itzin comments:

> Hare had chronicled the life and times of that almost mythological generation of the sixties in plays which repeatedly symbolized the state of the nation, microcosms of a country in decline, its citizens in despair. . . . Clearly Hare was sceptical about the impact of the sixties. . . . England—the ship—was sinking before the sixties, and was still sinking after the counterculture had come and gone.[138]

Maggie also personifies the themes of exploitation, manipulation, and marketing of popular entertainment. Because the audience is turned on by her public role-playing, she lives the scandalous life of the pop singer to excess: drink, drugs, promiscuity. In this she resembles the Piaf of Pam Gems's drama. But in sharp contrast to Piaf, she feels that she no longer has a personal life outside of her public image. In the end she deliberately chooses to go to jail in an effort to escape from the vicious circle of pop star fame.

The music to the songs of *Teeth 'n' Smiles* was composed by Nick Bicât (who later wrote the music for Bond's *Restoration*); the original lyrics are by his brother Tony Bicât. Most are sung as performance numbers during the sets of a disastrous Cambridge concert. Structurally they alternate with and contrast the more realistic scenes. In performance "the band's equipment is on a stage which, for the musical numbers, trucks down to the front,"[139] and they are sung directly to the audience. Some songs are generalized expressions of rebellion (for example, "Don't Let the Bastards Come Near You," pp 66–67). Others reflect the character portrayal of the drama. Maggie's opening number, for example, emphasizes her vulgarity, rootlessness and promiscuity:

> Mamma said I had the morals
> Of an alley cat
> . . . .
> Burning down the freeway
> Like a shootin' star
> . . . .
> Taking it from every mother-fucker's son.
>
> (p. 29)

Two numbers mock the mindless superficiality of many popular song lyrics. Maggie deliberately disrupts the performance by singing "Yeah yeah yeah" instead of the correct words (p. 54), and later the attempt to cultivate a new lead singer is satirized by an infantile text (p. 76). In accordance with his theme of disintegrating pop culture, Hare intentionally begins not with a rock number but with a long drawn-out anticlimax of frustration. The play closes with Maggie's symbolical "ship of state" song, performed not in a realistic context but as a kind of commentary musical coda. Thus, not only an emotional, but also a critical effect is achieved.

BARRIE KEEFFE

Barrie Keeffe, born in 1945 and raised in the East End of London, has a similar theme but a different perspective in *Bastard Angel* (1980). In his earlier plays, such as *Gimme Shelter* (1977) and *Barbarians* (1977), Keeffe depicted the life of young unemployed school dropouts having only a future

"Last Orders," lyrics by Tony Bicât, music by Nick Bicât, in David Hare, *Teeth 'n' Smiles* (London: Faber, 1976), pp. 91–93.

of hopelessness and more unemployment before them. As Catherine Itzin points out:

> Keeffe adopted the role of spokesperson for dispossessed youth, the victims of an inegalitarian social and educational system, the future unemployed, the unemployable.[140]

Bastard Angel may seem like a new departure in theme for Keeffe, but it is linked with his earlier plays both by the rock music that reverberates through them all and by its exploration of the world of popular entertainment available to the young dispossessed. The drama examines the reality behind the substitute ideals offered to those who will never have money or success.

While Hare approaches the world of rock music from the standpoint of Arthur, a decadent middle-class Cambridge intellectual, and Maggie, a neurotic failure, Keeffe explores pop entertainment through the eyes of a female lead singer who has come up from below and become successful in an intensely competitive, class-dominated society. Shelly is obsessed with the material aspects of success, partly because she believes it will give her a social power she has never known. She hates England and its class system, and her music thrives on hatred, as Maggie's did on pain.

Although set in 1979 and 1980, the drama reflects on the Angels' sixteen years in show business, that is, from 1963 on. The cult of youth and pleasure is ridiculed through the ageing members of the band; approaching middle age in real life, and saddled with alimony suits and tax problems, they are forced to project a public image of youth, vitality, and carefree existence—or drug-inspired orgy. As in *Teeth 'n' Smiles*, the idealism of the 1960s has been completely lost, and Shelly can no longer believe in the songs she sings. Nor can she, at the end, maintain the illusion that she has any meaningful power. As in the former play, the audience is left with the bitter recognition of the mechanisms of exploitation in popular culture and of the hollowness of the ideals it perpetrates:

> *Bill.* All your energy! And no direction.
> *Shelly.* That's why. No purpose. That's why . . . I'm in rock 'n' roll.[141]

In contrast to *Teeth 'n' Smiles*, which used newly-composed rock music, a majority of the songs introduced in *Bastard Angel* are familiar ones from the 1960s. Two are new songs with lyrics by Keeffe and music by Andrew Dickson. Most of the songs are either aggressive hard rock to warm up the audience or love songs that transport the listener into a dream world of illusion. In contrast with the anticlimactic beginning of *Teeth 'n' Smiles*, this drama opens with a rock and roll onslaught intended to create strong emotional response in the audience. The performance numbers of the Berlin gig are interspersed in the otherwise realistic action. The songs generally contrast with the surrounding action and sometimes create ironies. Keeffe thus forces reflection on the familiar texts in a new light. This is particularly true of the final song, "Stand by Me," a song from 1961. On the surface it is a personal declaration of Shelly's love for the dead Pimm, and as such moving and sincere. On the other hand, Pimm is a victim of drug addiction. In addition, Shelly no longer believes in the songs she sings—the sincerity is part of the image. Thus subtle ironies have been established that it is hoped would survive the emotional impact of performance.

The Entertainer, *Teeth 'n' Smiles*, and *Bastard Angel* all explore the world of singers and popular entertainment. Common to all three—especially at the end—is the sense of failure and disintegration, both of the singer and of the country. In *The Entertainer*, it is the disintegration of the British Empire after 1956; in the rock dramas the theme is the failure of the youth revolution of the 1960s to change the country and its class structure. All three alternate public performance scenes with naturalistic scenes of personal life. The performers are characterized by a feeling of deadness or drained emptiness. The realization of the exploitation mechanisms and hollow ideals of popular entertainment is balanced by a sense of loss, a nostalgia for the vitality of the Edwardian music hall in Osborne's case, or the aggressive optimism of the 1960s in the case of the younger dramatists.

The English characteristics of these two rock dramas come out clearly in a comparison with Sam Shepard's *The Tooth of Crime* (1972). Shepard's play also features a has-been rock singer and Elvis Presley imitator, Hoss, and an up-and-coming rock star, Crow. But in contrast with Hare and Keeffe, there is less concern with class conflict or even with social reality. The drama embodies more of a ritualized contest between two different styles and generations. The most striking difference between Shepard's play and the English ones is its language. In contrast with *The Tooth of Crime*, both *Teeth 'n' Smiles* and *Bastard Angel* seem realistic, even old-fashioned, in spite of their hip obscenity. The language of *The Tooth of Crime* is a medley of the styles and the slang of American pop culture. Shepard's dramatic idiom comprises, in Ruby Cohn's words,

> not only Western colloquialisms and rock slang, but also the vernaculars of sports, drugs, the underworld, science fiction, and the mass media. Shepard fuels his dramatic dialogue with these vocabularies, creating the most energetic language of today's American theater.[142]

For Shepard, language is closely interwoven with music. Indeed, ritual language and music merge in a hypnotic scene in *The Tooth of Crime*.[143] As Bruce Powe notes:

> In this play, Shepard creates a texture of language and music that echoes these distinctly American traditions and concerns by using songs, slang, profanity, quotations from rock hits, and words themselves as music. The form is surreal, yet anchored in a realistic frame, the rock music scene.[144]

On the power and function of music in drama Shepard says:

> I think music's really important, especially in plays and theatre—it adds a whole different kind of perspective, it immediately brings the audience to terms with an emotional reality. Because nothing communicates emotions better than music. . . . I wanted the music in *Tooth of Crime* so that you could step out of the play for a minute, every time a song comes, and be brought to an emotional comment on what's been taking place in the play. . . . I wanted the music to be used as a kind of sounding-board for the play.[145]

But in spite of Shepard's emphasis on music as comment, it still seems to me that Shepard's main intent is emotional impact.

Thus while the English rock plays are essentially psychological and social investigations of the role of rock music in England in the 1960s, *The Tooth of Crime* is more a dreamlike evocation of the emotional power and stylistic fascination of rock music. Although Hare and Keeffe employ the emotional effects of music to grip the audience, in the end effect the English plays are more intellectual—or at any rate more ironically critical and more nostalgic.

TREVOR GRIFFITHS

Trevor Griffiths is not of the rock generation, but as a radical left-wing political playwright he has taken a consistent interest in popular entertainment; its functions—and its dangers—for a mass audience. In *Comedians* he takes a look at what the music-hall tradition has become, and in *Oi for England* he focuses on a particularly topical contemporary phenomenon, skinheads and their music. Both dramas are set in working-class areas of Manchester.

Griffiths wants *Comedians* (1975) understood as a political play: "It's basically about two traditions—the social-democratic and the revolutionary tradition."[146] But these political positions are exemplified through dramatic figures from the sphere of popular culture and specifically the English music hall. The major conflict, as Griffiths sees it, is between the teacher, a music-hall comedian of the older generation, Eddie Waters, and his most gifted pupil, the radical Gethin Price. Secondarily the play is also about the conflict between the humanist Waters and the commercially adapted Bert Challenor, about challenging and escapist conceptions of art, and about "the function of comedy in a capitalist world."[147]

The drama does not make extensive use of song, but music enters into the action without being discussed on a theoretical level. The brothers Phil and Ged Murray, calling themselves "Night and Day" after the popular Cole Porter song, struggle with each other and muddle their act as they grapple with conflicting conceptions of comedy and success. As a result, most of their planned songs fail to materialize.[148] The innocuous and sentimental song, "Our Kid," with which they end their act, "gratefully rather than well" (pp. 45–46), forms an anticlimactic close to a poor performance. The uncompromising Gethin Price, in contrast, has already scrapped the song that he had in his act (p. 11) in an effort to achieve a more challenging and disturbing effect. In performance he ends not with a song, which might have reconciled the audience, but with a chilling and provocative rendition of "The Red Flag" on his miniature Grock-inspired violin (p. 53). Price has gone beyond comedy in his aggressive class hatred.

In his examination of popular culture and late twentieth-century music hall, Griffiths draws a pessimistic picture. Comparing the changes in comedy to the changes in music effected by the Beatles, Griffiths speaks of a "heightened realism, and a heightened cynicism and a heightened bitterness" that have become apparent in music and comedy in the 1970s.[149] In the 1970s it is established Challenor who can get the men jobs, and the apathetic bingo-playing audience in the workingmen's club bodes ill for performers such as Price. Political education via popular culture still has a long way to go.[150]

In *Comedians*, standup comedy lures the mostly working-class men and prospective entertainers, because it offers a chance to escape from menial and boring jobs. In Griffith's *Oi for England* (1982), music offers a temporary escape from a life with no employment and no future. It is no wonder that the group of young skinheads is desperate for a chance to perform in public and for money. What Griffiths is trying to demonstrate is that the conditions of performance may endow this music not only with a powerful emotional power, but also with a dangerous political power.

First presented on Central TV, then on tour in youth clubs and community centers, *Oi for England* is primarily aimed at an audience of young people, the peers of the band members, in an attempt to raise political consciousness. Griffiths prefers to write for television because he can there reach a massive working-class audience.[151] Finn, the most politically aware member of the young skinhead band, finally provokes the Man into a declaration of the political purpose of the mass meeting for which they are to play. On local election night the fascist National Front plans to bring in 20,000 unemployed white youngsters by bus to this free concert. The music is intended to subtly influence them in the direction of fascism: "Concerts, music: politics by other means."[152] The racial background is provided by the Asian-white riots raging in the streets outside the band's basement rehearsal room.

In contrast with the Man's calculating attitude, the songs of the skinheads are characterized by strong class consciousness, a sense of "Them" and "Us", but also by an aimless tendency to aggressiveness and destructive violence:

> Keep the light on, you in charge,
> You with the butter, us with the marge.
> Take extra precautions before you retire—
> This time a song, next time the FIRE!
>
> (p. 1)

They know what they are against, but they have only the vaguest of ideas what they are for. They call themselves AMMUNITION, and their second number reflects their anti-Establishment stance clearly. It is a parody of a patriotic song of World War II, "Praise the Lord and Pass the Ammunition" (1942). The final words of the original run:

> Praise the Lord, we're on a mighty mission!
> All aboard! We're not a-goin' fishin',

Praise the Lord, and pass the ammunition
And we'll all stay free.[153]

In the 1980s, all idealism and sense of purpose have been lost and the boys' energies are channelled into an ear-splitting emotional and political protest. Their lyrics represent a total rejection of the older values:

> *(The song deafens. Their involvement and passion are touchable: energy and spirit collect, cohere in performance)*
>
> . . . .
>
> Law and ORDER, up your ARSE!
> The orders are YOURS and the law's a FARCE!
> Watch out for the CRASH, the course is COLLISION.
> Sod the LORD—pass the AMMUNITION!

(p. 17)

In performance at the Royal Court Theatre Upstairs the aggressive beat, driving rhythm, and electronically amplified volume of the songs often made it hard to understand the words; their inaudibility is a serious drawback to this performance. Through the reactions of the various band members to the concert offer and to the riots—but also through the songs—the drama is trying to initiate political awareness.

The function of the Irish folk song that closes the play seems ambiguous. Finn chooses it after a moment of quiet intimacy with Gloria; perhaps it is intended to emphasize the values of personal commitment in the face of unrest. On the other hand, "its dense, sad, very Irish sound" (p. 37) provokes Finn to a sudden outburst of violence in which he destroys the equipment of the band. Has he rejected such values under the present circumstances in contemporary England, or has he despaired of them? In either case, it provides a strong musical contrast to the aggressive skinhead music. Griffiths typically wants to provoke discussion rather than provide definite answers.

Cultural values are shown to have strong political implications in Griffiths's plays. *Comedians* examines music-hall humor in ethical and political terms. In *Oi for England*, the playwright demonstrates that the strong emotional power of music is capable of political misuse and manipulation. This stance closely resembles that of Edward Bond and John McGrath. For Griffiths, as for other left-wing playwrights, awareness of the interconnections between music, politics and art is essential.

7. Summary

Popular song in all its variations from the nineteenth-century music hall ditty to the contemporary rock number exerts a pervading influence throughout modern drama. It is perhaps the most ubiquitous musical form today. Scarcely any dramatist alert to music can avoid taking a stand on this popular idiom. While responses range from rejection to wholehearted acceptance, most often the attitude is to ambivalently combine fondness for the tunes with criticism of some aspects of popular culture. The attraction may be rooted in the playwright's nostalgic longing for his or her own adolescent phase of development or based on a more general nostalgia for supposedly higher prewar cultural standards. Criticism may embody recognition of the vulgarity and triviality of this lowest common denominator of popular entertainment, or even rejection of the popular masses altogether.

Most often, however, the dramatists' stance is ambivalent; such songs are experienced as trivial, yet attractive, and their usefulness in the dramatic context lies precisely in their triviality. Thus Peter Barnes exploits the comic and satiric discrepancy between serious political themes and light, superficial tunes, as does Edward Bond also. John Osborne reflects through his use of shallow and vulgar song the decline of British imperial and cultural power in the twentieth century. Peter Nichols creates modern-day musicals that absorb the popular musical tradition and transform it into entertainment for today. Harold Pinter uses old tunes of the old times as a touchstone to evoke the elusive quicksand of shared common memories. And Tom Stoppard uses trivial melodies as part of his structural strategy to unsettle audience expectations and make spectators uncertain as to what is serious and where his true meaning lies. The rock music of the 1960s often symbolizes the erratic course of British politics in the decades following World War II.

Some dramatists emphasize the political implications of popular culture, while others exploit songs as a structural device. But all realize that popular music embodies a powerful attraction for the audience. Playwrights must find a way of coming to terms with this fact if they are to make the songs achieve their purpose in a serious dramatic context. Almost all seem to accept the music's power over the audience and develop their dramatic strategies building on this basis.

5

Other Musical Forms: From Religious Ritual to Political Song

No other category of music can compare quantitatively with the mass of popular song found in modern drama. The dramatists of the contemporary period do not frequently introduce either religious song or classical music into their work. With the exception of John Arden and Margaretta D'Arcy's work, folk song and working-class song also are much more limited in extent. Political lyrics, while pervasive, particularly in the more recent period, are not limited to any one style of music; sometimes they are combined with the popular idiom, sometimes with folk music. Nevertheless all of these categories do offer interesting variations on the theme of music in drama and provide alternatives to those who wish to explore musical idioms other than the popular.

1. Religious and Ritual Song

Among the religious examples represented are hymns, portions of the Catholic mass, other Christian airs such as plainsong, motets, chorales, and oratorios, and music associated with faiths and rituals other than Christian, such as Jewish songs or pre-Christian or non-Christian fertility rites. Several of the plays discussed earlier employed occasional religious songs. For example, one of the most moving scenes in *Oh What a Lovely War* was a musical religious service at the front, and the play as a whole contains several antiwar hymn parodies.

Both Edward Bond and Peter Barnes employ Christian hymns to satiric purpose in their attacks on the disastrous fusion of religious, class and patriotic norms in Western civilization. Bond also introduces melodies derived from ancient fertility rituals in both *The Fool* and *The Woman*. Elsewhere, hymns sometimes serve to create a religious atmosphere. Peter Barnes's *The Bewitched*, set in Spain during the Inquisition, reverberates with Christian music such as the "Te Deum" and "Magnificat." On the one hand, these establish an oppressive atmosphere of religious authority. On the other hand this atmosphere is undermined by juxtaposition with incongruous

271

popular tunes, and thus the negative effects of religious manipulation are revealed. Arnold Wesker introduces Jewish songs into several of his plays with both religious and cultural implications. John Osborne employs ritual church song for the creation of setting and atmosphere in *Luther* (1961), somewhat as T. S. Eliot had done much earlier in *Murder in the Cathedral;* and Arnold Wesker uses Catholic hymns similarly in *Caritas* (1981).

PETER SHAFFER

Most interesting among dramas using religious and ritual song is Peter Shaffer's *The Royal Hunt of the Sun* (1964). In the play Shaffer (born in 1926) uses theater itself as a kind of ritual, in an effort to create total theater:

> My hope was always to realise on stage a kind of 'total' theatre, involving not only words but rites, mimes, masks and magics. The text cries for illustration. It is . . . a pantomimist's piece, a musician's piece, a designer's piece.[1]

Most often mentioned as influences on Shaffer are the Japanese forms of Kabuki and Nō theater, which employ masks and music; and Antonin Artaud's theater of cruelty. Artaud himself was strongly influenced by oriental theater. Artaud proposes a metaphysical, ritual and magic theater, a "religious idea of the theater,"[2]

> a theater in which violent physical images crush and hypnotize the sensibility of the spectator. . . . A theater that induces trance . . .[3]

> This . . . language of the theater . . . turns words into incantations. . . . It pile-drives sounds. It seeks to exalt, to benumb, to charm, to arrest the sensibility.[4]

As Shaffer probably knew, Artaud in his Second Manifesto for "The Theater of Cruelty" described a stage spectacle concerning the conquest of Mexico.[5]

In *The Royal Hunt of the Sun* Shaffer also attempts to hypnotize the audience by means of spectacle, visual imagery, and music. In accordance with his nonintellectual concept of theater music, the meaning conveyed by the words of a song is secondary. Most of the music in this drama is instrumental or chanted, with no emphasis on lyrics. Only two pieces are actually sung, and one of these, a toil song, is in Indian dialect, in other words, in a language unknown to the audience. This toil song (p. 19) is a ritual work song and its effect is to bring out the peaceful, preordained, theocratically ritualized pattern of life among the Incas. It is accompanied by percussion instruments. During the following passage in which the Indian system is discussed, the hummed tune and the percussion continue, linking the rhythms of the song to the ritual rhythms of Inca life.[6] Because Atahuallpa is both king and God, most of the Inca music and chants have religious significance.

The one melody sung in English comes later in the play. The "Finch Song" (p. 52), first performed by Atahuallpa for Pizarro, is a parable warning against the fate of "robber birds." It calls attention to the fact that both leaders are robbers and foreshadows both the fall of the Inca kingdom and the degeneration of the Spanish *conquistadores:*

> So fell Peru. We gave her greed, hunger and the Cross: three gifts for the civilized life. *The family groups that sang on the terraces are gone.* In their place slaves shuffle underground and *they don't sing there.* Peru is a silent country, frozen in avarice. So fell Spain, gorged with gold; distended; now dying. (p. 79)[7]

The play ends with Pizarro forlornly singing fragments from this air over the body of Atahuallpa. This final song has personal, emotional, and thematic reverberations. It is presented unaccompanied, with a simple, almost monotonous melody and in an abrupt, precise manner, so that it too acquires the feeling of ritual.

Most of the music in *The Royal Hunt of the Sun* is ritual music, designed to overwhelm the audience aurally and emotionally. The listener is benumbed by sound, often in combination with mime and spectacle. Concerning the musical score by Marc Wilkinson, the dramatist writes:

> This extraordinary music I believe to be an integral part of any production of *The Royal Hunt of the Sun.* It embraces bird cries; plainchant; a fantasia for organ; freezing sounds for the Mime of the Great Ascent, and frightening ones for the Mime of the Great Massacre. To me its most memorable items are the exquisitely doleful lament which opens Act II, and, most amazing of all, the final Chant of Resurrection, to be whined and whispered, howled and hooted, over Atahuallpa's body in the darkness, before the last sunrise of the Inca Empire.[8]

It is evident that for Shaffer, inarticulate sound or music is more important dramatically than articulate words to music. Despite the fact that the play has epic features, it contains no songs with epic functions.

Shaffer's conception of theater music emerges clearly when compared with that of Peter Barnes. Barnes was also influenced by Artaud, especially in his use of inarticulate sounds, of music and song. But Barnes either quickly breaks the mood created by the music, or even uses music and satirical lyrics to disrupt an atmosphere already created. In these cases, the texts are crucial. His ultimate aim is to establish a critical awareness in his audience. Shaffer does not seek to disrupt but to involve, and his use of music is a powerful device to intensify audience involvement in his total theater.

2. Classical Music

Scattered references to classical music can be found throughout modern drama, but as in the case of religious song, its use does not compare quantitatively with the vast variety of popular songs. Often what seems to be important to the dramatist is the fact that a classical and respected composer is evoked, and not that the music is either instrumental or vocal. Indeed, in several instances playwrights seem to have deliberately chosen instrumental classical music for the purpose of greater contrast to popular songs. Stoppard's *Travesties* contrasts Beethoven's "Appassionata" with the "Mr. Gallagher and Mr. Shean" song; in Arnold Wesker's *Roots* Bizet's "L'Arlésienne" is compared with a pop song, to mention only two. Osborne in *A Patriot for Me* (1965) uses arias from Mozart operas to open and close his drag ball in act 2. These are chosen to contrast and to underline the element of theatricality in the scene. The singer's voice is inadequate, but "it has enough sweetness in feeling to immediately invoke the pang of Mozart."[9] In a world in which feelings must be disguised, Mozart seems to offer an emotional touchstone.

Three contemporary plays that are thematically concerned with classical music, both vocal and instrumental, are Peter Nichols's *Passion Play*, which contrasts classical Christian choral music with physical and emotional passion; Peter Shaffer's *Amadeus*, centering on Mozart's music; and David Rudkin's *Penda's Fen*, in which Edward Elgar's music becomes the vehicle through which an adolescent searches for identity.

PETER NICHOLS

Peter Nichols's *Passion Play* (1981) begins like a drawing-room comedy. And at one level, the level of plot, it can be understood as a combination of drawing-room comedy and bedroom farce. But quite suddenly a first burst of the "Dies Irae" from Mozart's *Requiem* drowns out the small talk, adding unusual dimensions to the theme. Throughout the drama, Nichols has employed classical choral music, passion music and requiem music by Verdi, Mozart, and Bach, and also other large choral works; for example, Beethoven's Ninth Symphony. His choice of vocal music is careful and deliberate, and the words of the sung passages are crucial to context and themes: trust, suffering, and wrath become multifold in their implications.

There is, of course, also a realistic reason for the introduction of music: Eleanor is a singer and music teacher and is rehearsing for a performance of Verdi's *Requiem* in the Albert Hall. James uses the opportunity to begin and carry on an affair with Kate while his wife is off rehearsing or performing. But this is almost incidental to the real significance of the choral music in this play. Nichols also experiments briefly in combining voices and music to create a kind of fugue.[10]

Gradually the audience comes to realize that there is a far deeper connection between the action and the sung passages. This becomes clear at the latest when Beethoven's "Ode to Joy" is placed in direct parallelism to the ecstasy of sexual passion:

You'll wait on the bed you and Albert used to share while on the radio Eleanor and a
hundred other choristers sing the Ode to Joy.
Again the music bursts out. (p. 36)

At the beginning of act 2 the thematic implications of the passion music
become explicit. Before the lights come up, the choir sings "O Haupt voll
Blut und Wunden" from Bach's *St. Matthew Passion.* James is restoring a
painting of the mocked Christ with a crown of thorns. As Eleanor and James
flounder to understand what James's infidelity means to them, the discussion
with each other and with their inner selves, Nell and Jim, widens to include
such questions as: the relationship between art (visual and musical) and
sexuality, the role of Christian tradition in modern life, and the meaning of
Christian art for community experience.

> *Jim.* . . . . This is all about *us,* what's happened to *us.* What's been happening for
> centuries. (p. 59)

> *Eleanor.* We're not Christians. I'm an atheist but I love church music and oratorio
> and hymns and Christmas carols. Hundreds of people singing together is the
> nearest we may ever come to heaven on earth. Communion. (p.60)

The passion of the title can thus be interpreted in subtly complex ways:
physical and sexual passion; individual emotional passion; the exhilaration of
artistic (especially musical) creation; spiritual communion; suffering in all its
gradations, physical, emotional and spiritual; and the passion of Christ. The
play links these concerns to a story that is not about marital strife alone but
also about human growth.

Unfortunately the conditions of production in commercial theater make a
full understanding of this complex play difficult, if not impossible. In the
performance I watched in the West End of London, for example, the audience chatted throughout the Chorale "O Haupt voll Blut und Wunden,"
which comes just after the intermission, and did not pay attention until the
resumption of what they considered to be a bedroom farce.[11] The true
fascination of the play could only emerge in a more thoughtful production for
a more thoughtful audience.

PETER SHAFFER

Shaffer's *Amadeus* (1979) has often been compared with melodrama because of its use of both music and spectacle in drama. The play is of only
secondary interest in the context of this study, for it is basically of little
importance to Shaffer whether this music is vocal or instrumental. True, the
playwright chooses many excerpts from Mozart operas, presumably for the-

atrical reasons, but it is irrelevant whether we understand the meaning of the text, and the nature of the experience conveyed by the music for the audience and for Salieri is similar whether it is operatic or instrumental music.

What is of interest is the association of classical music with religious feeling in this drama. The events of the play are seen through the eyes of Salieri, and for Salieri, Mozart's music is an example of divine inspiration. The man is "Amadeus," the beloved of God; the "voice of God"[12] speaks through his artistic creation. For a modern audience the music may or may not confirm this religious experience, but certainly it creates a feeling of awe, aesthetic beauty and creative genius. Indeed, in performance, the most moving moments are created simply by the replaying of Mozart's music. The emotional power of the music is by no means diminished or undermined either by Salieri's recognition of his own mediocrity or by Mozart's infantile character. On the contrary, because of these contrasts the audience becomes rather more overwhelmed when the music is played. The overall effect of the music in this drama is similar to that in *The Royal Hunt of the Sun*. Music is associated with religious experience in both, and the intention is to overpower the audience emotionally. In *Amadeus* one might even say that music takes on the function of a substitute religion.

DAVID RUDKIN

For David Rudkin (born in 1936) music and religious experience are also closely related. Coming from a family of strict evangelical Christians, Rudkin "as a teenager . . . became totally obsessed with music."[13] Later he became a music teacher and composer. (Peter Shaffer was a music critic for several years.) Rudkin possesses an intimate familiarity with classical music. *Ashes* (1974) is composed in three "movements," accompanied by music of Mahler, Schubert and Vaughan Williams. Often the music in Rudkin's drama is religious. In *The Sons of Light* (1977), he includes a hymn by Charles Wesley with music which he himself composed. In *The Triumph of Death* (1981) two hymns are sung.

With respect to music in drama, however, *Penda's Fen* (1974) is by far the most interesting of Rudkin's plays. Although designed for television, it could conceivably be produced on stage. In this drama the categories of classical music and religious song merge, as indeed they did in *Passion Play*. The play is permeated by the music of Edward Elgar, most notably the religious oratorio *The Dream of Gerontius* (1900). This oratorio is based on a visionary poem by Cardinal John Henry Newman and recounts the spiritual journey of the soul of the dead Gerontius to his judgment before his God. William Alwyn emphasizes the "essentially dramatic conception of the work."[14] It is this dramatic tension that makes it suitable to Rudkin's theme of the adolescent journey of self-discovery in *Penda's Fen*. Musically and dramatically the joyous, triumphant "Alleluia" of the Angel is contrasted with the crashing

Angel's "Alleluia," from *The Dream of Gerontius*, text by Cardinal Newman, music by Edward Elgar, in Elgar, *The Dream of Gerontius* (Borough Green, Sevenoaks, Kent: Novello, 1982).

dissonances that represent the "glance of God."[15] The soaring notes of praise are juxtaposed with the terror of the final moment of divine judgement.

Rudkin's play goes beyond the Roman Catholic faith of the oratorio and interprets the spiritual struggle between demons and angels in a wider sense as a "parable of power politics."[16] This is a psychological, political and visionary play, in which seventeen-year-old Stephen in an unreal dream-like sequence encounters the senile composer Elgar in person and is initiated into the secret of the "Enigma Variations" (scene 19). Stephen's father in turn introduces his son to his own dream "of some Second Coming Man himself must bring about. . . . Through some Last Disobedience and new . . . Resurrection" (p. 70).[17] He nurtures the idea of the survival or resurrection of the last "son of light" in England, the ancient King Penda who is keeping England's spiritual "deep dark flame" (p. 83) alive in the remoteness of the fens.

Under his new dawning awareness, Stephen's understanding of *The Dream of Gerontius* begins to expand and change. He is no longer satisfied with Elgar's dissonance of awe and faith, the acceptance of divine judgment. He now reaches out on the organ to create a "piercing discord of unbelievable obscenity" (p. 75) which represents the "sacred demon of ungovernableness

. . . secret, . . . strange: dark, true, impure and dissonant" (p. 83). In this symbolical scene the church cracks open to expose a black gulf as the air vibrates with the organ discord. In contrast, the following scene in which the schoolboys prepare to sing William Blake's "Jerusalem" seems more bland and realistic. But Stephen's new consciousness now reveals a mystic relevance of this "secondary British National Anthem"[18] to the ideas of ancient grace and the Second Coming. According to the Glastonbury legend that may have inspired Blake in the first stanzas of "Jerusalem," Christ as a young child came to England and lived there for a while.[19] Spiritual redemption and political vision merge both in the drama and in the song "Jerusalem":

> And did those feet in ancient time
> Walk upon Englands mountains green:
> And was the holy Lamb of God
> On Englands pleasant pastures seen!
>
> And did the Countenance Divine
> Shine forth upon our clouded hills?
> And was Jerusalem builded here,
> Among these dark Satanic Mills?
>
> Bring me my Bow of burning gold:
> Bring me my Arrows of desire:
> Bring me my Spear: O clouds unfold:
> Bring me my Chariot of Fire!
>
> I will not cease from Mental Fight,
> Nor shall my Sword sleep in my hand:
> Till we have built Jerusalem,
> In Englands green & pleasant Land.[20]

The music in this play is intended by the dramatist to touch the audience emotionally and spiritually. It is not just the immature schoolboy Stephen who finds *The Dream of Gerontius* shattering, the author's own stage directions say that the power of this music should "move us to tears and chill our spine" (p. 74). And yet the total effect is quite different from Shaffer's *Amadeus*. There, Mozart's music is the supreme standard by which creative genius and divine inspiration may be judged. There is nothing beyond that, and the audience is left to contemplate God's workings through the instrument of imperfect man. In *Penda's Fen* Stephen, and with him the audience, struggles to come to terms with the discipline of the music and the religious faith it expresses. Both the music and the meaning imparted by the sung words are questioned, and in the end are left behind for something new and more disturbing, the "sacred demon of ungovernableness." Emotional and intellectual quest are here embodied in the medium of vocal music. In this respect *Penda's Fen* is the more challenging play.

The attitude toward classical music most often to be found in contemporary drama is that of admiration or awe. If it is used to contrast popular music, the classical composer is usually favored. Only very seldom does classical music carry overtones of cultural and social snobbery (for example, David Mercer's *Then and Now*). Short lyrical songs by classical composers are seldom introduced; an infrequent example would be the fragment of Schubert's "Der Erlkönig" in Rudkin's *Ashes*. When sung passages from operas are employed, the words are often of little import. It is for this reason that the passion music in *Passion Play* and the Elgar oratorio in *Penda's Fen* are so interesting. In both cases the implications of the words have far-reaching significance for the meaning of the play and contribute to the enrichment of the whole.

3. Working-Class Song and Folk Song

In contrast to the extensive and varied use of popular song in contemporary English drama, folk song and working-class song are also much more limited. The most important dramatists to employ folk song are John Arden and Margaretta D'Arcy, John McGrath, and Arnold Wesker. Arden and D'Arcy go back to the folk song and ballad traditions to recapture the essential poetry of the English language, to tap the collective memory of the audience. In their later plays, they use working-class song to underline their socialist perspective. McGrath uses both the folk tradition and popular song to create a new popular political theater that will appeal directly to a working-class audience. Folk music is especially important in the plays for a Scottish audience. Wesker draws on English folk and workers' traditions as expression of a culture which is richer and more varied than modern commercialized popular culture.

ARNOLD WESKER

In his theoretical writings and in his plays, Wesker (born in 1932) speaks of contemporary culture in terms of "cultural bankruptcy" and "cultural exploitation." Both in his drama and in his work for Centre 42 Wesker actively tries to counteract the cynical attitude of the modern entertainment industry which seeks to sell its products as commercial commodities and appeals to the "lowest common denominator" in the audience:

> There is the problem of a vast army of commercial people exploiting what are genuine searchings for beauty, poetry, fun, enjoyment . . . by treating the public as a moron.[21]

For Wesker, positive cultural values are inextricably connected with socialist and humanist values. Through art, Wesker hopes to teach others to understand and enjoy life more fully:

> I believe that . . . the pursuit of art is also a . . . pursuit for an understanding of the complex world we live in, . . . I believe that the pursuit of art is a pursuit for sanity, self-respect, understanding and reassurance . . .[22]

These general attitudes towards popular culture and art can be applied also specifically to Wesker's approach to music as it appears in his plays. Rock and roll or bland sentimental popular tunes are often contrasted with either classical music or folk and industrial melodies as forms that possess deeper emotional truth and more rewarding variety.

Wesker has certainly learned from Sean O'Casey—an admitted influence—particularly in the introduction of folk airs at lyrical or emotional moments. Brechtian influence is usually seen as being at the most secondhand, perhaps transmitted via Joan Littlewood or others among the postwar dramatists such as Arden. Wesker's familiarity with Yiddish music and socialist hymns surely is conditioned by his family background and upbringing. His choice of rural English ballads is possibly inspired by the folk revival of the late 1950s.[23]

The Kitchen introduces tunes in realistic situations and exploits them in traditional functions. The songs serve to underline the portrayal of character and atmosphere. An international selection of melodies exemplifies the manifold origins of the kitchen staff, and the loud rock and roll music blaring from the radio corresponds to the fierce energy and hectic pace of the work. Here rock and pop music are not yet singled out and contrasted with classical or folk music as they are later in *The Wesker Trilogy*. In particular, Peter's song "Hi lee hi lo hi la" characterizes him as merry yet boisterous, good natured but nervous. This song also captures the atmosphere of the kitchen as a whole: "somehow its maniacal tone is part of the whole atmosphere of the kitchen."[24]

The playwright begins to explore his theme of modern cultural poverty as compared with traditional values in *The Wesker Trilogy*. This is articulated particularly clearly in *Roots*, and it will be taken up again later in *Chips With Everything*. *Chicken Soup With Barley* (1958) employs song to depict the fighting spirit of the working classes in 1936. But the patriotic "England Arise" and Brecht's "A Man is Only Human" ("Einheitsfrontlied," 1934), have ironic implications as well through the context in which they are introduced: Monty complains, "We've just won one of the biggest fights in working-class history and all we do is quarrel," and he begins to sing.[25] Human weakness and family squabbles counteract the spirit of solidarity, foreshadowing the loss of faith and energy in the later acts.

In *Roots* (1959) Ronnie's views on music are heard through Beatie's quota-

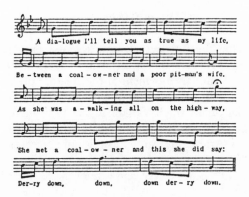

A dialogue I'll tell you as true as my life,
Between a coal-owner and a poor pitman's wife.
As she was a-walking all on the highway,
She met a coal-owner, and this she did say:
    Derry down, down, down derry down.

'Good morning, Lord Firedamp,' this woman she said,
'I'll do you no harm, sir, so don't be afraid.
If you'd been where I've been the most of my life,
You wouldn't turn pale at a poor pitman's wife.'
    Derry down, down, down derry down.

'Then where do you come from?' the owner he cries.
'I come from hell,' the poor woman replies.
'If you come from hell, then come tell me right plain,
How you contrived to get out again.'
    Derry down, down, down derry down.

'Aye, the way I got out, the truth I will tell,
They're turning the poor folk all out of hell.
This is to make room for the rich wicked race,
For there is a great number of them in that place.'
    Derry down, down down derry down.

'And the coal-owners is the next on command
To arrive in hell, as I understand,
For I heard the old devil say as I came out,
The coal-owners all had received their rout.'
    Derry down, down, down derry down.

'Then how does the old devil behave in that place?'
'O sir, he is cruel to the rich wicked race.
He's far more crueller than you could suppose.
He's like a mad bull with a ring through his nose.'
    Derry down, down, down derry down.

'If you be a coal-owner, sir, take my advice
And agree with your men and give them a fair price,
For if and you do not I know very well
You'll be in great danger of going to hell.'
    Derry down, down, down derry down.

'For all you coal-owners great fortunes has made
By those jovial men that works in the coal trade.
Now, how can you think to prosper and thrive
By wanting to starve your poor workmen alive?'
    Derry down, down, down derry down.

So come, ye poor pitmen, and join heart and hand;
For when you're off work, all trade's at a stand.
In the town of Newcastle all cry out amain:
Oh, gin the pits were at work once again!
    Derry down down, down derry down.

"The Coal-owner and the Pitman's Wife," from A. L. Lloyd, *Folk Song in England* (London: Lawrence and Wishart, 1967), pp. 344–46.

tions, but here too the intellectual, almost missionary fervor of Ronnie's words is ironically reflected through Beatie's imperfect understanding, and through her almost animal enjoyment of the creature pleasures of life. Musically, a popular melody, "I'll Wait for You in the Heavens Blue," is contrasted with an industrial tune (which Wesker in the stage directions calls a "folk song"), "The Coal-Owner and the Pitman's Wife," and later with classical music, Bizet's "L'Arlésienne Suite." In Ronnie's words the pop song is "third-rate" because it contains no passion.[26] Or as Beatie puts it, "it's sloshy and sickly" (p. 113). Beyond that she cannot make Ronnie's theory understood because she has not grasped it adequately herself. When she tries to illustrate its badness by singing it, she gets carried away and performs "with some enthusiasm" (p. 116), so that what emerges from this scene is more Beatie's energy and pleasure than Ronnie's point about commercialized culture. Beatie's presentation of "The Coal-Owner and the Pitman's Wife" (p. 113), a coalmining strike ballad, probably from the period of the 1844 Durham strike, is characterized more by her lively, ringing rendition than by her understanding of the words and their political implications. Ronnie presumably taught it to her as an example of industrial folk music and of early labor politics. (John Arden uses the same tune, but not the original words, in *Soldier, Soldier*.)

Similarly, when Beatie tries to teach her mother about Ronnie's theory of classical music, what is conveyed to the audience is not any theoretical appreciation, but more her animal pleasure in rhythm and movement, and her simple joy of being alive:

> (*She begins to dance a mixture of a cossack dance and a sailor's hornpipe. The music becomes fast and her spirits are young and high.*)
> . . . God, Mother, we could all be so much more happy and alive. Wheeeee . . .
> (*Beatie claps her hands and dances on and her Mother smiles and claps her hands . . .*).
>   (p. 130)

The enthusiasm and vitality of Beatie's renditions make Ronnie appear as a bit of a prig; this is surely part of Wesker's intention. Although the dramatist wants to contrast the poverty of pop culture with the richness of the folk and classical traditions, he is here too good a playwright to convey this dogmatically, without taking human nature into account.

In *Chips With Everything* (1962), one musical example in particular is perhaps too theoretical, too much an obvious demonstration of a principle on the author's part. At the Naafi Christmas party the Wing Commander expresses his contempt of the working-class recruits through his contempt for their pop culture and rock and roll music: "Look at them . . . Their wild dancing and their silly words."[27] To expose their despicability he calls for a talent show, cynically suggesting "a dirty recitation, or a pop song" (p. 35) as appropriate to their degenerate culture. Pip, understanding the challenge,

responds with a counter-demonstration. He prevents the recruits from singing an Elvis Presley number, and suggests instead a Burns poem and a
rendition of "The Cutty Wren" as expression of true folk culture. While this
rebellious song from the time of the peasant revolt is sung in full, the "Boys
join in gradually, menacing the officers" (p. 37). Edward Bond introduced a
more ritualistic version of this tune, "Hunting the Wren," in his drama *The
Fool* as expression of intact folk culture. But here the demonstration seems
too artificial on Wesker's part. The idea, according to John Russell Taylor, is
that

> the working-class will rebel against the ruling classes by refusing to accept any
> longer the rubbish of pop 'art' constantly foisted on them by commerce and
> returning instead to their folk song heritage.[28]

But the upper-class Pip has to prod them in this direction, and it is unlikely
that the working-class recruits would have been familiar with this song at all
in the early 1960s. Unrealistic as this episode may be, "The Cutty Wren"
serves to symbolize the class conflicts within this microcosm of society, the
military camp, and to contrast the concepts of folk and popular.

The Nottingham Captain: A Moral for Narrator, Voices and Orchestra (1962),
designed for a Centre 42 festival, is a musical documentary concerning the
Luddite riots of the early nineteenth century. This short piece combines both
spoken and sung passages, and one question and answer exchange is modeled
structurally on "The Cutty Wren."[29] There were both classical and jazz
scores composed for it. In the work of Centre 42 there was a strong emphasis
on bringing folk music, jazz, and classical music to the working classes.

In his later plays, Wesker continues to employ folk song and working-class
song, sometimes in new ways. Most interesting is perhaps the nonrealistic
and metaphorical *The Four Seasons* (1965). Here an old ballad, "The Unquiet
Grave" (Child, no. 78), is used to heighten the already lyrical language.[30] The
ballad reflects the "popular belief that excessive grieving for the dead inter-
feres with their repose."[31] Wesker has used the first two and last two of the
ballad stanzas, in a form almost identical to Child's Variant A. The substitu-
tion of death for God in the last line serves to emphasize Wesker's theme.
Adam's singing has symbolical implications: he is reaching out to Beatrice,
trying to bring her back from emotional death. This symbolism is particularly clear in the singing lesson in the "Spring" section of the drama
(pp. 19–22). Beatrice is at first incapable of singing, and singing here represents any joyous emotional reaction. She says, "Can you still teach me to
sing? Teach me to love myself, better—then perhaps I'll sing" (p. 22).
Gradually she learns to sing, and to respond to Adam's love. But this effect is
not lasting, and after this there are no further songs in the play. Wesker has
said that both the cooking scene and the singing lesson in *The Four Seasons*

The wind doth blow to-night my love and a
few small drops of rain I ne-ver had but
one true-love in cold grave she was lain.

A

Communicated to the Folk Lore Record, I, 60, by Miss Charlotte Latham, as written down from the lips of a girl in Sussex.

1 ' THE wind doth blow today, my love,
  And a few small drops of rain ;
I never had but one true-love,
  In cold grave she was lain.

2 ' I 'll do as much for my true-love
  As any young man may ;
I 'll sit and mourn all at her grave
  For a twelvemonth and a day.'

3 The twelvemonth and a day being up,
  The dead began to speak :
' Oh who sits weeping on my grave,
  And will not let me sleep ? '

4 ' 'T is I, my love, sits on your grave,
  And will not let you sleep ;
For I crave one kiss of your clay-cold lips,
  And that is all I seek.'

5 ' You crave one kiss of my clay-cold lips ;
  But my breath smells earthy strong ;
If you have one kiss of my clay-cold lips,
  Your time will not be long.

6 ' 'T is down in yonder garden green,
  Love, where we used to walk,
The finest flower that ere was seen
  Is withered to a stalk.

7 ' The stalk is withered dry, my love,
  So will our hearts decay ;
So make yourself content, my love,
  Till God calls you away.'

"The Unquiet Grave," tune as printed in Arnold Wesker, *The Four Seasons* (London: Jonathan Cape, 1966), p. 60; text from *The English and Scottish Popular Ballads*, ed. Francis James Child (New York: Folklore Press, 1956), ballad no. 78, variant A.

were "selected to convey a man trying to deepen, or rescue, his love by communicating something that had given him joy."[32] Singing is an ideal form of emotional communication.

Interestingly, in *The Friends* (1967) Wesker has written his own text to a song which echoes some of the themes of *The Four Seasons:*

> We've buried the winter
> Married the spring,
> And now we have a time
> To pause and think again and sing.[33]

This lyrical piece with music by Wilfred Josephs captures the mood of anticipation as the friends wait for Esther to die. It is calm and reflective rather than anguished and foreshadows the acceptance and renewal at the end of the play.

In *The Old Ones* (1972), Manny's singing of a socialist piece and a Hasidic song in Yiddish functions as an affirmation of the joy of life. That the tunes also serve to establish political, cultural, and religious identity is secondary. Just as Wesker says that "this play is essentially about defiant old age,"[34] so too we must see these songs as part of his characters' resilience. In spite of their weaknesses and doubts, the characters are drawn together by the music at the close of the play to a community of song, dance, and laughter. Only the pessimistic Boomy is left out, while his brother Manny, the taped singer, is finally able to laugh at him and defy him. Wesker was very aware of the patterning of this ending:

> I had envisaged . . . a triangle of tensions between a group singing in the background and a brother who is hurling quotations of doom from *Ecclesiastes* and the brother he is hurling them at, who is laughing.[35]

Here, too, the melodies communicate joy and emotional warmth. *The Merchant* (1976), in contrast, ends with the strains of a Sephardic air that both reflects on the theme of exile, as Shylock prepares to emigrate to the Holy Land, and strengthens the mood of sad and lonely longing at the end of the play.[36]

Song in Wesker's drama is associated with vitality and love of life, sometimes with more somber emotions. In this respect, Wesker is comparable to O'Casey. Whether it is young Beatie with her animal energy, or old Manny in his lonely defiance, singing for Wesker is part of the fullness of being alive. Beyond that he often draws a distinction in his plays between the vital but sentimental tunes of popular culture and folk or working-class traditions (both working-class hymns and industrial folk song) which he sees as being of

greater emotional depth and greater political and social significance, and
hence of greater value.

KEITH DEWHURST

   In addition to the work of Arden, D'Arcy and Wesker, folk song and new
pieces inspired by the folk tradition are sometimes used in alternative theater,
as will be seen in the example of John McGrath. In the established theater
works can also be found that have profited from the new awareness both of
popular theater and of folk traditions. A good example is Keith Dewhurst's
Lark Rise to Candleford, a dramatization of the Flora Thompson trilogy about
life in rural Oxfordshire in the 1880s, which was produced at the National
Theatre by Bill Bryden in 1978 and 1979. Dewhurst (born in 1931), calling
attention to the "epic and popular" in English dramatic tradition, and emphasizing the importance of Joan Littlewood for the continuation of these
traditions in England in the modern period, says of his collaboration with Bill
Bryden:

> We have developed over a number of years: epic plays with music that have
> gradually evolved into a promenade style.[37]

> We have always reached for what is epic and popular, and used music and spectacle
> because when there is a band . . . the event takes on vital aspects of a concert: the
> immediacy and the ability to speak directly to the audience.[38]

Best known of their collaborations are *The Passion* (1977), *The World Turned
Upside Down* (1978) and *Lark Rise to Candleford*.
   The latter employs both traditional folk song and ballad and newly written
tunes in the folk style. Elements of folk rock and music hall can also be heard
in the music.[39] The singing arises quite naturally out of the context. Because
the setting is rural England one hundred years ago, the musical heritage is
still part of living oral tradition. For example, a morris dance and a ballad,
"The Outlandish Knight" (Child, no. 4), are performed as the menfolk
gather in the pub (p. 89). Although the drama is epic in structure, the songs
fulfill more traditional functions: entertainment, celebration, establishment
of character, or atmosphere. They do not, as in the later work of Arden and
D'Arcy, help to bridge the epic time span, tell of events beyond the scope of
the stage, or comment on the action. Sandy Craig sums up this popular but
not radically inventive approach:

> While hardly presenting experimental work as was first promised, a core of actors
> under director Bill Bryden, and often with writer Keith Dewhurst, has developed a
> style through mainly folksy "promenade" productions that take a cosy look at
> England's history, apparently offering what the fringe does but without the edge.[40]

4. Song and Political Purpose in Alternative Theater

In contemporary alternative theater the use of song is so widespread that an entire book could be written on this subject alone. On the other hand many of the productions do not lay claim to any great literary value, and many of the texts have not been published. For these reasons treatment of alternative theater should be exemplary. The work of the playwright John McGrath and the 7:84 Theatre Company illustrates some major aims of music in political alternative theater.

JOHN MCGRATH AND THE 7:84 THEATRE COMPANY

For John McGrath all theater is political in the widest sense of the word:

The theatre is . . . the most public, the most clearly political of the art forms. . . . It is a place of recognition, of evaluation, of judgement. It shows the interaction of human beings and social forces.[41]

But McGrath distinguishes between his kind of alternative political theater and political drama that works within the "dominant mode"—established institutions or traditional dramatic forms—from Brecht and Piscator to Brenton and Hare.[42] His own basic aim is to create a new political theater for a working-class audience that makes use of working-class forms of entertainment: "a new kind of theatre developed from popular forms."[43] He wishes to evolve a

mode of theatre . . . which speaks the language of working-class entertainment and tries to develop that language to make critical, progressive theatre primarily for popular audiences.[44]

Based on his experience of more than ten years' work as director of the 7:84 theatre companies in England and later Scotland, McGrath in his important book *A Good Night Out. Popular Theatre: Audience, Class and Form* analyzes typical features of such popular entertainment. He lists and elucidates nine: directness, comedy, music, emotion, variety, effect, immediacy, localism and a sense of identity with the performer.[45] The songs in his plays contribute to the strengthening of many of these elements. What McGrath aims at is a critical and creative reassessment of such features in a new political theater. This may involve criticism of the audience and its popular traditions, as, for example, when a particularly sentimental form of popular music is ridiculed at the beginning of *Little Red Hen*. "Music can become mindlessness; emotion can become manipulative and can obscure judgement."[46] For this reason the lyrics of McGrath's songs, usually newly written, are of utmost importance. Often the form of his drama approaches that of musical documentary, a reassessment of a specific period in working-class history presented in a popular musical form.

For McGrath, the decision to use music in drama is a "very conscious quasi-political decision."[47] He is acutely aware of the interactions between author, text and audience. Communication for him is the essence of theater:

> It is, to me, the element of magic, of primitive communication, that makes the whole business of theatre mean more than films, television, novels, even most poetry.[48]

For this reason he takes as starting point popular forms of music familiar to the audience. He says:

> My theory of writing theatre is that you start with where the audience is. . . . We've used all kinds of music in 7 : 84. . . . The two important features of it, one of which is obvious, is that we try to use music which connects with the audience's entertainment expectations in some way. But the other bit, which is not recognized nearly enough, is that we also try to take it on, and use that basic music to, in some way, challenge the audience.

He emphasizes that 7 : 84 does not tailor its music to the audience's taste but always tries to do something new with it.

Because both 7 : 84 England and Scotland are touring companies, technical and economic necessities have often had a strong influence on the type of music and the number of musicians in their shows. Both companies have attempted large-scale ambitious musicals (*Bitter Apples* by 7 : 84 England in 1979, with music by Mark Brown; *Women in Power,* an adaptation of Aristophanes' *Ecclesiazousae* by 7 : 84 Scotland, with music by Thanos Mikroutsikos), but have found that they did not have the resources to produce them successfully. For these reasons, McGrath defines the successful 7 : 84 music in a more limited way:

> It is the kind of music we make with small groups, which connects with the audience, which is easy to travel, which depends very much on performance, solo or small group of singers' performances, and which really depends for its full effect on a commitment of the singers.

Elucidating what he means by "commitment of the singers," what emerges is a total commitment to all aspects of the show: participation in its conception and creation; a political commitment to its aims; theatrical commitment to its style; intellectual commitment to an overall perspective, so that a singer does not try to turn his or her song into the major number; and, above all, emotional commitment to the audience.

They have to commit themselves to that audience, to bringing out of the audience the response that they feel should be there to a song. That demands quite a bit of care and love.

The dramatist has also thought about the subtle effects that can be achieved with a song. He mentions emotional heightening, intense irony, satire, and solidarity:

> You can use it to reinforce solidarity amongst the audience, working-class consciousness through music. . . . People understand a statement in music far more than an intellectual or verbal appeal.

But McGrath, like Bond and Brecht, is also acutely aware of the dangers of music. In these playwrights, rational political consciousness is combined with a sensitivity to the emotional power of music, resulting in a critical distance to the medium. In an important statement McGrath warns against a sentimental, non-critical approach to music, even working-class collective music such as "Red Flag" sing-alongs; these "are to be distrusted because they work so easily."

> Music is dangerous because it can be so effective, even if its basic intellectual position is wrong. It worked in Nazi Germany very well. So you have to be very responsible about music, you have to let people know what you are doing. . . . You've just got to use music critically, is what I'm saying. . . . I think that one of the crucial things about the way we work in the theatre and the kind of music which I really admire, like Theodorakis, or Kurt Weill, or Eisler, is the critical content. That they all use forms which are popular, which relate to what people can listen to and appreciate. . . . But they all bring with them a kind of sensibility and a consciousness and a critical awareness—. . . not always a politically critical . . . often a musicologically critical awareness—to what they are doing, which makes the audience aware of the effect of the music. . . . One has to be very conscious. And I think very good composers and people who use music well in the theatre distrust the power of music and are very careful indeed what they do with it.

In considering McGrath's personal background and the musical and dramatic influences that entered into his playwriting career, the combination of popular and intellectual elements is distinctive. Born in 1935 into a Liverpool family of Irish Catholic origins ("That's a political background"[49]), both the Irish folk tradition and the popular musical theater played a role in determining McGrath's musical and theatrical leanings. He says about early influences that one

> main input into my expectation of theatre was panto, Christmas panto in the place I was brought up in. All my cousins . . . did acro and tap and danced in the panto line. So I associate the theatre with a lot of song of various kinds.

One of his uncles was a music-hall entertainer. The young McGrath experienced traditional music hall via radio:

> There were things on Saturday night that I listened to *every* Saturday night between eight and nine, called Variety Playhouse, when all the old music hall performers would come on and do their act. . . . It was terrific.

John Arden speaks of a similar exposure to music hall through radio in this period, but does not exhibit any great enthusiasm for it. McGrath sees a direct line from the ballad and folk tradition through music hall to modern pop. He finds that his working-class audiences do not relate as well to jazz or to American popular songs as to English tradition.

The second major early input into McGrath's stage song was of a much more intellectual nature: musical, cabaret, and revue at Oxford where he was a student from 1955 to 1958. Here he worked on productions of Aristophanes, Joyce, and satirical revues, all of which made extensive use of music. Among later influences, the playwright emphasizes especially those of Joan Littlewood, Brendan Behan (McGrath attended a dress rehearsal of *The Hostage* with Behan present) and John Arden.

> That whole Brendan and Joan Littlewood's tradition of using music in the theatre was very exciting, very exciting indeed. And I . . . ought to mention John Arden, whose *Musgrave* and particularly *Live Like Pigs* had a powerful effect on me as a young writer. I read *Live Like Pigs* before it was produced . . . and I was knocked out by it absolutely, by the language of it and by the poetry of it and by the music that was in it. So John was very, very important to me. . . . Arden, and the Joan Littlewood, Brendan Behan and later *Oh What a Lovely War* tradition meant a tremendous amount to me. It got me very, very excited and connected with things in me.

In his book *A Good Night Out*, McGrath shows an awareness of the fact that he is working within a long tradition of working-class theater. He makes special mention of many forms, emphasizing often their use of music: English Christmas pantomime; the prewar workers' theater (Blue Blouses, Living Newspaper) that also influenced Joan Littlewood; Brecht, Weill and Piscator; O'Casey and Odets. He stresses Littlewood's influence in passing on a popular, musical form of political theater to the postwar generations. He also singles out his own work in film and television, which—as in the case of Peter Barnes—has given him a sense of pace and intensity and paved the way for his later experiments in epic drama; and his love of pop and rock concerts, which has given him an awareness of the role popular music can play in theater. Throughout his book, McGrath exhibits a consciousness of the possibilities of live presentation as compared with dramatic texts. When he speaks of the "language of theatre"[50] he means all aspects of a performance:

visual and aural, physical and economic, from lighting and mime, music and songs, to the size of the theater, and the price of the tickets.

In his use of stage song, McGrath has thus combined a variety of influences and musical styles. Basically, he uses all kinds of English music. In this he is close to Arden; they both form a contrast to the large number of modern dramatists who employ American popular songs in their plays. Of the two, Arden is the more traditional musically, not employing modern popular music, whereas McGrath will use everything from folk music to pop and rock tunes. The 7:84 companies have worked together with a variety of composers, most notably Norman Smeddles and Mark Brown, and different musical bands and individual musicians.

McGrath's aims in introducing songs into his plays are determined by the overall aims of his political theater. They are an integral element in his creation of a new type of entertainment that is derived from popular forms. The tunes may be reminiscent of revue, variety entertainment, music hall, or rock concerts. 7:84 Scotland has based several shows, most notably *The Cheviot, the Stag and the Black, Black Oil* on the *ceilidh* form, a Scottish native local type of community get-together. Here the influence of the folk tradition is particularly strong. Whether the songs are intended as character introduction, caricature, action pieces, lyrical interludes, satire, commentary, or sung dialogue, the critical, creative approach of the texts is merged with the more popular nature of the tunes.

The type of the melodies in the plays is determined not only by the theme of the work, McGrath says, but also by the nature of the audience to which the production is playing:

> The cultural specificity of the English working class is very, very different from the cultural specificity of the Scottish working class. That's why we have two different companies.

McGrath points out that the Scottish company is usually a great success in Ireland, whereas the English company is often a disaster, "because of that cultural bridge not being there." 7:84 Scotland has a strong base in traditional music, while 7:84 England tends to use more rock. The element of audience participation in songs is much stronger in Scotland than it is in England: "It's a more alienated form with the English 7:84 than in Scotland." For these reasons it seems logical to distinguish between the work of 7:84 England and Scotland.

Not all of McGrath's earliest work included song. But since his period at Oxford, he has been interested in combining music with the theater. During the 1960s while he was working mostly for television and film, he experimented with connecting dramatic scenes by means of ballads with visual action links. One such work, originally written for television but withdrawn by McGrath when the producer wanted the songs cut, became *Soft or a Girl?*, presented by the Liverpool Everyman Theatre in 1971 with music by Norman Smeddles. This was the dramatist's first big musical play, containing "loads of songs," and it "was nearer to a concert with scenes than anything else."[51] From the late 1960s McGrath has written plays with songs and musicals.

In the development of a musical style by the English 7:84 Company the collaboration with John Arden and Margaretta D'Arcy proves very important. One of the first productions of the newly-formed company was Arden and D'Arcy's *The Ballygombeen Bequest* (1972). McGrath points out that 7:84's presentation style and also his own style as a playwright were already clearly developing in the direction of political plays with popular music. But *The Ballygombeen Bequest* gave new impulses: "We developed new ways of seeing music tying in with narrative. From then on the English 7:84 really grew a band." *Serjeant Musgrave Dances On*, an adaptation of Arden's *Serjeant Musgrave's Dance*, was also done in 1972. Although Arden is the older playwright and has influenced McGrath as a writer, I would say that there is a certain amount of reciprocal influence.

The next major work of 7:84 England was *Fish in the Sea*, which uses the musical form even more ambitiously. It employs pop and rock music to tell a story that combines a family plot with a factory occupation. McGrath writes about the songs:

> I was trying to write lyrics which would relate to the scene. . . . They were slightly like pop lyrics, but different—obviously in meaning, but also in style . . . just a little bit off the pop idiom, slightly more articulate, more literary than the pop idiom. Because they were to be listened to.[52]

When first presented by the Liverpool Everyman, the play had music by Norman Smeddles. The revision for the 7:84 Company in 1974–75 has a score by Mark Brown, who was to become the major composer for 7:84 England. As McGrath describes it, Brown's music is an effective combination of elements:

> What Mark did was to write . . . rock-based music, but for voices much more than for instruments. . . . The result was a very individualistic 7:84 style of music . . . where the bottom line, the rhythm and the piano players, . . . were very accomplished rock musicians, and the melodies were very near the rock or pop melodies, but were subtly not quite the same, and the harmonies and the melody lines related to a huge classical feeling that Mark had for old and early music, vocal music.

Music and text combine to involve the audience, while challenging, even alienating, them at the same time:

> The bottom line, the rhythm, is involving them, but the top line, what the words are saying and what the harmonies are doing, is challenging them. So it's quite a

complex relationship. It's very conscious, and it was worked out on every song, just what was going on and why we were doing it.[53]

Everything McGrath here says about the music to *Fish in the Sea* applies equally to *Yobbo Nowt* (1975), which represents the "high point" of the collaboration with Mark Brown. Here, the experimentation was more radical. The playwright distinguishes his drama, which integrates comedy, music, and political purpose, from traditional musical comedy with its implications of light, frivolous entertainment:

> In form it is not exactly a musical comedy—though it is definitely musical, and a comedy. With Mark Brown . . . I set out to explore several ways of relating music to speech and story-telling: the sung narrative, straightforward character- and situation-songs, plus scenes in which the characters cut from speech to song, and scenes completely set to music.[54]

The use of rock-inspired music is appropriate to the contemporary industrial setting and to the audience's entertainment expectations. Some tunes have traditional functions, such as "Marie's Ballad," which opens the drama by introducing setting, situation, mood, and characters. There are also several caricature pieces.

But singing is often used in new ways. For example, the scene at the Labour Exchange (pp. 14–17) alternates sung dialogue with realistic prose. These passages exemplify the incompatible standpoints of David and Marie: they sing at each other rather than with each other. Some of the lyrics embody a general commentary, presented by an impersonal singer:

> But now, they say society
> Is equal just and fair—
> You learn the world's reality
> As you fight to get your share.
>
> (p. 17)

At the beginning of Act Two McGrath experiments with "sing-talk": two factory girls are conversing lightly on personal topics with a chorus backing them up:

> *Chorus.* Men, men—
>   They're ever so boring men—
>   I don't know what we talk about them for—
>
> (p. 30)

Here the light form, approaching spoken discourse, exemplifies the triviality of the conversation.

In Marie's exchange with Lady Spike (pp. 43–45), sung couplets point up the inequality of their situations. Luxury and want are concisely contrasted. Marie complains:

> You've one black Jag, and one grey Rolls,
> And my lad's shoes is full of holes.
>
> . . . .
> You've bought a château down in France—
> Will *I* get t'Blackpool—not a chance.

(p. 43)

But just as the final scene is entitled "Where We Start From," so also the music at the end returns to the more traditional "Marie's Ballad" in a deliberate move to avoid an all too easy ending. McGrath in closing wants to pass the unsolved problems of the play on to the audience to think about:

> Now we've come to the end of our story,
> 　Not much happened, that is true—
> If you want an end, we're sorry,
> 　The rest is up to you.

(p. 62)

The use of music in *Yobbo Nowt* is so extensive that if one does not accept the term *musical comedy* because of its misleading implications, perhaps the term *political melodrama* would capture its unique mixture of political analysis and musical entertainment. It is at least as much a melodrama as John Arden's *The Workhouse Donkey,* with which it bears comparison.

The shows of 7:84 England have remained musical, but economic necessity has curtailed the size of the band, as McGrath explains:

> The economics of it are that in England we developed this band in *Fish in the Sea* in 1974 . . . and we kept that band very much together through . . . 1978. Then it just had to go . . . because we couldn't afford it. . . . We lost out in terms of inflation with the Arts Council.

In the production of D'Arcy and Arden's *Vandaleur's Folly* in 1978 the 7:84 England Company could afford no more than a single piano player, Terry Doherty (who had done the improvised music for the readings of *The Non-Stop Connolly Show* in London). McGrath notes:

> It became very much of a case of four actors and a piano through the Eighties in England. . . . . We have had to experiment desperately with ways of keeping the music in the shows at all.

Two or three of the most recent shows have had no music.

The songs in the shows of 7:84 Scotland have included both traditional folk tunes and more modern forms of music. Here, too, the music varies according to the type of audience the company is playing to. The dramas aimed at a Highland audience contain more folk melodies and Gaelic songs, those aimed at an audience in the industrial areas will include more rock-based music. *The Cheviot, the Stag and the Black, Black Oil* (1973) was 7 : 84 Scotland's first successful production on a Scottish theme. Here, McGrath modeled the structure on the popular variety show, using the theme of economic and cultural exploitation of the Scottish Highlands to hold the plot together:

> The plot is history. . . . They [*The Cheviot, Boom* and *Lay Off*] are different kinds of shows altogether, using a different kind of theatrical technique—variety, music, acting, singing—to relate more or less directly a series of events without the intervention of a fictional device.[55]

McGrath drew on a variant of variety entertainment with strong local traditions in the Highlands, the Scottish *ceilidh*. This is one of the few plays in which he introduces traditional songs in Gaelic. In this drama there is a stronger emphasis on folk music than in most of McGrath's other plays, although it is by no means the only kind of music used. "The music was what the people liked, and the songs, in Gaelic and English, went to the root of suppressed popular feeling."[56] In interview McGrath added: "There's a whole world of music up there, Gaelic folk music, and there's a world of Scottish popular music which is different from English popular music." It is "a much gentler, more lyrical, more Celtic . . . world of music, which has its own rhythms, its own scales actually."[57]

The drama begins with the musicians mixing in the arriving crowd and "THE FIDDLER playing Scottish and Irish fiddle tunes among the audience, in the bar, foyer, etc., as the audience are coming in."[58] McGrath uses many techniques aimed at involving the spectators, but song is perhaps the single most important factor in stimulating participation. The opening air is one with which the audience can sing along: the well-known popular tune "These Are My Mountains" by James Copeland. McGrath describes it as "mid-twentieth-century Scottish schmaltz, pure schmaltz." Emotional response is evoked by the ideas of childhood, exile and return to home. Immediately after this follow two Gaelic songs.

The role of the Gaelic songs in this play is vital. One of McGrath's themes is the destruction of traditional Gaelic culture. The dramatist thematizes this loss of language within the dramatic action when a vigorous Gaelic song provokes the following statements:

> M.C. It's no good singing in Gaelic any more—there's an awful lot of people here won't understand a word of it. . . .
> Because English is the language of the ruling class. . . . A whole culture was systematically destroyed—by economic power. (pp. 51–52)

McGrath says that in the original performances in the Highlands the audience not only understood the Gaelic songs but joined in. Elsewhere, where Gaelic is less widely understood, the lines, he says, are "meant to be a challenge to the audience." With the exception of the very last Gaelic tune, the lyrics are not translated in the Methuen edition. Part of their function is to evoke curiosity and the desire to retrieve what has been lost.

For those who do understand, the choice of texts and their placing create meaningful contrasts. For example, the first Gaelic piece, a Jacobite lament (p. 2), embodies older cultural, religious and political values. It strikes a note of sadness at the beginning. The next Gaelic melody, "Mo Dhachaidh" ("My Home") (p. 9), sings of the homely joys of the rustic cottage and of the singer's peace in the natural surroundings. It offers a strong contrast with the preceding "High Industry," which embodies the greedy mercenary attitude of the exploiters and the facile optimism with which they clothe their menace of cultural destruction. A reprise of "Mo Dhachaidh" (p. 72) brings an even sadder contrast, as the last of the native population are displaced by international progress. In one case a Gaelic song actually contradicts the words of an uncomprehending foreign landlord. Lord Crask remembers Mary MacPherson as a girl who was "always singing happily around the house" (p. 44). Mary's Gaelic text, however, is a heart-rending lament of an old grey-haired woman forced to live in exile and longing for her home on the misty islands. The piece thus exposes Lord Crask's ignorance of Gaelic culture and his indifference to the people who work for him.

McGrath, however, is also careful to include several lusty Gaelic work tunes and love songs, and not to end with a lament but with a Gaelic text of strength, pride, and militant confidence. He says in his introduction that part of his purpose in *The Cheviot, the Stag and the Black, Black Oil* is to combat the Gaelic "lament syndrome" (pp. xxvii–xxviii), and so the play ends not in resignation but with a call to fight the exploiter and with a vision of a freer future:

> Remember that you are a people and fight for your rights—
> . . . .
> Remember your hardships and keep up your struggle
> . . . .
> Everyone in the land will have a place
> And the exploiter will be driven out.
>
> (pp. 73–74)

In a kind of moral summary, it is maintained that the struggles and hardships of the past can enrich both present and future.

Other songs of the native population are sung in English to ensure audience understanding and participation. Two are vigorous action numbers: "The Battle of the Braes" (pp. 35–37) and "I Will Go" (pp. 53–55). Both recount

1   from *The Scottish Minstrel*

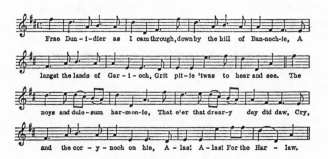

Frae Dun-i-dier as I cam through, down by the hill of Ban-noch-ie, A
langst the lands of Gar-i-och, Grit pit-ie 'twas to hear and see. The
noys and dule-sum har-mon-ie, That e'er that drear-y day did daw, Cry,
and the cor-y-noch on hie, A-las! A-las! For the Har-law.

2   from *The English & Scottish Popular Ballads — Child*

As I cam in by Dunidier,
An doun by Netherha,
There was fifty thousand Hielanmen
A-marching to Harlaw.
Wi a dree dree dradie drumtie dree.

As I cam on, an farther on,
An doun and by Balquhain,
Oh there I met Sir James the Rose,
Wi him Sir John the Gryme.

'O cam ye frae the Hielans, man,
An cam ye a' the wey?
Saw ye Macdonell an his men,
As they cam frae the Skee?'*   *Skye

'Yes, me cam frae ta Hielans, man,
An me cam a' ta wey,
An she saw Macdonnel an his men,
As they cam frae to Skee.'

**From "The Battle of Harlaw," in Michael Brander, *Scottish and Border Battles
and Ballads* (London: Seeley Service, 1975), pp. 51–52.**

historical episodes that are not portrayed scenically, thus fulfilling epic and narrative functions. The first celebrates a victory of resistance to eviction in a comic heroic tone. The tune used is an old Scottish ballad melody, "The Battle of Harlow" (Child, no. 163), but aside from the basic idea of battle there seems to be no connection intended with the original text. The rousing chorus invites audience participation. The second of these melodies begins sadly, like a lament, but modulates to a tone of defiance and ends in an attitude of pride in a fight well won and with determination to continue the battle:

> But we'll fight
> Once again
> For this country is the people's
> Yes we'll fight, once again.

(p. 55)

Both celebrate the strength, energy and vitality of the people, and illustrate how to resist.

The songs of the exploiters, in contrast, tend to employ heavy irony, satire, or even caricature to criticize negative aims, policies, and attitudes. In "It's Awfully, Frightfully, Nice" (pp. 41–43), the ruling class is caricatured through absurdly primitive rhymes (nice/grice [grouse], right/trite [trout]), exaggerated vocabulary and a ridiculously superficial interest in Highland culture. In this way, the snobbery and ignorance of the outside intruder are exposed. The tone is superficially gay and comically distorted until the last stanzas, when the reality of cultural and economic exploitation is made brutally clear.

The domination of the modern American oil industry is caricatured in the figure of Texas Jim. He is introduced singing "My Grannie's Hielan' Home" (p. 58), a nostalgic and sentimental piece. The irony emerges as it becomes clear that Texas Jim has come to Scotland for profit motives only. "Hoe Down," with American square dance music, is comic in its aggressive exaggeration and in its juxtaposition of incompatible cultural spheres. But it, too, becomes acutely menacing as Texas Jim "gets more and more frenzied" (p. 61) and finally freaks out in a passion of greed and contempt:

> I'll go home when I see fit
> All I'll leave is a heap of shit.

(p. 61)

The parody of an American square dance ends up illustrating the reality of cultural alienation in contemporary Scotland. Fun and shock effect are combined; the audience is warned not to let the entertainment lure them into an acceptance of the values represented.

Much the same is true of the reprise of "High Industry" in a "souped-up version" (p. 63) as American pop song. As in the square dance a contradiction exists between the tune, which sounds like harmless entertainment, and the text, which is a blatantly open expression of exploitation. The backup chorus, which in this type of popular ditty often consists of meaningless syllables, is here the embodiment of multinational oil power: "*Girls. (As backing group.)* Conoco, Amoco, Shell-Esso, Texaco, British Petroleum, yum, yum, yum *(Twice.)*" (p. 63). The effect of this on the listener is amusing. But the lesson for the audience is serious: keep your eyes and ears open, exploitation can creep in in a multitude of entertaining ways.

The songs in *The Cheviot, the Stag and the Black, Black Oil* thus cover a wide range of emotional and didactic effects. The emotional functions are strongest in the traditional Gaelic melodies that express both the sadness and the defiance of a dying culture. The didactic functions are most obvious in the caricatures: here the contradiction between musical form and content cannot be overlooked. And the epic and commentary functions are most in evidence in the action pieces that illustrate a point through historical example. In this play McGrath has achieved a successful combination of older traditions, modern popular musical elements, and progressive political intention.

In contrast with *The Cheviot, the Stag and the Black, Black Oil*, which toured mainly in rural and Highland areas, *Little Red Hen* (1975), another play with a Scottish theme, was aimed primarily at the industrial population of Scotland and toured in industrial areas. As a result, the rural folk and Gaelic heritage no longer play so important a role as in the earlier drama. Here, the emphasis is more on other forms of popular entertainment: working-class song, urban children's street ditties, music-hall, pop, and newly written and composed pieces, often of a humorous nature. Says McGrath,

> For a show . . . which was going to originate in the industrial belt of Scotland and play to industrial workers, we went for a more modern, rock-based style. That rock-based music . . . also incorporated kid's songs, street songs, music-hall songs. . . . *Little Red Hen* has got a whole slew of street songs which are fabulous.

McGrath thus adapts to a different audience by using a different type of localism and immediacy in his music, more urban and industrial in nature.

As in most of McGrath's dramas, music and comedy are combined with serious political purpose. In *Little Red Hen* the drama is held together not only by the historical theme—Scottish working-class history from the 1920s to the present—but also by the fictitious family story and character of the Old Hen. The play begins with a good example of McGrath's critical approach to popular tradition. As in *The Cheviot*, the opening sequence invites audience participation. It is derived from the routines of Harry Lauder, a Scottish music-hall comedian and singer best known for his extreme sentimentality.

Old Hen's protest "He made the Scottish people look damn stupid all over the world,"[59] coming as it does after the audience has joined in, is also directed toward audience members and asks them to reassess their attitude toward this kind of artificial and sentimental entertainment. Old Hen then sets both mood and scene for her historical survey of the 1920s by singing a rousing "shimmy" song (p. 3). In performance, this brings down the house and presents a good contrast to the sentimental Harry Lauder numbers.[60] The attack is directed not against popular culture per se, but only against its more mindless and cruder excesses. Act 1 ends on a rousing medley of Glasgow children's street songs (pp. 30–32), a heritage which is common to most of the audience and which again invites participation, this time without criticism.

Among the texts written by McGrath, with music by Dave Anderson, some are satirical and some are serious. The lyrics in the London scenes are reminiscent of the caricatures in *The Cheviot*. The stilted vocabulary, crude rhyme and reactionary sentiments all ridicule the singers (for example, pp. 14–17). The "Red Hen Song" serves both the purposes of characterization of the titular figure and didactic commentary:

> Planting little seeds to grow one day
> Grow up into fields of wheat
> Little Red Hen, like the story books say
> Works so one day we can eat.

(p. 10)

The tune is quiet but determined and skillfully blends folk and music-hall elements. The final number closes the play on a note of exhortation, serious political commentary and visionary prophecy:

> You working folk of Scotland,
> All you who want her free
> Remember John Maclean right well
> Or free you'll never be
>
> . . . .
> Not England alone but the tyrants at home
> Must go before we've won.
>
> . . . .
> We'll proudly build a Scotland
> Where landlords' fences fall
> Whose industry's for you and me
> Where each can work for all.

(p. 51)

Whereas the "Red Hen Song" is sung by an impersonal singer, the final tune is begun by this singer straight to the audience, and the whole company gradually joins in. It thus creates a feeling of community and solidarity,

summing up the lessons of the play and strengthening the emotional communication between singers and audience. Although they lack the longing
and poignancy of the Gaelic melodies in *The Cheviot*, the songs in *Little Red
Hen* successfully combine emotion and entertainment with political information and didactic commentary.

One later show by 7:84 Scotland that McGrath feels very strongly about is
Out of Our Heads (1976). It was directed toward a Scottish industrial
working-class audience, yet had a universal theme (alcohol) and used music
by Mark Brown, the composer associated with 7:84 England. McGrath says:

> It was I think the show that challenged the audience most, socially and politi-
> cally. . . . It was about drinking, Scottish male working-class drinking, and it was
> playing very often in clubs which were mirror images of the stage. . . . It was about
> . . . the connection between alienation, drink, and the abuse of women.

The music worked on two levels: there were naturalistic, sentimental pop
tunes, the typical fare of a workingmen's club, "a very Scottish kind of music
you would hear in any bar any night in Glasgow." Then, with a change of
lighting, there were pieces that placed the action of the play in perspective
and provided a comment on it. These had more alienating, "just slightly
distanced" music by Mark Brown. "The music was very tricky and subtle in
many ways . . . It challenged all kinds of assumptions, musically as well as
socially," McGrath says. As textual example one might cite the closing
number of the play:

> Drowning your sorrow
> Is drowning to-morrow
> And crying in your drink won't make things good
> Forget your sorrow
> And drink to to-morrow
> For things won't change unless we think they could.[61]

In 1978 a number of the musicians of the 7:84 Scotland band left to form
their own group, Wildcat, which became specialized in political band theater.
Since that time the remaining 7:84 Scotland Company has been using music
more sparingly, employing more traditional and more vocal music. "The
music has tended to become now less instrumental for the simple reason that
. . . we can no longer afford to keep a band," McGrath says. In addition to
economic factors, artistic factors play a role in McGrath's decision to use less
music. In *Swings and Roundabouts* for example, he removed the songs he had
written, explaining, "Because it was about detailed behaviour patterns, you
didn't need music." *Blood Red Roses* (1980) is a domestic epic linked by
Scottish ballads. Here, the songs most often introduce or close the scenes
with a generalized commentary.

The 7:84 Company's attempt to recreate working-class forms and transform them into a new socialist drama has been criticized by David Edgar who claims that "we don't have a popular tradition that is still feasible."[62] McGrath, while clearly recognizing the dangers of commercialized and debased popular culture, defends his critical and constructive use of these forms:

> Forms of popular culture can both retain their vitality and relationship with a mass audience, *and* work within a more complex theatrical construct.[63]

John McGrath seems the writer among contemporary dramatists whose work most resembles that of John Arden. As has been mentioned, there seems to be a reciprocal influence here, and the two have collaborated. The 7:84 Theatre Company has presented Arden and D'Arcy's *The Ballygombeen Bequest* (1972), *Serjeant Musgrave Dances On* (1972) and *Vandaleur's Folly* (1976). Aside from other similarities, both dramatists have consistently developed a strongly musical style of drama. Both have become radically political playwrights and both now prefer to work for alternative theater.

Their original impulses for turning to song in drama seem to stem from different sources. Whereas Arden—in his early plays—was looking for methods to increase the lyrical and poetic potentials of the language, McGrath was seeking to develop theatrical techniques that would attract a popular rather than an elite audience. One could say that Arden's motivation was aesthetic, McGrath's political. This difference is reflected in the fact that Arden also makes extensive use of verse in his drama; both verse and song increase the emotional and poetical intensity. Arden throughout his career has consistently employed folk melodies and ballads (or new texts to folk tunes), sometimes including street ballad or music-hall songs in his repertoire. His choice of music is largely determined by his subject matter: medieval carols in a nativity play, eighteenth-century song in a drama about Nelson, and street ballads for modern gypsies. McGrath's use of musical idioms in contrast is mainly adapted to the potential audience, only to a lesser extent to the topic. He uses any kind of popular music with which the audience will be familiar, from folk for rural areas to music hall and contemporary rock for more urban listeners. He sums up his approach in the words:

> Form is . . . a means of communication between one lot of people and another and . . . you have to be conscious of the way it works between those two groups.[64]

Song for McGrath is an important initiator of audience participation, a motive which plays little role for the early Arden.

In spite of these initial differences, their use of music in drama appears to become increasingly similar as their careers progress. Both have experimented widely with new forms. Both have developed a variety of epic and narrative functions: for example, describing journeys, reporting on off-stage action, visualizing battles. Both have become experts at political caricature through song. Both Arden and McGrath create satiric effects by writing new texts to traditional tunes. Both create alienation effects by breaking the mood of a song or scene through abrupt contrast. Arden/D'Arcy and McGrath exhibit an increasing tendency to employ commentaries, with lyrics that not only sum up the lessons of the specific play but also evaluate wider social and political issues. While retaining the more traditional functions of dramatic song to create atmosphere, establish setting and character, they have helped to expand epic and commentary functions in contemporary drama.

5. Further Vistas

Contemporary alternative theater in Britain accepts music as an integral part of drama; song is omnipresent. Having used the work of John McGrath and the 7:84 companies to exemplify the aims and techniques of song in a new political popular theater, I can do no more than summarize other developments of the 1970s and 1980s. Among the politically-oriented playwrights active in alternative theater who have turned to song in their drama, mention should be made of Steve Gooch, David Edgar, Caryl Churchill, Howard Brenton, and Barrie Keeffe. Gooch is perhaps the most consistently musical, whereas the others will employ song or not, according to the style they are aiming at and the nature of the company they are cooperating with. It is characteristic of many plays in alternative theater that they are written for, or in collaboration with, a specific company and are adapted to the resources of this company, musical and otherwise. On the whole I have concentrated on published plays.

OTHER PLAYWRIGHTS

Steve Gooch's *Will Wat? If Not, What Will?* (1972) and *Female Transport* (1973) were both created in conjunction with the Half Moon Theatre. (Gooch was born in 1945.) The former concerns Wat Tyler's uprising of 1381 and employs music by Robin Marsden. The instruments included "a 2 cwt anvil, two out-of-tune church bells, a 98 gallon hogshead drum . . . and a jaw harp."[65] The latter portrays the transportation of six women convicted of petty crimes to Australia in the nineteenth century and uses Australian folk melodies and transport songs. *The Motor Show* (1974) with music by Paul Thompson, is a musical documentary of the Ford motor company, first presented to car workers in Dagenham and later transferred to the Half Moon Theatre. *The Women Pirates Ann Bonney and Mary Read* (1978) originated in alternative theater but was finally premiered by the Royal Shakespeare Company. It portrays two female pirates of the eighteenth century and presents a broad social and historical panorama. The music is by Guy Woolfenden and many of the songs are sung by impersonal narrating singers. Most of Gooch's plays have been for community theater, and he emphasizes that this means close communication with the audience. The songs aid considerably in achieving this aim. Gooch has also written a book on community theater entitled *All Together Now* (1984).

David Edgar (born in 1948) has been closely associated with the theater company General Will. Because this group was skilled musically, he included songs in several of his early plays. *Dick Deterred* (1974) is a musical parody of Shakespeare's *Richard III*, and at the same time a political satire on Nixon and the Watergate affair. *Destiny* (1976), presented by the Royal Shakespeare Company, contains a Fascist party song and a Kipling ballad, set to music by Anthony Perrins. *Wreckers* (1977)[66] is a collaboration with 7:84 England, a company that at that time employed four musicians regularly. As a consequence it contains numerous songs, many of them narrative and commentary. The tunes by the 7:84 band are printed at the back. Edgar studied drama at Manchester University, researching the Living Newspaper and writing a dissertation on postrevolutionary Russian drama. Perhaps he has also received some musical ideas from these sources.[67]

Caryl Churchill (born in 1938), in her collaborations with the Joint Stock Company and with Monstrous Regiment, has also experimented with song in drama. Perhaps most interesting to me is *Vinegar Tom* (Monstrous Regiment, 1976) with music by Helen Glavin, in which the songs constitute the bridge between the theme of seventeenth-century witchcraft and the idea of discrimination against women in the present:

> Look in the mirror tonight.
> Would they have hanged you then?
> Ask how they're stopping you now.
> Where have the witches gone?
> Who are the witches now?[68]

Cloud Nine (Joint Stock, 1979) employs both traditional and original songs, among them the title song, "Cloud Nine," with music by Andy Roberts. *Fen* (Joint Stock, 1983) includes an excerpt from the first of Rainer Maria Rilke's famous *Duino Elegies*, "Who, if I cried, would hear me among the angelic orders?" ("Wer, wenn ich schriee, hörte mich denn aus der Engel Ordnungen?")[69] The melody, composed by Ilona Sekacz, is printed at the back of the published edition. Rilke's lyrics hint at the helplessness and essential inarticulateness of these East Anglian fen country rural women, but also their search for spiritual answers.

Howard Brenton (born in 1942), who says of himself that he is a strongly verbal playwright who does not feel the need for other non-verbal theatrical idioms (for example rock music),[70] nevertheless sometimes does include music in his drama. *Hitler Dances* (1972) has original songs with music by "Bread, Love and Dreams." The title song, "The Hitler Dances Song," is one of concentrated lyricism and political vision:

> Can you hear
> The voices calling
> Can you see
> The buildings falling
> Rising from the ruins
> The carrion cabal
> Dancing on the banks
> Of the boiling canal.[71]

It is no coincidence that Brenton, like Bond, has published his theater songs and poems separately.[72] In contrast, *Brassneck* (1973), a collaboration with David Hare, uses recordings of popular music from Bing Crosby to the Rolling Stones to open the scenes. In one case the words of a Rolling Stones' song are projected onto a screen.

Barrie Keeffe (born in 1945) makes use of contemporary rock music in his portrayals of the dispossessed, unemployed youth of today. In many cases the function is atmospheric and social, and the music is interchangeable. Keeffe says: "This may be changed—the more contemporary the music, the better."[73] In other cases songs have given the dramas their titles, for example "Gimme Shelter" by the Rolling Stones. In *Sus* (1979), one moving moment is created through the medium of a reggae song by Bob Marley, "No Woman, No Cry."[74] Here words and music incorporate all the desperation and homesickness, but also all the hope and social cohesion of the West Indians in Britain.

Among the alternative political groups that regularly employ music and song are CAST (Cartoon Archetypical Slogan Theatre), Red Ladder, and Belt and Braces, all of which have published collective plays. CAST's *Confessions of a Socialist* (1978) and Red Ladder's *Taking Our Time* (1978) are published by Pluto Press; Red Ladder's *A Woman's Work is Never Done* (or *Strike While the Iron is Hot*) (1974) and Belt and Braces' *England Expects* (1976) by Journeyman Press. Leading feminist companies such as Monstrous Regiment and the Women's Theatre Group (*My Mother Says I Never Should,* 1974) and gay theater groups (*Two Gay Sweatshop Plays*) also have published dramatic works with songs that may be consulted.[75]

PERFORMANCE ART

In the case of performance art, the situation is more difficult to document because so many of the productions are ephemeral and the texts have seldom

been printed. Relying as performance art does on improvisation and spontaneity for its major effects, the scripts may differ from day to day and seldom
have a firm literary basis. Performance art is nonverbal, oriented toward
visual effect, and it borrows from film and television, as John Ashford notes:

> It must include performance which plays upon the expectations of theatre, which is
> a collaborative compilation, without any one writer, director or designer, and the
> substance of which is the unpredictable but structured interplay of sound, object
> and action.[76]

It need hardly be said that music can play a pivotal role in performance art,
though song, due to its semiverbal nature, is less dominant. Some performance art song texts seem almost surreal.[77] Foremost performance art groups
in contemporary Britain are the People Show, Welfare State, the Pip Simmons
Theatre Company and, more recently, IOU. Music in such shows is not
employed to explain what is happening but to immerse and envelop the
audience in a multimedia environment of light and sound montage.[78] In
pursuing these goals, the groups follow some of the earlier ideas about music
and lighting in theater put forward by Adolphe Appia and Gordon Craig.

The Pip Simmons Group produced an interesting show in 1975 entitled *An
die Musik*, which was concerned with music in a Nazi concentration camp.
One scenario of the Pip Simmons Theatre Group, *Superman*, has been published. The company emphasizes the constant communal revision process
and does not consider this a working script for future performances. In their
portrayal of the comic-strip rock and roll Superman they try to capture some
of the vital energy of the rock and roll era. The script contains songs for
which they have "plagiarized and borrowed unscrupulously." The lyrics
range from sentimental pop to comic strip diction: "Splat. Zap. Zonk. Pow./
Oufff. Ouch. Aagh. Eyow."[79]

DOCUMENTARY MUSICALS

More literary than performance art, but still essentially communal and
collaborative, are the works known as documentary musicals. The activities
of Peter Cheeseman, Alan Plater and Alan Cullen are strongly influenced by
Joan Littlewood, Ewan MacColl, and the Theatre Workshop, and have in
turn inspired younger drama in the direction of musical theater. These
documentaries are oriented toward a local audience, usually in the midlands
or north of England, and record some aspect of local industrial history in a
popular musical form. Cheeseman began in the Victoria Theatre, Stoke-on-
Trent, in the early 1960s. *The Knotty* (1966) concerns the railways in North
Staffordshire. *Fight for Shelton Bar* (1974, published in 1977), portrays the
fight of the Shelton Works Action Committee to keep a steel mill open.

Cheeseman explains the principles of such dramatic documentaries in his introductory notes:

> The Stoke documentaries are . . . collations of the utterances of the people in-volved in the real events themselves, collected from written records of those events, . . . newspaper and other eyewitness accounts and by means of the tape-recorder.[80]

In this case the songs have newly-written lyrics, but these are in a robust traditional folk style. The methods are almost identical with those of Ewan MacColl in creating his radio documentaries such as *The Ballad of John Axon*, *The Big Hewer*, or *The Travelling People* in the years after the war.[81]

Alan Cullen, working in Sheffield, created a documentary musical *The Stirrings in Sheffield on Saturday Night* (1966) with a slightly different method. Here, authentic local folk song lyrics of the nineteenth century are mainly employed, but with new tunes in the folk style by Roderick Horn.[82] Yet another style of music is achieved in Alan Plater's *Close the Coalhouse Door*, produced in Newcastle in 1968 and performed for local audiences of miners. It portrays mining life in present-day England. Plater emphasizes that such local community theater relies on collective improvisation, and the printed script should not be taken as definitive. Concerning the songs he says:

> Half the songs were written specially for the show and the rest—including the title song—were from Alex Glasgow's extensive collected works. Contrary to some speculation, they are not based on traditional ballads, nor are they 'folk songs.' They are out of the composer's own head, drawing their inspiration from a long tradition of Tyneside music-hall songs. The music-hall element is very important.[83]

Music hall of course had a strong Northern tradition in England. The title song emphasizes the modern critical perspective rather than folk atmosphere:

> Close the coalhouse door, lad,
> There's blood inside.
> Blood from broken hands and feet
> Blood from hearts that know no beat
> Close the coalhouse door, lad,
> There's blood inside.[84]

Whatever musical style these local documentaries choose, their spoken dialogue is always based on historical fact and aims to present some aspect of working-class history to a local audience familiar with the setting. Their themes are most often working and living conditions of some special profession such as potters, steel workers or miners. Documentary musicals illustrate the strength and vigor of local regional theater in the contemporary period. A major element of their liveliness and local appeal is provided by the songs, whether these are traditional folk tunes, newly-written airs, or melodies based on popular heritage such as music hall.

6. Conclusion

This study has illustrated the range and depth of dramatic song in the contemporary period. The use of music in drama goes back to the ritual origins of Western theater. Although religious ritual is no longer crucial to our experience of theater, a drama that makes uninhibited use of song and other visual and aural techniques usually indicates a strong affinity to the popular tradition. The liveliness of the theater landscape in postwar Britain is documented in its musical basis.

Not all of the songs are sung by actors on stage. While this is certainly the most traditional manner of presentation, it is not the only one, even in earlier periods. One need only think of the music from beneath the stage in Shakespeare's *Antony and Cleopatra*, or the burden of Ariel's song in *The Tempest*, which is sung by various invisible actors positioned around the stage. In the modern period a new technical apparatus has increased the possibilities for variation. In addition to rock musicals using amplifying equipment and microphones, there are also the possibilities offered by tape recordings and hidden loud speakers.

Among dramatists who consistently employ song there seems to be a typical pattern of development. Often, younger playwrights begin with traditional melodies that they employ in ironic or satiric fashion. As they proceed in their careers, a need develops to write their own song lyrics and sometimes to have these set to new tunes also, rather than to traditional airs. This observation applies (with slight modifications) to Sean O'Casey, Bertolt Brecht, Edward Bond, Peter Barnes, and John Arden, to name only a few.

Insofar as they say anything about their theory of dramatic song, the playwrights indicate an awareness of both the emotional and rational powers of music, particularly of the emotional. The authors considered here employ song because it combines the possibilities of text and musicality. Their texts range from lyrical sentiment to rational commentary. But the sensuous powers of the tunes balance the words. Especially striking is the awareness of the potentiality for misuse, and manipulation through music. This has been ascertained in O'Casey, where political parties rally their forces through song, and in Theater Workshop's *Oh What a Lovely War*, where song is employed by the authorities to manipulate the emotions of a people at war. Brecht distrusts Wagner's emotionally overwhelming music, and Bond, Barnes, and McGrath point out the successful misuse of music in Fascist Germany.

The two major poles among the traditional sources introduced into modern drama are folk and popular sentimental. Classical art music is much less frequent. Seldom, however, are folk tunes or popular tunes allowed to stand on their own terms. Usually they form some contrast to the dramatic situation, and are given functions and dramatic meaning far beyond the mere atmospheric.

That is indeed one of the major conclusions of this study: that contemporary playwrights do recognize the possibilities of dramatic song as a genre of its own. Not only the potentiality of the lyric poem in a dramatic context appeals to them. It is the possibility of using these foregrounded or heightened moments of song to make points of wider dramatic significance. No matter what their political convictions or artistic styles, the playwrights generally fit their dramatic songs into the structure of the drama in subtle and satisfying ways. Lyrics are related to themes, characterization, action, or imagery of the whole. Not just the textual but also the musical potentialities of these interludes are realized to the full. Musical contrasts or ironies make points as effectively as do the lyrics. Almost never in serious contemporary drama does song have a merely decorative or entertaining function alone.

Among the song lyrics written by the dramatists themselves can be found lyrical, satirical, and rational commentary texts. Whereas the purely commentary texts work less well when printed out of context from the play, some of the best of modern theater songs combine concentrated commentary with metaphorical lyricism in a fascinating way. Brecht, Auden, Bond, and Brenton have published collections of theater songs that can also be read as compelling poetry. But a dramatic song must always be seen not only within the context of the play but also envisioned or heard within the context of musical performance in order to display its full powers.

Notes

Introduction

1. Peter Davison, *Contemporary Drama and the Popular Dramatic Tradition in England* (London: Macmillan, 1982); Katharine J. Worth, *Revolutions in Modern English Drama* (London: Bell, 1973); David Bradby, Louis James, and Bernard Sharratt, eds., *Performance and Politics in Popular Drama: Aspects of Popular Entertainment in Theatre, Film and Television 1800–1976* (Cambridge: Cambridge University Press, 1980); Ruby Cohn, "Theater in Recent English Theater," *Modern Drama* 30, no. 1 (March 1987): 1–13.

2. James Anderson Winn, *Unsuspected Eloquence: A History of the Relations between Poetry and Music* (New Haven: Yale University Press, 1981). Other useful studies are: Cecil Day Lewis, *The Lyric Impulse* (Cambridge: Harvard University Press, 1965); John Hollander, *The Untuning of the Sky* (Princeton: Princeton University Press, 1961); Calvin S. Brown, *Music and Literature* (Athens: University of Georgia Press, 1948); V. C. Clinton-Baddeley, *Words for Music* (Cambridge: Cambridge University Press, 1941); Jakob Knaus, ed., *Sprache, Dichtung, Musik* (Tübingen, W. Germany: Max Niemeyer, 1973); Johannes Mittenzwei, *Das Musikalische in der Literatur: Ein Überblick von Gottfried von Strassburg bis Brecht* (Halle, E. Germany: VEB Verlag Sprache und Literatur, 1962); Horst Petri, *Literatur und Musik* (Göttingen, W. Germany: Sachse und Pohl, 1964); Helmut Schmidt-Garre, *Von Shakespeare bis Brecht: Dichter und ihre Beziehung zur Musik* (Wilhelmshaven, W. Germany: Heinrichshofen, 1979).

3. *Comparative Literature* 22, no. 2 (Spring 1970); *Mosaic* 18, no. 4 (Fall 1985): Music and Literature Issue.

4. Mark W. Booth, *The Experience of Songs* (New Haven: Yale University Press, 1981).

5. Frederick S. Boas, ed., *Songs and Lyrics from the English Playbooks* (London: Cresset Press, 1945); Edward Bliss Reed, ed., *Songs from the British Drama* (New Haven: Yale University Press, 1925).

6. William R. Bowden, *The English Dramatic Lyric, 1603–42* (New Haven: Yale University Press, 1951); J. S. Manifold, *The Music in English Drama: From Shakespeare to Purcell* (London: Rockliff, 1956).

7. James Redmond, ed., *Themes in Drama 3: Drama, Dance and Music* (Cambridge: Cambridge University Press, 1981).

8. *Gambit: International Theatre Review* 10, no. 38 (1981): Theater and Music Issue.

9. Cf. Booth, *The Experience of Songs*, pp. 94–96.

Chapter 1. Dramatic Song: Theoretical and Historical Considerations

1. *Grove's Dictionary of Music and Musicians*, ed. H. C. Colles, 3d ed. (New York: Macmillan, 1947), s.v. "song."

2. Booth, *The Experience of Songs*, p. 7; see entire "Introduction," especially pp. 5–28.

3. W. H. Auden, Chester Kallman, and Noah Greenberg, eds., *An Elizabethan Song Book*, new ed. (London: Faber, 1968), "Introduction," pp. vii–x.

4. Clinton-Baddeley, *Words for Music*, p. 141.

5. Charles O. Hartman, "The Criticism of Song," *The Centennial Review* 19 (1975): 97 and 106.

6. Lawrence Kramer, *Music and Poetry* (Berkeley and Los Angeles: University of California Press, 1984), p. 127.

7. Ibid.

8. Ibid., p. 130.

9. Booth, *The Experience of Songs*, p. 34.

10. Ibid., p. 33.

11. Booth doubts audience capacity to perceive complexities in performance, but he fails to consider the interaction of viewing *and* rereading: see his entire chapter on "Theater Song," ibid., pp. 116–24.

12. Bernard Dort, "The Liberated Performance," *Modern Drama* 25, no. 1 (March 1982): 63, 66, and 67.

13. Jindřich Honzl, "Dynamics of the Sign in the Theater," in *Semiotics of Art: Prague School Contributions*, ed. Ladislav Matejka and Irwin R. Titunik (Cambridge: MIT Press, 1976), pp. 74–93.

14. Anne Ubersfeld, "The Pleasure of the Spectator," *Modern Drama* 25, no. 1 (March 1982): 131.

15. Marco De Marinis, "Dramaturgy of the Spectator," *The Drama Review* 31, no. 2 (Summer 1987): 107.

16. Peter Hacks, "Über Lieder zu Stücken," *Sinn und Form* 14, no. 3 (1962): 421–29.

17. Umberto Eco, "Semiotics of Theatrical Performance," *The Drama Review* 21, no. 1 (March 1977): 112.

18. See František Deák, "Structuralism in Theatre: The Prague School Contribution," *The Drama Review* 20, no. 4 (December 1976): 87; and Keir Elam, *The Semiotics of Theatre and Drama* (London: Methuen, 1980), p. 50.

19. Elam, *The Semiotics of Theatre*, pp. 50–51.

20. The German theoretician Manfred Pfister, who attempts to categorize the codes and systems of theater in exhaustive detail, surprisingly stops short where music is concerned, never even mentioning dramatic song as an expressive possibility: *Das Drama* (Munich: Fink, 1977), see graph on p. 27. English translation as *The Theory and Analysis of Drama*, trans. John Halliday (Cambridge: Cambridge University Press, 1988).

21. Elam, *The Semiotics of Theatre*, pp. 37–39.

22. Ibid., p. 44.

23. Joseph Melançon, "Theatre as Semiotic Practice," *Modern Drama* 25, no. 1 (March 1982): 18.

24. Patrice Pavis, *Languages of the Stage* (New York: Performing Arts Journal Publications, 1982), pp. 30–31.

25. Ibid., p. 17.

26. Rose Rosengard Subotnik, "The Cultural Message of Musical Semiology," *Critical Inquiry* 4, no. 4 (Summer 1978): esp. 741–46.

27. Eco, "Semiotics of Theatrical Performance," p. 117.

28. Pavis, *Languages of the Stage*, p. 20.

29. Ibid., pp. 138–39.

30. See Jonathan Culler, *The Pursuit of Signs* (Ithaca: Cornell University Press, 1981), chap. 5: "Presupposition and Intertextuality"; and Ulrich Broich and Manfred Pfister, eds., *Intertextualität* (Tübingen, W. Germany: Niemeyer, 1985).

31. Paul R. Farnsworth, *The Social Psychology of Music*, 2d ed. (Ames: Iowa State University Press, 1969), pp. 94–95.

32. W. H. Auden, "Music in Shakespeare," in *The Dyer's Hand and Other Essays* (London: Faber, 1963), pp. 505–06.

33. Kramer, *Music and Poetry*, pp. 130–31.

34. For a discussion of this theory, see Booth, *The Experience of Songs*, pp. 67–70.

35. See Karl H. Pribram, "Brain Mechanism in Music," in *Music, Mind and Brain*, ed. Manfred Clynes (New York: Plenum, 1982), pp. 21–35.

36. Farnsworth, *The Social Psychology of Music*, p. 80.

37. Alan Lomax, "Song Structure and Social Structure," in *The Sociology of Art and Literature: A Reader*, ed. Milton C. Albrecht, James H. Barnett and Mason Griff (London: Gerald Duckworth, 1970), p. 56.

38. See for example G. Révész, "Die Tonartencharakteristik," *Einführung in die Musikpsychologie* (Bern: Francke, 1946), pp. 134–45; A. L. Lloyd, *Folk Song in England* (St. Albans,

Hertfordshire: Granada/Paladin, 1975), pp. 38–42; or Farnsworth, *The Social Psychology of Music*, pp. 72–76.

39. Booth, *The Experience of Songs*, p. 21; see also the entire section on "Song as Transcendence," pp. 17–23.

40. Bernard Gredley, "Dance and Greek Drama," in *Themes in Drama 3: Drama, Dance and Music*, ed. James Redmond (Cambridge: Cambridge University Press, 1981), p. 25. For a newer theory of the origins of Greek drama and an excellent discussion of the role of music and song in Greek theater, see John Herington, *Poetry into Drama: Early Tragedy and the Greek Poetic Tradition* (Berkeley and Los Angeles: University of California Press, 1985.

41. Winn, *Unsuspected Eloquence*, pp. 5 and 9.

42. Ibid., p. 17.

43. John Herington, *Poetry into Drama*, p. 3; for a discussion of the musical fragments see p. 44.

44. F. H. Sandbach, *The Comic Theatre of Greece and Rome* (London: Chatto and Windus, 1977), pp. 120–22.

45. The following section summarizes the main points of the article by John Stevens, "Music in Some Early Medieval Plays," in *Studies in the Arts*, ed. Francis Warner (Oxford: Basil Blackwell, 1968), pp. 21–40.

46. Ibid., p. 39.

47. Ibid., pp. 39–40. Cf. also E. D. Mackerness, *A Social History of English Music* (London: Routledge and Kegan Paul, 1964), chap. 1: "Music and Society in the Middle Ages."

48. J. M. Nosworthy, "Music and its Function in the Romances of Shakespeare," *Shakespeare Survey* 11 (1958), p. 60; the emphasis is mine. See also W. H. Auden, "Music in Shakespeare," and John Hollander, "*Musica Mundana* and *Twelfth Night*," in *Literary Criticism: Idea and Act*, ed. W. K. Wimsatt (Berkeley and Los Angeles: University of California Press, 1974), pp. 265–83.

49. William Shakespeare, *The Merchant of Venice*, in The Arden Shakespeare, ed. John Russell Brown, 7th rev. ed. (London: Methuen, 1955), pp. 128–29.

50. John H. Long, *Shakespeare's Use of Music: A Study of the Music and its Performance in the Original Production of Seven Comedies* (1955; reprint, Gainesville: University of Florida Press, 1961), p. 187.

51. Richmond Noble, *Shakespeare's Use of Song* (1923; reprint, Oxford: Clarendon, 1966), p. 12.

52. Henry Raynor, *Music in England* (London: Robert Hale, 1980), p. 69.

53. Nosworthy, "Music and its Function in the Romances of Shakespeare," pp. 63–64.

54. Noble, *Shakespeare's Use of Song*; Long, *Shakespeare's Use of Music: A Study of the Music and its Performance in the Original Production of Seven Comedies*; J. Long, *Shakespeare's Use of Music: The Final Comedies* (Gainesville: University of Florida Press, 1961); Peter J. Seng, *The Vocal Songs in the Plays of Shakespeare: A Critical History* (Cambridge: Harvard University Press, 1967).

55. Long, *Shakespeare's Use of Music in Seven Comedies*, pp. 183–85.

56. Mary Chan, *Music in the Theatre of Ben Jonson* (Oxford: Clarendon Press, 1980), p. 3.

57. William Bowden, *The English Dramatic Lyric, 1603–42* (New Haven: Yale University Press, 1951), p. 16.

58. Cf. A. E. H. Swaen, "The Airs and tunes of John Gay's *Beggar's Opera*," *Anglia* 43 (1919): 152–90; William Eben Schultz, *Gay's Beggar's Opera* (1923; reprint New York: Russell and Russell, 1967).

59. David Mayer, "The Music of Melodrama," in *Performance and Politics in Popular Drama*, ed. Bradby, James, and Sharratt (Cambridge: Cambridge University Press, 1980), p. 51.

60. Cf. David F. Cheshire, *Music Hall in Britain* (Newton Abbot, Devon: David and Charles, 1974); Peter Davison, *Songs of the British Music Hall* (New York: Oak, 1971); Raymond Mander and Joe Mitchenson, *British Music Hall: A Story in Pictures* (London: Studio Vista, 1965); Laurence Senelick, "Politics as Entertainment: Victorian Music Hall Songs," *Victorian Studies* 19 (December 1975): 149–180.

61. Mayer, "The Music of Melodrama," p. 49.

62. John Arden, "Ecce Hobo Sapiens: O'Casey's Theatre," in *Sean O'Casey: A Collection of Critical Essays*, ed. Thomas Kilroy (Englewood Cliffs, N.J.: Prentice Hall, 1975), p. 76.

63. Sean O'Casey, "Art is the Song of Life," in *Blasts and Benedictions* (London: Macmillan, 1967), pp. 80–81.

64. Sean O'Casey, Letter to Charles B. Cochran (2 August 1933) in *The Letters of Sean O'Casey 1910–41*, vol. 1, ed. David Krause (London: Cassell, 1975), p. 461.

65. For a detailed discussion of the way in which the song exploits multiple ironies see Ronald Gene Rollins, *Sean O'Casey's Drama: Verisimilitude and Vision* (Tuscaloosa: University of Alabama Press, 1979), pp. 37–38. Cf. also Robert Hogan, "The Haunted Inkbottle," *James Joyce Quarterly* 8, no. 1 (Fall 1970): 76–95; Ilse Karlson, *Die Funktion der Lieder in den Dublin Plays von Sean O'Casey* (Diss. Kiel, W. Germany, 1978); Naomi Pasachoff, "O'Casey's Not Quite Festive Comedies," *Eire-Ireland* 12, no. 3 (1977): 41–61; and Burchard Winkler, *Wirkstrategische Verwendung populärliterarischer Elemente in Sean O'Caseys dramatischem Werk* (Göppingen, W. Germany: Alfred Kümmerle, 1977).

66. V. C. Clinton-Baddeley, "W. B. Yeats and the Art of Song," in *Words for Music*, p. 154; Cf. also Gerhard Hoffman, "Die Funktion der Lieder in Yeats' Dramen," *Anglia* 89 (1971): 87–116; and Colin Meir, *The Ballads and Songs of W. B. Yeats* (London: Macmillan, 1974). Mention should also be made of an excellent book on James Joyce: Zack Bowen, *Musical Allusions in the Works of James Joyce: Early Poetry Through Ulysses* (Albany: State University of New York Press, 1975).

67. Ulrich Weisstein, "Cocteau, Stravinsky, Brecht, and the Birth of Epic Opera," *Modern Drama* 5 (Fall 1962): 142–53.

68. Cf. Sammy McLean, *The Bänkelsang and the Work of Bertolt Brecht* (The Hague: Mouton, 1972); Bernward Thole, *Die Gesänge in den Stücken Bertolt Brechts* (Göppingen, W. Germany: Alfred Kümmerle, 1973); Gottfried Wagner, *Weill und Brecht: Das musikalische Zeittheater* (Munich: Kindler, 1977); John Willett, *The Theatre of Bertolt Brecht* (1959; rev. ed., London: Eyre Methuen, 1977).

69. Bertolt Brecht, "Anmerkungen zur Oper 'Aufstieg und Fall der Stadt Mahagonny,'" in *Gesammelte Werke 17: Schriften zum Theater 3* (Frankfurt am Main: Suhrkamp, Werkausgabe edition Suhrkamp, 1967): 1009–11; English translation as "The Modern Theatre is Epic Theatre," in *Brecht on Theatre*, ed. and trans. John Willett (New York: Hill and Wang, 1964), pp. 33–42.

70. Cf. Martin Esslin, "Brecht and the English Theater," *Tulane Drama Review* 11, no. 2 (Winter 1966): 63–70; Wolf-Dietrich Weise, *Die 'Neuen englischen Dramatiker' in ihrem Verhältnis zu Brecht* (Bad Homburg, W. Germany: Gehlen, 1969); and Margrit Hahnloser-Ingold, *Das englische Theater und Bert Brecht* (Bern: Francke, 1970).

71. T. S. Eliot, *Sweeney Agonistes*, in *The Complete Poems and Plays* (London: Faber, 1969), pp. 115–26.

72. Cf. Auden's brief theoretical statement on theater in *The English Auden: Poems, Essays, and Dramatic Writings, 1927–1939*, ed. Edward Mendelson (London: Faber, 1977), p. 273. The lyrics to many of Auden's dramatic songs are printed on pp. 273–89.

73. Katharine Worth, *Revolutions in Modern English Drama*, pp. 107–8.

74. Julian Symons, *The Thirties: A Dream Revolved* (1960; reprint Westport, Conn.: Greenwood Press, 1973), p. 83.

75. There is a recording of this song cycle: Benjamin Britten, *Our Hunting Fathers*, op. 8, A Symphonic Cycle for Voice and Orchestra, text by W. H. Auden (from a B.B.C. Third Programme broadcast on 11 June 1961), (BBC, 1981).

76. W. H. Auden and Christopher Isherwood, *The Ascent of F6 and On the Frontier* (London: Faber, 1958), p. 92; a revised version of the song text is printed in *The English Auden*, p. 163; text and music are published as Benjamin Britten and W. H. Auden, *Four Cabaret Songs* (London: Faber Music, 1980), pp. 7–11.

77. Donald Mitchell, *Britten and Auden in the Thirties: The Year 1936* (London: Faber, 1981), p. 122.

78. Cf. Ulrich Weisstein, "Reflections on a Golden Style: W. H. Auden's Theory of Opera," *Comparative Literature* 22, no. 2 (Spring 1970): 108–24.

79. Cf. Howard Goorney, *The Theatre Workshop Story* (London: Eyre Methuen, 1981).

80. Sandy Craig, ed., *Dreams and Deconstructions: Alternative Theatre in Britain* (Ambergate, Derbyshire: Amber Lane Press, 1980), p. 32.

81. Arthur Arent, "The Techniques of the Living Newspaper," *Theatre Quarterly* 1, no. 4

(October–December 1971): 57–59; and John O'Connor and Lorraine Brown, eds., *The Federal Theatre Project* (London: Eyre Methuen, 1980).

82. Ewen MacColl, "Grass Roots of Theatre Workshop," *Theatre Quarterly* 3, no. 9 (January–March 1973): 69.

83. An unpublished manuscript translation was available to me: Brendan Behan, *The Hostage*, translated from the original Irish text and annotated by Richard Wall. See also Richard Wall, "*An Giall* and *The Hostage* Compared," *Modern Drama* 18 (1975): 165–72. The two plays have now been printed in a single volume: Brendan Behan, *An Giall/The Hostage*, trans. and ed. Richard Wall (Washington, D.C.: The Catholic University of America Press, 1987).

84. MacColl as quoted in Goorney, *The Theatre Workshop Story*, p. 128.

85. Theatre Workshop, Charles Chilton and the members of the original cast, *Oh What a Lovely War* (1965; reprint, London: Methuen, 1967), pp. 20–22. All further references to this play will be made parenthetically in the text. I have also consulted the original cast recording, *Oh, What a Lovely War* (Decca PA27/SPA27, 1969).

86. The emphasis is mine.

87. *Oh! It's a Lovely War: Songs, Ballads and Parodies of the Great War* (London: EMI Music Publishing, 1978), p. 5.

Chapter 2. Folk Tradition and Theatrical Experimentation: The Drama of John Arden and Margaretta D'Arcy

1. Katharine J. Worth, *Revolutions in Modern English Drama* (London: Bell, 1973), p. 126.

2. Michael Cohen, "The Politics of the Earlier Arden," *Modern Drama* 28, no. 2 (June 1985): 198–210.

3. "John Arden," interview, in *The Playwrights Speak*, ed. Walter Wager (London: Longmans, Green, 1967), p. 211.

4. "John Arden," interview, in *The Poet Speaks: Interviews with Contemporary Poets*, ed. Peter Orr (London: Routledge and Kegan Paul, 1966), p. 1.

5. John Arden, "Telling a True Tale," in *New Theatre Voices of the Fifties and Sixties*, ed. Charles Marowitz, Tom Milne, and Owen Hale (1965; reissued London: Eyre Methuen, 1981), p. 127. The emphasis is mine.

6. This and all other statements by John Arden and Margaretta D'Arcy not otherwise identified are from an unpublished interview with the author on 9 May 1984.

7. Arden, "Telling a True Tale," p. 127.

8. John Arden, "The Reps and New Plays," *New Theatre Magazine* 1, no. 2 (January 1960): 25, as quoted in John Russell Brown, *Theatre Language: A Study of Arden, Osborne, Pinter and Wesker* (London: Allen Lane, 1972), p. 193.

9. Arden, "Telling a True Tale," p. 125.

10. Ibid., p. 128.

11. Ibid., p. 126. n. 1.

12. Ibid., p. 125.

13. Ibid., p. 128.

14. Ibid., p. 129.

15. John Arden, "Verse in the Theatre," *New Theatre Magazine* 2, no. 3 (1961), reprinted in *English Dramatic Theories IV: 20th Century*, ed. Paul Goetsch (Tübingen, W. Germany: Niemeyer, 1972), pp. 116–17.

16. Ibid., p. 117.

17. John Arden, "Preface and Production Notes," *The Business of Good Government* (London: Eyre Methuen, 1963), p. 13.

18. Arden, "Verse in the Theatre," p. 115.

19. John Arden, "Playwrights and Play-Writers," in *To Present the Pretence* (London: Eyre Methuen, 1977), pp. 194–95.

20. On Arden and the melodrama tradition see also Worth, *Revolutions in Modern English Drama*, pp. 126–35.

21. "Arden of Chichester: John Arden talks to Frank Cox about 'The Workhouse Donkey' at Chichester this month," *Plays and Players* (August 1963): 18.

22. Arden, *To Present the Pretence*, p. 103.

23. Arden, "Telling a True Tale," p. 127; note, however, that in " Verse in the Theatre," p. 113, he speaks of verse rather than song in this context.

24. Arden, "Telling a True Tale," p. 126.

25. "John Arden," interview, in *Theatre at Work: Playwrights and Productions in the Modern British Theatre*, ed. Charles Marowitz and Simon Trussler (London: Methuen, 1967), p. 42. The emphasis is mine.

26. "John Arden," in Wager, *The Playwrights Speak*, p. 206.

27. John Arden and Margaretta D'Arcy kindly made me a copy of the taped performance of this adaptation.

28. Andrew Kennedy, *Six Dramatists in Search of a Language* (Cambridge: Cambridge University Press, 1975), p. 213.

29. Letter to the author of 24 August 1984.

30. Kennedy, *Six Dramatists*, p. 215.

31. Ibid., p. 215 n. 7.

32. BBC Radio 4, produced by Alfred Bradley. A recording of this production is in the National Sound Archive, London.

33. Authorized version, verses 1–4. A popular nineteenth-century parlor song also used a watered-down version of these words.

34. John Arden, *The Waters of Babylon*, in Arden, *Three Plays* (Harmondsworth: Penguin, 1964), pp. 21–22. All further quotations are from this edition. For a detailed discussion of this one song see Frances Gray, *John Arden* (London: Macmillan, 1982), pp. 33–36.

35. John Arden, *Live Like Pigs* in Arden, *Three Plays*, p. 104. All further quotations are from this edition.

36. Albert Hunt, *Arden: A Study of His Plays* (London: Eyre Methuen, 1974), pp. 47–51. Cf. also Arden's "Introductory Note," *Three Plays*, p. 101.

37. Albert Hunt, "Arden's Stagecraft," in *Modern British Dramatists: A Collection of Critical Essays*, ed. John Russell Brown (Englewood Cliffs, N.J.: Prentice Hall, 1968), p. 102.

38. Arden, "Introductory Note," p. 101.

39. Kennedy, *Six Dramatists*, p. 219.

40. Ibid., p. 220.

41. Arden, "Telling a True Tale," p. 127.

42. John Arden, *Serjeant Musgrave's Dance* (London: Methuen 1960), p. 52. All further references are to this edition. One of Karno's favorite slapstick routines was the drill of inept raw military recruits.

43. In an American production, for example, which transferred the action to an American setting, the tunes, with the exception of "Michael Finnegan" and "Blow Away the Morning Dew" were replaced by "historical or original melodies which served to define the American setting." R. Skloot: "Spreading the Word: The Meaning of Musgrave's Logic," *Educational Theatre Journal* 27, no. 2 (1975): 219.

44. Quoted from Timothy John, ed., *The Great Song Book* (Garden City, N.Y.: Doubleday, 1978), p. 18.

45. Hunt, *Arden: A Study of His Plays*, p. 59.

46. "John Arden," in Marowitz and Trussler, *Theatre at Work*, p. 45.

47. Peter Brook, *The Empty Space* (Harmondsworth: Penguin, 1972), p. 79.

48. Frances Gray compares two very different performances of this song and dance sequence, one frenzied and one subdued: *John Arden* (London: Macmillan, 1982), pp. 116–17.

49. The Irish version, with more dotted notes.

50. John Arden, *Soldier, Soldier*, in *Soldier, Soldier and Other Plays* (London: Methuen, 1967), p. 77. All further references are to this edition.

51. This song was probably written during the angry 1840s and has been associated with the 1844 Durham strike: A. L. Lloyd, *Folk Song in England* (Frogmore, St. Albans, Hertfordshire: Paladin, 1975), pp. 323–25.

52. It is an Arden *with* D'Arcy play, which indicates a slightly different form of collaboration from the Arden *and* D'Arcy joint-authorship dramas. The playwrights wish these distinctions to be noted.

53. Hunt, *Arden: A Study of His Plays*, p. 63.

54. John Arden, *The Happy Haven* in *Three Plays*, pp. 203 and 205–6. All further references are to this edition.

55. *The Oxford Dictionary of Nursery Rhymes*, ed. Iona and Peter Opie, 2d corrected impression (Oxford: Clarendon Press, 1952), no. 75.

56. John Arden, "Author's Preface," *The Workhouse Donkey* (London: Methuen, 1964), p. 7. All further references to the play are to this edition.

57. "Arden of Chichester," p. 18.

58. Ibid.

59. Arden, "Author's Preface," *The Workhouse Donkey*, p. 9.

60. John Arden, "Correspondence to the Editors," *Encore* 20 (May–June 1959): p. 42.

61. Hunt, *Arden: A Study of His Plays*, p. 88.

62. "Arden of Chichester," p. 18.

63. The score for John Addison's music is available on request from London Management. The page numbers I quote refer to the vocal score.

64. Francis James Child, ed., *The English and Scottish Popular Ballads*, 5 vols. 1882–1898 (New York: The Folklore Press/Pageant Book Co., 1956), ballad no. 56, variant A.

65. J. R. Brown, *Theatre Language*, pp. 213–16. About half of his examples are from sung, half from spoken passages.

66. "John Arden," in Marowitz and Trussler, *Theatre at Work*, p. 53.

67. John Arden, "General Notes," in *Armstrong's Last Goodnight* (London: Methuen, 1965), p. 8. All further references to the play will be to this edition.

68. See note to the introduction to ballad no. 169 in F. J. Child, *The English and Scottish Popular Ballads*, p. 363; and James Reed, *The Border Ballads* (London: Athlone Press, 1973), pp. 42–43.

69. Evelyn Kendrick Wells, *The Ballad Tree* (London: Methuen, 1950), p. 58.

70. Ibid., p. 62.

71. Child, *English and Scottish Popular Ballads*, no. 169, variant C, stanza 17. All further quotations from the ballad are from this source.

72. Wells, *The Ballad Tree*, pp. 61–62.

73. Child, introduction to ballad no. 169, *English and Scottish Popular Ballads*, p. 364.

74. Ibid., p. 366.

75. Ronald Bryden, "Ballad Country," *New Statesman* (15 May 1964): p. 783.

76. Child, *English and Scottish Popular Ballads*, no. 193, variant B, stanza 7. All further quotations from the ballad are from this source.

77. Michael Brander, *Scottish and Border Battles and Ballads* (London: Seeley Service, 1975), p. 73, note.

78. John Arden, "Preface and Production Notes," in John Arden and Margaretta D'Arcy, *The Business of Good Government* (London: Eyre Methuen, 1963), [p. 7]. All further quotations are from this edition.

79. Cecil Sharp, *English Folk Song*, chap. 8, p. 124, as quoted in Douglas Brice, *The Folk Carol of England* (London: Herbert Jenkins, 1967), p. 3.

80. See Erik Routley, *The English Carol* (London: Herbert Jenkins, 1958), chap. 6, "The Wrath of the Puritans."

81. Brice, *The Folk Carol of England*, p. 4.

82. Routley, *The English Carol*, p. 28.

83. Lloyd, *Folk Song in England*, p. 111.

84. In certain versions of this carol the burden is a separate stanza.

85. Routley, *The English Carol*, pp. 60–61.

86. For detailed interpretations of this carol see Routley, *The English Carol*, pp. 50–52; and Brice, *The Folk Carol of England*, pp. 42–47.

87. Cf. Lloyd, *Folk Song in England*, pp. 112–13; and Brice, *The Folk Carol of England*, p. 43.

88. Routley, *The English Carol*, p. 52.

89. See note to "Down in Yon Forest" in *The Oxford Book of Carols*, ed. Percy Dearmer, Ralph Vaughan Williams, and Martin Shaw (1928; reprint, London: Oxford University Press, 1950), p. 127.

90. Routley, *The English Carol*, p. 64. For detailed interpretations of the entire carol see Routley, pp. 61–64 and Brice, *The Folk Carol of England*, pp. 70–77.

91. Arden, "Preface and Production Notes," *The Business of Good Government*, [p. 13].

92. John Arden and Margaretta D'Arcy, "Authors' Note," *The Royal Pardon* (London: Methuen, 1967), p. 7. All further quotations are from this edition.

93. Ibid.

94. Ibid.

95. "John Arden," in Marowitz and Trussler, *Theatre at Work*, p. 54.

96. For an account of the difficulties Arden and D'Arcy encountered in trying to realize their conception at the Round House see Hunt, *Arden: A Study of His Plays*, pp. 138–43.

97. John Arden and Margaretta D'Arcy, "An Asymmetrical Authors' Preface," *The Hero Rises Up* (London: Methuen, 1969), p. 8. All further references will be to this edition.

98. Ibid.

99. Hunt, *Arden: A Study of His Plays*, p. 140.

100. Ibid., p. 132.

101. Note to "All Things are Quite Silent," *The Penguin Book of English Folk Songs*, ed. Ralph Vaughan Williams and A. L. Lloyd (1959; reprint, Harmondsworth: Penguin, 1976), p. 109.

102. Lloyd, *Folk Song in England*, p. 250.

103. *The Penguin Book of English Folk Songs*, p. 13.

104. Claude M. Simpson, *The British Broadside Ballad and its Music* (New Brunswick, N.J.: Rutgers University Press, 1966), p. 299.

105. Ibid., p. 300.

106. *The Oxford Song Book*, ed. Percy C. Buck (London: Oxford University Press, 1916), p. 157.

107. Cohen, "The Politics of the Earlier Arden," p. 208.

108. John Arden, "Playwrights on Picket," (written in collaboration with Margaretta D'Arcy), in *To Present the Pretence*, p. 159.

109. Ibid., p. 169.

110. Brecht in a late essay says: "Das Verhalten des Musikers zu seinem Text . . . zeigt den Grad seiner politischen und damit menschlichen Reife an," "Über gestische Musik," *Gesammelte Werke 15: Schriften zum Theater 1* (Frankfurt am Main: Suhrkamp, 1967), p. 484; English translation by John Willett in *Brecht on Theatre*, p. 105: "The musician's attitude to his text . . . shows the extent of his political, and so of his human maturity." Carl Davis has made a career composing stage music for the National Theatre and the Royal Shakespeare Company, and music for television features and films.

111. John Lahr, *"The Island of the Mighty," Plays and Players* (February 1973): 32.

112. Cf. "A Socialist Hero on the Stage," *To Present the Pretence*, p. 103.

113. Margaretta D'Arcy, "Author's Preface (2)," *The Island of the Mighty* (London: Eyre Methuen, 1974), pp. 20–21. All further references to the play will be to this edition.

114. "The Island of the Ardens: Pam Gems talks to John Arden," *Plays and Players* (January 1973): 18.

115. Arden and D'Arcy, "A Socialist Hero on the Stage," *To Present the Pretence*, p. 103. The emphasis is mine.

116. Ibid., p. 104.

117. There is a good photograph of these masks in Lahr, *"The Island of the Mighty,"* p. 31.

118. *The Oxford Dictionary of Nursery Rhymes*, no. 508, p. 408.

119. Arden, "The Matter of Britain," *To Present the Pretence*, p. 157.

120. Catherine Itzin, *Stages in the Revolution: Political Theatre in Britain Since 1968* (London: Eyre Methuen, 1980), p. 31.

121. See Elizabeth Hale Winkler, "Reflections of Derry's Bloody Sunday in Literature," in *Studies in Anglo-Irish Literature*, ed. Heinz Kosok (Bonn: Bouvier, 1982), pp. 411–421.

122. Because I am quoting from an unpublished manuscript of *The Ballygombeen Bequest*, I will cite only the scene numbers. The quotation here is from the initial "Production Notes."

123. See introductory note to "Lilliburlero," in Simpson, *The British Broadside Ballad*, p. 449ff.

124. This song is also sung in Brendan Behan's *The Quare Fellow* (London: Methuen, reprint 1960), p. 3.

125. Margaretta D'Arcy and John Arden, *The Little Gray Home in the West* (London: Pluto, 1982), pp. 31–33 and 36–38. All further references to the play are from this edition. For an account of the court case see Itzin, *Stages in the Revolution*, pp. 35–36.

126. John Arden, "Author's Preface," *The Workhouse Donkey*, p. 8.

127. Margaretta D'Arcy and John Arden, *The Non-Stop Connolly Show*, part 6 (London: Pluto, 1978), p. 7. Hereafter, the references will be to part and page number only. The publication data of the separate parts are as follows: parts 1 and 2 (London: Pluto, 1977); part 3 (London: Pluto, 1978); part 4 (London: Pluto, 1978; part 5 (London: Pluto: 1978); part 6 (London: Pluto, 1978). See also Arden and D'Arcy, "A Socialist Hero on the Stage," *To Present the Pretence*, pp. 92–138.

128. D'Arcy and Arden, "Authors' Preface" to all parts of *The Non-Stop Connolly Show*, p. vii.

129. Paddy Marsh, "Easter at Liberty Hall: The Ardens' *Non-Stop Connolly Show*," *Theatre Quarterly* 5, no. 20 (December 1975–February 1976), p. 140.

130. Edith Fowke and Joe Glazer, *Songs of Work and Protest* (New York: Dover, 1973), p. 131.

131. Margaretta D'Arcy and John Arden, "Preface," *Vandaleur's Folly* (London: Eyre Methuen, 1981), p. xii. All further references to the play will be from this edition.

132. Albert Hunt, "Passions and Issues," *New Society* (18 January 1979): 151.

Chapter 3. "Men Run Camps of Mass Murder and Sing Carols": The "Rational Theatre" of Edward Bond

1. See the songs "From an Unfinished Ballet," in Edward Bond, *Theatre Poems and Songs* (London: Eyre Methuen, 1978), pp. 123–132.

2. David L. Hirst, *Edward Bond* (Houndmills, Basingstoke, Hampshire: Macmillan, 1985), p. 16.

3. Edward Bond, "Types of Drama," *The Activists Papers* in *The Worlds with The Activists Papers* (London: Eyre Methuen, 1980), p. 131.

4. These and all other statements by Edward Bond not otherwise identified are from an unpublished interview with the author on 18 May 1984.

5. Edward Bond, "Author's Note," *Theatre Poems and Songs*, no page.

6. Bond, "On Music," *Theatre Poems and Songs*, p. 78.

7. Ibid.

8. In *The Bundle* Tiger's tongue is cut out, but this cannot check the course of the revolution. The incident of breaking a musician's hands is also referred to by John McGrath in *The Game's a Bogey* (1974), where a song by this musician, Victor Jara, is sung on stage and commented on. John McGrath, *The Game's a Bogey* (Edinburgh: EUSPB, 1975), pp. 43–44.

9. Bond, *Theatre Poems and Songs*, p. 78.

10. Ibid., p. 79.

11. Ibid., p. 83.

12. Bond, *Orpheus: A Story in Six Scenes* and "Canzoni to Orpheus," in *Orpheus: Materialien* (Stuttgart, W. Germany: Würtembergisches Staatstheater, 1979); Hans Werner Henze and Edward Bond, *Orpheus Behind the Wire* (Mainz, W. Germany: B. Schott's Söhne, 1984); Bond, "Orpheus and the Wire," in *Poems 1978–1985* (London: Methuen, 1987), pp. 114–20.

13. Hans Werner Henze, "Über die Entstehung der Musik zu Edward Bonds Orpheus. Aus einem Brief an Joseph Rufer," *Orpheus: Materialien* (Stuttgart, W. Germany: Würtembergisches Staatstheater, 1979), p. 39; translation by Peter Labanyi in Henze, *Music and Politics* (Ithaca: Cornell University Press, 1982), p. 250.

14. Bond, *Orpheus: A Story in Six Scenes*, in *Orpheus: Materialien*, p. 30.

15. Bond, "Orpheus and the Wire," in *Poems 1978–1985*, pp. 114–15.

16. Ibid., pp. 119–20.

17. Bond, *Summer and Fables*, rev. ed. (London: Methuen, 1982), p. 22.

18. Bond, *The Worlds*, p. 78.

19. Bond, "Hans Werner Henze," B.B.C. Radio 3 (1 July 1976), B.B.C. Script Library transcript, p. 3.

20. Ibid., p. 5.

21. Bond, *The Activists Papers*, p. 111.

22. Bond, "Hans Werner Henze," pp. 3–4.

23. Bond in Malcolm Hay and Philip Roberts, *Edward Bond: A Companion to the Plays* (London: TQ [Theatre Quarterly] Publications, 1978), p. 7.

24. Unpublished statement by Bond, quoted in Tony Coult, *The Plays of Edward Bond* (London: Eyre Methuen, 1977), p. 73.

25. Ibid., p. 11.

26. Bond in conversation with Philip Roberts (31 March 1977), LSA Recorded Interview No. RI 2010, The British Council, 1978, [p. 5].

27. Bond, letter of 18 May 1983 to the author.

28. Frances Rademacher points out that in these two early plays there is an intimate connection between the comic bantering and violence: "Violence and the Comic in the Plays of Edward Bond," *Modern Drama* 23, no. 3 (September 1980): 258–68.

29. Bond in conversation with Philip Roberts, British Council interview, [p. 23].

30. Edward Bond, *The Pope's Wedding*, in *Plays: One* (London: Eyre Methuen, 1977), p. 241. All further quotations from the play will refer to this edition.

31. "Sing, my tongue, the glorious battle," in *Hymns Ancient and Modern*, standard edition (London: Clowes, 1916), no. 97. Compare also nos. 96 and 105.

32. "A Discussion with Edward Bond," *Gambit* 5, no. 17 (October 1970), p. 19.

33. *The Oxford Dictionary of Nursery Rhymes*, no. 22.

34. Ibid., pp. 61–62 n.

35. Bond, *Saved*, in *Plays: One*, p. 73. All further quotations from the play will refer to this edition.

36. Edward Bond, *Narrow Road to the Deep North*, revised ed. in *Plays: Two* (London: Eyre Methuen, 1978), p. 199. All further quotations from the play will refer to this edition).

37. 1975, available at the National Sound Archive, London.

38. *The Oxford Song Book*, pp. 24–25.

39. See note to hymn no. 27 in Maurice Frost, ed., *Historical Companion to Hymns Ancient and Modern* (London: Clowes, 1962).

40. *Hymns Ancient and Modern*, no. 27. Cf. also the commentary in John Julian, ed., *A Dictionary of Hymnology*, rev. ed. 2 vols. (1907; reprint, New York: Dover, 1956).

41. Bond, "The Writer's Theatre," in Hay and Roberts, *Edward Bond: A Companion to the Plays*, p. 45.

42. My ellipses are marked by square brackets. The rest are indications of Georgina's distraction.

43. *Hymns Ancient and Modern*, no. 573.

44. The emphasis is mine.

45. "A Discussion with Edward Bond," *Gambit*, p. 7.

46. Bond, *Narrow Road to the Deep North* (London: Methuen, 1968), p. 56.

47. Bond, *Lear*, revised ed. in *Plays: Two*, p. 22.

48. Gregory Dark, "Production Casebook No. 5: Edward Bond's *Lear* at the Royal Court," *Theatre Quarterly* 2, no. 5 (January–March 1972): p. 27.

49. Hirst, *Edward Bond*, p. 34.

50. Bond, *Passion*, revised ed. in *Plays: Two*, p. 238. All further quotations from the play will refer to this edition.

51. *Fireside Book of Folk Songs*, ed. Margaret Bradford Boni (New York: Simon and Schuster, 1947), pp. 64–65.

52. *The Parlour Song Book*, ed. Michael Turner (London: Michael Joseph, 1972), pp. 101–4.

53. Frost, *Historical Companion to Hymns Ancient and Modern*, no. 577.

54. Bond, *The Sea*, revised ed. in *Plays: Two*, p. 105. All further quotations from the play will refer to this edition.

55. Hay and Roberts, *Edward Bond: A Companion to the Plays*, p. 56.

56. *The Parlour Song Book*, pp. 140–43.

57. Turner, note to "Home Sweet Home," in *The Parlour Song Book*, pp. 143–44.

58. Ibid., p. 144. For an example of even more negative criticism cf. J. S. Bratton, *The Victorian Popular Ballad* (London: Macmillan, 1975), p. 90: "It illustrates the lack of any but the most primitive emotional connection between the words and images which is common in these songs."

59. Coult, *The Plays of Edward Bond*, p. 70.

60. Bond, "The Author's Note for Programmes," *The Sea* (London: Eyre Methuen, 1975), p. 67.

61. Coult, *The Plays of Edward Bond*, p. 69.

62. Ibid., p. 70.

63. Malcolm Hay and Philip Roberts, *Bond, A Study of His Plays* (London: Eyre Methuen, 1980), p. 221.

64. Ibid., p. 216.

65. Edward Bond, *Grandma Faust*, in *A-A-America! and Stone*, rev. ed. (London: Eyre Methuen, 1981), pp. 11–12. All quotations from the play will refer to this edition, unless otherwise specified.

66. Edward Bond, *A-A-America and Stone* (London: Eyre Methuen, A Methuen New Theatrescript, 1976), p. 20.

67. Edward Bond, *The Swing*, in *A-A-America and Stone*, rev. ed. (London: Eyre Methuen, 1981), pp. 67–68. All further quotations from the play will refer to this edition.

68. "Letter to Angela Praesent," in Hay and Roberts, *Edward Bond: A Companion to the Plays*, pp. 71–72.

69. Bond, "Author's Note," *The Swing*, [p. 34].

70. "Letter to Angela Praesent," in Hay and Roberts, *Edward Bond: A Companion to the Plays*, p. 72.

71. Ibid.

72. Ibid.

73. E. K. Chambers, *The English Folk-Play* (Oxford: Clarendon, 1933), p. 12.

74. Ibid., p. 220.

75. E. K. Chambers, *The Medieval Stage*, vol. 1 (London: Oxford University Press, 1903), p. 218; see also A. L. Lloyd, *Folk Song in England*, p. 92.

76. Edward Bond, *The Fool and We Come to the River* (London: Eyre Methuen, 1976), p. 4. All further references to the play will be to this edition.

77. The emphasis is mine. Bond's version is quite close to that printed in the notes to *The Folk Songs of Britain, vol. 9: Songs of Ceremony* (Topic Records 12T197, 1961); a slightly different version entitled "Helston Furry Dance" is included in *Everyman's Book of English Country Songs*, ed. Roy Palmer (London: Dent, 1979).

78. Cf. Chambers *The English Folk-Play*, p. 66.

79. Lloyd, *Folk Song in England*, p. 91.

80. Ibid., p. 88.

81. Ibid., p. 89.

82. Ibid., p. 88; cf. also "Hunting the Wren" in Christina Hole, *A Dictionary of British Folk Customs* (London: Granada, Paladin Books, 1978), pp. 163–67.

83. *Stories of Britain in Song*, compiled with commentaries by Forbes Stuart (London: Longman, 1972), p. 33.

84. *Songs of Struggle and Protest*, ed. John McDonnell (Skerries, Co. Dublin, Ireland: Gilbert Dalton, 1979), p. 8.

85. Arnold Wesker, *Chips With Everything, The Friends, The Old Ones, Love Letters on Blue Paper*, vol. 3 (Harmondsworth: Penguin, 1980), pp. 37–38.

86. "Letter to Louis Scheeder," in Hay and Roberts, *Edward Bond: A Companion to the Plays*, p. 63.

87. Edward Bond, *The Woman* (London: Eyre Methuen, 1979), p. 48. All further references to the play will be to this edition.

88. Edward Bond, "Us, Our Drama and the National Theatre," *Plays and Players* (October 1978): 9.

89. Hay and Roberts, *Bond: A Study of His Plays*, p. 256.

90. Chambers, *The English Folk-Play*, pp. 206–10.

91. Hay and Roberts, *Bond: A Study of His Plays*, pp. 256–57.

92. A tape of the National Theatre production, recorded in January 1979, is available at the National Sound Archive.

93. Unpublished interview with Tony Coult, as quoted in Hay and Roberts, *Bond: A Study of His Plays*, p. 257.

94. Heinrich F. Plett, "Edward Bond: *The Woman*. Mythos und Geschichte in einer 'sozialistischen Rhapsodie,'" in *Englisches Drama von Beckett bis Bond*, ed. Heinrich F. Plett (Munich: Fink, 1982), pp. 376–77.

95. Hay and Roberts, *Bond: A Study of His Plays*, p. 230.

96. Bond, "Us, Our Drama and the National Theatre," p. 8.

97. I have consulted both the score (Studienpartitur) and a tape recording of the opera lent to me by the Schott Verlag. All quotations from *We Come to the River* will be from the Methuen edition: Edward Bond, *The Fool and We Come to the River* (London: Eyre Methuen, 1976). My textual analysis is based mainly on the Methuen edition. The scene numbers correspond to those of this edition. The titles of the songs are from Bond's *Theatre Poems and Songs*. The texts of the songs in both these editions are almost identical. In addition, I have compared the Methuen with the Schott edition: Edward Bond and Hans Werner Henze, *We Come to the River: Actions for Music* (Mainz, W. Germany: B. Schott's Söhne, 1976). The latter exists in both English and German versions. The text differs from that of the Methuen edition—in several cases lines or even whole stanzas of the songs are not included or are placed in different positions. The Schott edition contains numerous printing errors that render its authority as text questionable. It is, however, particularly useful in that it prints the simultaneous scenes in parallel columns. (The Methuen edition does this only at the end of the final scene.) One can thus determine throughout which words of the scenes are sung simultaneously. Ironies and contrasts are perceived more clearly in this manner.

98. Hans Werner Henze, "We Come to the River," in *Musik und Politik: Schriften und Gespräche 1955–1975* (Munich: Deutscher Taschenbuch Verlag, 1976), p. 252; English translation in Henze, *Music and Politics*, p. 231.

99. Bond as quoted in Hay and Roberts, *Edward Bond: A Companion to the Plays*, p. 23.

100. Hans Werner Henze in his diary, as quoted in Hans-Klaus Jungheinrich, "Zwei Autoren nähern sich einem Stoff: Hans Werner Henzes Zusammenarbeit mit Edward Bond bei 'We Come to the River,'" *Akzente* 24, no. 2 (April 1977): 173. The translation is mine.

101. Bond as quoted in Tony Coult, *The Plays of Edward Bond*, p. 83.

102. Hans Werner Henze, "Musica impura—Musik als Sprache," in *Musik und Politik*, p. 187. The translation is mine.

103. Jens Brockmeier, "Vorwort des Herausgebers," in *Musik und Politik*, p. 11.

104. On Henze's political consciousness and its reflection in his music see *Musik und Politik*, pp. 262–63; and Ernst H. Flammer, *Politisch engagierte Musik als kompositorisches Problem* (Baden-Baden, W. Germany: Valentin Koerner, 1981), pp. 108ff.

105. For those who cannot consult score or tape, there is much useful information in Henze, "We Come to the River," in *Musik und Politik*, pp. 251–65; *Music and Politics*, pp. 230–42; and an essay that follows Henze quite closely: Theo Becker and Irmtraut Müller, "Befreiungskampf auf der Opernbühne," *Theater Heute* (November 1976): 30–33.

106. The Schott edition of *We Come to the River* specifies which actions are to be played on each stage.

107. Hans Werner Henze, *We Come to the River*, actions for music by Edward Bond, Studienpartitur [score], Edition Schott 6682 (Mainz, W. Germany: B. Schott's Söhne, n. d.), p. x.

108. Edward Bond, "Note on 'We Come to the River,'" written with Hans Werner Henze, in Hay and Roberts, *Edward Bond: A Companion to the Plays*, p. 70.

109. Edward Bond, "Orpheus and the Wire," in *Poems 1978–1985*, p. 120.

110. Edward Bond in conversation with Philip Roberts, British Council Interview, [p. 22].

111. Edward Bond, "On Music," in *Theatre Poems and Songs*, p. 78.

112. Hans Werner Henze, "We Come to the River," in *Musik und Politik*, p. 261; translation in *Music and Politics*, p. 239.

113. Bond/Henze, *We Come to the River* (Mainz, W. Germany: Schott, 1976), p. 13.

114. Becker and Müller, "Befreiungskampf auf der Opernbühne," p. 31. The translation is mine.

115. See the elaborate drawing in the score, ibid., p. 286.

116. The stanzas beginning "A white horse is nibbling the wet grass" and "The soldiers marched by in the night" (pp. 121–22) are lacking in the Schott edition and in the score; they seem to be a later addition by Bond.

117. Henze, *We Come to the River*, score, p. 553.

118. Henze, "We Come to the River," in *Musik und Politik*, pp. 264–65; translation in *Music and Politics*, p. 242.

119. Henze as quoted in Hay and Roberts, *Bond: A Study of His Plays*, p. 178.

120. Cf. also Henze, "We Come to the River," in *Musik und Politik*, pp. 253–54.

121. Edward Bond, *A-A-America! and Stone* (London: Eyre Methuen/A Methuen New Theatrescript, 1976).

122. Edward Bond, *A-A-America! and Stone*, rev. ed. (London: Eyre Methuen, 1981). All quotations from the play will be taken from this edition.

123. Hay and Roberts, *Bond: A Study of His Plays*, p. 229.

124. Ibid., pp. 235–37.

125. Edward Bond, "From an Unfinished Ballet," in *Theatre Poems and Songs*. All quotations are from this edition.

126. Hay and Roberts, *Bond: A Study of His Plays*, p. 236.

127. Edward Bond, *The Activists Papers*, in *The Worlds with the Activists Papers* (London: Eyre Methuen, 1980), p. 139.

128. Ibid., p. 141.

129. Katharine Worth, "Bond's *Restoration*," *Modern Drama* 24, no. 4 (December 1981), p. 479.

130. Ibid., p. 483.

131. Bond in "Kaleidoscope," B.B.C. Radio 4 (22 July 1981), B.B.C. Script Library transcript, pp. 1–2.

132. The traditional tune is "Bogie's Bonnie Belle" (scene 11). The rehearsal edition includes a second folk tune, "The False Bride": Edward Bond, *Restoration* (London: Eyre Methuen in association with the Royal Court Theatre, 1981), p. 42. This is eliminated from the revised edition.

133. "The Music Men: Stephen Oliver and Nick Bicât talk to Anthony Masters," *Plays and Players* (November 1981), p. 21. Information concerning the accompaniment to Bicât's tunes comes from the unpublished piano score with orchestration by Terry Davies, the manuscript of which was lent to me by his agent at London Management.

134. For a more positive assessment of the music that emphasizes its aggressive style, see Katharine Worth, "Bond's *Restoration*," pp. 482–83.

135. Edward Bond, *Restoration and the Cat*, revised ed. (London: Methuen, 1982). All quotations from the play will refer to this edition.

136. Cf. Philip Roberts, "The Search for Epic Drama: Edward Bond's Recent Work," *Modern Drama* 24, no. 4 (December 1981), pp. 470–71.

137. Bond, *The Activists Papers*, in *The Worlds with the Activists Papers*, p. 140.

138. Ibid.

139. In the original 1981 edition two further stanzas of "Man is What He Knows" are included at this point that elaborate didactically on the idea of mental slavery. The fact that Bond removed them in the revised edition of 1982 indicates that he did not want didactic commentary to entirely dominate this final song.

140. Edward Bond, *Derek and Choruses from After the Assassinations* (London: Methuen, 1983), "Author's Note." All further quotations from the play refer to this edition.

141. Edward Bond, *Human Cannon* (London: Methuen, 1985). All further references are to this edition.

142. Hans Werner Henze, *Die englische Katze: Ein Arbeitstagebuch 1978–1982* (Frankfurt am Main: Fischer, 1983).

143. Edward Bond, letter to Hans Werner Henze (24 September 1979), quoted (in German translation), ibid., p. 34.

144. Ibid., p. 35.

145. Ibid., p. 75. The translation is mine.

146. Edward Bond, letter to Hans Werner Henze (3 October 1979); Henze translates the entire letter into German, and also reproduces one page of the English original with Bond's sketch. I have quoted from the latter, ibid., p. 45.

147. Ibid.

148. Edward Bond, *The Cat*, in *Restoration and The Cat* (London: Methuen, 1982), p. 117. All further quotations are from this edition.

149. Henze, *Die englische Katze*, p. 339.

150. Bond, "On Music," in *Theatre Poems and Songs*, p. 78.

151. John McGrath, unpublished interview with the author (26 May 1984).

152. Ibid.

153. See the conclusion to the chapter on Peter Barnes.

154. For a further discussion of the symbolism see Coult, *The Plays of Edward Bond*, pp. 33–34.

Chapter 4. The Dominance of Popular Song: Music Hall to Rock

1. Peter Barnes, *Collected Plays* (London: Heinemann, 1981), p. viii.

2. Ibid., p. 122.

3. Ibid., p. ix.

4. Ibid., p. viii.

5. "Peter Barnes," interview with Brendan Hennessy, *The Transatlantic Review* 37/38 (Autumn/Winter 1970–71), p. 120.

6. Ibid.

7. All statements by Barnes not otherwise identified are from an unpublished interview with the author on 14 May 1984.

8. Cf. also Bernard F. Dukore, *The Theatre of Peter Barnes* (London: Heinemann, 1981), pp. 60ff.

9. Cf. Dukore, *The Theatre of Peter Barnes*, pp. 62ff.

10. Cf. Dukore, *The Theatre of Peter Barnes*, pp. 54ff.

11. "Peter Barnes," *Transatlantic Review*, p. 118.

12. "Liberating Laughter: Peter Barnes and Peter Nichols in Interview with Jim Hiley," *Plays and Players* (March 1978): 17.

13. "Peter Barnes," *Transatlantic Review*, p. 124.

14. Ibid.

15. Barnes, *Collected Plays*, p. viii.

16. "Peter Barnes," *Transatlantic Review*, p. 121.

17. Barnes, *The Ruling Class*, in *Collected Plays*, p. 19. All further quotations from *The Ruling Class* are from this edition.

18. *Hymns, Ancient and Modern*, no. 573.

19. This film may be viewed at the National Film Archive, London. All quotations from *Leonardo's Last Supper* are from Barnes, *Collected Plays*.

20. Barnes, *Collected Plays*, p. 122.

21. Introduction to *The Bewitched*, ibid., p. 188.

22. Lothar Černy, "Peter Barnes, *The Bewitched*," in *Englische Literatur der Gegenwart 1971–1975*, ed. Rainer Lengeler (Düsseldorf, W. Germany: Bagel, 1977), pp. 94–106.

23. *Oxford Dictionary of Nursery Rhymes*, pp. 330–31.

24. Dukore, *The Theatre of Peter Barnes*, p. 56.

25. "Liberating Laughter," p. 17.

26. Peter Barnes, *Red Noses* (London: Faber, 1985), p. 52. All further quotations are from this edition. It is surely no coincidence that Antonin Artaud in *The Theater and its Double* spends an entire chapter on the parallelism between theater and plague. "The Theater and the Plague," in *The Theater and its Double* (New York: Grove, 1958), pp. 15–32.

27. Peter Mortimer, "C. P. Taylor—An appreciation of his work and life," *Drama* (Autumn 1982): 16.

28. C. P. Taylor, "Author's Note," *Good* (London: Methuen, 1982). All further quotations from the play are from this edition.

29. Ibid.

30. These pauses are part of the original text.

31. My ellipses are indicated by square brackets.

32. Bond, "On Music," *Theatre Poems and Songs*, p. 78.

33. Mervyn Jones, "Peter Nichols, The playwright who has had enough," *Drama* (Summer 1983): 7.

34. John Osborne, "Note," *The Entertainer* (London: Faber, 1961). All further quotations from the play are from this edition, unless otherwise noted.

35. Osborne, "The Writer in His Age," In John Russell Taylor, ed., *John Osborne: Look Back in Anger, a Casebook* (London: Macmillan, 1963), p. 61.

36. Ibid., p. 60.

37. Ibid., p. 61.

38. Ibid.

39. Osborne, "That Awful Museum," in Taylor, *Look Back in Anger, a Casebook*, p. 65.

40. Osborne, "They Call it Cricket," *Declaration*, ed. Tom Maschler (New York: Dutton, 1958), p. 47.

41. Ibid., p. 65.

42. "That Awful Museum," in Taylor, *Look Back in Anger, a Casebook*, p. 66.

43. John Osborne, *A Better Class of Person: An Autobiography 1929–1956* (London: Faber, 1981), p. 23.

44. Ibid., p. 41.

45. Ibid., p. 27.

46. Peter Davison, *Songs of the British Music Hall* (New York: Oak, 1971), p. 72.

47. Osborne, *A Better Class of Person*, p. 203.

48. Ibid., p. 174.

49. Compare Dukore, *The Theatre of Peter Barnes*, pp. 5–6 and Osborne, *A Better Class of Person*, pp. 86–88.

50. John Osborne, *Look Back in Anger* (London: Faber, 1960), pp. 81–82.

51. "Production Note," Osborne, *The Entertainer* (London: Evans Acting Edition, 1959), no page.

52. The film may be viewed at the National Film Archive, London.

53. Katharine J. Worth, *Revolutions in Modern English Drama* (London: Bell, 1973), p. 73.

54. "They Call It Cricket," in *Declaration*, p. 51.

55. John Russell Brown, *Theatre Language: A Study of Arden, Osborne, Pinter and Wesker* (London: Allen Lane, 1972), p. 147.

56. Davison, *Songs of The British Music Hall*, p. 235.

57. Peter Davison, *Contemporary Drama and the Popular Dramatic Tradition in England* (London: Macmillan, 1982), pp. 99–101. Robert Weimann also sees an element of alienation in the songs but comes to the conclusion that there is a contradiction between the effect of the songs and the intention in the rest of the play: "Die Literatur der *Angry Young Men*," *Zeitschrift für Anglistik und Amerikanistik* 7 (1959): 159–60.

58. Rudyard Kipling, *The Complete Barrack-Room Ballads*, ed. Charles Carrington (London: Methuen, 1974), pp. 111–13 and 170–71.

59. Worth, *Revolutions in Modern English Drama*, p. 75.

60. Dietrich Schwanitz, "John Osborne: The Entertainer," in *Englisches Drama von Beckett bis Bond*, ed. Heinrich Plett (Munich: Fink, 1982), p. 101.

61. Raymond Williams, *The Long Revolution* (Harmondsworth: Penguin, 1965), p. 291.

62. This recording may be heard at the National Sound Archive, London.

63. John Osborne, *A Sense of Detachment* (London: Faber, 1973), p. 12. All further quotations are taken from this edition.

64. Günter Ahrends, "John Osborne, A Sense of Detachment," in *Englische Literatur der Gegenwart, 1971–1975*, ed. Rainer Lengeler (Düsseldorf, W. Germany: Bagel, 1977), p. 76.

65. Peter Nichols, *Forget-me-not Lane* (London: Faber, 1971), no page. All further quotations are taken from this edition.

66. John Russell Taylor, *The Second Wave: British Drama for the Seventies* (London: Methuen, 1971), p. 34. In his autobiography, Nichols recalls his adolescent passion for jazz, comedians, and films in the 1940s and sees this in relation to the experience of other boys of his generation. Peter Nichols, *Feeling You're Behind* (London: Weidenfeld and Nicholson, 1984), p. 45. The autobiography also makes clear that many of the episodes portrayed in the play are recreations of Nichols's own experience.

67. David Mercer, *The Monster of Karlovy Vary* and *Then and Now* (London: Eyre Methuen, 1979), p. 104. All further quotations are from this edition.

68. C. P. Taylor, *And A Nightingale Sang . . .* (London: Eyre Methuen, 1979), pp. 49–51. All further quotations are from this edition.

69. Harold Pinter, *Old Times* (London: Eyre Methuen, 1971), p. 26. All further quotations are from this edition.

70. Esslin for example refers to "the popular tunes of the early fifties" and speaks of "evocations of life in postwar London." Martin Esslin, *Pinter: A Study of His Plays*, rev. ed. (London: Eyre Methuen, 1973), p. 188. As the date of the film *Odd Man Out* is 1946 one could also argue for the late 1940s as the time of the play.

71. Colin Blakely, "Old Times," *Plays and Players* (July 1971): 22.

72. "A Conversation with Harold Pinter," *The New York Times Magazine* (5 December 1971), p. 133.

73. For example Peter Hall, "Directing Pinter," *Theatre Quarterly* 4, no. 16 (November 1974–January 1975), p. 5; and Kennedy, *Six Dramatists*, p. 178.

74. Worth, *Revolutions in Modern English Drama*, p. 99.

75. The National Sound Archive has a recording of the production of the Royal Shakespeare Company at the Aldwych, recorded in 1972.

76. Alan Hughes, " 'They Can't Take That Away from Me'; Myth and Memory in Pinter's *Old Times*," *Modern Drama* 17 (1974): 471.

77. Harold Pinter, "Writing for the Theatre" (1964), in *English Dramatic Theories: 20th Century*, ed. Paul Goetsch (Tübingen, W. Germany: Max Niemeyer, 1972), pp. 120–21.

78. Arthur E. McGuinness, "Memory and Betrayal: The Symbolic Landscape of *Old Times*," in *Themes in Drama 4: Drama and Symbolism*, ed. James Redmond (Cambridge: Cambridge University Press, 1982), p. 102.

79. Samuel Beckett, *Waiting for Godot*, 2d ed. (London: Faber, 1965), p. 70.

80. Ibid., pp. 57–58.

81. Samuel Beckett, *Happy Days* (London: Faber, 1966), p. 30.

82. Kennedy, *Six Dramatists*, p. 150.

83. Beckett, *Happy Days*, p. 42.

84. C. W. E. Bigsby, "Tom Stoppard," in *Contemporary Dramatists*, ed. James Vinson (London: St. James Press, 1977), p. 762.

85. Tom Stoppard, "Ambushes for the Audience: Towards a High Comedy of Ideas," *Theatre Quarterly* 4, no. 14 (May–July 1974): 13.

86. Michael Hinden, "*Jumpers:* Stoppard and the Theater of Exhaustion," *Twentieth Century Literature* 27 (1981): 12.

87. Victor L. Cahn, *Beyond Absurdity: The Plays of Tom Stoppard* (Rutherford, N.J.: Fairleigh Dickinson University Press, 1979), p. 153.

88. "First Interview with Tom Stoppard, 12 June 1974," in Ronald Hayman, *Tom Stoppard* (London: Heinemann, 1977), p. 7.

89. "Tom Stoppard," in *Behind the Scenes: Theatre and Film Interviews from the Transatlantic Review*, ed. Joseph McCrindle (New York: Holt, Rinehart and Winston, 1971), p. 84.

90. "Ambushes for the Audience," p. 7.

91. "An Interview with Tom Stoppard," *Dutch Quarterly Review* 10 (1980): 57.

92. Ibid., pp. 56–57.

93. "First Interview with Tom Stoppard," in Hayman, p. 8.

94. Ibid., p. 5.

95. Tom Stoppard, *Jumpers* (London: Faber, 1972), p. 72. All further quotations are from this edition.

96. Bigsby, "Tom Stoppard," in Vinson, p. 762.

97. C. W. E. Bigsby, *Tom Stoppard* (Burnt Mill, Harlow, Essex: Longman, 1976), p. 23.

98. Stoppard, "Ambushes for the Audience," p. 17.

99. Hinden, "*Jumpers:* Stoppard and The Theater of Exhaustion," p. 9.

100. Bigsby "Tom Stoppard," in Vinson, p. 763.

101. Tom Stoppard, *Travesties* (London: Faber, 1975), p. 21. All further quotations are from this edition.

102. "Second Interview with Tom Stoppard, 20 August 1976," in Hayman, *Tom Stoppard*, p. 140.

103. Ronald Hayman, "Profile 9: Tom Stoppard," *The New Review* (December 1974): 21.

104. "First Interview with Tom Stoppard," in Hayman, *Tom Stoppard*, p. 10.

105. Tom Stoppard, "Introduction," in *Every Good Boy Deserves Favour* and *Professional Foul* (London: Faber, 1978), p. 7. All quotations from the play are from this edition.

106. Ibid., p. 5.

107. Cf. The recorded version of *Every Good Boy Deserves Favour* on RCA stereo (1978) BL 12855; the play was televised in 1979.

108. Tom Stoppard, *Night and Day*, 2d ed. (London: Faber, 1979), p. 19. All quotations are from this edition.

109. Richard Kislan, *The Musical: A Look at the American Musical Theater* (Englewood Cliffs, N.J.: Prentice Hall, 1980), pp. 2–7.

110. Simon Trussler, *The Plays of John Osborne: An Assessment* (London: Granada/Panther, 1971), p. 71.

111. Richard Findlater, "The Case of P. Slickey," *Twentieth Century* 167 (January 1960): 32.

112. "Liberating Laughter," pp. 16–17.

113. Ibid., p. 17.

114. Mervyn Jones, "Peter Nichols, the playwright who has had enough," *Drama* 148 (Summer 1983): 8.

115. Ibid.

116. "Liberating Laughter," p. 15.

117. Ibid.

118. Ibid.

119. Peter Nichols, *Privates on Parade: A Play with Songs in Two Acts* (London: Faber, 1977), p. 68. All quotations are from this edition.

120. National Sound Archive recording of the Royal Shakespeare Company production at the Aldwych (March 1977).

121. Charles Marowitz, "Privates on Parade," (review) *Plays and Players* (April 1977): 24.

122. Ibid., p. 22.

123. Jones, "Peter Nichols," p. 8; cf. also Desmond Christy, "Poppy," (review) *Plays and Players* (January 1984): 40–41.

124. Peter Nichols, *Poppy* (London: Methuen, 1982), p. 113. All further quotations are from this edition.

125. John Russell Taylor, "Plays in Performance: London," *Drama* 147 (Spring 1983): 27.

126. There is a phonograph record with the original cast: RSC 25-0000-1 (1982).

127. John Russell Taylor, "Poppy," (review) *Plays and Players* (December 1982): 23.

128. Jones, "Peter Nichols," p. 8.

129. Christy, "Poppy," p. 41.

130. Jones, "Peter Nichols," p. 8.

131. Pam Gems, introductory note to *Piaf* (Oxford: Amber Lane Press, 1979), no page. All quotations from the play are from this edition.

132. Michelene Wandor, *Understudies: Theatre and Sexual Politics* (London: Eyre Methuen, 1981), p. 64.

133. David Hare, "From Portable Theatre to Joint Stock . . . via Shaftesbury Avenue," (interview) *Theatre Quarterly* 5, no. 20 (December 1975–February 1976): 113.

134. David Hare, "A Lecture, given at King's College, Cambridge, March 5 1978," in *Licking Hitler* (London: Faber, 1978), p. 67.

135. Catherine Itzin, *Stages in the Revolution: Political Theatre in Britain since 1968* (London: Eyre Methuen, 1980), p. 333.

136. Hare, "A Lecture," in *Licking Hitler*, p. 70.

137. David Hare, *Teeth 'n' Smiles* (London: Faber, 1976), p. 88. All further quotations are from this edition.

138. Itzin, *Stages in the Revolution*, p. 333.

139. Hare, *Teeth 'n' Smiles*, introductory note, no page.

140. Itzin, *Stages in the Revolution*, p. 244.

141. Barrie Keeffe, *Bastard Angel* (London: Eyre Methuen, 1980), p. 56. All further quotations are from this edition.

142. Ruby Cohn, "Sam Shepard: Today's Passionate Shepard and His Loves," in *Essays on*

Contemporary American Drama, ed. Hedwig Bock and Albert Wertheim (Munich: Hueber, 1981), p. 161.

143. Sam Shepard, *The Tooth of Crime*, in Shepard, *Four Two-Act Plays* (London: Faber, 1981), pp. 97ff.

144. Bruce W. Powe, *"The Tooth of Crime:* Sam Shepard's Way with Music," *Modern Drama* 24, no. 1 (March 1981): 16.

145. Sam Shepard, "Metaphors, Mad Dogs and Old Time Cowboys" (interview), *Theatre Quarterly* 4, no. 15 (August–October 1974): 12.

146. Trevor Griffiths, "Transforming the Husk of Capitalism" (interview), *Theatre Quarterly* 6, no. 22 (Summer 1976): 42.

147. Itzin, *Stages in the Revolution*, pp. 173–74.

148. Trevor Griffiths, *Comedians* (London: Faber, 1976), pp. 43 and 45. All quotations are from this edition.

149. Griffiths, "Transforming the Husk of Capitalism," p. 44.

150. Compare John McGrath's description of a typical bill of entertainment in a workingmen's club in *A Good Night Out. Popular Theatre: Audience, Class and Form* (London: Eyre Methuen, 1981), pp. 22–25.

151. Cf. Itzin, *Stages in the Revolution*, pp. 165–75.

152. Trevor Griffiths, *Oi For England* (London: Faber, 1982), p. 25. All quotations are from this edition. Text and tune of the song "As I Roved Out" may be found in Seán O'Boyle, *The Irish Song Tradition* (Dublin: Gilbert Dalton, 1976), p. 42.

153. *I'll Be Seeing You . . . Featuring the Songs, the Artists and the Memories of the Second World War* (London: EMI Music Publishing, 1979), p. 100.

Chapter 5. Other Musical Forms: From Religious Ritual to Political Song

1. Peter Shaffer, "Author's Notes," in *The Royal Hunt of the Sun* (Burnt Mill, Harlow, Essex: Longman, 1966), p. xviii. All further quotations from the play refer to this edition.

2. Antonin Artaud, *The Theater and its Double*, translated from the French by Mary Caroline Richards (New York: Grove, 1958), p. 80.

3. Ibid., pp. 82–83.

4. Ibid., p. 91.

5. Ibid., pp. 126–32.

6. The National Sound Archive, London, has a recording of the National Theatre production with the music by Marc Wilkinson, recorded at The Old Vic in 1964.

7. The emphasis is mine.

8. Shaffer, "Author's Notes," *Royal Hunt of The Sun*, p. xviii.

9. John Osborne, *A Patriot for Me* (London: Faber, 1966), p. 71.

10. Peter Nichols, *Passion Play* (London: Eyre Methuen, 1981), pp. 55–57. All further quotations are from this edition.

11. A Leicester Haymarket production at Wyndham's Theatre, May 1984.

12. Peter Shaffer, *Amadeus* (London: Andre Deutsch, 1980), p. 37.

13. John Russell Taylor, "David Rudkin," in Vinson, *Contemporary Dramatists*, p. 676.

14. William Alwyn, "Edward Elgar (1857–1934)," notes to the record of *The Dream of Gerontius* (Decca SET 525–6, 1972), p. 6.

15. David Rudkin, *Penda's Fen* (London: Davis-Poynter, 1975); see especially the passages pp. 1–5 and pp. 73–75. All further quotations are from this edition.

16. Itzin, *Stages in the Revolution*, p. 185 uses this term for Rudkin's *The Sons of Light*, but I believe that it can also be applied to *Penda's Fen*.

17. The ellipses are part of Rudkin's text.

18. *The Concise Oxford Dictionary of Music*, 2d ed. (London: Oxford University Press, 1964), p. 298.

19. Erik Routley, *The English Carol*, pp. 63–64.

20. William Blake, from *Milton*, in *William Blake's Writings*, ed. G. E. Bentley Jr., vol. 1

(Oxford: Clarendon, 1978), p. 318. This song from *Milton* (1804) is known popularly as "Jerusalem," or "The New Jerusalem," and should not be confused with Blake's long poem *Jerusalem*. The tune, by Hubert Parry, was not composed until 1916.

21. Arnold Wesker, "Art and Action," *The Listener* (10 May 1962): 808.

22. Arnold Wesker, *Fears of Fragmentation* (London: Jonathan Cape, 1970), p. 65.

23. Wesker told me, for example, that he had first heard the ballad "The Unquiet Grave" on the radio.

24. Arnold Wesker, *The Kitchen*, in *Three Plays* (Harmondsworth: Penguin, 1976), p. 11.

25. Arnold Wesker, *Chicken Soup with Barley*, in *The Wesker Trilogy* (London: Jonathan Cape, 1960), p. 29. All further quotations are from this edition.

26. Wesker, *Roots*, in *The Wesker Trilogy*, p. 115. All further quotations are from this edition.

27. Arnold Wesker, *Penguin Plays, Vol. 3: Chips with Everything, The Friends, The Old Ones, Love Letters on Blue Paper* (Harmondsworth: Penguin, 1980), p. 31. All further quotations are from this edition.

28. John Russell Taylor, *Anger and After*, rev. ed. (Harmondsworth: Penguin, 1963), p. 148.

29. Arnold Wesker, *The Nottingham Captain*, in *Six Sundays in January* (London: Jonathan Cape, 1971), pp. 51–53.

30. Arnold Wesker, *The Four Seasons* (London: Jonathan Cape, 1966), p. 6. All further quotations are from this edition.

31. Francis James Child, introductory note to ballad 78, in *The English and Scottish Popular Ballads*, 5 vols. (New York: The Folklore Press in association with Pageant Book Co., 1956), p. 234.

32. Arnold Wesker, "Casual Condemnations," *Theatre Quarterly* 1, no. 2 (April–June 1971): 22.

33. Arnold Wesker, *The Friends*, in *Penguin Plays, Vol. 3*, p. 104.

34. Arnold Wesker, *The Old Ones* in *Penguin Plays, Vol. 3*, p. 128. All further quotations are from this edition.

35. Arnold Wesker, "A Sense of What Should Follow" (interview), *Theatre Quarterly* 7, no. 28 (Winter 1977–78): 12.

36. Arnold Wesker, *The Merchant*, in *Penguin Plays, Vol. 4: The Journalists, The Merchant, The Wedding Feast* (Harmondsworth: Penguin, 1980), pp. 264–66.

37. Keith Dewhurst, "Introduction," in *Lark Rise to Candleford* (London: Hutchinson, 1980), p. 11. All quotations are from this edition.

38. Ibid., p. 13.

39. There is a phonograph record of the National Theatre production (1979) Charisma CDS 4020.

40. *Dreams and Deconstructions: Alternative Theatre in Britain*, ed. Sandy Craig (Ambergate, Derbyshire: Amber Lane Press, 1980), p. 114.

41. McGrath, *A Good Night Out*, p. 83.

42. Ibid., pp. 61–62.

43. Ibid., p. 62.

44. Ibid., p. 100.

45. Ibid., pp. 54–59.

46. Ibid., p. 59.

47. This and all other statements by John McGrath not otherwise identified are from an unpublished interview with the author on 26 May 1984.

48. McGrath, *A Good Night Out*, p. 94.

49. John McGrath, "Better a Bad Night in Bootle" (interview), *Theatre Quarterly* 5, no. 19 (September–November 1975): 39.

50. McGrath, *A Good Night Out*, pp. 4ff.

51. McGrath, "Better a Bad Night in Bootle," p. 50.

52. Ibid., p. 51.

53. The best example of Mark Brown's music available to me was a record of *Lay Off* (1975), kindly lent to me by John McGrath. Here it is indeed the harmony that is unusual. There is also a small record of *The Life and Times of Joe of England* with music by Mark Brown and the 7:84 Band, 7:84 Theatre Company (England) Record no. 784005S.

54. John McGrath, "Yobbo Nowt," [Author's Note], in *Yobbo Nowt* (London: Pluto, 1978, no page). All further references to the play will be to this edition.

55. McGrath, "Better a Bad Night in Bootle," p. 51.

56. McGrath, *A Good Night Out*, p. 122.

57. There is a good recording of the music to this play: *The Cheviot, the Stag and the Black, Black Oil*, 7:84 Theatre Company (Scotland), Record no. 784002S.

58. John McGrath, *The Cheviot, the Stag and the Black, Black Oil*, rev. illus. ed. (London: Eyre Methuen, 1981), p. 1. All further quotations are from this edition.

59. John McGrath, *Little Red Hen* (London: Pluto, 1977), p. 2. All further quotations are from this edition.

60. 7:84 made a tape of this show that gives a good impression of the music and of the liveliness of the performance.

61. To my knowledge the play has not been published. I am quoting from a manuscript copy.

62. David Edgar, "Towards a Theatre of Dynamic Ambiguities" (interview), *Theatre Quarterly* 9 no. 33 (Spring 1979): 14.

63. McGrath, *A Good Night Out*, p. 62.

64. John McGrath, "Interview," *Scottish Marxist* 26 (Spring 1983): 8.

65. Steve Gooch, *Will Wat? If Not, What Will?* (London: Pluto, 1975), "Writer's Note," no page; Steve Gooch, *Female Transport* (London: Pluto, 1974); Steve Gooch and Paul Thompson, *The Motor Show* (London: Pluto, 1975); Steve Gooch, *The Women Pirates Ann Bonney and Mary Read* (London: Pluto, 1978); Steve Gooch, *All Together Now: An Alternative View of Theatre and the Community* (London: Methuen, 1984).

66. David Edgar, *Dick Deterred* (New York: Monthly Review Press, 1974); David Edgar, *Destiny* (London: Methuen, 1976); David Edgar, *Wreckers* (London: Methuen New Theatrescript, 1977).

67. David Edgar, "Ten Years of Political Theatre, 1968–78," *Theatre Quarterly* 8, no. 32 (Winter 1979): 25–33; and David Edgar, "Towards a Theatre of Dynamic Ambiguities," *Theatre Quarterly* 9, no. 33 (Spring 1979): 3–23.

68. Caryl Churchill, *Vinegar Tom*, in *Plays by Women, Vol. I*, ed. Michelene Wandor (London: Methuen, 1982), p. 37; Caryl Churchill, *Cloud Nine* (London: Pluto and Joint Stock, 1979).

69. Caryl Churchill, *Fen* (London: Methuen in association with Joint Stock, 1983), p. 19; Rainer Maria Rilke, *Duineser Elegien* (Zürich: Manesse, 1951), p. 7.

70. Howard Brenton, "Petrol Bombs Through the Proscenium Arch," *Theatre Quarterly* 5, no. 17 (March–May 1975): 12.

71. Howard Brenton, *Hitler Dances* (London: Methuen, 1982), p. 75; Howard Brenton and David Hare, *Brassneck* (London: Eyre Methuen, 1974).

72. Cf. Paul Merchant, "The Theatre Poems of Bertolt Brecht, Edward Bond, and Howard Brenton," *Theatre Quarterly* 9, no. 34 (Summer 1979): 49–51.

73. Barrie Keeffe, *Gimme Shelter* (London: Eyre Methuen, 1977), "Note" [p. 6].

74. Barrie Keeffe, *Sus* (London: Eyre Methuen, Methuen New Theatrescript, 1979), p. 23.

75. CAST (Cartoon Archetypical Slogan Theatre), *Confessions of a Socialist* (London: Pluto, 1979); Red Ladder, *Taking Our Time* (London: Pluto, 1979); Red Ladder, *Strike While the Iron is Hot*, in *Strike While the Iron is Hot: Three Plays on Sexual Politics*, ed. Michelene Wandor (London: Journeyman, 1980); Gavin Richards (Belt and Braces), *England Expects* (London: Journeyman, 1977); Women's Theatre Group, *My Mother Says I Never Should*, in *Strike While the Iron is Hot*, ed. Michelene Wandor; *Two Gay Sweatshop Plays*, (London: Gay Men's Press, 1981).

76. John Ashford, "The Jazz of Dreams: Performance Art," in *Dreams and Deconstructions*, ed. Sandy Craig, p. 95.

77. Susan Burt and Clive Barker print some interesting song texts in "IOU and the New Vocabulary of Performance Art," *Theatre Quarterly* 10, no. 37 (Spring 1980): 70–94.

78. Cf. Clive Barker, "Pip Simmons in Residence," *Theatre Quarterly* 9, no. 35 (Autumn 1979): 17–30.

79. Pip Simmons Theatre Group, *Superman*, in *New Short Plays: 3* (London: Eyre Methuen, 1972), pp. 90–91.

80. Peter Cheeseman, *Fight for Shelton Bar* (London: Eyre Methuen, Methuen New Theatrescript, 1977), "The Text," no page.

81. Ewan MacColl and Charles Parker, *The Big Hewer: A Radio Ballad* (ARGO DA140, 1967); Ewan MacColl and Charles Parker, *The Ballad of John Axon* (ARGO DA139, 1965); Ewan MacColl, Peggy Seeger and Charles Parker, *The Travelling People* (ARGO DA133, 1969).

82. Alan Cullen, *The Stirrings in Sheffield on Saturday Night* (London: Eyre Methuen, 1974).

83. Alan Plater, *Close the Coalhouse Door* (London: Methuen, 1969), "Introduction," no page.

84. Ibid., p. 11; See also Alan Plater, "The Playwright and His People," *Theatre Quarterly* 1, no. 2 (April–June 1971), 67–70; and Alan Plater, "Twenty-Five Years Hard: A Playwright's Personal Retrospective," *Theatre Quarterly* 7, no. 25 (Spring 1977): 34–46.

Bibliography

Primary Sources

Addison, John. Unpublished piano/vocal score to John Arden, *The Workhouse Donkey*. London Management, Regent Street, London.

Arden, John. *Armstrong's Last Goodnight*. London: Methuen, 1965.

———. *Serjeant Musgrave's Dance*. London: Methuen, 1960.

———. *Soldier, Soldier and Other Plays*. London: Methuen, 1967.

———. *Three Plays*. Harmondsworth: Penguin, 1964.

———. *The Workhouse Donkey*. London: Methuen, 1964.

Arden, John, and Margaretta D'Arcy. *The Ballygombeen Bequest*. Unpublished type-script.

———. *The Business of Good Government*. London: Eyre Methuen, 1963.

———. *The Hero Rises Up*. London: Methuen, 1969.

———. *The Island of the Mighty*. London: Eyre Methuen, 1974.

———. *The Royal Pardon*. London: Methuen, 1967.

Auden, W. H. *The Dance of Death*. London: Faber, 1933.

———. *The English Auden: Poems, Essays and Dramatic Writings, 1927–1939*. Edited by Edward Mendelson. London: Faber, 1977.

Auden, W. H., and Christopher Isherwood. *The Ascent of F6 and On the Frontier*. London: Faber, 1958.

Barnes, Peter. *Collected Plays*. London: Heinemann, 1981.

———. *Red Noses*. London: Faber, 1985.

Bart, Lionel. *Fings Ain't Wot They Used T'Be*. Vocal Score. Words and music by Lionel Bart. London: EMI Music Publishing, 1960.

Beckett, Samuel. *Happy Days*. 1961. London: Faber, 1966.

———. *Waiting for Godot*. 1956. 2d ed. London: Faber, 1965.

Behan, Brendan. *An Giall / The Hostage*. Translated and edited by Richard Wall. Washington, D.C.: The Catholic University of America Press, 1987.

———. *The Hostage*. Translated from the original Gaelic *An Giall* and annotated by Richard Wall. Unpublished manuscript translation.

———. *The Hostage*. London: Methuen, 1958.

———. *The Quare Fellow*. London: Methuen, paperback ed., 1960.

Bicât, Nick. Unpublished score to Edward Bond's *Restoration*. Music by Nick Bicât, piano score by Terry Davies. London Management, Regent Street, London.

Blake, William. *William Blake's Writings*. Ed. G. E. Bentley Jr. Vol. 1. Oxford: Clarendon, 1978.

Bond, Edward. *A-A-America! and Stone*. Methuen New Theatrescript. London: Methuen, 1976.

——. *A-A-America! and Stone*. Revised ed. London: Eyre Methuen, 1981.

——. *Bingo*. London: Eyre Methuen, 1974.

——. *The Bundle*. London: Eyre Methuen, 1978.

——. "Canzoni to Orpheus." In *Orpheus: Materialien*, 78–88. Stuttgart, W. Germany: Würtembergisches Staatstheater, 1979.

——. *Derek and Choruses from After the Assassinations*. A Methuen New Theatrescript. London: Methuen, 1983.

——. *The Fool and We Come to the River*. London: Eyre Methuen, 1976.

——. *Human Cannon*. *A Methuen New Theatrescript. London: Methuen, 1985*.

——.*Narrow Road to the Deep North*. London: Methuen, 1968.

——. *Orpheus*. In *Orpheus: Materialien*, 10–30. Stuttgart, W. Germany: Würtembergisches Staatstheater, 1979.

——. *Plays: One*. London: Eyre Methuen, 1977.

——. *Plays: Two*. London: Eyre Methuen, 1978.

——. *Poems 1978–1985*. London: Methuen, 1987.

——. *Restoration*. The Royal Court Writers Series. London: Eyre Methuen in association with the Royal Court Theatre, 1981.

——. *Restoration and the Cat*. Revised ed. London: Methuen, 1982.

——. *The Sea*. 1973. Reprinted with Author's Note. London: Eyre Methuen, 1975.

——. *Summer and Fables*. 1982. Revised ed. Methuen Modern Plays. London: Methuen, 1982.

——. *Theatre Poems and Songs*. Edited by Malcolm Hay and Philip Roberts. London: Eyre Methuen, 1978.

——. *The War Plays: A Trilogy*. Part 1: *Red Black and Ignorant*. Part 2: *The Tin Can People*. Methuen New Theatrescript. London: Methuen, 1985.

——. *The War Plays: A Trilogy*. Part 3: *Great Peace*. Methuen New Theatrescript. London: Methuen, 1985.

——. *The Woman*. London: Eyre Methuen, 1979.

——. *The Worlds with The Activists Papers*. London: Eyre Methuen, 1980.

Bond, Edward and Hans Werner Henze. *We Come to the River: Actions for Music*. Mainz, W. Germany: B. Schott's Söhne, 1976.

——. *Wir erreichen den Fluss: Handlungen für Musik*. Deutsche Fassung vom Komponisten Hans Werner Henze. Mainz, W. Germany: B. Schott's Söhne, 1976.

Brecht, Bertolt. *Gesammelte Werke*. 20 vols. Werkausgabe edition suhrkamp. Frankfurt am Main: Suhrkamp, 1967.

Brenton, Howard. *Hitler Dances*. London: Methuen, 1982.

Brenton, Howard and David Hare. *Brassneck*. London: Eyre Methuen, 1974.

Britten, Benjamin and W. H. Auden. *Four Cabaret Songs*. London: Faber Music, 1980.

CAST (Cartoon Archetypical Slogan Theatre). *Confessions of a Socialist*. London: Pluto, 1979.

Cheeseman, Peter. *Fight for Shelton Bar*. London: Methuen, 1977.

Churchill, Caryl. *Cloud Nine*. London: Pluto and Joint Stock Theatre Company, 1979.

——. *Fen*. London: Methuen in association with Joint Stock Theatre Company, 1983.

————. *Vinegar Tom*. In *Plays by Women, Vol. 1*. Edited by Michelene Wandor. London: Methuen, 1982.

Cullen, Alan. *The Stirrings in Sheffield on Saturday Night*. London: Methuen, 1974.

D'Arcy, Margaretta and John Arden. *The Little Gray Home in the West*. London: Pluto, 1982.

————. *The Non-Stop Connolly Show*. 5 vols. London: Pluto, 1977–78.

————. *Vandaleur's Folly*. London: Eyre Methuen, 1981.

Dewhurst, Keith. *Lark Rise to Candleford*. London: Hutchinson, 1980.

Edgar, David. *Destiny*. London: Methuen, 1976.

————. *Dick Deterred*. New York: Monthly Review Press, 1974.

————. *Wreckers*. London: Methuen, 1977.

Eliot, T. S. *Sweeney Agonistes: Fragments of an Aristophanic Melodrama*. In *The Complete Poems and Plays*, 115–26. London: Faber, 1969.

Gems, Pam. *Piaf.* Oxford: Amber Lane Press, 1979.

Gooch, Steve. *Female Transport*. London: Pluto, 1974.

————. *Will Wat? If Not, What Will?* London: Pluto, 1975.

————. *The Women Pirates Ann Bonney and Mary Read*. London: Pluto, 1978.

Gooch, Steve and Paul Thompson. *The Motor Show*. London: Pluto, 1975.

Griffiths, Trevor. *Comedians*. London: Faber, 1976.

————. *Oi for England*. London: Faber, 1982.

Hare, David. *Licking Hitler*. London: Faber, 1978.

————. *Teeth 'n' Smiles*. London: Faber, 1976.

Henze, Hans Werner. *We Come to the River: Actions for Music by Edward Bond*. Studien-Partitur [score]. Edition Schott 6682. Mainz, W. Germany: B. Schott's Söhne, n.d.

Henze, Hans Werner and Edward Bond. *Orpheus Behind the Wire*. Schott Kammerchor-Reihe. SKR 20007. Mainz, W. Germany: B. Schatt's Söhne, 1984.

Keeffe, Barrie. *Barbarians*. London: Eyre Methuen, 1978.

————. *Bastard Angel*. London: Eyre Methuen, 1980.

————. *Gimme Shelter*. London: Eyre Methuen, 1977.

————. *Sus*. London: Methuen, 1979.

Kipling, Rudyard. *The Complete Barrack-Room Ballads*. Ed. Charles Carrington. London: Methuen, 1974.

McGrath, John. *The Cheviot, the Stag and the Black, Black Oil*. 1974. Revised, illustrated ed. London: Eyre Methuen, 1981.

————. *The Game's a Bogey*. Edinburgh: EUSPB, 1975.

————. *Fish in the Sea*. London: Pluto, 1977.

————. *Little Red Hen*. London: Pluto, 1977.

————. *Out of Our Heads*. Unpublished manuscript.

————. *Two Plays for the Eighties: Blood Red Roses and Swings and Roundabouts*. Aberdeen, Scotland: 7:84 Theatre Company and Aberdeen People's Press, 1981.

————. *Yobbo-Nowt*. London: Pluto, 1978.

Mankowitz, Wolf. *Make Me an Offer*. Vocal score. Music and lyrics by Monty Norman and David Heneker. London: Britannia Music Co., 1961.

Mercer, David. *Then and Now.* In *The Monster of Karlovy Vary and Then and Now.* London: Eyre Methuen, 1979.

Nichols, Peter. *Forget-Me-Not Lane.* London: Faber, 1971.

———. *The National Health.* London: Faber, 1970.

———. *Passion Play.* London: Eyre Methuen, 1981.

———. *Poppy.* London: Methuen, 1982.

———. *Privates on Parade.* London: Faber, 1977.

Osborne, John. *The End of Me Old Cigar.* London: Faber, 1975.

———. *The Entertainer.* Acting Edition. London: Evans, 1959.

———. *The Entertainer.*1957. London: Faber, 1961.

———. *Look Back in Anger.* 1957. London: Faber, 1960.

———. *Luther.* London: Faber, 1961.

———. *A Patriot for Me.* London: Faber, 1971.

———. *A Sense of Detachment.* London: Faber, 1973.

———. *The World of Paul Slickey.* London: Faber, 1959.

Pinter, Harold. *Old Times.* London: Eyre Methuen, 1971.

Pip Simmons Theatre Group. *Superman.* In *New Short Plays: 3.* London: Eyre Methuen, 1972.

Plater, Alan. *Close the Coalhouse Door.* London: Methuen, 1969.

Red Ladder. *Taking Our Time.* London: Pluto, 1979.

Richards, Gavin. *England Expects.* London: Journeyman, 1977.

Rilke, Rainer Maria. *Duineser Elegien.* Zürich: Manesse, 1951.

Rudkin, David. *Ashes.* London: Pluto, 1978.

———. *Penda's Fen.* London: Davis-Poynter, 1975.

———. *The Sons of Light.* London: Eyre Methuen, 1981.

———. *The Triumph of Death.* London: Eyre Methuen, 1981.

Shaffer, Peter. *Amadeus.* London: Andre Deutsch, 1980.

———. *The Royal Hunt of the Sun.*, Burnt Mill, Harlow, Essex: Longman, 1966.

Shakespeare, William. *The Merchant of Venice.* Edited by John Russell Brown. The Arden Shakespeare. 1905. 7th edition, revised and reset. London: Methuen, 1955.

Shepard, Sam. *The Tooth of Crime.* In *Four Two-Act Plays.* London: Faber, 1981.

Stoppard, Tom. *Every Good Boy Deserves Favour and Professional Foul.* London: Faber, 1978.

———. *Jumpers.* London: Faber, 1972.

———. *Night and Day.* 1978. 2d edition. London: Faber, 1979.

———. *Travesties.* London: Faber, 1975.

Taylor, Cecil P. *And a Nightingale Sang . . .* London: Eyre Methuen, 1979.

———. *Good.* London: Methuen, 1982.

Theatre Workshop, Charles Chilton and members of the original cast. *Oh What a Lovely War.* 1965. Paperback ed. London: Methuen, 1967.

Two Gay Sweatshop Plays. London: Gay Men's Press, 1981.

Wandor, Michelene, Ed. *Strike While the Iron is Hot: Three Plays on Sexual Politics.* London: Journeyman Press, 1980.

Wesker, Arnold. *Caritas.* London: Jonathan Cape, 1981.

———. *The Four Seasons*. London: Jonathan Cape, 1966.

———. *The Kitchen*. In *Three Plays*. 1961. Harmondsworth: Penguin, 1976.

———. *The Nottingham Captain*. In *Six Sundays in January*, 41–60. London: Jonathan Cape, 1971.

———. *Plays, Vol. 3*. Harmondsworth: Penguin, 1980.

———. *Plays, Vol. 4*. Harmondsworth: Penguin, 1980.

———. *The Wesker Trilogy*. London: Jonathan Cape, 1960.

Cited Secondary Sources

N.B. All statements by the dramatists John Arden, Peter Barnes, Edward Bond, Margaretta D'Arcy, and John McGrath that are not otherwise identified are taken from unpublished personal interviews with the author in May 1984.

Ahrends, Günter. "John Osborne: *A Sense of Detachment*." In *Englische Literatur der Gegenwart 1971–1975*, edited by Rainer Lengeler, 68–80. Düsseldorf, W. Germany: Bagel, 1977.

Arent, Arthur. "The Techniques of the Living Newspaper." *Theatre Quarterly* 1, no. 4 (October–December 1971): 57–79. Reprinted from *Theatre Arts* 22 (November 1938): 820ff.

Arden, John. "Arden of Chichester: John Arden talks to Frank Cox about 'The Workhouse Donkey' at Chichester this month." *Plays and Players*, August 1963, 16–18.

———. "Ecce Hobo Sapiens: O'Casey's Theatre." In *Sean O'Casey: A Collection of Critical Essays*, edited by Thomas Kilroy, 61–76. Englewood Cliffs, N.J.: Prentice Hall, 1975.

———. "The Island of the Ardens: Pam Gems talks to John Arden." *Plays and Players*, January 1973, 16–19.

———. "John Arden" (interview). In *Theatre at Work: Playwrights and Productions in the Modern British Theatre*, edited by Charles Marowitz and Simon Trussler, 36–57. London: Methuen, 1967.

———. "John Arden" (interview). In *The Poet Speaks: Interviews with Contemporary Poets*, edited by Peter Orr, 1–6. London: Routledge and Kegan Paul, 1966.

———. "John Arden" (interview). In *The Playwrights Speak*, edited by Walter Wager, 189–212. London: Longmans, Green, 1967.

———. Personal interview with Elizabeth Hale Winkler. 9 May 1984.

———. "Poetry and Theatre." *Times Literary Supplement* 6 August 1964, 705.

———. *To Present the Pretence: Essays on the Theatre and its Public*. London: Eyre Methuen, 1977.

———. "The Reps and New Plays—A Writer's Viewpoint." *New Theatre Magazine* 1, no. 2 (January 1960): 23–26.

———. "Telling a True Tale." *Encore* 7 no. 3 (1960): 41–43. Reprinted in *New Theatre Voices of the Fifties and Sixties: Selections from Encore Magazine 1956–1963*, edited by Charles Marowitz, Tom Milne, and Owen Hale, 125–29. 1965. Reissued. London: Eyre Methuen, 1981.

———. "Verse in the Theatre." *New Theatre Magazine* 2, no. 3 (1961): 200–206.

Reprinted in *English Dramatic Theories IV: 20th Century*, edited by Paul Goetsch, 111–18. Tübingen, W. Germany: Niemeyer, 1972.

Artaud, Antonin. *The Theater and Its Double*. Translated from the French by Mary Caroline Richards. New York: Grove, 1958.

Auden, Wystan Hugh. "Music in Shakespeare." In *The Dyer's Hand and Other Essays*, 500–27. London: Faber, 1963.

Barker, Clive. "Pip Simmons in Residence." *Theatre Quarterly* 9, no. 35 (Autumn 1979): 17–30.

Barnes, Peter. "Peter Barnes interviewed by Brendan Hennessy." *The Transatlantic Review* 37/38 (Autumn/Winter 1970–71): 188–24.

———. "Liberating Laughter: Peter Barnes and Peter Nichols in interview with Jim Hiley." *Plays and Players*, March 1978, 14–17.

———. Personal interview with Elizabeth Hale Winkler. 14 May 1984.

Becker, Theo and Irmtraut Müller. "Befreiungskampf auf der Opernbühne: Ein Versuch, Hans Werner Henzes 'Wir erreichen den Fluss' zu rehabilitieren." *Theater Heute*, November 1976, 30–33.

Belz, Carl. *The Story of Rock*. 1969. 2d ed. New York: Harper and Row, 1972.

Bicât, Nick. "The Music Men: Stephen Oliver and Nick Bicât talk to Anthony Masters." *Plays and Players*, November 1981, 20–21.

Bigsby, C. W. E. *Tom Stoppard*. Burnt Mill, Harlow, Essex: Longman, 1976.

———. "Tom Stoppard." In *Contemporary Dramatists*, 2d ed. edited by James Vinson, 760–63. London: St. James Press, 1977.

Blakely, Colin. "*Old Times:* Colin Blakely talks to *Plays and Players*." *Plays and Players*, July 1971, 22–24.

Boas, Frederick S., ed. *Songs and Lyrics from the English Playbooks*. London: Cresset Press, 1945.

Bond, Edward. "A Discussion with Edward Bond." *Gambit: International Theatre Review* 5, no. 17 (October 1970): 5–38.

———. "Hans Werner Henze." BBC Radio 3 (1 July 1976). BBC Script Library transcript.

———. "Edward Bond in Conversation with Philip Roberts." 31 March 1977. LSA Recorded Interview No. RI 2010. The British Council, 1978.

———. "Interviews with Edward Bond and Arnold Wesker." By Karl-Heinz Stoll. *Twentieth Century Literature* 22, no. 4 (December 1976): 411–32.

———. "Kaleidoscope." BBC Radio 4 (22 July 1981). BBC Script Library Transcript.

———. Personal interview with Elizabeth Hale Winkler. 18 May 1984.

———. "Us, Our Drama and the National Theatre." *Plays and Players*, October 1978, 8–9.

Booth, Mark W. *The Experience of Songs*. New Haven: Yale University Press, 1981.

Bowden, William R. *The English Dramatic Lyric, 1603–42; A Study in Stuart Dramatic Technique*. New Haven: Yale University Press, 1951.

Bowen, Zack. *Musical Allusions in the Work of James Joyce: Early Poetry through Ulysses*. Albany: State University of New York Press, 1975.

Bradby, David, Louis James, and Bernard Sharratt, eds. *Performance and Politics in Popular Drama: Aspects of Popular Entertainment in Theatre, Film and Television 1800–1976*. Cambridge: Cambridge University Press, 1980.

Brander, Michael. *Scottish and Border Battles and Ballads*. London: Seeley Service and Co., 1975.

Bratton, J. S. *The Victorian Popular Ballad*. London: Macmillan, 1975.

Brecht, Bertolt. *Brecht on Theatre: The Development of an Aesthetic*. Edited and translated by John Willett. New York: Hill and Wang, 1964.

Brenton, Howard. "Petrol Bombs Through the Proscenium Arch." *Theatre Quarterly* 5, no. 17 (March–May 1975): 4–20.

Brice, Douglas. *The Folk-Carol of England*. London: Herbert Jenkins, 1967.

Broich, Ulrich and Manfred Pfister, eds. *Intertextualität: Formen, Funktionen, anglistische Fallstudien*. Tübingen, W. Germany: Niemeyer, 1985.

Bronson, Bertrand Harris. *The Ballad as Song*. Berkeley and Los Angeles: University of California Press, 1969.

———. *The Traditional Tunes of the Child Ballads*. 4 vols. Princeton: Princeton University Press, 1959–1972.

———. "The Interdependence of Ballad Tunes and Texts." In *The Critics and the Ballad: Readings*, edited by M. Leach and T. Coffin, 77–102. Carbondale: Southern Illinois University Press, 1961.

Brook, Peter. *The Empty Space*. 1968. Harmondsworth: Penguin, 1972.

Brown, Calvin S. *Music and Literature: A Comparison of the Arts*. Athens: University of Georgia Press, 1948.

Brown, John Russell. *Theatre Language: A Study of Arden, Osborne, Pinter and Wesker*. London: Allen Lane, 1972.

Bryden, Ronald. "Ballad Country." *New Statesman* 15 May 1964, 782–83.

Burt, Susan and Clive Barker. "IOU and the New Vocabulary of Performance Art." *Theatre Quarterly* 10, no. 37 (Spring 1980): 70–94.

Cahn, Victor. *Beyond Absurdity: The Plays of Tom Stoppard*. Rutherford, N.J.: Fairleigh Dickinson University Press, 1979.

Černy, Lothar. "Peter Barnes, *The Bewitched*." In *Englische Literatur der Gegenwart 1971–1975*, edited by Rainer Lengeler, 94–106. Düsseldorf, W. Germany: Bagel, 1977.

Chambers, E. K. *The English Folk-Play*. Oxford: Clarendon, 1933.

———. *The Medieval Stage*. 2 vols. London: Oxford University Press, 1903.

Chan, Mary. *Music in the Theatre of Ben Jonson*. Oxford: Clarendon, 1980.

Cheshire, David F. *Music Hall in Britain*. Newton Abbot, Devon: David and Charles, 1974.

Child, Francis James, ed. *The English and Scottish Popular Ballads*, 1882–98. 5 vols. New York: The Folklore Press in association with Pageant Book Co., 1956.

Christy, Desmond. *"Poppy."* *Plays and Players*, January 1984, 40–41.

Clinton-Baddeley, V. C. *Words for Music*. Cambridge: Cambridge University Press, 1941.

Cohen, Michael. "The Politics of the Earlier Arden." *Modern Drama* 28, no. 2 (June 1985): 198–210.

Cohn, Ruby. "Sam Shepard: Today's Passionate Shepard and His Loves." In *Essays on Contemporary American Drama*, edited by Hedwig Bock and Albert Wertheim, 161–72. Munich: Hueber, 1981.

———. "Theater in Recent English Theater." *Modern Drama* 30, no. 1 (March 1987): 1–13.

Comparative Literature 22, no. 2 (Spring 1970).

The Concise Oxford Dictionary of Music. 2d ed. Edited by John Owen Ward. London: Oxford University Press, 1964.

Coult, Tony. *The Plays of Edward Bond*. London: Eyre Methuen, 1977.

Craig, Sandy, ed. *Dreams and Deconstructions: Alternative Theatre in Britain*. Ambergate, Derbyshire: Amber Lane Press, 1980.

Culler, Jonathan. *The Pursuit of Signs: Semiotics, Literature, Deconstruction*. Ithaca: Cornell University Press, 1981.

Cutts, John P. "Music and the Supernatural in *The Tempest*." *Music and Letters* 39 (1958): 347–58. Reprinted in *Shakespeare, The Tempest: A Casebook*, edited by D. J. Palmer, 196–211. London: Macmillan, 1968.

D'Arcy, Margaretta. Personal interview with Elizabeth Hale Winkler. 9 May 1984.

Dark, Gregory. "Production Casebook No. 5: Edward Bond's *Lear* at the Royal Court." *Theatre Quarterly* 2, no. 5 (January–March 1972): 20–31.

Davison, Peter. *Contemporary Drama and the Popular Dramatic Tradition in England*. London: Macmillan, 1982.

———. *Songs of the British Music Hall*. New York: Oak, 1971.

Deák, František. "Structuralism in Theatre: The Prague School Contribution." *The Drama Review* 20, no. 4 (December 1976):83–94.

De Marinis, Marco. "Dramaturgy of the Spectator." *The Drama Review* 31, no. 2 (Summer 1987): 100–114.

A Dictionary of British Folk Customs. Edited by Christina Hole. London: Granada/ Paladin, 1978.

Dort, Bernard. "The Liberated Performance." *Modern Drama* 25, no. 1 (March 1982): 60–68.

Dukore, Bernard F. *The Theatre of Peter Barnes*. London: Heinemann, 1981.

Dutton, Richard. *Modern Tragicomedy and the British Tradition*. Norman: University of Oklahoma Press, 1986.

Eco, Umberto. "Semiotics of Theatrical Performance." *The Drama Review* 21, no. 1 (March 1977): 107–17.

Edgar, David. "Ten Years of Political Theatre." *Theatre Quarterly* 8, no. 32 (Winter 1979): 25–33.

———. "Towards a Theatre of Dynamic Ambiguities" (interview). *Theatre Quarterly* 9, no. 33 (Spring 1979): 3–23.

Elam, Keir. *The Semiotics of Theatre and Drama*. London: Methuen, 1980.

Esslin, Martin. "Brecht and the English Theatre." *Tulane Drama Review* 11, no. 2 (Winter 1966): 63–70.

———. *Pinter: A Study of His Plays*. Revised, retitled ed. London: Eyre Methuen, 1973.

Ewen, David. *All the Years of American Popular Music*. Englewood Cliffs, N.J.: Prentice Hall, 1977.

Farnsworth, Paul R. *The Social Psychology of Music*. 2d ed. Ames: Iowa State University Press, 1969.

Findlater, Richard, ed. *At the Royal Court: 25 Years of the English Stage Company*. Ambergate, Derbyshire: Amber Lane Press, 1981.

———. "The Case of P. Slickey." *Twentieth Century* 167, (January 1960): 29–38.

Finnegan, Ruth. *Oral Poetry: Its Nature, Significance and Social Context.* 1977. Paperback ed. Cambridge: Cambridge University Press, 1979.

Flammer, Ernst H. *Politisch engagierte Musik als kompositorisches Problem: Dargestellt am Beispiel von Luigi Nono und Hans Werner Henze.* Sammlung musikwissenschaftlicher Abhandlungen, Bd. 65. Baden-Baden, W. Germany: Valentin Koerner, 1981.

Frost, Maurice, ed. *Historical Companion to Hymns Ancient and Modern.* London: William Clowes and Sons, 1962.

Gambit: International Theatre Review. 10, no. 38 (1982). Theatre and Music Issue.

Gooch, Steve. *All Together Now: An Alternative View of Theatre and the Community.* London: Methuen, 1984.

Goorney, Howard. *The Theatre Workshop Story.* London: Eyre Methuen, 1981.

Gray, Frances. *John Arden.* London: Macmillan, 1982.

Gredley, Bernard. "Dance and Greek Drama." In *Themes in Drama 3: Drama, Dance and Music,* edited by James Redmond, 25–29. Cambridge: Cambridge University Press, 1981.

Griffiths, Trevor. "Transforming the Husk of Capitalism" (interview). *Theatre Quarterly* 6, no. 22 (Summer 1976): 25–46.

Grove's Dictionary of Music and Musicians. 3d ed. Edited by H. C. Colles. New York: Macmillan, 1947.

Hacks, Peter. "Über Lieder zu Stücken." *Sinn und Form* 14, no. 3 (1962): 421–29.

Hahnloser-Ingold, Margrit. *Das englische Theater und Bert Brecht.* Bern: Francke, 1970.

Hall, Peter. "Directing Pinter." *Theatre Quarterly* 4, no. 16 (November 1974–January 1975): 4–17.

Hare, David. "A Lecture." Given at King's College, Cambridge (5 March 1978). In *Licking Hitler,* 57–71. London: Faber, 1978.

———. "From Portable Theatre to Joint Stock . . . via Shaftesbury Avenue" (interview). *Theatre Quarterly* 5, no. 20 (December 1975–February 1976): 108–15.

Hartman, Charles O. "The Criticism of Song." *The Centennial Review* 19 (1975): 96–107.

Hay, Malcolm and Philip Roberts. *Bond: A Study of His Plays.* London: Eyre Methuen, 1980.

———. *Edward Bond: A Companion to the Plays.* London: Theatre Quarterly Publications, 1978.

Hayman, Ronald. "Profile 9: Tom Stoppard." *The New Review,* December 1974, 15–22.

Henze, Hans Werner. *Die englische Katze: Ein Arbeitstagebuch 1978–1982.* Frankfurt am Main: Fischer, 1983.

———. *Music and Politics: Collected Writings 1953–81.* Translated by Peter Labanyi. Ithaca: Cornell University Press, 1982.

———. *Musik und Politik: Schriften und Gespräche 1955–1975.* Munich: Deutscher Taschenbuch Verlag, 1976.

Henze, Hans Werner and Edward Bond. *Wir erreichen den Fluss.* Programheft der Deutschen Oper Berlin zur deutschen Erstaufführung am 18. September 1976.

Herington, John. *Poetry into Drama: Early Tragedy and the Greek Poetic Tradition.* Berkeley and Los Angeles: University of California Press, 1985.

Hinden, Michael. "*Jumpers:* Stoppard and the Theatre of Exhaustion." *Twentieth Century Literature* 27 (1981): 1–15.

Hirst, David L. *Edward Bond*. Houndmills, Basingstoke, Hampshire: Macmillan, 1985.

Hogan, Robert. "The Haunted Inkbottle: A Preliminary Study of Rhetorical Devices in the Late Plays of Sean O'Casey." *James Joyce Quarterly* 8, no. 1 (Fall 1970): 76–95.

Hoffmann, Gerhard. "Die Funktion der Lieder in Yeats Dramen." *Anglia* 89 (1971): 87–116.

Hollander, John. *Musica Mundana* and *Twelfth Night.*" In *Literary Criticism: Idea and Act*, edited by W. K. Wimsatt, 265–83. Berkeley and Los Angeles: University of California Press, 1974.

————. *The Untuning of the Sky: Ideas of Music in English Poetry 1500–1700*. Princeton: Princeton University Press, 1961.

Holy Bible. Authorized King James edition of 1611. New York: Thomas Nelson, no date.

Honzl, Jindřich. "Dynamics of the Sign in the Theater." In *Semiotics of Art: Praque School Contributions*, edited by Ladislav Matejka and Irwin R. Titunik, 74–93. Cambridge: MIT Press, 1976.

Hughes, Alan. "'They Can't Take That Away From Me'; Myth and Memory in Pinter's *Old Times.*" *Modern Drama* 17 (1974): 467–76.

Hunt, Albert. "Arden's Stagecraft." *Encore* 12, no. 5 (1965): 9–12. Reprinted in *Modern British Dramatists*, edited by John Russell Brown, 98–103. Englewood Cliffs, N.J.: Prentice Hall, 1968.

————. *Arden: A Study of His Plays*. London: Eyre Methuen, 1974.

————. "Passions and Issues." *New Society* 18 (January 1979): 51.

Itzin, Catherine. *Stages in the Revolution: Political Theatre in Britain Since 1968*. London: Eyre Methuen, 1980.

Jones, Mervyn. "Peter Nichols, the Playwright Who Has Had Enough." *Drama: The Quarterly Theatre Review* 148 (Summer 1983): 7–8.

Julian, John, ed. *A Dictionary of Hymnology*. 2 vols. Revised ed. 1907. Reprint New York: Dover, 1957.

Jungheinrich, Hans-Klaus. "Zwei Autoren nähern sich einem Stoff: Hans Werner Henzes Zusammenarbeit mit Edward Bond bei *We Come to the River.*" *Akzente* 24, no. 2 (April 1977): 168–76.

Karlson, Ilse. Die Funktion der Lieder in den Dublin Plays von Sean O'Casey. Dissertation Kiel, 1978. Privately printed.

Kennedy, Andrew. "Mimesis and the Language of Drama: A Reply to Michael Anderson." In *Themes in Drama 3: Drama, Dance and Music*, edited by James Redmond, 225–33. Cambridge: Cambridge University Press, 1981.

————. *Six Dramatists in Search of a Language: Shaw, Eliot, Beckett, Pinter, Osborne, Arden*. Cambridge: Cambridge University Press, 1975.

Kislan, Richard. *The Musical: A Look at the American Musical Theater*. Englewood Cliffs, N.J.: Prentice Hall, 1980.

Knaus, Jakob. *Sprache, Dichtung, Musik: Zu ihrem gegenseitigen Verständnis*. Tübingen, W. Germany: Max Niemeyer, 1973.

Kramer, Lawrence. *Music and Poetry: The Nineteenth Century and After.* Berkeley and Los Angeles: University of California Press, 1984.

Lahr, John. *"The Island of the Mighty." Plays and Players,* February 1973, 31–33.

Lewis, Cecil Day. *The Lyric Impulse.* Cambridge: Harvard University Press, 1965.

Lloyd, A. L. *Folk Song in England.* 1967. Reprint Frogmore, St. Albans, Hertfordshire: Granada/Paladin, 1975.

Lomax, Alan. "Song Structure and Social Structure." In *The Sociology of Art and Literature: A Reader,* edited by Milton C. Albrecht, James H. Barnett, and Mason Griff, 55–71. London: Gerald Duckworth, 1970.

Long, John H. *Shakespeare's Use of Music: The Final Comedies.* Gainesville: University of Florida Press, 1961.

———. *Shakespeare's Use of Music: A Study of the Music and its Performance in the Original Production of Seven Comedies.* Gainesville: University of Florida Press, 1955.

MacColl, Ewan. "Grass Roots of Theatre Workshop." *Theatre Quarterly* 3, no. 9 (January–March 1973): 58–68.

McGrath, John. "Better a Bad Night in Bootle . . . " (interview). *Theatre Quarterly* 5, no. 19 (September–November 1975): 39–54.

———. *A Good Night Out. Popular Theatre: Audience, Class and Form.* London: Eyre Methuen, 1981.

———. "Interview." *Scottish Marxist* 26 (Spring 1983): 7–9.

———. Personal Interview with Elizabeth Hale Winkler. 26 May 1984.

McGuinness, Arthur E. "Memory and Betrayal: The Symbolic Landscape of *Old Times.*" In *Themes in Drama 4: Drama and Symbolism,* edited by James Redmond, 101–11. Cambridge: Cambridge University Press, 1982.

Mackerness, E. D. *A Social History of English Music.* London: Routledge and Kegan Paul, 1964.

McLean, Sammy. *The Bänkelsang and the Work of Bertolt Brecht.* The Hague: Mouton, 1972.

Mander, Raymond and Joe Mitchenson. *British Music Hall: A Story in Pictures.* London: Studio Vista, 1965.

Manifold, J. S. *The Music in English Drama From Shakespeare to Purcell.* London: Rockliff, 1956.

Marowitz, Charles. "Privates on Parade." *Plays and Players,* April 1977, 22–25.

Marowitz, Charles, Tom Milne, and Owen Hale, eds. *New Theatre Voices of the Fifties and Sixties: Selections from Encore Magazine 1956–1963.* London: Eyre Methuen, 1981.

Marsh, Paddy. "Easter at Liberty Hall: The Ardens' *Non-Stop Connolly Show.*" *Theatre Quarterly* 5, no. 20 (December 1975–February 1976): 133–41.

Maschler, Tom, ed. *Declaration.* New York: Dutton, 1958.

Mayer, David. "The Music of Melodrama." In *Performance and Politics in Popular Drama,* edited by David Bradby, Louis James, and Bernard Sharratt, 49–63. Cambridge: Cambridge University Press, 1980.

Meir, Colin. *The Ballads and Songs of W. B. Yeats: The Anglo-Irish Heritage in Subject and Style.* London: Macmillan, 1974.

Melançon, Joseph. "Theatre as Semiotic Practice." *Modern Drama* 25, no. 1 (March 1982): 17–24.

Merchant, Paul. "The Theatre Poems of Bertolt Brecht, Edward Bond and Howard Brenton." *Theatre Quarterly* 9, no. 34 (Summer 1979): 49–51.

Mitchell, Donald. *Britten and Auden in the Thirties: The Year 1936.* London: Faber, 1981.

Mittenzwei, Johannes. *Das Musikalische in der Literatur: Ein Überblick von Gottfried von Strassburg bis Brecht.* Halle, E. Germany: VEB Verlag Sprache und Literatur, 1962.

Mortimer, Peter. "C. P. Taylor: An Appreciation of His Work and Life." *Drama: The Quarterly Theatre Review* 145 (Autumn 1982): 16–17.

Mosaic 18, no. 4 (Fall 1985): Music and Literature Issue.

Nichols, Peter. *Feeling You're Behind.* London: Weidenfeld and Nicholson, 1984.

———. "Liberating Laughter: Peter Barnes and Peter Nichols in Interview with Jim Hiley." *Plays and Players,* March 1978, 14–17.

Noble, Richmond. *Shakespeare's Use of Song.* 1923. Oxford: Clarendon, 1966.

Nosworthy, J. M. "Music and its Function in the Romances of Shakespeare." *Shakespeare Survey* 11 (1958), 60–69.

O Boyle, Seán. *The Irish Song Tradition.* Dublin: Gilbert Dalton, 1976.

O'Casey, Sean. *Blasts and Benedictions.* London: Macmillan, 1967.

———. *The Letters of Sean O'Casey 1910–41.* Vol. 1. Edited by David Krause. London: Cassell, 1975.

O'Connor, John and Lorraine Brown, eds. *The Federal Theatre Project.* London: Eyre Methuen, 1980.

O'Neill, P. G. "Music, Dance and Text in *nō* Drama." In *Themes in Drama 3: Drama, Dance and Music,* edited by James Redmond, 103–21. Cambridge: Cambridge University Press, 1981.

Orpheus, Materialien. Redaktion Jens Brockmeier. Stuttgart, W. Germany: Würtembergisches Staatstheater, 1979.

Osborne, John. *A Better Class of Person: An Autobiography 1929–1956.* London: Faber, 1981.

———. "That Awful Museum." In *John Osborne, Look Back in Anger: A Casebook,* edited by John Russell Taylor, 63–67. London: Macmillan, 1968.

———. "They Call It Cricket." In *Declaration,* edited by Tom Maschler, 45–66. New York: Dutton, 1958.

———. "The Writer in His Age." In *John Osborne, Look Back in Anger: A Casebook,* edited by John Russell Taylor, 59–62. London: Macmillan, 1968.

The Oxford Dictionary of Nursery Rhymes. Edited by Iona and Peter Opie. 1951. Reprinted with corrections. Oxford: Clarendon, 1952.

Pafford, J. H. P. "Music and the Songs in *The Winter's Tale.*" *Shakespeare Quarterly* 10 (1959): 161–75.

Pasachoff, Naomi. "O'Casey's Not Quite Festive Comedies." *Eire-Ireland* 12, no. 3 (1977): 41–61.

Pavis, Patrice. *Languages of the Stage: Essays in the Semiology of the Theatre.* New York: Performing Arts Journal Publications, 1982.

Petri, Horst. *Literatur und Musik.* Göttingen, W. Germany: Sachse und Pohl, 1964.

Pfister, Manfred. *Das Drama.* Munich: Wilhelm Fink, 1977.

————. *The Theory and Analysis of Drama*. Trans. John Halliday. Cambridge: Cambridge University Press, 1988.

Pinter, Harold. "A Conversation (Pause) with Harold Pinter." By Mel Gussow. *The New York Times Magazine* 5 December 1971, 42–43 and 126–36.

————. "Writing for the Theatre." In *English Dramatic Theories IV: 20th Century*, edited by Paul Goetsch, 118–24. Tübingen, W. Germany: Max Niemeyer, 1972.

Plater, Alan. "The Playwright and His People." *Theatre Quarterly* 1, no. 2 (April–June 1971): 67–70.

————. "Twenty-Five Years Hard: A Playwright's Personal Retrospective." *Theatre Quarterly* 7, no. 25 (Spring 1977): 34–46.

Plett, Heinrich F. "Edward Bond, *The Woman:* Mythos und Geschichte in einer 'sozialistischen Rhapsodie.'" In *Englisches Drama von Beckett bis Bond*, edited by Heinrich Plett, 359–94. Munich: Fink, 1982.

————, ed. *Englisches Drama von Beckett bis Bond*. Munich: Fink, 1982.

Powe, Bruce W. "*The Tooth of Crime:* Sam Shepard's Way With Music." *Modern Drama* 24, no. 1 (March 1981): 13–25.

Pribram, Karl H. "Brain Mechanism in Music." In *Music, Mind and Brain: The Neuropsychology of Music*, edited by Manfred Clynes, 21–35. New York: Plenum, 1982.

Rabey, David Ian. *British and Irish Political Drama in the Twentieth Century: Implicating the Audience*. New York: St. Martin's Press, 1986.

Rabillard, Sheila. "Sam Shepard: Theatrical Power and American Dreams." *Modern Drama* 30, no. 1 (March 1987): 58–71.

Rademacher, Frances. "Violence and the Comic in the Plays of Edward Bond." *Modern Drama* 23, no. 3 (September 1980): 258–68.

Raynor, Henry. *Music in England*. London: Robert Hale, 1980.

Redmond, James, ed. *Themes in Drama 3: Drama, Dance and Music*. Cambridge: Cambridge University Press, 1981.

Reed, Edward Bliss, ed. *Songs from the British Drama*. New Haven: Yale University Press, 1925.

Reed, James. *The Border Ballads*. London: Athlone Press, University of London, 1973.

Révész, G. *Einführung in die Musikpsychologie*. Bern: Francke, 1946.

Roberts, Philip. "The Search for Epic Drama: Edward Bond's Recent Work." *Modern Drama* 24, no. 4 (December 1981): 458–78.

Rollins, Ronald Gene. *Sean O'Casey's Drama: Verisimilitude and Vision*. Tuscaloosa: University of Alabama Press, 1979.

Routley, Erik. *The English Carol*. London: Herbert Jenkins, 1958.

Sandbach, F. H. *The Comic Theatre of Greece and Rome*. London: Chatto and Windus, 1977.

Schmidt-Garre, Helmut. *Von Shakespeare bis Brecht: Dichter und ihre Beziehung zur Musik*. Wilhelmshaven, W. Germany: Heinrichshofen, 1979.

Schultz, William Eben. *Gay's Beggar's Opera: Its Content, History and Influence*. 1923. Reprint New York: Russell and Russell, 1967.

Schwanitz, Dietrich. "John Osborne, *The Entertainer*." In *Englisches Drama von Beckett bis Bond*, edited by Heinrich F. Plett, 100–117. Munich: Fink, 1982.

Senelick, Laurence. "Politics as Entertainment: Victorian Music-Hall Songs." *Victorian Studies* 19 (December 1975): 149–80.

Seng, Peter. *The Vocal Songs in the Plays of Shakespeare: A Critical History.* Cambridge: Harvard University Press, 1967.

Shepard, Sam. "Metaphors, Mad Dogs and Old Time Cowboys." (Interview with the editors and Kenneth Chubb). *Theatre Quarterly* 4, no. 15 (August–October 1974): 3–25.

Simpson, Claude M. *The British Broadside Ballad and Its Music.* New Brunswick, N.J.: Rutgers University Press, 1966.

Skloot, R. "Spreading the Word: The Meaning of Musgrave's Logic." *Educational Theatre Journal* 27, no. 2 (1975): 208–19.

Stevens, John. "Music in Some Early Medieval Plays." In *Studies in the Arts,* edited by Francis Warner, 21–40. Oxford: Basil Blackwell, 1968.

Stoppard, Tom. "Ambushes for the Audience: Towards a High Comedy of Ideas" (interview). *Theatre Quarterly* 4, no. 14 (May–July 1974): 3–17.

———. "First Interview." 12 June 1974. In *Tom Stoppard,* by Ronald Hayman, 1–13. London: Heinemann, 1977.

———. "Interview with Giles Gordon." In *Behind the Scenes: Theatre and Film Interviews from the Transatlantic Review,* edited by Joseph McCrindle, 77–87. New York: Holt, Rinehart and Winston, 1971.

———. "An Interview with Tom Stoppard." With Joost Kuurman. *Dutch Quarterly Review* 10 (1980): 41–57.

———. "Second Interview." 20 August 1976. In *Tom Stoppard,* by Ronald Hayman, 135–43. London: Heinemann, 1977.

Subotnik, Rose Rosengard. "The Cultural Message of Musical Semiology: Some Thoughts on Music, Language, and Criticism Since the Enlightenment." *Critical Inquiry* 4, no. 4 (Summer 1978): 741–68.

Swaen, A. E. H. "The Airs and Tunes of John Gay's *Beggar's Opera.*" *Anglia* 43 (1919): 152–90.

Symons, Julian. *The Thirties: A Dream Revolved.* 1960. Reprint. Westport, Conn.: Greenwood Press, 1973.

Taylor, John Russell. *Anger and After: A Guide to the New British Drama.* 1962. Revised ed. Harmondsworth: Penguin, 1963.

———, ed. *John Osborne, Look Back in Anger: A Casebook.* London: Macmillan, 1968.

———. "Plays in Performance: London." *Drama* 147 (Spring 1983): 26ff.

———. *"Poppy." Plays and Players,* December 1982, 22–23.

———. *The Second Wave: British Drama for the Seventies.* London: Methuen, 1971.

Thole, Bernward. *Die Gesänge in den Stücken Bertolt Brechts: Zur Geschichte und Ästhetik des Liedes im Drama.* Göppingen, W. Germany: Alfred Kümmerle, 1973.

Toll, Robert C. *Blacking Up: The Minstrel Show in Nineteenth-Century America.* London: Oxford University Press, 1974.

Trussler, Simon. *The Plays of John Osborne: An Assessment.* 1969. Reprint London: Granada/Panther, 1971.

Ubersfeld, Anne. "The Pleasure of the Spectator." *Modern Drama* 25, no. 1 (March 1982): 127–39.

Vinson, James, ed. *Contemporary Dramatists.* 2d ed. London: St. James Press, 1977.

Wagner, Gottfried. *Weill und Brecht: Das musikalische Zeittheater.* Munich: Kindler, 1977.

Wall, Richard. "*An Giall* and *The Hostage* Compared." *Modern Drama* 18 (1975): 165–72.

Wandor, Michelene. *Understudies: Theatre and Sexual Politics.* London: Eyre Methuen, 1981.

Weimann, Robert. "Die Literatur der *Angry Young Men:* Ein Beitrag zur Deutung englischer Gegenwartsliteratur." *Zeitschrift für Anglistik und Amerikanistik* 7 (1959): 117–89.

Weise, Wolf-Dietrich. *Die "Neuen englischen Dramatiker" in ihrem Verhältnis zu Brecht.* Bad Homburg, W. Germany: Gehlen, 1969.

Weisstein, Ulrich. "Cocteau, Stravinsky, Brecht, and the Birth of Epic Opera." *Modern Drama* 5 (Fall 1962): 142–53.

———. "Reflections on a Golden Style: W. H. Auden's Theory of Opera." *Comparative Literature* 22, no. 2 (Spring 1970): 108–24.

Wells, Evelyn Kendrick. *The Ballad Tree.* London: Methuen, 1950.

Wesker, Arnold. "Art and Action." *The Listener,* 67, no. 1728 (10 May 1962): 806–8.

———. "Casual Condemnations: A Brief Study of the Critic as Censor." *Theatre Quarterly* 1, no. 2 (April–June 1971): 16–30.

———. *Fears of Fragmentation.* London: Jonathan Cape, 1970.

———. "A Sense of What Should Follow" (interview). *Theatre Quarterly* 7, no. 28 (Winter 1977–78): 5–24.

Willett, John. *The Theatre of Bertolt Brecht.* 1959. Revised, paperback ed. London: Eyre Methuen, 1977.

Williams, Raymond. *The Long Revolution.* 1961. Harmondsworth: Penguin, 1965.

Winkler, Burchard. *Wirkstrategische Verwendung populärliterarischer Elemente in Sean O'Caseys dramatischem Werk.* Göppingen, W. Germany: Alfred Kümmerle, 1977.

Winkler, Elizabeth Hale. "Reflections of Derry's Bloody Sunday in Literature." In *Studies in Anglo-Irish Literature,* edited by Heinz Kosok. 411–21. Bonn: Bouvier, 1982.

Winn, James Anderson. *Unsuspected Eloquence: A History of the Relations between Poetry and Music.* New Haven: Yale University Press, 1981.

Worth, Katharine J. "Bond's *Restoration.*" *Modern Drama* 24, no. 4 (December 1981): 479–93.

———. *Revolutions in Modern English Drama.* London: Bell, 1973.

Cited Musical Recordings

Britten, Benjamin. *Our Hunting Fathers.* Op. 8: A Symphonic Cycle for Voice and Orchestra. Text by W. H. Auden. From a BBC Third Programme Broadcast on 11 June 1961. BBC, 1981.

Dewhurst, Keith. *Lark Rise to Candleford.* Recording of the National Theatre Production. Charisma CDS 4020, 1979.

Elgar, Edward. *The Dream of Gerontius.* Decca Recording SET 525–6, 1972.

The Folk Songs of Britain, Vol. 9: Songs of Ceremony. Topic Records 12T197, 1961.

Händel, Georg Friedrich. *Rinaldo.* CBS Recording, 1977.

Henze, Hans Werner. *We Come to the River.* Unpublished tape recording in possession of the Schott Verlag, Mainz, W. Germany.

MacColl, Ewan and Charles Parker. *The Ballad of John Axon.* ARGO DA 139, 1965.

——. *The Big Hewer: A Radio Ballad.* ARGO DA 140, 1967.

MacColl, Ewan, Peggy Seeger and Charles Parker. *The Travelling People: A Radio Ballad.* ARGO DA 133, 1969.

McGrath, John. *The Cheviot, the Stag and the Black, Black Oil.* 7:84 Theatre Company (Scotland). Record no. 784002 S, 1974.

——. *Lay Off.* Music by Mark Brown and the 7:84 Band. 7:84 Theatre Company (England), 1975.

——. *The Life and Times of Joe of England.* Music by Mark Brown and the 7:84 Band. 7:84 Theatre Company (England). Record no. 784005 S, 1978.

——. *Little Red Hen.* Unpublished tape recording of the 7:84 Theatre Company. Live in Scotland, 1975.

Nichols, Peter. *Poppy.* Music by Monty Norman. Royal Shakespeare Company recording no. 25–000–1, 1982.

Oh What a Lovely War. Original Cast Recording. DECCA PA 27/SPA 27, 1969.

Stoppard, Tom. *Every Good Boy Deserves Favour: A Play for Actors and Orchestra.* RCA Recording BL 12855, 1978. Music by André Previn.

Cited Films

Barnes, Peter. *Leonardo's Last Supper.* With Joe Melia and Dilys Laye. Directed by Peter Barnes. 1977. Available through National Film Archive, London.

Nichols, Peter. *Privates on Parade.* Music by Denis King. With Denis Quilley, Joe Melia and other members of the original cast. Directed by Michael Blakemore. 1983.

Osborne, John. *The Entertainer.* Music by John Addison. With Sir Laurence Olivier. Directed by Tony Richardson. A Woodfall Production. Available through National Film Archive, London.

Song Books

A Ballad History of England from 1588 to the Present Day. Edited by Roy Pamler. London: Batsford, 1979.

Ballads from the Pubs of Ireland. 4th ed. Edited by James N. Healy. Cork, Ireland: Mercier, 1971.

Bawdy Songs of the Early Music Hall. Edited by George Speaight. London: Pan 1977.

Best Music Hall and Variety Songs. Edited by Peter Gammond. London: Wolfe, 1972.

Big Red Songbook. Compiled by Mal Collins, Dave Harker, and Geoff White. London: Pluto, 1977.

A Centenary Selection of Moore's Melodies. Edited by David Hammond. Skerries, Co. Dublin, Ireland: Gilbert Dalton, 1979.

Classic George Gershwin. Ilford, Essex: International Music Publications, 1983.

Classic Jerome Kern. Ilford, Essex: International Music Publications, 1983.

Cockney Ding Dong. Edited by Charles Keeping. Harmondsworth: Penguin; and London: EMI Music Publishing, 1975.

Community Book of Music Hall Songs. London: EMI Music Publishing, 1977.

The Constant Lovers. More English Folk Songs from the Hammond and Gardiner MSS. Edited by Frank Purslow. London: English Folk Dance and Song Society, 1972.

Daily Express Community Song Book. Edited by John Goss. London: Daily Express, 1927.

An Elizabethan Song Book. Edited by W. H. Auden, Chester Kallman, and Noah Greenberg. 1957. New ed. London: Faber, 1968.

English Folk Songs from the Southern Appalachians. Edited by Maude Karpeles. 2 vols. 1932. 2d impression. London: Oxford University Press, 1952.

The English and Scottish Popular Ballads. Edited by Francis James Child. 5 vols. 1882–98. New York: The Folklore Press in association with Pageant Book Co., 1956.

The Ernest Newton Community Song Book. London: Keith Prowse Music Publishing. Distributed by EMI Music Publishing. No date.

Everyman's Book of British Ballads. Edited by Roy Palmer. London: Dent, 1980.

Everyman's Book of English Country Songs. Edited by Roy Palmer. London: Dent, 1979.

Fireside Book of Favorite American Songs. Edited by Margaret Bradford Boni. New York: Simon and Schuster, 1952.

Fireside Book of Folk Songs. Edited by Margaret Bradford Boni. New York: Simon and Schuster, 1947.

The First Book of Irish Ballads. Edited by Daniel D. O'Keefe. Revised ed. Cork, Ireland: Mercier, 1968.

The Foggy Dew. More English Folk Songs from the Hammond and Gardiner MSS. Edited by Frank Purslow. London: English Folk Dance and Song Society, 1974.

Folksongs of Britain and Ireland. Edited by Peter Kennedy. London: Cassell, 1975.

Forty Years On: An Anthology of School Songs. Edited by Gavin Ewart. London: Sidgwick and Jackson, 1969.

The Great Song Book. Edited by Timothy John. Garden City, N.Y.: Doubleday, 1978.

Hymns, Ancient and Modern. Standard edition. London: Clowes, 1916.

Ideal Songs: A Collection of Rare and Popular Songs. Vol. 2. New York: Saalfield, 1885.

I'll Be Seeing You . . . Featuring the Songs, the Artists and the Memories of the Second World War. London: EMI Music Publishing, 1979.

Irische Lieder und Balladen. Edited by Frederik Hetmann. Frankfurt am Main: Fischer, 1979.

Irish Songs of Resistance (1169–1923). Edited by Patrick Galvin. London: Oak, 1962.

Irish Street Ballads. Edited by Colm O Lochlainn. 1939. London: Pan Books, 1978.

Just a Song at Twilight: The Second Parlour Song Book. Edited by Michael Ralph Turner and Antony Miall. London: Michael Joseph, 1975.

Marrow Bones. English Folk Songs from the Hammond and Gardiner MSS. Edited by Frank Purslow. London: English Folk Dance and Song Society, 1965.

A Medley of Folk-Songs. Edited by Stuart Forbes. London: Longman, 1971.

More Irish Street Ballads. Edited by Colm O Lochlainn. 1965. London: Pan Books, 1978.

Mud, Songs and Blighty: A Scrapbook of the First World War. Edited by Colin Walsh. London: Hutchinson, 1975.

The National Song Book. Edited by Charles Villes Stanford. London: Boosey, 1906.

O! It's a Lovely War: Songs, Ballads and Parodies of the Great War. Edited by Cecil Bolton. London: EMI Music Publishing, 1978.

Oh, What a Lovely War. A Selection of Songs from the Theatre Workshop Production. London: Essex Music, 1963.

One Hundred Songs of Toil. Edited by Karl Dallas. London: Wolfe, 1974.

The Oxford Book of Carols. Edited by Percy Dearmer, R. Vaughan Williams, and Martin Shaw. 1928. London: Oxford University Press, 1950.

The Oxford Song Book. Edited by Percy C. Buck. London: Oxford University Press, 1916.

The Parlour Song Book: A Casquet of Vocal Gems. Edited by Michael R. Turner. London: Michael Joseph, 1972.

The Penguin Book of English Folk Songs. Edited by R. Vaughan Williams and A. L. Lloyd. Harmondsworth: Penguin, 1959.

Political Verse and Song from Britain and Ireland. Edited by Mary Ashraf. London: Lawrence and Wishart, 1975.

Poverty Knock. A Picture of Industrial Life in the Nineteenth Century through Songs, Ballads and Contemporary Accounts. Edited by Roy Palmer. Cambridge: Cambridge University Press, 1974.

The Rigs of the Fair. Popular Sports and Pastimes in the Nineteenth Century through Songs, Ballads and Contemporary Accounts. Edited by Roy Palmer and Jon Raven. Cambridge: Cambridge University Press, 1976.

Scottish and Border Battles and Ballads. Edited by Michael Brander. London: Seeley Service, 1975.

The Scottish Students' Song Book. Edited by A. G. Abbie. London: Bayley and Ferguson, 1897.

The Second Book of Irish Ballads. Edited by James N. Healy. Revised ed. Cork, Ireland: Mercier, 1968.

The Service Song Book. New York: Association Press, 1941.

Shanties from the Seven Seas. Edited by Stan Hugill. London: Routledge and Kegan Paul, 1961.

Sixty Old-Time Variety Songs. London: EMI Music Publishing, 1977.

Songs of Belfast. Edited by David Hammond. Skerries, Co. Dublin, Ireland: Gilbert Dalton, 1978.

Songs of the British Music Hall. Edited by Peter Davison. New York: Oak, 1971.

Songs of a Changing World. Edited by Jon Raven. London: Ginn, 1972.

Songs of County Down. Edited by Cathal O'Boyle. Skerries, Co. Dublin, Ireland: Gilbert Dalton, 1979.

Songs of Dublin. Edited by Frank Harte. Skerries, Co. Dublin, Ireland: Gilbert Dalton, 1978.

The Songs of England. Vol 1. Edited by J. L. Hatton. London: Boosey, no date.

Songs of the Four Nations. Edited by Harold Boulton. London: Cramer, 1893.

The Songs of Ireland. Edited by J. L. Molloy. London: Boosey, no date.

Songs of the Irish in America. Edited by Bill Meek. Skerries, Co. Dublin, Ireland: Gilbert Dalton, 1978.

Songs of Irish Rebellion: Political Street Ballads and Rebel Songs 1780–1900. Edited by Georges-Denis Zimmerman. Dublin, Ireland: A. Figgis, 1967.

Songs of the People: Selections from the Sam Henry Collection. Part 1. Edited by John Moulden. Belfast: Blackstaff, 1979.

Songs of Struggle and Protest. Edited by John McDonnell. Skerries, Co. Dublin, Ireland: Gilbert Dalton, 1979.

Songs of Work and Protest. 100 favorite songs of American workers complete with music and historical notes. Edited by Edith Fowke and Joe Glazer. New York: Dover, 1973.

Stories of Britain in Song. Compiled with commentaries by Stuart Forbes. London: Longman, 1972.

There Goes That Song Again. One Hundred Years of Popular Song. Edited by Colin Walsh. London: Elm Tree Books in association with EMI Music Publishing, 1977.

The Thirties. London: EMI Music Publishing, no date.

A Touch on the Times: Songs of Social Change 1770 to 1914. Edited by Roy Palmer. Harmondsworth: Penguin, 1974.

The Traditional Tunes of the Child Ballads. 4 vols. Edited by Bertrand Harris Bronson. Princeton: Princeton University Press, 1959–1972.

Travellers' Songs from England and Scotland. Edited by Ewan MacColl and Peggy Seeger. Knoxville: University of Tennessee Press, 1977.

The Treasury of Negro Spirituals. Edited by H. A. Chambers. Poole, Dorset: Blandford Press, 1953.

The Twenties. London: EMI Music Publishing, no date.

The Valiant Sailor. Sea songs and ballads and prose passages illustrating life on the lower deck in Nelson's navy. Edited by Roy Palmer. Cambridge: Cambridge University Press, 1973.

Victorian Folk Songs. Edited by Charles Chilton. London: Essex Music, 1965.

The Wanton Seed. More English Folk Songs from the Hammond and Gardiner MSS. Edited by Frank Purslow. London: English Folk Dance and Song Society, 1968.

General Index

Numbers in italics refer to the musical illustrations.

351

Musical Index

Numbers in italics refer to the musical illustrations.